# Black Women's Portrayals
on Reality Television

# Black Women's Portrayals on Reality Television

## *The New Sapphire*

### Edited by Donnetrice C. Allison

LEXINGTON BOOKS
Lanham • Boulder • New York • London

Published by Lexington Books
An imprint of The Rowman & Littlefield Publishing Group, Inc.
4501 Forbes Boulevard, Suite 200, Lanham, Maryland 20706
www.rowman.com

Unit A, Whitacre Mews, 26-34 Stannary Street, London SE11 4AB

British Library Cataloguing in Publication Information Available

**Library of Congress Cataloging-in-Publication Data**

Allison, Donnetrice C., editor.
Black women's portrayals on reality television : the new Sapphire / edited by Donnetrice C. Allison.
Lanham : Lexington Books, 2016. | Includes bibliographical references and index.
LCCN 2015045413 (print) | LCCN 2015047338 (ebook)
    ISBN 9781498519328 (cloth : alk. paper)
    ISBN 9781498519335 (Electronic)
Reality television programs--United States--History and criticism. | African American women on
    television.
LCC PN1992.8.A34 B58 2016 (print) | LCC PN1992.8.A34 (ebook) | DDC 791.45/652208996073--
    dc23 LC record available at http://lccn.loc.gov/2015045413

# Contents

# Acknowledgments

This project has been a labor of love for over three years. It began with a wonderful panel of young, female scholars at the 2012 convention of the National Communication Association, who so inspired me that I initiated the process of soliciting contributors for this book right then and there. I have since consulted many friends and colleagues, from the preparation of the original proposal to this final product. I want to first thank my friend and colleague Dr. Ron Jackson, who assisted me with great ideas for my original proposal. His guidance was invaluable. I'd also like to thank my sister-friend, Dr. Donyale Padgett. Words cannot express how much you have meant to me in this process and in my life in general. Your guidance and suggestions mean the world to me and your ability to always say exactly what I need to hear when I need to hear it, have been priceless. My friendship with you, Dr. Tosin Adegbola, Dr. Cheryl Jenkins, and Natasha Myers has been a saving grace.

I am also blessed to have great mentors in my life–wonderful women–in my educational pursuits, in my career, and in my personal life. These women include my professors–Dr. Brenda Williams, Dr. Carolyn Stroman, Dr. Brenda J. Allen and Dr. Melbourne Cummings; and my colleagues–Dr. Patricia Reid-Merritt, Dr. Linda Nelson and Dr. Beverly Vaughn. Of course, I am further blessed to have been raised by a wonderful mother, Esther Barbee, and five big sisters–Debra Barnett, Cynthia Barbee-Wallace, Dollinda Barbee, Dyanne Barbee and Donna Barbee. All of these women gave me the truest sense of what it mean to be a Black woman, with a level of intelligence, grace, dignity and supportiveness that is too often absent on television.

Last, but never least in my life, are the four people I share my every day with–my husband, Albert Allison, who has supported and encouraged every goal that I set. He is not only a phenomenal cheerleader, but he is also a wonderful editor, who pays great attention to detail. I could not have completed this process without you. Thank you! And I must also thank my children–Akili, Adia and Ameer–for their love and patience when I needed to work. You are the loves of my life!

# Introduction

## *A Historical Overview*

## Donnetrice C. Allison

The first African American woman to appear on television was Ethel Waters in a one-night-only variety show called, *The Ethel Waters Show*. The year was 1939 and the show was deemed an "experimental broadcast" for the new medium of television.[1] That same year, however, World War II began, and plans to grow the new medium were put on hold. It wasn't until the late 1940s, after WWII ended, that significant efforts were made to create regular programming for the newly minted television networks—CBS, NBC and ABC—all of which had transitioned from radio. And, according to MacDonald (1992), author of *Blacks and White TV: African Americans in Television Since 1948*, "early television seemed to be almost color blind"[2] and many believed that the new medium brought new hope to blacks who had previously been stereotypically portrayed— in the early film industry—as slaves, servants and buffoons. In contrast, on the variety shows of the late 1940s—such as *The Ed Sullivan Show* and *The Steve Allen Show*—black performers were invited to appear in their elegant evening gowns and tuxedos to perform musical numbers. Unfortunately, that era was short-lived and networks caved in to advertising pressure. MacDonald (1992) asserted that "TV executives and advertisers feared alienating the white consumer,"[3] due to preconceived notions about appropriate roles for blacks to portray. In her historic book, *Ain't I a Woman*, bell hooks (1981) speaks to the challenges that black women had long faced being taken seriously and deemed as "ladies." She states:

> When slavery ended . . . everywhere black women went—on public streets, in shops, or at their places of work—they were accosted and subjected to obscene comments and even physical abuse . . . those Black women suffered most whose behavior best exemplified that of a "lady." A Black woman dressed tidy and clean, carrying herself in a dignified manner, was usually the object of mud-slinging by White men who ridiculed and mocked her self-improvement efforts. They reminded her that in the eyes of the White public she would never be seen as worthy of consideration or respect.[4]

Hence, the stereotypical roles quickly re-emerged. Those most common for African American women on television were the "Mammy," the "Sapphire" and the "Jezebel."

According to Bogle (2001), Mammy is usually "big, fat and cantankerous."[5] Her counterpart—Aunt Jemima—on the other hand, is typically portrayed as "sweet, jolly and good tempered." She is "more polite than Mammy and certainly never as headstrong."[6] What the two have in common, however, is that each is fiercely loyal to the white family she serves; often to the detriment of her own black family. Both Mammy and Aunt Jemima were the dominant depictions of black women on television in the 1950s. In fact, for the most part, black women were either completely absent or there to serve others. As such, the first starring role for an African American actress on television went, once again, to Ethel Waters in the ABC sitcom *Beulah* (1950–1953); and the elegant evening gowns were replaced by an apron. Although Waters left the show after only one season, the show continued until 1953—first with *Gone with the Wind*'s Hattie McDaniel and later with *Imitation of Life*'s Louise Beavers.[7]

The "Sapphire" depiction made its television debut on *Amos 'n' Andy* in 1951. The wife of one of the main characters—George 'Kingfish' Stevens—was named Sapphire and she was the antithesis to the good natured Aunt Jemima. According to hooks (1981), she was depicted as "evil, treacherous, bitchy, stubborn and hateful."[8] The author went on to contend that:

> The Sapphire image had as its base one of the oldest negative stereotypes of woman—the image of the female as inherently evil. Christian mythology depicted woman as the source of sin and evil; racist-sexist mythology simply designated black women the epitome of female evil and sinfulness.[9]

*Amos 'n' Andy* was originally a 15-minute radio broadcast, beginning in 1928 on NBC. As a result of the show's popularity, by 1943 it became a 30-minute sitcom and moved to CBS. Then, in 1951, like many popular radio sitcoms, soap operas and variety shows, *Amos 'n' Andy* transitioned to television. The transitioning process took longer than many other shows, however, because the stars of the radio sitcom were white males portraying a pair of "bumbling, stumbling, dim-witted black men,"[10] who chased one get-rich-quick scheme after another. For television, on the other hand, network executives decided it best to search for black male actors to portray the beloved caricatures;[11] rather than have the original actors perform in blackface—which they'd also considered. Once African American actors were selected, the show debuted in June of 1951 and lasted only two years. It was cancelled in 1953—largely due to pressure from the NAACP that had threatened to lead a boycott against the show's sponsor—the Blatz Brewing Company.[12] The NAACP also drafted a listed of grievances about the show, asserting that, "It tends to strengthen the conclusion among uninformed and prejudiced people that Negroes are inferior, lazy, dumb and dishonest."[13] Nonetheless, Sapphire and her buffoon of a husband remained on television—in syndication—for more than an additional decade. And that stereotype of the "angry black woman" continues to appeal to network executives to this very day, which is further dissected throughout this book.

The remainder of the 1950s included occasional appearances of blacks on television as ancillary characters—maids, butlers, doormen and other service workers—on popular sitcoms such as: *The Trouble with Father, My Little Margie, The Danny Thomas Show* and *The Jack Benny Show*.[14] These appearances were so few and far between that "*Jet Magazine* began to publish listings of every African American appearance on TV," just so that African American families could be informed and tune in.[15] Conversely, some of the most prominent appearances of blacks on television in the 1950s and 1960s came in the form of television news. The Civil Rights Movement was heating up by the mid-1950s and broadcast journalists were there to cover every aspect—from the non-violent protests themselves, to the violent responses of whites towards those protestors and other blacks in the south. According to Torres (2003) in *Black, White and in Color: Television and Black Civil Rights*, the growth of television—particularly telejournalism—and the growth of the Civil Rights Movement had a somewhat reciprocal relationship.[16] Torres (2003) asserted that "Telejournalism, obviously, needed vivid pictures and clear-cut stories; less obviously, it also sought political and cultural *gravitas*. For its part, The Civil Rights Movement...needed to have its picture taken and its stories told."[17] The author further noted that while stories of civil rights played a major role in 1950s television, it did not eclipse the stereotyped depictions of African Americans.

> With respect to black televisuality, to claim that televisual racial representation in information genres was dominated by images of the Civil Rights Movement in the late '50s and early '60s is not to claim that stereotypical representation in other genres was eradicated or even came temporarily to a screeching halt during the period. It is rather to note that such representation existed alongside representations of many of the most forceful and articulate African Americans that the nation has known.[18]

What is most interesting about this point is the fact that, while these "most forceful and articulate" African American voices were ever present throughout the decade, the voices of the inarticulate buffoon portrayals of African Americans on scripted television seemed to have the most memorable and endearing impact on white audiences. According to Gray (2005), in shows like *Beulah* and *Amos 'n' Andy*, white audiences "found comforting reminders of whiteness and the ideology of white supremacy."[19] In many ways, this continues to ring true with today's oversaturation of black women—or, more pointedly, black "Sapphires"—on reality television. Most assuredly, the "bad black girl" and/or the "sistah with an attitude" (SWA) offers much validation for those who seek to justify the continued subjugation of black women—politically and socially—in today's society.

In the late 1960s, characterizations were said to have "improved" and become more positive, but for critics this too was problematic because it ignored the real racial injustices that were occurring in the United States at that time. As noted in the documentary, *Color Adjustment (1991)*:

> It was almost as if there were two Black Americas. There was the Black America that you saw on the news, which confronted racial issues head on. And then there was the Black America that you saw the rest of the evening on prime time television, where racial hostility was virtually absent, where harmony dictated the neighborhood, where there were no signs of any kinds of struggles with segregation. So you get on screen this idealized view of how Blacks and Whites work together that most people knew were inaccurately depicting the reality.[20]

In the 1968, Diahann Carroll made waves as the first African American actress to star in her own weekly network series;[21] and "the first black nondomestic female character on television."[22] The show, *Julia*, ran for three seasons, until 1971; and it faced a great deal of criticism, largely from African American audiences. The most common criticism of the show was that it was attempting to sugarcoat the harsh realities of black life post-Civil Rights Movement; and it "offered white viewers the attractive illusion that America's race problems had been solved."[23]

> Julia lived in an integrated California environment as a widowed, professional nurse, raising her son. This fictional integration aired across a real-life backdrop of white homeowners fleeing neighborhoods where blacks moved. With government funds made available for the construction of federal freeways leading out of the city and government assistance for those who wanted to buy homes in the suburbs, whites left the city in droves—taking their dollars with them.[24]

Was such criticism harsh and unfair? According to network executive, Hal Kanter, it was. He stated, "In those days, our mandate was to amuse an audience, not to excite them. And I stuck to that mandate to try and amuse as many people as I possibly could."[25] On the other hand, it was also noted in the documentary that, "because prime time images of us were so rare, each image became precious, [and] involuntarily bore the burden of representing the race."[26] This rings true today as well, except that images of African Americans are not as "rare" as they were in the 1950s and 1960s; instead, they are commonly outrageous, violent, uncivilized, overdramatized, and downright embarrassing.

There were a few exceptions to those characterizations noted above, however. Beginning in 1966, Nichelle Nichols took on the role of Lieutenant Uhura on *Star Trek* (1966–1969), where she was portrayed as a Communications Officer—from the United States of Africa—fluent in several languages, including Swahili.[27] Additionally, Gail Fisher won an Emmy and two Golden Globe awards for her role as Peggy Fair on *Mannix* (1967–1975),[28] where she portrayed the witty and charming secretary of private investigator, Joe Mannix. Fisher was the first African American actress to win either of the awards noted.

In the 1970s, Black women gained more television roles, but most continued to be primarily portrayed as Mammies and Sapphires. In fact, Flip Wilson garnered enormous laughs portraying the Sapphire—Geraldine—on *The Flip Wilson Show*, which ran from 1970–1974. The show was so popular that it drew an average of 40 million viewers per week, during its first season.[29] And while it did receive its share of criticism for the many stereotyped portrayals in the comedy sketches, the show also included a host of African American guest stars—such as Lena Horne, Diahann Carroll, James Brown, Stevie Wonder, and many more.[30]

Also in the 1970s, Isabel Sanford transitioned from an occasional appearance as a domestic worker in *All in the Family*, to a high society wife of a successful businessman in *The Jeffersons*. The spinoff continued, however, to include the portrayal of a domestic worker in the character Florence—the laziest maid on television. She wasn't the eternally lovable and nurturing sage that we saw in Alice from *The Brady Bunch*. Nor was she anything like the ever-obedient Mammies and Aunt Jemimas of the 1950s—though she may have been had she worked for a white family, instead of for the newly-successful Jeffersons. Nonetheless, the show garnered popularity and ran for a record ten seasons[31]—some believe due to the popularity of Florence and her Sapphire-like interactions with George. On the other hand, it could also be argued that she demonstrated a power and influence over George that even Mrs. Jefferson did not; in that, she was often able to convince, or manipulate, him into doing things that he had otherwise refused to do—things which were often considered the "right" thing to do, both morally and ethically.

Just as in the movies, with the string of Blaxploitation films, the 1970s saw a record number of African American faces on television; though most continued in stereotypical roles. As previously noted, the women often fell into either the Mammy or Sapphire category. The Sapphires included LaWanda Page as Aunt Esther on *Sanford and Son* (1972–1977); Danielle Spencer portrayed a "mini-Sapphire" as Dee on *What's Happening* (1976-1979); and Marla Gibbs was much more of a Sapphire than a Mammy as Florence—the never-working maid—on *The Jeffersons* (1975–1985). The Mammies included Esther Rolle as Florida Evans on *Good Times* (1974–1979), Theresa Merritt as Mama Curtis on *That's My Mama* (1974–1975), and Mabel King as Mama Thomas on *What's Happening* (1976–1979). These women primarily worked as domestic workers, but the difference in their portrayals as compared to the 1950s Mammy, was that these women were shown most often interacting with their families, rather than with the white families they worked for. One of the few television shows that offered an exception to the Mammies and Sapphires of the 1970s was *Get Christie Love*, where Teresa Graves portrayed a tough, smart and attractive undercover cop for the LAPD. Unfortunately, the show was short lived and ran for only one season.[32]

One of the most popular and beloved shows of all those mentioned above was *Good Times*, which holds the distinction of being "the first prime-time series to feature a black family with both mother and father."[33] And while it too faced criticism for the buffooning depiction of J.J., the eldest son, for many black families it was the first authentic television portrayal of what they were going through in the real world—the real financial hardships, and the political and social divide between blacks and whites. On the other hand, critics of the show—and others like it—argued that it glorified the ghetto, even making it seem like a fun, hip place to grow up.

> These programs were problematic because they represented the hell holes of the ghetto as places where human beings could survive. They made the ghetto palatable to the larger American society precisely when the social programs of the 1960s, such as the war on poverty and the Great Society were ending. These programs were saying let them end. Let them end, because the people are happy. They have good lives. They can survive there, and they can thrive.[34]

The 1980s were a mixed bag of black women's portrayals on television. It started with a re-make of Mammy, but ended with NBC introducing viewers to the HBCU experience (Historically Black College/University). In 1981, *Gimme a Break!* (1981–1987) premiered, featuring Nell Carter as the housekeeper to a widowed Police Chief and his three daughters. According to Bogle, "*Gimme a Break!* was little more than a remake of *Beulah*," in that Nell was fully devoted to her white family, with little need or desire for a life outside of their home.[35] On the other hand, in 1984 Diahann Carroll made her return to television with a most memorable entrance onto the set of *Dynasty*, a primetime soap opera following the lives of The Carrington's—a wealthy White family that made its fortune in the oil business in Denver, Colorado. Carroll joined the cast as the glamorous half-sister of family patriarch, Blake Carrington, who had returned to claim her share of the fortune. "Haughty, outspoken, glamorous as all get-out, the black woman was now depicted as a formidable combatant in a tough, competitive, dog-eat-dog, mink-lined world."[36] In fact, it was Carroll who called herself "the first black bitch" of television in press interviews. Yet again, her role was met with criticism. According to some, Dominique Deveraux was simply "an old-style tragic mulatto, simply grateful to be seated in the Big House."[37] Her entrée onto the show did bring a significant spike in black viewership, however;[38] and, for those fans, it was an accomplishment just to have her present in a world that few African Americans in the 1980s could imagine.

The 1980s also included the return of *The Jeffersons* alumni, Marla Gibbs and Sherman Hemsley. Gibbs led the cast of *227*—about a group of black women who often sat out on the front stoop in their working-class neighborhood, sharing gossip and getting in and out of various zany situations. While Gibbs often played a very sensible character and the "voice of reason" for the other ladies—much different than Florence on *The Jeffersons*—her character was often overshadowed by Jackee Harry's character, Sandra, the "Jezebel" of the show. Sandra's clothes were always tight, highlighting her voluptuous curves; she often spoke baby talk; and she was always on the prowl for a man. Her character became such a popular feature of the show that some critics suggested that she was the reason the show lasted as long as five seasons,[39] from 1985–1990. Sherman Helmsley also carved out a moderate success with his show *Amen* (1986–1991) where he portrayed a lawyer and a church deacon, who lived with his grown daughter—played by Anna Maria Horsford. On the show, Horsford also portrayed a man-hungry woman; but unlike Harry's character, she was less experienced in the art of flirtation and flamboyance. Furthermore, she only had eyes for one man, Reverend Reuben Gregory, who she ultimately "landed" and married in season four. She was, however, a bit of a screw-up, "constantly getting herself into the most absurd of situations."[40]

Nonetheless, with the variety of portrayals of black women in 1980s, none was more impactful than that of Attorney Claire Huxtable on *The Cosby Show* (1984–1992); and while the show also heard its share of criticism—as an "unrealistic" portrayal of black life"—it was incredibly successful with both black and white audiences alike. In fact, *The Cosby Show* held the number one spot on the Nielsen ratings chart for five consecutive seasons.[41] And for many African American viewers, whether the Huxtable's lives mirrored their lives or not, they aspired to be like them. In her portrayal of Claire Huxtable, Phylicia Rashad truly offered black women a role model—sophisticated, smart, beautiful, poised, and loving. Claire was living the dream—married to a successful doctor, mother of five gorgeous children, and holding down a prominent career. She had it all and she was unlike any other black woman previously portrayed on television. The success of *The Cosby Show* soon led to a spin-off show—*A Different World* (1987–1993)—where Cosby's daughter, Denise, portrayed by Lisa Bonet, was off to college at her parents' Alma Mater. The show was set on the campus of a fictional HBCU—Hillman College—and included a diverse cast of characters. Coleman (2000) called it "one of the best initiatives of the period," in that, "it was firmly rooted in black culture."[42] The author went on to say that:

Thanks to a large, co-ed cast of characters representing a variety of socioeconomic backgrounds, there was ample room to engage a multitude of economic, class-based, educative, personal, romantic, familial, employment, among other situations from a variety of sociocultural vantage points as they intersect and/or were informed by varying black cultural experiences. [43]

The 1990s also added more variety in black women's portrayals with shows like: *In Living Color* (1990–1994), *The Fresh Prince of Bel Air* (1990–1996), *Roc* (1991–1994), *Martin* (1992–1997), and *Living Single* (1993–1998). [44] *In Living Color* was a sketch comedy show, very popular among African American viewers during its four-season run; however, many stereotypical black female characters emerged. For example, there was the noisy neighbor, Benita Butrell, who always wore rollers in her hair as she aired everyone's dirty laundry; and Wanda, a character brought to life by comedian Jamie Foxx, who was a very unattractive woman with the exaggerated features of large lips, large behind and cross-eyes. She was always on the look-out for Mr. Right, but she was too physically, socially, and politically unattractive to ever succeed at finding him.

*The Fresh Prince of Bel Air* was also criticized for the buffoonery of Will Smith's character. There was, however, an interesting mix of women on the show: Aunt Vivian (first portrayed by Janet Hubert and later by Daphne Reid) was a poised and dignified woman who had earned a PhD and taught from time to time at Bel-Air Academy; Hilary Banks was portrayed as a spoiled, materialistic and privileged, fair-skinned eldest daughter of the family—who didn't care about much more than fulfilling her superficial needs; and Ashley was a sweet, innocent, and impressionable young girl who grew up right in front of the camera throughout the six-year run of the show. In some ways, all of the women were sassy, strong-willed and independent—including Will's mother Vy and his Aunt Helen. And this trend seemed to follow the common thread of the decade—the sassy, sharp-tongued, independent black woman—i.e., a revamped Sapphire.

On the other hand, Ella Joyce played the loving, supportive wife of garbage man—Roc Emerson—on *Roc*. She always had a kind word to say and lots of hugs and kisses for her husband. The year after *Roc* premiered, *Martin* came on the scene—in an effort to raise the profile of the fledgling FOX network. *Martin* was also the network's hope to find ratings gold, which *Roc* had not done because its storylines were often too political and socially conscious. [45] On the other hand, *Martin* was rude and crude, slapstick comedy, marketed to a younger generation. The show was purely out for laughs and it faced its share of criticism for its stereotypical portrayals. For example, one of its most popular portrayals was that of Martin Lawrence—dressed in drag—with large gaudy earrings, clothes and colorful hair weaves; yelling; fighting; and butchering the English language as Sheneneh. Coleman (2000) even called the character a female brutal buck.[46] *Martin* also played out the old "light-skin versus dark-skin" conflicts, with Martin's constant lust after his girlfriend Gina, played by the fair-skinned Tisha Campbell; and his constant criticism of her friend Pam, played by the darker-skinned Tichina Arnold.[47] Additionally, Coleman (2000) asserted that "Martin was so antagonistic to women, the series was largely misogynistic."[48]

Another television program of the 1990s portraying an all-black cast was *Living Single*, which focused on the lives of four African American women. The main character of the show—Khadijah James—was played by Hip Hop artist, Queen Latifah. She portrayed the owner and editor of *Flavor*, an independent magazine; Erika Alexander portrayed Khadijah's best friend—Maxine Shaw, a cut-throat attorney; Kim Coles portrayed Khadijah's naïve cousin and receptionist—Synclaire James; and Kim Fields portrayed Khadijah's gold-digging roommate—Regine Hunter. The show offered a depiction of black women as educated, goal-oriented and upwardly-mobile; it also offered a depiction of loyalty, friendship and solidarity among the African American women. Unfortunately, while the decade could boast some progress in black women's images, such as these, two new and potentially more problematic images were emerging—the video vixen, reminiscent of the old Jezebel stereotype; and the SWA (sistah with an attitude), reminiscent of Sapphire.

The notion of the black woman as a Jezebel has been around since the time of enslavement.

> The designation of all black women as sexually depraved, immoral, and loose had its roots in the slave system. White women and men justified the sexual exploitation of enslaved black women by arguing that they were the initiators of sexual relationships with men. From such thinking emerged the stereotype of black women as sexual savages...[49]

Collins (2005) fully dissected the modern conceptualization of the Jezebel in her book, *Black Sexual Politics*, and she explained that the stereotype can be further analyzed in terms of categories. On one hand, the "ho" is depicted as one who trades sexual favors for jobs, money, drugs or other material items; while the "bitch" controls her own sexuality; and finally, the "female hustler" uses her sexuality to "catch" a man with money, a man who can take care of all of her material needs.[50] Many of the 90s primetime dramas offered cameo appearances of black women in these modern Jezebel roles; but she was overwhelmingly promoted in Hip Hop music videos.

In 1992, on his triple platinum album *The Chronic*, Dr. Dre released a song that would become an ongoing characterization of black women. The song was called, *Bitches Ain't Shit*, and it implied that all women—particularly women of color given that they were his primary reference group growing up in the predominantly black and Latino Compton, California—were only good for sex, and only out for money."[51] And visually, this phenomenon of the gold-digging black "ho" began to play out in music videos. According to the documentary—*The Tanning of America*—the first music video to transition from having a few neighborhood girls dancing in music videos to having dozens of "video models" was Heavy D's *Nuthin But Love* in 1994.[52] The video opens with several black women of various complexions at a table, and one says, "Girl, all I know is, what's mine is mine and what's his is MINE." Then she receives high fives and affirmations from the rest of the group. Once the music starts, the four or five women at the table multiplies, and the camera pans along a wall of women dancing in their seats—presumably to be divided between Heavy D., his dancer and two friends. Eventually this trend became the norm, and in nearly every rap video thereafter the women have outnumbered the men on average ten to one.

> In a sense, the *celebration* of black women's bodies and how they handled them that had long appeared in earlier black cultural production . . . became increasingly replaced by the objectification of black women's bodies as part of a commodified black Culture. Contemporary music videos of black male artists in particular became increasingly populated with legions of young black women who dance, strut, and serve as visually appealing props for the rapper in question. The women in these videos typically share two attributes—they are rarely acknowledged as individuals and they are scantily clad.[53]

And while this trend continues in Hip Hop today, the new millennium did breathe some new life into portrayals of black womanhood on television through the creative visions of two young, African American, female writers/producers—Mara Brock Akil and Shonda Rhimes. Brock Akil is the writer/executive producer of *Girlfriends* (2000–2008), *The Game* (2006–2015) and *Being Mary Jane*, which aired its first season in 2013. Shonda Rhimes has become a power-house writer/executive producer of several hit shows on network television; and she has seen greater mainstream success than Brock Akil. Rhimes' shows include: *Grey's Anatomy*, which began airing in 2005 and just completed its eleventh season; *Private Practice*, which aired for six seasons, from 2007–2013; *Scandal*, which began airing in 2012 and just completed its fourth season; and *How to Get Away with Murder* (*HGAM*), which Rhimes produces but does not write.[54] According to Nielson, both *Scandal* and *HGAM* consistently rank among the top ten primetime programs nation-wide—as did *Grey's Anatomy*'s earlier seasons. Among African American audiences, however, all of the above-named shows ranked among the top ten at some point during their respective seasons.[55] On the other hand, a newcomer to television, *Empire*, written and created by Lee Daniels and Danny Strong, uses hip hop culture as a backdrop to advance its storylines.

Nonetheless, regarding the new millennium, *Girlfriends*—similar to *Living Single*—depicted four progressive, young, African American women trying to balance their career goals, dating lives and friendship. *The Game* also portrays black female friendships, but set against the backdrop of wealth and relationships with professional football players. According to Lewis:

> The enduring legacies of *Girlfriends* and *The Game* are their positioning and location of black women's experiences within rounded narratives of identity, sexuality, health and authority. These negotiations serve not so much to countervail as to complicate the reduced projections of black female subjectivity and sexuality.[56]

More recently, *Being Mary Jane* continues that legacy of portraying a black woman in all of her complexities—well put together professionally, but unravelling personally.

Rhimes also portrays complex, three-dimensional, African American women. Her niche, however, is that nearly all of her black female characters are brilliant, professionally accomplished and powerful; yet, they are often unsuccessful or unfulfilled in their personal relationships. Still, these characters have enjoyed significant mainstream attention and acclaim—Dr. Miranda Bailey and Dr. Maggie Pierce of *Grey's Anatomy*, Dr. Naomi Bennet of *Private Practice*, Olivia Pope of *Scandal*, and Defense Attorney Annalise Keating of *How to Get Away with Murder*.

Although there has been criticism that Rhimes' black female protagonists often do portray the "Angry Black Woman" stereotype, I would argue that the ABW characteristic is a mere portion of the complexities these women depict. In addition to displays of anger, these women also display affection, compassion, generosity, high intelligence, independence, strength and vulnerability. On the other hand, reality television seems to undermine the portrayal of these well-rounded women with a barrage of images of black women scantily clad and scheming to "catch" rich men, all while scratching and clawing at one another—literally in many cases—to gain social status and material wealth.

## REALITY TELEVISION

The notion of television depicting the real lives of real people is not new. As early as the 1950s, when *Candid Camera* aired, there was a certain pleasure audiences gained from peeking into the real lives—and sometimes misfortunes—of others. *Candid Camera* was a show that set out to capture "unsuspecting people placed in confusing, impossible, embarrassing, ridiculous, and hilarious positions" on a hidden camera.[57] And like many other television shows of the 1950s, *Candid Camera* was first broadcast on radio—then called *Candid Microphone*—and later transitioned to television in 1948.[58] The show switched from ABC to NBC a year later, and finally settled on CBS from 1960–1967.[59] According to McCarthy, the show's host, Allen Funt, saw himself as both "an aesthetic pioneer in the realm of minimalist realism and a social scientist."[60]

Another early television program about "real people" was *An American Family*, which aired on PBS in 1973. The program consisted of twelve one-hour episodes and it followed the lives of an "average, upper-middle-class family." However, as with many "reality" shows today, there was an ulterior motive. Show creator, Craig Gilbert, purportedly "manipulated everything from casting to editing to publicity in order to assert that family and marriage were 'dying institutions' and the American dream was in decay."[61] He set out to find a "traditional" nuclear family that was falling apart, and could provide high drama for viewers. The chosen family was that of William C. Loud, which included a mother, father, five children and two dogs. Right before the eyes of America, the Loud's marriage crumbled and the children rebelled; and to add further drama to the show, one of the Loud sons "came out as a homosexual on national television."[62] According to Gilbert, in his introduction of the first episode in 1973, "There is no question that the camera crews and our equipment had an effect on the Louds—one which is impossible to evaluate."[63] At the time, this genre of television was called "reality documentary;" but today, it is called "reality television." Clearly, *An American Family* set the stage for the manipulated drama that airs today.

The 1980s brought a new type of "reality" to television, with shows like *Unsolved Mysteries* (1987–current) and *Cops* (1989–current). Both portrayed real-life crime, but each took a different approach. *Unsolved Mysteries* described real crimes that were unsolved, and offered dramatic re-enactments of the facts of each case. *Cops*, on the other hand, followed law enforcement officers in the day-to-day interactions with the public. From its first season, *Cops* faced criticism for racial profiling. In fact, it is purported that the show first began airing on the FOX network in order to broadcast "The War on Crack" for the entire world to see; and that war was being waged in poor, black neighborhoods across the country.[64] In the documentary *Planet Rock: The Story of Hip Hop and the Crack Generation*, narrator Ice T stated: "The crack raids in this pilot episode [of *Cops*] formed a template that makes *Cops* the first successful reality TV show in the history of commercial television."[65] A few years later, however; the show that truly set the stage for high drama between "real people" on television aired on MTV. The show was called, *The Real World*, and it premiered in 1992 on MTV—which had previously focused on airing music videos. In the opening credits, cast members stated, "This is the true story of seven strangers; picked to live in a loft and have their lives taped; to find out what happens when people stop being polite and start getting real."[66] It was this show that re-introduced the black female as

Sapphire; but this time it was under the guise of being "reality." In many ways, this depiction was far more harmful and impactful than all of the previous depictions of black women, because "reality"—by its very definition—implies "truth" and "accuracy."

In thirty seasons of *The Real World*, nearly all have included at least one black female; and nearly all of those black females have been described by their roommates using terms like: "controlling," "harsh," "overbearing," "bossy," "quick-tempered," "independent," "diva," "outspoken," and "gold-digger."[67] Additionally, most of those black females have engaged in yelling matches during their time on the show, with many even engaged in physical altercations. Moreover, in several seasons, the black women were unflatteringly portrayed in direct conflict with black men on the show. In short, the black female cast members were almost always projected as the Sapphire of the household. And, in some cases, they were both Sapphire and Jezebel wrapped in one! Many deem *The Real World* to be the catalyst for modern reality television; and in some ways it was—based on the element of cohabitation. But it was the new millennium when reality television truly exploded—based on the introduction of competition, elimination and financial gain.

In 2000 both *Survivor* and *Big Brother* debuted. Both introduced a new element to reality television—competition and cash prizes. *Survivor* was the first to premiere—on May 31, 2000. According to Huff:

> It was an odd, contrived test of sorts to see how people would live together without creature comforts. It was a test to see how they interacted with each other when at times they would have to rely on each other to survive, and yet would also have to turn on one another in the voting process.[68]

The show struck ratings gold for CBS; and the competitive premise left much room for dramatic conflicts to occur. As such, many believe that *Survivor*—rather than *The Real World*—was the true catalyst for the modern reality television phenomenon. Huff (2006) contended, "thanks to *Survivor*, reality would become a true staple of television programming, finding a spot on every network's schedule."[69] A barrage of other shows followed—*Big Brother* (2000), *The Bachelor* (2002), *Top Model* (2003), *The Apprentice* (2004), *Flavor of Love* (2006)—and most followed the competition formula, whereby the "winner" would either take home a cash prize or win the affections of a romantic interest. And each show typically cast one black female each season, perhaps in hopes that she would "let loose" on someone at some point during taping. Wiltz coined the term "sistah with an attitude" (SWA) to describe this common casting tactic, and in her *Washington Post* article she stated:

> If you've ever seen a reality TV show, chances are you've seen her: a perpetually perturbed, tooth-sucking, eye-rolling, finger-wagging harpy, creating confrontations in her wake and perceiving racial slights

from the flimsiest provocations. At the very sight of her, her cast mates tremble in fear. And no wonder. She is the Sista with an Attitude. [70]

The Wiltz's (2004) article was initially published after the debut of NBC's *The Apprentice* — with the casting of Omarosa Manigault Stallworth — a tall, intelligent, sophisticated doctoral candidate from Howard University. She carried herself like a model; she wore business suits; and she boasted of accomplishments that included working for the White House. Yet, on this show, hosted by business tycoon — Donald Trump — where contestants were competing for the opportunity to work for him, Omarosa quickly became the "bitch" of the show. And in many ways, her entrée into the reality television phenomenon was different — in that she was portrayed as a professional. On the *Real World, Survivor,* and *Big Brother* that had not been the case; for although some of the black women on *Survivor* were professionals in their real lives, when trapped on a desert island or in an isolated house, none of that was apparent. With Omarosa, however, it was very apparent — from her clothes, shoes, handbags and condescending attitude. Moreover, in her initial audition video, Omarosa stated, "I know exactly what it takes to be a winner. I'm competitive. I'm fierce in my energy and my commitment, and more important, is my focus and my determination to be the best I can be. So pick me." [71] They did; and for nine weeks she became the woman that everyone loved to hate. In fact, in her nine-week appearance on the show, she was called a "bitch" by another contestant — either to her face or during a "confessional" — seven times. We can only speculate if that was the desired outcome when she was selected.

According to Friedman (2002), producers of reality programs create drama through the editing process, particularly in cases when there is a "winner." [72] Dates (2004) agreed, but added that casting plays a significant role in reality television manipulation. She asserted that producers exploit the vulnerability of contestants on reality programs, and they create distorted images of participants. [73] Dates (2004) further contended that when contestants do not conform to the roles producers desire, they are either not selected at all or they are eventually cut from the program. [74] In several post-show interviews, Omarosa argued that same notion, asserting that she was mischaracterized through the editing of the show; and she further argued that although she made several good friends during the taping of the show, she was never shown smiling or interacting positively with any of her roommates. [75]

In 2006, reality television made yet another transition with the premiere of *The Real Housewives of Orange County*. The show was inspired by the successful night-time drama, *Desperate Housewives*, which ran on ABC from 2004–2012, [76] and ranked in the top five on the Nielsen ratings chart for the first two seasons. [77] *Desperate Housewives* followed the lives of four women — touted as "housewives," living on a fictional suburban street called Wisteria Lane. The show was filled with bad behavior on the part of these women—cheating, screaming matches and physical altercations—just to name a few. Viewers seemed to enjoy the drama, so executives at the Bravo network decided to re-create that drama in the world of reality television. As a result of the success of the first installment—*The Real Housewives of Orange County*—several others began shooting in cities across the country—New York, Atlanta, New Jersey, Washington, D.C., Beverly Hills, and Miami. Ironically, the only version of *The Real Housewives* franchise to have a predominantly black cast is *The Real Housewives of Atlanta*; and it has become the highest-rated installment of the show and the most-watched series airing on the Bravo network.[78] And while all of the installments of *The Real Housewives* include bad behavior—drinks thrown, screaming matches and back-stabbing—apparently these behaviors are more palatable to audiences coming from black women, as *The Real Housewives of Atlanta* has become the most-watched show on the network.[79] Furthermore, what makes the show different from previous portrayals of black women on reality television is that these women display a great deal of material wealth. They drive the finest cars and wear the hottest designer fashions—including the matching shoes and handbags. Some of them have also managed to "land" wealthy husbands and boyfriends, who are typically responsible for the material wealth these women display. In other words, some of these women are portrayed as gold-diggers who've successfully struck gold.

As described on *BravoTV.com*, "The series delves into the lives of six *sassy* women from Atlanta's social elite."[80] It is important to note, however, that none of the ladies on the other installments are described this way. And this "sassy," "angry," "gold-digging," black woman is depicted over and over again on reality television today; and ratings for the shows that feature her continue to grow. In sum, *The Real Housewives of Atlanta* blew open the doors for more soap-opera-style reality shows featuring predominantly black female casts—*Bad Girls Club* premiered in 2006; *Basketball Wives* in 2010; *Love & Hip Hop* in 2011; *Hollywood Exes* in 2012; and *R&B Divas* in 2012.[81] And it seems that every few months a new show, like those named above, premieres—such as *Sisterhood of Hip Hop*, which premiered in August of 2014. Why? They are ratings grabbers. And who is watching? According to a Nielsen report, African Americans are the primary audience.[82] In fact, Nielsen (2013) reports that "Blacks watch 37 percent more television than any other group, spending seven hours and 17 minutes per day viewing TV."[83] In addition, black women watch more television than black men. And what are African Americans watching? The report determined that six of the top ten shows watched by African American audiences were in the "reality television" genre—with *Love and Hip Hop Atlanta 2* ranked number one among African Americans age 18–49.[84] So, why are we contributing to our own subjugation and misinterpretation? Nielsen (2013) further reported that, "Black viewers tend to mostly watch programs that provide diversity in casts or characters who are reflective of the black lifestyle and culture"[85] even if those characters are not accurately reflective of viewers' own behaviors and lifestyles. In other words, we want to see ourselves on television, even if the depictions are distorted and inaccurate.

In contrast to the distorted images offered on reality television, the new millennium has also introduced audiences to some very powerful and complex African American female characters—particularly those imagined by writer/producer extraordinaire, Shonda Rhimes, who brought viewers: Dr. Miranda Bailey on *Grey's Anatomy*; Dr. Naomi Bennett on *Private Practice*; Olivia Pope on *Scandal*—which ranks number two among African American viewers age 18–49;[86] and Annalise Keating on *How to Get Away with Murder*. Yet, both Ms. Rhimes and her characters have been placed in the "Angry Black Woman" box, time and time again, by critics and social commentators. In fact, *New York Times* contributor, Alessandra Stanley (2014), faced criticism when she suggested that a show recently produced by Ms. Rhimes, starring yet another black woman should be titled: *How to Get Away With Being an Angry Black Woman.*[87] Although later in the article she attempted to praise Rhimes' portrayals of black women on television, her comment set the stage for yet another heated debate.

Moreover, the "Angry Black Woman" is a persistent stereotype that not even First Lady Michelle Obama has been able to escape.[88] A part of this problem lies at the feet of network executives and reality television producers who continue to manipulate these images and offer them as truth—as reality. The unfortunate consequence of projecting this false reality is that—even when talented writers, like Rhimes, try to add layers of complexity to black female characters (and the real-life black women who embody their traits)—perceptions of those characters persist to conform with the same false notions that black women are angry, aggressive, intimidating, sassy and LOUD! I believe author, James Baldwin, put it best in his 1961 article for *Esquire Magazine*, when he stated:

> All roles are dangerous. The world tends to trap you in the role you play and it is always extremely hard to maintain a watchful, mocking distance between oneself as one appears to be and oneself as one actually is.[89]

## IN THIS BOOK

The following chapters in this book will dissect images of black women on various reality television programs today. The book is divided into three thematic sections: Section One is entitled, *Portrayals of Christianity and Motherhood*; Section Two is entitled, *Portrayals of the Angry Black Woman*; and Section Three is entitled, *Portrayals of Black Women as Spouses,*

*Girlfriends and Lovers*. The first section examines the portrayal of black women on shows such as, *Preachers of L.A.*, *Mary Mary*, *T.I. & Tiny: The Family Hustle*, *Welcome to Sweetie Pie's*, *Raising Whitley*, and *Mom's Got Game*. The chapters in this section highlight portrayals of black women's spirituality and their roles as mothers.

The first chapter in Section One—*Chapter One*—examines the women of *Preachers of L.A.*, which debuted on the Oxygen Network in 2013. Specifically, the chapter uses critical race feminism to analyze the roles of the pastor's wives, as portrayed in Season One of the show; and it examines their relationships with one another. The chapter also analyzes the conversations they have on issues of sex, marriage, relationships, and friendships. The second chapter in Section One—*Chapter Two*—examines the role of faith, religion and spirituality in the lives of the two main characters on the show *Mary, Mary*. *Mary Mary* follows the personal lives and careers of the gospel duo—sisters Tina Campbell and Erica Campbell. And, according to Erica Campbell in an interview with V-103 FM in Atlanta, "Our show is really our real life . . . we are very honest and very open, but one thing is for sure, God gets the glory out of all of it."[90] The third chapter in Section One—*Chapter Three*—focuses on Tameka "Tiny" Cottle, wife of rap superstar T.I. It explores the portrayals of Tiny as stage mother and celebrity wife in two reality shows—*Tiny & Toya* and *T.I. & Tiny: The Family Hustle*. The chapter also compares her role as mother and wife to historical portrayals of black women as mothers and wives on television. The fourth chapter in Section One—*Chapter Four*—explores the female-led reality programming on the Oprah Winfrey Network (OWN), paying particular attention to depictions of motherhood on programs such as *Welcome to Sweetie Pie's*, *Raising Whitley*, and *Mom's Got Game*. The final chapter in this section—*Chapter Five*—examines the portrayal of black motherhood on the shows *Dance Moms*, *Tia and Tamera*, and *Run's House*—paying particular attention to the fact that all of the black mothers on these reality programs are of a light complexion, and all are of a higher socio-economic status than the average black woman on television. As such, the chapter implies that in some ways their portrayals are more "positive" than other portrayals of black women on reality television.

Section Two—*Portrayals of the Angry Black Woman*—dissects the notion of the "Angry Black Woman," by examining the outbursts of black women portrayed on *Bad Girls Club*, *The Apprentice*, and *America's Next Top Model*. *Chapter Six* is the first chapter in this section and it examines displays of anger—that can be considered either positive or negative—on *Bad Girls Club*; and the chapter places these behavioral illustrations into historical context, with respect to notions of Sapphires versus notions of strong, powerful black women. The chapter further delves into potential reasons behind these displays of anger. *Chapter Seven* examines a 2007 episode of *America's Next Top Model*, dubbed "The Tyra Tirade," in which supermodel Tyra Banks yelled at a contestant that she had eliminated from the show. The chapter not only examines the episode, but it also examines the many parodies of that episode and the ways in which those parodies continue to perpetuate negative stereotypes of black woman- hood. The final chapter in this section—*Chapter Eight*—examines portray- als of black womanhood on *NBC's The Apprentice*. The chapter focuses specifically on the seven seasons of the show that did not include "celeb- rities," given that those seasons might be more prone to manufactured drama. Instead, the chapter analyzes the roles of unknown black women, who gained "celebrity" solely based on their appearance on the show, such as Omarosa Manigault, who became the infamous "Bitch" of *The Apprentice*.

Section Three of this book—*Portrayals of Black Women as Spouses, Girl- friends and Lovers*—discusses the portrayal of black women as girlfriends, wives and potential lovers on shows such as *Love & Hip Hop: Atlanta* and *The Real Housewives of Atlanta*. *Chapter Nine*—the first chapter in this sec- tion—uses Hip Hop Feminism as a theory to deconstruct the ways in which *Love & Hip Hop: Atlanta* reinforces misogynistic and stereotypical understandings of black women. Additionally, one of the authors of the chapter—a black male—offers his own self-reflection to examine ways in which he himself has been complicit in accepting these views. *Chapter Ten* also examines *Love & Hip Hop: Atlanta*, in addition to the original install- ment of *Love & Hip Hop*, set in New York City; however, it focuses on deconstructing the notion of the "Down-ass-Bitch" in Hip Hop and her depiction on reality television. The final chapter in Section Three—*Chap- ter Eleven*—analyzes *The Real Housewives of Atlanta*, and the ways in which the show has re-conceptualized what it means to be a housewife, as de- fined by the modern discourse of women's empowerment. The author argues that the reality of the "housewife" construct is called into question because of the financial resources available to the women on the show, and because of the reality format of the show. The author further exam- ines the loud, rude and brash portrayals of the women on the show, and questions their authenticity.

The book concludes with a discussion chapter that reflects upon the potential impact of these images and depictions of black women in reality television. The chapter reviews literature about media influence on view- ers' perceptions of African Americans and others—such as the contention made by Gates (2012) that audiences are "well aware that the portrayals they see are manipulated in various ways by the process of produc- tion."[91] The chapter also examines the implications of previous re- search—such as a series of extensive interviews conducted by Coleman (2000) analyzing black viewers' perceptions of black situation come- dies.[92] Finally, the chapter offers suggestions for future analyses of black women's portrayals in television; and ways to improve those portrayals.

One final note: throughout the book, readers will notice that the terms African American and black are used interchangeably. This is simply due to the fact that those terms are used interchangeably in most of the literature cited throughout the book. Moreover, both terms continue to be accepted ways to discuss and describe people of African descent across the diaspora.

## NOTES

1. Donald Bogle, *Prime Time Blues: African Americans on Network Television* (New York, NY: Farrar, Straus and Giroux, 2001), 9.
2. J. Fred MacDonald, *Blacks and White TV: African Americans in Television Since 1948*, 2nd Edition (Chicago, IL: Nelson-Hall Publishers, 1992), 3.
3. Ibid., 8.
4. bell hooks, *Ain't I a Woman: Black Women and Feminism* (Boston, MA: South End Press, 1981), 55.
5. Bogle, Donald, *Toms, Coons, Mulattoes, Mammies & Bucks: An Interpretive History of Blacks in American Films*, 4th Edition (New York: NY: Continuum, 2001), 9.
6. Ibid.
7. Bogle, *Prime Time Blues*, 25.
8. Hooks, *Ain't I a Woman*, 85.
9. Ibid.
10. Bogle, *Prime Time Blues*, 27.
11. Ibid. 28.
12. Robin R. Means Coleman, *African American Viewers and the Black Situation Comedy* (New York, NY: Garland Publishing, Inc, 2000), 60–61.
13. Ibid. 61.
14. *IMDB.com*, accessed November 2014, http://www.imdb.com/?ref_=nv_home.
15. Devorah Heitner, *Black Power TV* (Durham, NC: Duke University Press, 2013), 6.
16. Sasha Torres, *Black, White and in Color: Television and Black Civil Rights* (Princeton, NJ: Princeton University Press, 2003), 15.
17. Ibid.
18. Ibid. 7.
19. Herman Gray, "The Politics of Representation in Network Television" in *Channeling Blackness: Studies on Television and Race in America*, ed. Darnell M. Hunt (New York, NY: Oxford University Press, 2004), 158.
20. Ruby Dee (narrator), "Two Black Americas: News and Prime Time," *Color Adjustment*, directed by Marlon T. Riggs (San Francisco, CA: California Newsreel, 1991). Videocassette (VHS).
21. Donald Bogle, *Brown Sugar: Eighty Years of America's Black Female Superstars* (New York, NY: Harmony Books, 1980), 150.
22. Beretta E. Smith-Shomade, *Shaded Lives: African-American Women and Television* (New Brunswick, NJ: Rutgers University Press, 2002), 13.
23. Heitner, *Black Power TV*, 7.
24. Smith-Shomade, *Shaded Lives*, 13.
25. Hal Kanter (commentary), "Mandate to Amuse," *Color Adjustment*, directed by Marlon T. Riggs (San Francisco, CA: California Newsreel, 1991). Videocassette (VHS).
26. Ruby Dee (narrator), *Color Adjustment*.
27. Bogle, *Prime Time Blues*, 132.
28. *IMDB.com*, "Gail Fisher," accessed November 2014, http://www.imdb.com.
29. Bogle, *Prime Time Blues*, 180.
30. Ibid.
31. *IMDB.com*, "The Jeffersons," accessed November 2014, http://www.imdb.com.

32. Accessed November 2014, http://www.imdb.com/?ref_=nv_home.

33. Ruby Dee (narrator), "Good Times," *Color Adjustment*.

34. Henry Louis Gates (commentary), "Ghetto Sitcoms of the 70s," *Color Adjustment*.

35. Bogle, *Prime Time Blues*, 257.

36. Ibid. 262.

37. Ibid.

38. Ibid.

39. Ibid. 311.

40. Ibid. 314.

41. *Encyclopedia Britannica Online*, s.v. "The Cosby Show," accessed November 2014 , http://www.britannica.com/topic/The-Cosby-Show.

42. Coleman, *African American Viewers and the Black Situation Comedy*, 98.

43. Ibid.

44. *IMDB.com*, accessed November 2014, http://www.imdb.com/?ref_=nv_home.

45. Coleman, *African American Viewers and the Black Situation Comedy*, 117.

46. Ibid.

47. Bogle, *Prime Time Blues*, 418.

48. Coleman, *African American Viewers and the Black Situation Comedy*, 116.

49. Hooks, *Ain't I a Woman: Black Women and Feminism*, 52.

50. Patricia Hill Collins, *Black Sexual Politics: African Americans, Gender, and the New Racism* (New York: Routledge, 2005), 127–128.

51. Andre Romelle Young, a.k.a Dr. Dre, *The Chronic*, Death Row Records, 1992, CD.

52. *The Tanning of America*, VH1 Productions, February 24, 2014, directed by Bill Corbin and narrated by Ice T., television documentary/mini-series.

53. Collins, *Black Sexual Politics*, 128.

54. *IMDB.com*, accessed November 2014, http://www.imdb.com/?ref_=nv_home.

55. *Nielsen.com*, accessed November 2014, http://www.nielsen.com/us/en/insights/reports.html.

56. Nghana Lewis, "Prioritized: The Hip Hop (Re) construction of Black Womanhood in *Girlfriends* and *The Game*" in *Watching While Black: Centering the Television of Black Audiences*, ed. Beretta E. Smith-Shomade (New Brunswick, NJ: Rutgers University Press, 2002), 158.

57. *IMDB.com*, "Candid Camera," accessed November 2014, http://www.imdb.com.

58. Fred Nadis, "Surveillance as Cold War Entertainment," in *The Tube has Spoken: Reality TV & History*, eds. Julie Taddeo & Ken Dvorak (Lexington, KY: The University Press of Kentucky, 2010), 15.

59. Ibid.

60. Anna McCarthy, "Stanley Milgram, Allen Funt, and Me": Postwar Social Science and the 'First Wave' of Reality TV," in *Reality TV: Remaking Television Culture*, eds. Susan Murray & Laurie Ouellette (New York, NY: New York University Press, 2004), 26.

61. Laurie Rupert & Sayanti Ganguly Puckett, "Disillusionment, Divorce, and the Destruction of the American Dream: *An American Family* and the Rise of Reality TV," in *The Tube has Spoken: Reality TV & History*, eds. Julie Taddeo & Ken Dvorak (Lexington, KY: The University Press of Kentucky, 2010), 83.

62. Ibid. 88.

63. *An American Family*, "Pilot Episode," PBS, January 11, 1973, created and produced by Craig Gilbert.

64. *Planet Rock: The Story of Hip-Hop and the Crack Generation*, VH1 Productions, September 18, 2011, written and directed by Richard Lowe & Martin Torgoff, narrated by Ice T.

65. Ibid.

66. *The Real World*, MTV, premiere episode aired May 21, 1992, written by Mary-Ellis Bunim & Jonathan Murray, directed by George Verschoor.

67. *MTV.com*, accessed November 2014, http://www.mtv.com/.

68. Richard M. Huff, *Reality Television* (Westport, CT: Praeger, 2006), 3.

69. Ibid. 10.

70. Teresa Wiltz, "The Evil Sista of Reality Television: Shows Trot Out Old Stereotypes to Spice Up Stagnant Story Lines," *The Washington Post* (February 25, 2004): C1.

71. *The Apprentice*, "Audition Tapes," NBC, premiere episode aired January 8, 2004, created by Mark Burnett.

72. James Friedman, *Reality Squared: Televisual Discourse on the Real* (Piscataway, NJ: Rutgers University Press, 2002), 8.

73. Janette L. Dates, "A Stereotypical Grip on 'Reality,'" *The Washington Post* (March 13, 2004): A17.

74. Ibid.

75. Omarosa Manigualt on *The Donnie Simpson Morning Show*, WPGC-FM radio, Washington, DC, 2004.

76. *IMDB.com*, accessed November 2014, http://www.imdb.com.

77. *Nielsen.com*, accessed November 2014, http://www.nielsen.com/us/en.html.

78. *BravoTV.com*, accessed November 2014, http://www.bravotv.com/.

79. Ibid.

80. Ibid.

81. *IMDB.com*, accessed November 2014, http://www.imdb.com.

82. Nielsen staff writers, *Resilient, Receptive and Relevant: The African American Consumer* (New York, NY: The Nielson Company, 2013).

83. Ibid. 15.

84. Ibid. 17.

85. Ibid. 16.

86. Ibid. 17.

87. Alessandra Stanley, "Wrought in Their Creator's Image Viola Davis Plays Shonda Rhimes' Latest Tough Heroine," *The New York Times* (September 18, 2014) accessed November 2014, http://www.nytimes.com/.

88. Melissa Harris-Perry, *Sister Citizen: Shame, Stereotypes, and Black Women in America* (New Haven, NJ: Yale University Press, 2011), 86–87.

89. James Baldwin, "The Black Boy Looks at the White Boy," *Esquire Magazine*, May 1961.

90. *Pastor Murray & Erica Campbell Of Mary Mary Talk Religion In Current Times/ Reality TV*, YouTube video, 6:50, posted by "V-103 Atlanta," November 20, 2013, https://www.youtube.com/watch?v=10LFHRp0vVM.

91. Racquel Gates, "Keepin' it Reality Television," in *Watching While Black: Centering the Television of Black Audiences*, ed. Beretta E. Smith-Shomade (New Brunswick, NJ: Rutgers University Press, 2002), 144.

92. Coleman, *African American Viewers and the Black Situation Comedy*.

# I

# Portrayals of
# Christianity and Motherhood

# ONE

# High Tea, Church Hats, Pastor Wives, and Friendships

### *A critical race feminism analysis of Black women in* Preachers of L.A.

## Elizabeth Whittington Cooper

In October 2013, a new series titled, *Preachers of L.A.*, debuted on the Oxygen network. The show, which centers on the personal lives of six pastors and their families, was rated in the "Top 10 most social cable reality program in October and November."[1] According to Oxygen's Media Senior Vice President of Original Programming and Development, Rod Aissa:

> *Preachers of L.A.* is powerful, impactful and touches the viewers' spirit. These six men of God and the amazing women alongside them are brave and transparent about their journey in life, which is why it resonates so well with Oxygen's young, female audience.[2]

The premise of the show revolves around six preachers in the Los Angeles area. They each pastor churches ranging from 3,500–4,000 members; however, one pastor's church has nearly 20,000 members (season 1: episode 1). A multitude of cameras follow the stories of each of the pastors' lives, their relationships with each other, as well as their wives relationships with one another. The show has five black male preachers and one white male preacher. In season 1, all of the pastors—except for two— are married; one of the unmarried pastors is engaged to the mother of his child, and the other has a long-standing relationship with a female friend who frequently appears on the show.

3

As viewers watch the show, they are given a glimpse into the world of evangelical preachers. Although at first glance the show seems to only focus on the men, the women provide an interesting glimpse at what it means to be a preacher's wife, fiancée, or female companion. There were a total of eight episodes that aired over the course of two months. This chapter explores how black women and their friendships are portrayed on *Preachers of L.A.*—including the one white woman on the show. It also examines their discourse between one another—using critical race feminism to analyze the roles of these women as first ladies (a term used to describe the wives of pastors), their relationship with one other, and the conversations they have surrounding sex, marriage, relationships, and friendships. The chapter focuses on the first season of the show, which began in the fall of 2013. The show was later renewed for a second season, which began airing late summer 2014. This critique attempts to bring awareness to black women in the church and the discourse that perpetuates the stereotypes of black women on television. It also aims to initiate further conversations on various stereotypes—regardless of context—that have the potential to bear negatively on black women.

## BLACK WOMEN'S IMAGES IN MAINSTREAM MEDIA

Although media representations of African American women are increasing in mainstream media, it is still important to understand how black women are portrayed.[3] The term "mainstream" is conceptualized as having the purpose of gaining viewership or readership from the majority of the public. This does not include special interest groups, or media targeting special populations such as ethnic minorities.[4] Mainstream media images of blacks, however, are not consistent with the way blacks view themselves.[5] This can be attributed—in part—to stereotypes. Black women's misrepresentation continues to dominate media—from television shows and commercials, to print ads in magazines and newspapers. This misrepresentation in media comes from a misinterpretation of black women's history.[6] As discussed in chapter one, black women were historically represented in mainstream media as Mammies and Jezebels.

A known media analyst, K. Sue Jewell (1993),[7] argued that the way media perpetuates stereotypes is a reflection of the larger mindset of society; and media must change these stereotypes in order for mainstream society to begin to change theirs. However, some argue that even the re-construction of the black woman will still be a stereotype that would simply change from negative to positive.[8] For example, even when black women are seen "as strong and independent" these same attributes have been blamed for the demise of the black family.[9] Hence, media images will never encompass all aspects of black women, as no social entity can.[10] However, yet another representation of these women purports to represent the "real" black woman, when in actuality it represents more of the idea of the black woman. This "idea" does not create a direct relationship between how black women actually identify themselves and how media portrays them. As such, with the rise of reality television and more black women being represented in them, viewers are given another version of what they consider to be the "real" black woman.

## CRITICAL RACE FEMINISM

Critical Race Feminism (CRF) is a derivative of Critical Race Theory (CRT). Roots of CRF can also be found in legal research, but the theory made its debut into the academy approximately ten years ago—to explain the intersections of race in the context of gender oppression.[11] CRF examines how "structural racism actively works against non-white people."[12] CRF further extends CRT to include "the experiences of women of color [which] are not adequately conceptualized within race or gender-only theories and social movements."[13] Therefore, CRF's foundations include intersectionality, which "complicates the demarcation of social identities by demonstrating how race is intertwined with other categories of identity difference."[14] The experiences of women of color need to be situated within all of their social identities to understand the lived experiences of these women. However, CRF does argue that there is still "no all-encompassing gender experience or race experience that is independent of other identities."[15] Thus, for the purpose of this study—in order to examine how black women are portrayed within the reality show *Preachers of L.A.*—an analysis of how the intersections of race, gender, and class are illustrated when the women are together is conducted to examine the structural racism of reality television in the portrayal of black women.

Sule (2014) stated, "CRF employs storytelling to explicate the intricacies of how institutions and social practices are lived by women of color."[16] The analysis of these women and their relationships with each other tells a story of black women's friendships as illustrated on reality television. "CRF facilitates an analysis of the relationship between systems of power and agency—the ability to identify and select options."[17] This study is situated within the concepts of agency and power, those who have agency and how it is achieved, and the lack of power of those outside the dominant discourse. All of these are illustrated through the various gatherings the ladies have on the show. Moreover, the roles of these women are important to analyze in order to understand how "agency can manifest on a continuum from actions that reproduce social structure to actions that transform social structure."[18]

CRF provides a framework that centers these black women's experiences to understand how their raced and gendered bodies are displaced for mainstream television as an authentic experience of black women. This framework further explains how black women are perceived through the eyes of mainstream society with how they are represented through this religious reality show. The character types that emerge in how these black women are perceived take it a step further than previously examined stereotypes, to also understand how religion impacts the black women in this reality show. However, many of the conflicts and discourse within the show are anything but "amazing," as one network executive proclaimed.

The analysis of the images of black women on *Preachers of L.A.* will extend the conversation on black women's experiences with the intersections of race, class, and gender to understand the multiple identities prevalent in the show. My ability, as a black woman, to analyze and understand these women's stories as not all equal—but representations of their own experiences—can help to deconstruct how some may interpret the women's portrayals on the show. Furthermore, the deconstruction of these women's stories will help in understanding how black women are perceived in the media, and how the portrayals speak to a greater story of the black woman's experience.

## METHOD OF ANALYSIS

CRF is beneficial to investigate how media representations potentially impact perceptions of black women. As a methodology in this study, CRF unpacks how race, gender, and class explain the varying representations of black women in reality television specifically—and media in general— which seems to represent them more than mainstream television. This analysis will examine the first season of *Preachers of L.A.*, specifically focusing on the interactions of the women in the show. Each scene was viewed several times and the conversations were thoroughly transcribed (including nonverbal expressions and the positionality of the women in comparison to one other).

From there, I analyzed the conversations based on the themes present within CRF. In addition to that, I examined how these black women's relationships existed within the realm of black culture and in contrast to mainstream culture. Furthermore, the themes employed in this analysis emerged from a previous study by Evans-Winters and Esposito (2010) on applying a theoretical framework of CRF to black girls' education. Through their lens of CRF it is clear the connection to using this lens in media to understand black women's representation. The themes include:

1. Critical race feminism is a theoretical lens and movement purports that women of color's experiences, thus perspectives, are different from experiences of men of color and those of white women;
2. Critical race feminism focuses on the lives of women of color who face multiple forms of discrimination, due to the intersections of race, class, and gender within a system of white male patriarchy and racist oppression;
3. Critical race feminism asserts the multiple identities and consciousness of women of color (i.e., anti-essentialist);
4. Critical race feminism is multidisciplinary in scope and breadth; and
5. Critical race feminism calls for theories and practices that simultaneously study and combat gender and racial oppression.[19]

Through a CRF lens, I illustrate the types of characters that are embodied within this reality television show to understand how these images do not portray the black woman from a CRF perspective and instead the show continues to essentialize black women and their experience by silencing their race, class, and gender.

## BLACK WOMEN CHARACTER TYPES IN *PREACHERS OF L.A.*

The following section examines the friendships between the women in *Preachers of L.A.* According to Niles Goins (2011),[20] Black women's friendships are an important and integral part of black women's existence. These friendships serve as a place of safety and security, as a place where black women can be themselves. In the show, there are six women who are married, engaged, or in a relationship with the pastors represented on the show. Minister Deitrick Haddon is engaged to Dominique. He was a pastor of a church in Detroit, but now focuses on his music ministry. Bishop Gibson is married to First Lady LaVette. As stated by Lady LaVette, "a First Lady is a term of respect and honor" for the wives of senior pastors at a church (sometimes the term is shortened simply to 'Lady' and their first name). Pastor Jay Haizlip is married to First Lady Christy. Lady Christy is the only white woman on the show, but they pastor a diverse, multicultural congregation. Pastor Wayne Chaney is married to First Lady Myesha. And Bishop Clarence McClendon is married to First Lady Priscilla. Lady Priscilla is the only woman on *Preachers of L.A.* who does not actively participate in friendship-building with the other women, for reasons not clarified on the show. Lady Priscilla is also racially ambiguous—meaning that her racial background is not clearly expressed or defined on the show. Lastly, Bishop Noel Jones has a special "lady friend" named Loretta. Loretta and Bishop Noel have been friends for sixteen years; the dynamics of their relationship will be discussed further in the chapter. Hence, this analysis focuses on the six types of characters that emerged during the course of season one, as the women interacted with one another.

## THE VICTIM

In episode three—*Tea and Sympathy*—the women met together as a group for the first time for a high tea party, hosted by Lady Myesha. *The Victim* is a term that Bishop Noel Jones used when Loretta told him that she was invited to the First Lady tea. Loretta asked what he thought about her going to the tea. Bishop Noel replied, "So they're the first ladies and you are going to be the victim." He was suggesting that she does not have a place there and that they are only inviting her to interrogate her about their relationship. He warned that it would be them against her. *The Victim* is the woman who is being taken advantage of by a man and needs to learn her value by giving him an ultimatum. And what Bishop Jones described is exactly what happened when Loretta attended the tea party. During a question and answer session, Loretta stated, "I know I am not married to a pastor but . . ." Lady LaVette then interrupted her and asked, "You're not married [pause] yet? Are you and Bishop engaged?" Other questions followed, "How long have you been friends?" and "So are you happy being unmarried?" Loretta then became defensive and felt like a victim that needed sympathy, because she has been "friends" with a man who will not marry her. She then turned the tables by saying, "Let me be clear. Let's just not assume that I'm here to be his wife." This was Loretta's way of taking back her agency and power. She proclaimed that she is happy with who she is, and that she is not defined by marriage. On the other hand, she added that if marriage eventually happened she would be very happy; and she asked the women to "pray for her." In this instance, Loretta rejected the dominant institution of marriage, but also embraced the idea of marriage in the future.

Within black women's friendships, the idea of navigating the contradictions forced by society—but also trying to find a place in other ways—is a key component to the need for these friendships.[21] At first, it seems that the women are attacking Loretta, but then they seem to remember their place as "Godly women" and the purpose for the group, which is for support and freedom to discuss their issues. It is also supposed to be a place for fellowship, and healing. Lady LaVette then switched her tone towards the end of the tea party and reminded Loretta of her worth—though still placing her in the role of the victim—yet with a more loving and less judgmental tone.

## MATERIALISTIC MARTHA

The majority of the women on the show embody materialism and consumerism. Most of them drive very expensive luxury cars—except for the two women who are not married. For the tea party, they were expected to wear hats, gloves, and pearls. A high tea party is considered a luxury in England, which these women are trying to emulate. Most of the women's hats were intricate and beautifully designed. In fact, Lady Loretta considered herself a hat connoisseur—with hats ranging from $50 to over $200. Additionally, their attire was also very expensive. During one conversation about friendship, Lady Christy was lamenting about developing a close female friendship with someone who can say to her, "you can get in my convertible." The assumption, of course, was that her friend would even have a convertible. She was not wishing for a friend to say, "Let's grab a cup of coffee or go for a walk," but specifically, "let's go for a drive in an expensive car." By the end of episode three, Lady Myesha and Lady Christy were spending time together shopping and Lady Christy said, "I want to be a blessing to you." Lady Myesha responded to that by saying, "Well I'm gonna go ahead and let you buy me something." There was an assumption there that being a blessing meant something financial or material. And although finances are sometimes discussed among black female friends, this type of display seems grossly exaggerated, as though it is one of the most important things to them.[22] Additionally, throughout the show, large, extravagant homes, Bentleys, Land Rovers, Mercedes, and expensive jewelry and clothes surround these women. It appears excessive and superficial.

## COMPASSIONATE CANDACE

As mentioned earlier, stereotypes can also be positive. One of the attributes that many of the women portrayed in the show was compassion. During the high tea party, they talked about being a support system for one another. Words such as "I am going to support you," "I am there for you," "I get you," and "you are all unique, all lovely, all special" were commonly used throughout the tea party event. Moreover, there were several hugs and kisses exchanged. During one emotional scene, the women all comforted one another as a few others welled up with tears about friendship and the need for friendship. The purpose of the tea party was to provide a community for Pastor's wives to come together, talk to each other, spend time together, and to be a support system for the unique issues that they go through. Additionally, during other episodes when some of the ladies would get together, they did seem to demonstrate genuine concern for one another's wellbeing.

## MESSY MARY AND JUDGING JANICE

*Messy Mary* is a character stereotype that describes a woman who likes to delve into the personal lives of other women; and also included within this framework is *Judging Janice*. Both of these characters are similar, in that, they tend to appear simultaneously. Judging Janice is a woman who judges another woman's experience as inappropriate. Not only does she think that what the woman is doing is inappropriate, but she also offers unsolicited advice to make it better—by her terms. At first, when planning the gathering, Lady LaVette suggested that only women who can truly understand their experiences should attend—so that they can "get down to the nitty gritty." Later, however, she seemed to enjoy probing into the lives of some of the other women, particularly those whose lives were not aligned with the Christian lifestyle that she felt they should follow. For instance, Lady LaVette did not want Loretta to come to the tea party, because she was not engaged or married to Bishop Noel. She felt that her lifestyle was not the same as the rest of the women. In fact, prior to the event, when Lady Myesha asked Lady LaVette whom she should invite to the tea, Lady LaVette stated, "girlfriends don't have the same level of commitment and shouldn't be allowed because she is not able to relate to the first lady's experience." Lady Myesha decided to invite Loretta anyway. Then, when Lady LaVette saw Loretta, she gave her a look of disapproval. Later, during Loretta's "interrogation," Lady LaVette asked her if she was engaged to Bishop Jones, even though she already knew that the couple was not engaged. When Loretta responded, Lady LaVette gasped and said, "You're not." Then she said that she was about to go "Preacher wifey" on her, as she attempted to delve further in Loretta's personal business. Lady LaVette also suggested that Loretta show more value for herself and require marriage from the Bishop. At this point, Lady LaVette had become a Judging Janice. She took it upon herself to assume that something was wrong with Loretta for not requiring marriage, and she suggested that Loretta use scripture to fix the situation.

After the tea party, Lady LaVette pulled Dominique aside to tell her that she does not need to live with Minister Haddon before they get married, and she suggested that Dominique follow what the Bible says. Again, this was unsolicited advice, insinuating that Dominique was having premarital sex with Minister Haddon and that is why she wants to live with him. Lady LaVette also stated—during a confessional scene—that she hoped Dominique was helping Minister Haddon to deal with some of the issues that caused his first marriage to fail. She was insinuating that Minister Haddon was unfaithful to his first wife and may do the same to Dominique. Of course, none of this information was of any concern of Lady LaVette, but she went on to tell her husband everything that transpired at the tea.

Another example of *Messy Mary* and *Judging Janice* was during a meeting with Lady Myesha, Lady Christy, and Loretta at Loretta's restaurant—JJs Bistro—in episode six. They began a conversation about Dominique and Minister Haddon's upcoming wedding. Loretta said, "I don't know all of the details of the relationship, but I do know this is a great new beginning for the both of them." It was unclear how she would know or not know about either parts of this statement. However, Lady Myesha went on to clarify what Loretta could have meant by that statement by saying, "So do you guys think that people should have babies and not be married?" Both of these statements related to the fact that Dominique had become pregnant by Minister Haddon while he was in the process of divorcing his first wife. All of the ladies knew the details of this story, because it was widely publicized within the Christian community. Loretta then went on to say, "Everybody has free will to do what they want. I don't judge people for the actions they take. I don't judge Lady Christy for her tattoos." In short, the entire conversation centered on judgment, even as both ladies argued that they were not judging. Nonetheless, not only were they judging Dominique, they were also judging Lady Christy by bringing up her tattoos. Both Loretta and Lady Myesha were embodying a Messy Mary, by talking about Dominique and her personal life when she was not present. Overall, these women offered a negative portrayal of black womanhood, by suggesting that within black female friendships there is a lack of trust surrounding how much information can be shared, because there is always a perceived possibility that what is shared will be talked about in separate conversations—behind your back. This can also cause difficulty in women's desire to share; and because this is a religious context, judgment may be even harsher. Although historically the black church "functioned as a place of solace and strength,"[23] a new question has emerged. That is—what is the function of the black church now, particularly with character stereotypes such as Messy Mary and Judging Janice, as portrayed by these First Ladies on television?

## THE PEACEMAKER AND THE PLEASER

*The Peacemaker* and *The Pleaser* are characters that do not necessarily involve interactions between the women, but interactions with their husbands. *The Peacemaker* is a woman who calms her husband or significant other down when they are angry or upset. During several episodes, the women act as peacemakers and the "voice of reason" for their husbands. For instance, in episode one, Minister Haddon became involved in a verbal altercation with Bishop Clarence McClendon. In episode two, he and Dominique were in the studio, and she asked him about what happened at the "Man Cave." He was still furious about the incident and the way that Bishop McClendon spoke to him. Dominique asked several questions to get to the bottom of what happened. After she listened to his side of the story she commented, "How can you guys reconcile? Whether you have a relationship or not, but just to clear the air. So if you do see each other it's not tense . . . praying that you come as humble as you want him to be. That is my prayer for you." In this situation, she offered a levelhead to help him see the entirety of the situation. By the end of their conversation, he was calm and more levelheaded. Throughout the season, Minister Haddon spoke many times of how Dominique was his peace and has helped him come out of a really dark place in his life.

In another scene, Pastor Jay Haizlip and Lady Christy were discussing an issue about one of their church members who is transitioning from female to male. They were speaking with another member of the executive team at the church, and Pastor Haizlip was struggling with how to deal with the situation. Lady Christy said, "We have to show the love of Jesus. We have to adhere to the way our belief system would handle it . . . and that would be with love." Hence, she provided the assurance that, at the end of the day despite how they may personally feel, they have an obligation to reach out to this member and love him. She did not know exactly how to handle it, but she provided a peace and comfort about the situation. There were several episodes in which the women provided a sense of reason and rationale to the men of the show.

The other character is *The Pleaser*. This one did not manifest until nearly the end of the season. Dominique, Lady Christy, Lady Myesha, and Lady LaVette were having lunch together, when Dominique asked how they make time to be with their husbands outside of the church. Lady Myesha began making insinuations about her sexual relationship with her husband. Then all of the women agreed that sex was a key component in their relationships. Comments ranged from: "Have sex in different places," "say yes as often as possible," and "you always say yes unless it's something extreme." These women offered themselves as pleasers to their husbands with no concern for what they individually wanted. Although, based on their facial expressions, it did not appear as though they always wanted to have sex. It came across as though they felt obligated as wives. Within the Christian community there is a theme that 'women's bodies no longer belong to them, but to their husbands.' In other words, their first responsibility is to please their husbands. Therefore, the question becomes—what about their own pleasure? What if they do not want to have sex? These questions are not addressed on the show. Dominique was given the advice that these women were probably given at some point in their lives, "please your husband; that is your responsibility." This type of character places the woman as objects, not subjects. This is a common stereotype of how women in general—not just Black women—are viewed throughout media, whether in advertisements or television shows.

## DISCUSSION AND CONCLUSION

This chapter examines various portrayals of black women on the show, *Preachers of L.A.* The characters seem to have intersecting layers of not just race and gender, but also class and religion. Throughout the shows, each of the women embody one or more of the characters listed above. Critical Race Feminism (CRF) examines the social construction of race in the larger context of societal institutions. Although race is not specifically discussed on the show, the absence of race on a television show that revolves around a predominantly black cast speaks volumes; and the lack of discussion on race leaves the show lacking on how these black women's experiences are actually influenced by race. Additionally, the materialism that is evident on the show seems to only involve the black members of the cast, as the white couple on the show rarely speaks of material things. The white couple lives in a more modest home and dresses more casually than the black cast members. Conversely, the black couples seem to flaunt their wealth more often on the show, which speaks to how class is demonstrated on the show, but not really discussed among the women. Their experiences of race, class, and gender are silenced throughout the show and instead they focus on more relational elements of the characters. This silencing explains the need for CRF in this study, because it addresses how these women still operate in a society in which they still face "multiple forms of discrimination, due to intersections of race, class, and gender within a system of white male patriarchy and racist oppression," yet in reality television these ideas are silenced.[24] Why is that? CRF purports that the experiences of women of color are different than "the experiences of men of color and those of white women."[25] How does a show that revolves around both black and white men and women continue to portray the black women as having essentialist characters instead of embracing the "multiple identities and consciousness of women of color?"[26]

Many such questions emerge after viewing season one of *Preachers of L.A.* Another question to emerge asks—What was the rationale behind taking race out of the issues that they deal with on a day-to-day basis? In my experience as a black woman in friendships with other black women, issues of race seem inevitable. Niles Goins (2011)[27] discussed this as one of the many tensions that black women's friendship groups experience. "These groups allow the females to speak with freedom, to strengthen their souls, and to tell stories that reinforce their identities, particularly in a society that magnifies their differences."[28] Race is a topic that, although not overtly discussed, is mentioned at various times when discussing certain topics in black women's friendship groups. The fact that in *Preachers of L.A.* it is never mentioned says something about how the black female experience is perceived by the people producing the show, who appear to leave race absent from the conversation. In fact, the only time race was mentioned on the show was when Pastor Haizlip said at a Gospel concert, where most of the audience was black, "I was a little too white when I was standing next to Ron Gibson." In this particular case, by not mentioning race as an integral part of these women's lives, the show seems to promote a colorblind theme—whereby race is not an issue that black women experience on a day to day basis.

On the other hand, the character themes that do emerge in season one provide interesting narratives for how these black women interact with one another. Their stories provide an array of different experiences that many black women can attest to—from finding true friendships, to getting married and finding time for the marriage while balancing other work-life circumstances. These women seem to have real experiences that illustrate them in a different lens. The characters are not extremely evil or extremely good. They experience real life issues that could be seen as controversial to some, but they are everyday situations that many women experience. These narratives are important in understanding feminist discourse and they provide a way of examining the inequalities within their experiences[29]—as seen in the characters of *The Peacemaker* and *The Pleaser*. These roles are controversial to some, particularly within the Christian community, because they suggest that the role of a woman is to be submissive to her mate. This inequality leads women to find their value and worth in their husbands, and when women are not married—such as Loretta—they are seen as deviants of the Christian community.

The last two themes deal with a woman of color's experience, and the ways it differs from those of men of color. The woman of color's experience cannot be essentialized to other women's experiences.[30] The experiences of these women are definitely different from their significant others, yet throughout the show—because race is not discussed—there is not an equivalent sampling of the women's experience as compared to the men's experiences. Moreover, these women's stories cannot be essentialized as one black woman's experience. The character themes provide a deeper understanding of what some pastors' wives experience. They can be relatable to other women, but each of these narratives is unique and different, given that each one of these women have lived and experienced life very differently. However, some watching the show may feel that all First Ladies are like these women and that the "Church" may not be a place for them. These character themes only provide a broad view of the experiences of these women; and they allow a different view of black women's portrayals in reality television. *Preachers of L.A.* gives a glimpse into the lives of six women building friendships, and their personal lives with their significant others. Their images represent black women within a religious context; and the issues discussed include sex, marriage, relationships, and friendships. These characters are not new portrayals of old stereotypes, but some display gender in a way previously seen—such as women being submissive—while others provide more of a view into the experiences of these specific women. These representations are not inherently dysfunctional, but they could be viewed—within the context of religion—as stereotypical. In the end, the portrayals of black women on reality television should only be viewed as snapshots into certain black women's experiences, which are molded and manipulated by producers for a certain type of audience. It is up to researchers to unpack their narratives, provide an examination into the impact of these stories, and start conversations about how the portrayals impact black women and the society as a whole.

## NOTES

1. Oxygen Announces 'Preachers of L.A.' Season Two Premiere Date (Video). *Huff Post Black Voices.* Last modified June 27, 2014. http://www.huffingtonpost.com/2014/06/24/preachers-of-la-season-two-premiere-date_n_5525337.html.
2. Ibid.
3. Juanita J. Covert and Travis L. Dixon, "A Changing View: Representation and Effects of the Portrayal of Women of Color in Mainstream Women's Magazines," *Communication Research,* 35 (2008): 232–233.
4. Ibid.
5. Jannette Dates and William Barlow, *Split Image: African Americans in the Mass Media* (2nd ed.), (Washington, DC: Howard University Press, 1993), 10.
6. Shawna V. Hudson, "Re-creational Television: The Paradox of Change and Continuity within Stereotypical Iconography, *Sociological Inquiry* 68 (1998): 242.
7. K. Sue Jewell, *From Mammy to Miss America and Beyond: Cultural Images and the Shaping of US Social Policy* (London: Routledge, 1993), 1–256.
8. Linda L. Ammons, "Mules, Madonnas, Babies, Bathwater, Racial Imagery, and Stereotypes: The African American Woman and the Battered Woman Syndrome," in *Critical Race Feminism: A reader* (2nd ed), ed. Adrien Katherine Wing (New York: New York University Press, 2011), 261–269.
9. Ibid.
10. Hudson, "The Paradox of Change and Continuity," 245.
11. Ayanna F. Brown, "Descendants of 'Ruth:' Black Girls Coping Through the 'Black male crisis,'" *Urban Review* 43 (2011): 597–598.
12. Ibid., 602.
13. Venice Thandi Sulé, "Enact, Discard, and Transform: A Critical Race Feminist Perspective on Professional Socialization among Tenured Black Female Faculty," *International Journal of Qualitative Studies in Education,* 27 (2014): 435.
14. Ibid.
15. Ibid., 436.
16. Ibid.
17. Ibid.
18. Ibid., 437.
19. Venus E. Evans-Winters and Jennifer Esposito, "Other People's Daughters: Critical Race Feminism and Black Girls' Education," *Educational Foundations,* 24 (2010): 20.
20. Marnel Niles Goins, "Playing with Dialectics: Black Female Friendship Groups as Homeplace," *Communication Studies,* 62 (2011): 540.
21. Ibid., 535.
22. Ibid., 537.
23. Brown, "Black Girls coping," 599.
24. Evans-Winters and Esposito, "Other People's Daughters," 20.
25. Ibid.
26. Ibid.

27. Niles Goins, "Black Female Friendship Groups," 531.

28. Ibid., 532.

29. Adrien Katherine Wing, "Introduction," *Critical Race Feminism: A Reader* (2nd ed.), (New York: New York University Press, 2011), 7.

30. Ibid.

# TWO

## The God in Me

*Faith, Reality TV, and Black Women*

### Chetachi A. Egwu

The display of spirituality, faith and religion is not a new phenomenon among black women in the United States, nor is it new to the world of media. Africans came to the Americas with their own sense of spirituality and religion, and the awareness of a higher being became the mortar that bound the community together during the trials of enslavement and subsequent oppression. Not surprisingly, this legacy of worship continues to provide solace and strength, with black women at the helm.

In fact, a *Washington Post*-Keiser Family Foundation Study (2012) found that black women are among the most religious people in America, with 74 percent of black women responding that living a religious life is very important to them personally; compared with 70 percent of black men, 57 percent of white women and 43 percent of white men. In tumultuous times, the *Washington Post* indicates that 87 percent of black women turn to faith as a coping mechanism.[1] Since black women play such a pivotal role in faith, spirituality and religion, understanding the role of these concepts in the lives of black women is critical to gaining insight on this population.

While there is a body of research concerned with investigating perceptions, images and stereotypes of black women on reality television, no work thus far has investigated the role of faith, religion and spirituality in the lives of the main characters. The research presented in this chapter attempts to examine the functions of faith, spirituality and religion in the televised lives of black women. Through careful analysis of Season 3 of the reality show *Mary Mary*—and the two lead cast members, Tina and Erica Campbell—this chapter will begin a discussion and form a foundation for subsequent studies on black women, reality television and faith.

## AFRICAN AMERICANS AND THE
## IMPORTANCE OF RELIGION

The fact that faith has been and continues to be a large part of African American life is beyond debate. Beliefs and practices steeped in spirituality and religiosity provide a meaningful context within which African Americans interpret and respond to critical life events. Further, churches exist as forums where black men and women can cultivate and assert traits such as personal and organizational leadership, skills that are often discouraged in larger society.[2]

In exploring religion and black people within a historical context, Africans in sub-Saharan Africa observed their own traditional religious beliefs, rooted in the reverence for nature and the land.[3] Islam spread throughout North Africa and then to countries in Sub-Saharan eastern and western Africa through Arab influence. In asserting the historical context of the struggle for recognition and civil treatment, the function of black religions is paramount. Ross (2012) writes that early religious efforts by Africans in the Americas sought to "preserve functions of cultural systems disrupted through colonization and enslavement."[4] Essentially, Ross (2012) contends that black religions and para-religious groups provided structure for black civil society.[5] She further asserts that the purpose of the religious journey among African Americans paralleled the purpose of religion for continental Africans, which was to affirm humanity and cultivate social cohesion.[6]

Through religious institutions such as Islam, practices rooted in African traditions and brotherhoods, such as Prince Hall freemasonry, had a presence in early black America. Eventually Protestant-style Christianity became the predominant religious practice among African Americans—resulting from planters' fervor for Christianity as a justification for enslavement, coupled with state-sanctioned subjugation of Africans' varied religious practices. Such support for widespread African Christianity worked to significantly diminish, though not completely abolish, the diverse black religious practices.[7] African acceptance of Christianity, then, served two functions. For the European oppressors it provided solace and safety in that the enslaved Africans' foreign, pagan ways had been eliminated; and for the enslaved Africans, it provided a means of acceptable worship, thus making them—presumably—more acceptable to society.

Historians have also documented the pivotal role that religion played in the mobilization and humanization of enslaved Africans. Protestant

Christianity acted as preservation factor for the humanity of many slaves, while encouraging resistance and escape for others.[8] The historical cultivation of the African Christian in the European likeness, and later in the form of religions that incorporated the unique background of Africans in the Americas—such as the African Methodist Episcopal Church—has resulted in African Americans fiercely adhering to faith. According to the Pew Research Religions and Public Life Project, over half of African-Americans (53 percent) reported attending religious services at least once a week, more than three-in-four (76 percent) reported praying at least daily and nearly nine-in-ten (88 percent) said that they have absolute certainty in the existence of God. On each of these measures, African-Americans stood out as the most religiously committed racial or ethnic group in the nation.[9] These findings are consistent with the *Washington Post*-Keiser Family Foundation Study, where 74 percent of black women attested to the importance of living a religious life and 70 percent of black men echoing this assertion.[10]

Black faith has also taken a front seat in terms of politics. The influence of religion in the political realm is well documented. Clyde Wilcox and Leopoldo Gomez (1990) detailed that endorsements by black ministers have been pivotal in the election of black mayors.[11] They also assert that churches serve as places for political organization and getting out the vote, as well as a possible important financial resource. The authors note that Jesse Jackson raised large sums prior to the Super Tuesday primaries in the 1980s, through collections gathered at black churches.[12] Further, black churches were shown to be instrumental in John F. Kennedy's victory over Richard Nixon.[13]

Not all views of the politics and black religion are rooted in the ability to mobilize. Reed's (1986) evaluation of the 1984 presidential campaign of Jesse Jackson argues that the idea that the black church encourages political participation among blacks is a myth; instead, the church encourages "political quietism" among African Americans, suppressing mass activism among African Americans.[14] In a more recent example, Cauchon (2012) reports that black churches were conflicted about president Obama's stance on gay marriage.[15]

In a study examining three separate cohorts of African Americans and variables affecting an African American belief system, Allen and Bagozzi (2001) theorized that religiosity would have a positive correlation to a collective African belief system across the studied cohorts.[16] They further hypothesized that African Americans who display greater religiosity would "feel closer to black masses, feel closer to black elites, possess stronger positive stereotypes, and possess a stronger sense of self-esteem."[17] Finally, the researchers speculated that greater religiosity would cultivate a solid perception of well-being among African Americans, coupled with a more critical view of the social system (i.e., express greater system blame, more system cynicism, and more perceived racial discrimination).

Their findings indicated that there was indeed a positive correlation between level of religiosity and certain variables; the higher the level of religiosity, the greater participants reported feeling close to the black masses and black elites. Those who reported high religiosity also held more positive stereotypes of African Americans and greater self-esteem. However, the results did not show that the participants had a greater sense of well-being or were more critical of the system. In fact, in one cohort, those with a high level of religious belief were shown to be less critical of the system, indicating that their faith caused them to regard negative situations through the lens of religious teaching.[18] This is demonstrative of the importance of faith in the outlook of African Americans regarding their life contexts.

Linda Chatters, Jeffrey Levin and Robert Joseph Taylor (1999) developed a three-dimensional model of African American religious involvement based on their research.[19] *Organizational religious participation* references behaviors occurring within a religious setting, such as a church or a mosque. *Non-organizational religious participation* cites activities such as private prayer and reading religious materials, and *subjective religiosity* measures phenomena such as the perceived salience of religion.[20]

Using this three-pronged approach, Taylor, Mattis and Chatters (1999) investigated African American subjective religiosity from five large national probability samples.[21] The findings showed that African Americans demonstrate high levels of various indicators of subjective religiosity compared to whites. The findings show that black Americans indicated (a) religious comfort and support was extremely helpful in coping with life problems and difficulties, (b) religious and spiritual beliefs were important in their daily lives, (c) they felt close to God, and (d) they considered themselves to be religious.[22]

## BLACK WOMEN AND THE CONCEPT OF FAITH

As previously discussed, the concept of faith has long been germane to the black female experience. Black churches are of particular value for African American women, as the numerous social ills affecting them—i.e., racism and sexism—are often handled through religious and spiritual convictions and beliefs.[23] In addition to turning to faith as solace in times of distress, research indicates that women may be more religious because of prescribed gender roles. Mol (1985) suggests that males in Western societies are socialized to value aggressiveness and goal achievement rather than conflict resolution.[24] Conversely, Francis (1997) cites that female socialization encourages conflict resolution and traits such as nurturance, gentleness, and submission, all which comply with the tenets of Western religious teachings.[25] African American women have been socialized to believe in the power associated with aligning one's behavior with mainstream values; hence, as a devalued group, it makes sense that many would forgo the earthly satisfaction of mainstream respect and acceptance for the divine promise of the everlasting life outlined in religious texts.[26]

Numerous studies demonstrate the key role that faith plays in the lives of African American women, attesting to the fact that this group exhibits a higher level of spirituality and religiosity. Taylor et al. (1999) found their study to be consistent with other research in terms of gender. Participants reported that subjective religious involvement substantiates the characterization that African American women are more religiously involved than men.[27] It is notable that despite life disappointments that could cause many to turn away from the concept of spirituality, African American women still find peace in knowing that something greater than themselves exists and that the hope for better is still possible.

## STEREOTYPING REALITY AND BLACK WOMEN

How real are the story lines and actions in a 'reality' series? According to Tyree (2011), not very. The author contends that many reality television shows contain scripting and staging and consequently are re-imagined as situation comedies or dramas.[28] Darling (2004) further posits that in this repositioning, reality-based programming must have conflict and resolution as well as heroes and villains.[29] Following a traditional narrative structure with easily identifiable characters helps to move the story along from episode to episode. These recognizable characters often have stereotypical behavior. Wilson and Gutierrez (1995) write that such stereotyping serves as a substitute for character development.[30]

In the characterization of black women, the stereotyping has taken both old and new forms. In a textual analysis of ten reality shows, on both broadcast and cable networks featuring African American cast members, Tyree (2011) examined the gamedoc, talent competition and docusoap—sub genres of reality television—to discover the occurrences of historic and new stereotypes of African American cast members.[31] She discovered that African American women in these programs were mainly characterized under three stereotype genres: the angry black woman whose wrath is a hair-trigger away; the hoochie, whose primary offering is sex, and who is usually uneducated, possessing little social status; and the chicken head, or modern-day jezebel. The chicken head (also known as the hood rat) exhibits moral bankruptcy in her sexual exploits and gold digging behavior.[32]

The advent of such anger and extreme sexual disregard apparently provides a media-prescribed formula for entertainment. The recent physical squabbles that have taken place between women on VH1's *Basketball Wives*, such as the infamous drink and bottle throwing incidents by cast member Evelyn Lozada, seemed to set off similar incidences on other programs (Mayte from *Hollywood Exes* and Karli Redd from *Love and Hip Hop Atlanta* both engaged in beverage throwing after Lozada's initial incident.) *Love and Hip Hop Atlanta*'s Joseline Hernandez does not shy away from the fact that she "loves sex." Hernandez's character is positioned as both the hoochie and the chicken head; there is friction between her and some of the other cast members; thus, her past as a stripper is constantly hurled back at her as a weapon. Although the men in the cast are sometimes the antecedents for the women's irrational behavior, rarely are they called out or held responsible for it. Ironically, the creators and executive producers of both the *Basketball Wives* and *Love and Hip Hop* franchises, Shaunie O'Neal and Mona Scott-Young respectively, are black women. In their quest to commodify the black female image, O'Neal and Young miss critical opportunities to speak for black women's sexual agency, projecting sexually empowered women rather than whores, and to display conflict resolution skills, dispelling angry black woman representations.

Such stereotypes of black women persist because they are still an inherent part of the American cultural landscape. Hence, media portrayals and everyday American life are not mutually exclusive.[33] The key point, however, is not that other groups are always fairly depicted in reality programming—as evidenced by shows such as TLC's *Breaking Amish*, and *Return to Amish* and Bravos' *Shahs of Sunset*, all which evidently deal with religious themes as part of the storyline. Bravo's *Shahs of Sunset* explores the paradox in stereotyping. The cast is comprised of predominantly Iranian (Persian) American Muslims living in Los Angeles—with the exception of Mike who is a Persian Jew. Though they are shown as overly concerned with opulence and appearance, these traits are often viewed as desirable by mainstream society, thus making them acceptable. The production also humanizes the struggles that they have come from in Iran, further humanizing them for the audience. In one episode, Asa and Lily have a conversation about going to visit Turkey, as travel to bordering Iran was not possible. Despite the obvious pain Asa felt by being unable to freely visit her family members, her emotions and feeling about her family's escape from Iran also deems her human, a complete departure from current news reports and media depictions of people from the Arab world.

Despite criticism, being wealthy and attractive makes the flawed female cast members acceptable. *Shahs* cast member, Golnesa, often displays a complete lack of self-control, lashing out at people for what seems insignificant. The same criteria applied to black female cast members on similar shows would have them deemed irresponsible for their displays of wealth and angry outbursts. The difference here is that all Arab

American women are not labeled as angry because of Golnesa's actions; yet, all black women are angry because of Kenya Moore (*Real Housewives of Atlanta*).

## THE BLACK CHURCH AND THE MEDIA

The presence of the black church in media is far from a new occurrence. In some shape or form, religion, spirituality and faith have been synonymous with black existence in the broadcasted space. Filmmaker Oscar Micheaux tackled the issue of charlatan preachers in *Within Our Gates* (1919).[34] Popularity has led to the expansion of the black church into mega churches, with charismatic pastors, music filled services, and doctrines of economic development.[35] Evidence of the power of televised black ministries can be seen in examples like Fred K.C. Price's *Crenshaw Christian Center* broadcast and *The Potter's House*, with popular minister and author Bishop T.D. Jakes at the helm.

In fact, in a study exploring religious media use by African-Americans, black Caribbeans and non-Hispanic whites, Taylor and Chatters (2011) found that about half of African Americans, 49.46 percent, and 36.68 percent of Caribbean blacks listened to religious radio programming nearly every day and at least once per week.[36] In terms of viewing religious television, 32 percent of African Americans and 24 percent of black Caribbeans report watching at least once a week, in contrast to 14 percent of non-Hispanic whites. The results speak to the fact that blacks are higher consumers of media than whites—watching more television (Nielsen 2013)—and blacks also display higher levels of religiosity.[37]

Moreover, the importance of gospel music has made its way from relegation, to Sunday music video programs, to primetime television, as BET's *Sunday Best*—a gospel singing competition featuring gospel icons as judges—is now in its seventh season. The fact that African Americans value spirituality has also been recognized in sitcoms with predominantly black casts. *The Flip Wilson Show* (NBC, 1970–1974) featured Wilson as the materialistic Reverend Leroy of the 'Church of What's Happening Now.' Race and faith led the storyline in *Good Times* (CBS, 1974–1979), when JJ created a painting he called black Jesus (1974, Season 1, Episode 2). *The Cosby Show* (NBC, 1984–1992) frequently showed the family discussing church attendance and showed family matriarch, Claire Huxtable (Phylicia Rashad), singing 'All Good Things Will Be Added Unto You' with the Hillman Choir (1987, Season 3, Episode 25). The Chris Rock-produced *Everybody Hates Chris* featured an episode where his mother was on a quest to find the largest hat, so she could dominate the church fashion on Easter Sunday (The CW Network, 2005–2009). And faith, religion and spirituality were the main topics on *Amen* (NBC, 1986–1991),

UPN's *Good News* (1997–1998) and on TV Land's *The Soul Man*, which debuted in 2012.

According to Seikaly (2014), network executives have now taken notice of the long ignored faith-based market.[38] Seikaly (2014) notes that Eli Lehrer, Lifetime Network's senior VP of nonfiction programming, says this new trend of televising religion is demonstrative of the increase in programming targeted toward other demographics, like African-Americans.[39] We TV's *Mary*, A&E's *Duck Dynasty*, GSN's (Game Show Network) *American Bible Challenge* and Lifetime's *Preachers' Daughters* are a few examples of the growing number of shows highlighting faith on TV. In addition to *American Bible Challenge*, GSN premiered *It Takes a Church* in 2014, a dating reality show where church members attempt to find a mate for one of their single congregants. Clearly, network executives see the financial opportunities that lie in targeting the devout.

Moreover, in 2012, TLC debuted *The Sisterhood*, a show that provides a detailed look at the lives of the first ladies of Atlanta-based churches. This was followed by BET's *The Sheards*, about the famous Detroit-based gospel music family; Oxygen's *The Preachers of L.A.*; and *Thicker than Water*, on Bravo, about millionaire gospel recording artist Ben Tankard. In a 2013 article for *The Washington Post*, however, Rahiel Tesfamariam wrote that while such shows may provide a much desired and needed look into the lives of pastors and their families, it may also serve to further embarrass and polarize the religious community, already wrought with ridicule.[40] Tesfamariam (2013) further suggested that the depictions of opulence among the reality religious makes a mockery of black wealth in general, positioning wealthy African Americans as irresponsible—a view made worse by highlighting prosperity in ministries.[41] This stance is also reported by Jonathan Hicks of BET.com, citing that numerous pastors gave the show a strong, negative reaction.[42]

On the other hand, upon examining "religious" reality programs, the significance or insignificance of the black women is twofold. The shows feature black female cast members—often prominently as in the case of *The Sisterhood*—as subordinates to the male characters. For instance, in *The Sisterhood* the emphasis is on the female characters as a support system for the male cast, even if they are also instrumental in the ministry. Stereotypes about the woman's lack of ability to lead persist in the black church, whether based on interpretation of Biblical history or rooted in Western hegemony. This ideology further suggests that her existence as a faithful, religious and spiritual being can only be facilitated through male intervention.

Political Analyst and television host, Roland Martin, mentioned to a panel on his show, *NewsOne Now*, asserted that he "can't watch ignorance," after watching the second episode of *The Sisterhood*.[43] Martin also noted that unlike the majority of pastor's wives, very little of the show's contents had anything to do with the church. In essence, the show is not an accurate depiction of what most first ladies endure. While Martin may not have intended to indicate that the women on the show are ignorant, it does set the stage for an important discussion. Additionally, a photo recap on the website for Oxygen's *Preachers of LA* is captioned "Big Hats, Bigger Gossip," which implies that the women on the show are unsuitable, with utility in little more than stirring up trouble.[44] This is consistent with stereotypes of black women as messy, gossipy, and in Christian circles, unfit for church leadership.

## ANALYSIS OF MARY MARY

As previously mentioned, black women on reality TV have been framed as a series of stereotypes, both new and old. Though these stereotypes continue to persist in the media, there has been little recognition that the cast members, like all humans, are multi-faceted beings. As such, it is natural to assume that because faith plays such a large part in the lives of African American women it would be reflected on reality television. This section examines the exhibitions of faith, religion and spirituality of Tina and Erica Campbell on WE TV's *Mary*. This program was selected for evaluation because of its faith-based nature, and the depth and diversity of experiences that occurred during Season 3. In addition to the episodes aired during Season 3, this chapter also analyzes the text in both women's social media commentary to gauge their expressions of faith, given that contemporary television tends to rely on its social media presence. The major queries that guide this evaluation are: (1) In what ways do the sisters' behaviors express faith, religion and spirituality; (2) Which of the three are more prominently displayed by the sisters within the context of the program; and (3) How does operating within the secular space of the show affect their expression of these concepts. In dissecting the text related to *Mary Mary*, my intention is to uncover another side of black women on current reality television programs, the side that gives conscious thought in a realm of often unconscionable actions. This analysis may further give insight as to how viewing audiences may regard the sisters' spiritual presence on the show.

## TEXTUAL ANALYSIS

As humans, we make sense of our world not only through interaction with others, but also through our experiences with cultural products — e.g. film, television, magazines, clothing, jewelry, etc. These texts are cultural productions from which individuals make meaning, therefore gaining a sense of how they act upon the world, and what it means when factions in the world act upon them. Employing a textual analysis methodology serves researchers in fields such as mass communication, cultural studies and media studies, in that it sheds light on the multitude of ways in which we interpret reality.[45] Alan McKee (2003) further states that using textual analysis as an interpretation technique involves an 'educated guess' by the researcher to determine the likely interpretations.[46]

The analysis of text guided by specific research questions using this approach does not often produce singular, unified answers as to the meaning of the text. Hence, different researchers could be given the same group of texts and draw completely different conclusions, as they rely on their cultural knowledge from which the texts emanate. It is then possible to understand some researchers' arguments against the post-structuralist textual analysis. However, McKee (2003) contends that it is difficult to examine human sense-making through a purely scientific scope. While chemical reactions may show the same result over repeated tests, human reactions differ.[47]

Though different from statistical facts, textual analysis provides a useful way to begin the conversation of what the text is saying and why the viewpoint is useful. In this manner, it is no less truthful than numerical quantification. Simply performing a content analysis to count the number of times the pair said 'Jesus,' 'pray,' 'Lord' or 'God' as a measure of their faith would not have provided differentiation between *Mary Mary* and the methods used for a televised religious service, or a film that is a spoof of religion. In this case, the analysis leans on Leanne Newman's (2004) model to explore Tina and Erica's faith and moments in the show that depict it.[48]

## NEWMAN'S MODEL OF SPIRITUALITY AND RELIGION AS FUNCTION OF FAITH

As previously discussed, both religion and spirituality require faith as a foundation. According to Newman (2004), *faith* is the prevailing tenet by which individuals claim either religiosity or spirituality, and it serves as both the source and the target of such.[49] It is a sense of *knowing*. Moreover, Newman's (2004) assertion suggests that an individual's commitment to religion or the appearance of maturation in spirituality may be viewed as a gauge of greater understanding of one's faith.[50] In *religion*, the expression of faith exists in the act of *doing*—attending worship services and praying are examples. *Spirituality* draws its essence from a life guided by the spirit of one's faith. Newman (2004) quantifies spirituality by saying that "persons may meditate, pray, or make conscious decisions regarding their actions based on how they sense the Spirit leading them," in short a state of *being*.[51]

Newman (2004) further maintains that religion and spirituality can be mutually exclusive. Hence, it is possible to have faith, or *knowing*, that a higher being exists, without exhibiting an allegiance to a particular religion by attending a prescribed church, or *doing*.[52] One may also have faith and engage in spirituality, or *being*, without religiosity. For example, an individual may not be very religious, but feels they are a good person (e.g. may not attend church services, but meditates daily).[53]

A similar pattern is seen in the Chatters, Levin and Taylor (1992) three-dimensional model of African American religious behaviors.[54] Their three-pronged approach of organizational religious participation, non-organizational religious participation, and subjective religiosity, loosely correlates to some aspects of the Newman model.

## NEWMAN'S MODEL OF FAITH, SPIRITUALITY AND RELIGION

While the model and definitions are by no means exhaustive, its simplicity provides an adequate starting point for a discussion on black women, faith and reality tv; and as the basis for subsequent research on the topic. Note that the discussion can only take place within the frame of behaviors revealed on the show and spoken about through social media, which may not always be an accurate reflection of a cast member's actual feelings or behaviors.

## A TALE OF TWO MARYS: TESTS OF FAITH, RELIGION, AND SPIRITUALITY

Tina Campbell and Erica Atkins-Campbell comprise the award winning gospel group *Mary Mary*. Hailing from a family of nine siblings, with an evangelist/choir director mother and a youth minister father, the pair has been a force on the gospel music scene since 2000, with their crossover hit "Shackles." Since then, the group has gone on to win numerous awards (three Grammys, two American Music Awards, a BET Award and an NAACP Image Award), solidifying their place in gospel music, and arguably pop/R&B given their crossover appeal. In 2012, their reality program *Mary Mary* debuted on WE TV.[55] It follows the balancing act of their very public lives as gospel artists trying to raise and expand their families.

The show puts the sisters' beliefs on full display. For instance, they are shown on several episodes holding group prayer before performances and meals. In a 2009 interview with PBS's Tavis Smiley, Erica refers to herself as a "vessel," asserting that "to be able to be used by God in that way is amazing . . . we should all be open to be vessels, to be used for the greater good and to make a change in this world."[56] This vessel approach expresses Erica's sense of religiosity—the action of doing. The pair cite on their official website the endeavor to spread the message of faith to both youth and adults through their music.

In another interview on the *Arsenio Hall Show*, Tina responds to a question about being on the show, by saying:

> I don't think I ever imagined when I was sitting on the couch watching Arsenio Hall for countless years that I would end up on the couch talking to him, I never even thought or dreamed that. So as Erica said, God can always dream a bigger dream for you than you can. And I like the way you dreaming, God, I like it.[57]

The concept of dreaming is often as abstract as the conceptualization of God. The fact that Tina feels that God has a larger plan is her process of knowing—a process that has helped her cope with the difficult situations she encounters.

Now in its third season, the sisters experienced an onslaught of faith-testing events on the show. It was revealed in the first episode of Season 3 that Tina's husband, drummer Teddy Campbell, had engaged in numerous instances of infidelity. Tina, while hurt, was forgiving at first, but discovered in a later episode that there had been more than one indiscretion. In Episode 7, we see an explosive scene between Erica and Tina, where Erica questions Tina's faith and how to proceed in the situation.

> You all want me to be more saved than I am! I love Jesus, I wanna be like him, but I'm not Jesus! Y'all gotta let me be broken, let me get it out.[58]

The level of exasperation appears to be Tina's response to the undue pressure that visible people of faith feel—an expectation to react within the parameters of their faith. There is also the expectation, as Tina expresses, for Christians to 'be like Jesus.' This view is also upheld by Tara Lewis, a pastor's wife in *The Sisterhood*. On the inaugural episode she stated, "When you're married to a pastor, you're held to a higher standard."[59]

The phrase 'What Would Jesus Do?' (WWJD) comes to mind in discussing the previously mentioned scene in Episode 7. The popular phrase is seen on a myriad of artifacts, and acts as semiotic reminder, or sign, that those who walk the Christian walk should aspire to mirror Christ's behavior. Thus, Christians, especially those in the public eye, continuously wear an invisible WWJD bracelet.

Tina eventually solidifies her faithfulness, saying that she loves Jesus and wants to be like him, a goal for followers of Christianity.[60] In a proverbial sense, she puts her bracelet back on. Though still extremely angry, and with her husband out of the house, she eventually exhibits a major tenet of those professing Christianity and other religions—forgiveness. Tina does so twice, when she initially discovers her husband's infidelity, and after discovering that he had withheld the actual number of affairs.[61] Her sense of religion is front and center—demonstrating her adherence to the Biblical doctrine of how often one must forgive. In Matthew 18:21–22 it states:

> Then Peter came to Jesus and asked, "Lord, how many times shall I forgive my brother or sister who sins against me? Up to seven times?" Jesus answered, "I tell you, not seven times, but seventy times seven."[62]

This passage implies that one should forgive those who have transgressed against him/her for eternity and beyond. The same creed is heard in *The Lord's Prayer*, which states, "Forgive us our trespasses as we forgive those who trespass against us . . ."[63]

Tina's initial response to her husband's infidelity is a human one, as opposed to a Biblical one. Later in the clip, Tina strongly affirms "I don't want him, I don't want him. I don't want him . . . he doesn't deserve me."[64] Her initial refusal to forgive her husband, but proclaiming her love for and desire to be like Jesus indicates that while she questions her religion, she recognizes a spiritual force outside of herself. Nonetheless, Tina's faith remains intact, as she somehow manages to transcend her anger, and rely on religiosity to come to the ultimate display of her combined faith and religion in the form of forgiveness. Waffling through the two aspects of faith is probable, as Newman's (2004) model suggests that while faith is foundational and within the individual, religion and spirituality are in flux.[65]

Tina discusses her husband's infidelity with her mother, who tries to comfort her with religious principles. Tina replies:

> I understand what you're saying, but I can't just say, Ooh, well to God be the Glory, real life happens and it hurts.[66]

Her mother responded with understanding, as she also had been "to hell and back," hinting at the fact that she had also faced infidelity, and that "you shake it off after a while."[67] Going back to Francis's (1997) contention of female socialization, conflict resolution and submission comply with the doctrines of Western religious philosophy, possibly a partial rationale for women's willingness to forgive infidelity.[68]

This willingness of black people to forgive those who hurt them is not by accident, it is deeply imbedded in a faith-based approach conflict resolution. This "letting go" is observable throughout history, despite the acts of anti-black terrorism that took place in the segregated south of the 1960s, after the legal crumbling of the apartheid system in South Africa, and most recently, by the families of the nine individuals who were slain by a white gunman at Emanuel African Methodist Episcopal Church in June 2015.

In fact, in a June 20, 2015 article for the BBC News, Adam Harris explores the concept of forgiveness in the African American church, noting that this ability to forgive serves as both an act of mercy and a method of dealing with systematic oppression.[69] Patton (2015) notes, however, that the expectation of black forgiveness and the expediency with which African Americans are expected to grant it does not allow for processing, grieving or healing and is deeply problematic.[70] The marital infidelity Tina faced played out publicly, and was therefore open to societal scrutiny. Thus, before she had the proper chance to process her situation, her role as a representative of African American Christian values dictated that she exercise forgiveness toward her husband. It remains to be seen what affect her seemingly premature mercy has on her marriage and the future course of the show.

Erica also has a bout with tribulation in Episode 7. After years of vigorous singing, her vocal cords are beginning to show signs of wear and tear. In response to the doctor informing her that she had a nodule on her left cord and needed to slow down to facilitate healing, Erica acknowledged the testing of her faith in the confessional:

> The moment I got a shot, I got blood on my vocal chords? [looking to the sky] Come on God. . . . What am I supposed to do? I can't rest . . .[71]

Her acknowledgment of God shows that her sense of faith and spirituality remain, while her religious principles bend. Yet, we see her renewed sense of faith in a tweet after one of her followers/fans urges her to rest her voice. Her fan tweets, "Girl, you are straining your voice. Not good. Why not lip-sync instead? You need to do that." Erica responds in all caps, "MY GOD IS A HEALER AND I'M HEALED IN JESUS NAME!"

In this tweet, Erica asserts that it is her sense of faith that will help her overcome the struggles with her voice. As evidenced by the generations of black women who held on to faith in troubled times, Erica remains faithful while simultaneously loosely holding on to fear and doubt.

As committed as the sisters are to their musical careers, they are more staunch in their "family first" commitment. In fact, the catalyst to Erica embarking on a solo career is because Tina declared her need to take a break to focus more on her family. The show makes full use of these moments to solidify adherence to family values: an eight-month pregnant Tina takes her daughter with her to a show in New Orleans and they go to an amusement park. Erica's oldest daughter is shown crying when her mom leaves to go to another show. Moreover, there are rarely times where their mother or siblings do not make an appearance. These instances exemplify their religiosity, as marriage and family are cornerstones of Christian values.

Additionally, there are other situations that occur in season 3, such as: (1) Erica and Tina take a break from *Mary Mary* to allow Tina to focus on her family and rebuild her relationship with Teddy, and for Erica to build a solo career; (2) the family also experiences the death of their father, and (3) they part ways with their manager, Mitchell.[72] In all of these situations, they lean on faith and religion in the form of prayer, giving counsel, and of course, performing gospel. These physical signs of faith appear to signify the sisters'/family's deep commitment to the hopefulness of faith and religious action.

## SOCIAL MEDIA AS TEXT

Because social media today is intertwined with and pivotal to the success of contemporary television, it is key to also explore these platforms. Furthermore, social media provides an outlet for reality stars (seemingly) away from the camera, where their unscripted thoughts, and true personalities may shine through.

According to the Pew Internet and American Life Project (2013), 29 percent of black adults use Twitter. Facebook garnered more hits, with 76 percent of black adults online. Upon examining the official *Mary Mary* Facebook page, it was discovered that it was probably linked to Twitter, as the bulk of the message used Twitter's 140 character format and contained the same messages. From this, it was then determined that for Erica and Tina, their primary form of social media use is Twitter. Search phrases in Twitter all contained their names, Erica & Tina, and/or their Twitter handle, @therealmarymary plus God, Jesus, father, death, solo, cheating, or infidelity.

This analysis included all tweets from the June 2012 debut of the series until the end of season 3. Their tweets were primarily messages of faith and inspiration for their followers, and updates about upcoming live performances and new developments. Additionally, the pair would tweet about God, Jesus and other aspects of their Christian faith. For instance, posted on @therealmarymary in November of 2012 was the tweet, "Know more than just what U hear on Sunday in church! Study and know God for yourself. Seek search learn grow, Think & Expand & LIVE!!"

This tweet seems to suggest the importance of reaching beyond religion to know spirituality (being), and it implies that the physical church is more of a manifestation of religion (doing). Their suggestion that followers come to know and determine their own concept of God in addition to church edict, is an example of spirituality. Other examples of messages on Twitter attest to the tradition of religion, in the form of recognizable prayers. From @therealmarymary, they tweet:

> God grant me the serenity to accept the things I cannot change,
> The courage to change the things I can,
> And the wisdom to know the difference.[73]

*The Serenity Prayer* is demonstration of the mix of faith, spirituality and religion that the sisters exhibit, though their expressions tend toward a combination of faith and religion more so than spirituality.

In their tweets, the pair is primarily concerned with inspiring others, while offering limited self-disclosure. For instance, there were numerous tweets from followers, including other gospel artists, sending condolences for the death of their father. Yet if they responded, they did not do so publicly. This was also the case when followers commented on Tina's husband's infidelity; however, they did forward links of interviews with themselves speaking on the topics. The guarded nature of their tweets appears to give them control about the information that is circulated about *Mary Mary*, and control of their spiritual image.

Tina's actions, in response to her husband's infidelity, seem to be in keeping with the concept of not airing one's dirty laundry in public spaces, an important adage taught in many African American households. This line of thinking dictates that information that makes others (particularly whites) regard African Americans negatively should be kept private. Evelyn Simien (2006) explores this viewpoint in discussing black feminism. She writes about the belief by some black men and women that rather than fight black patriarchy, black feminists' efforts would be better directed toward protecting black men from racism.[74] Essentially, this division in ideology indicates a lack of unity among the black community, a roadblock to black liberation in the eyes of some in the African American community. Nonetheless, the irony of the situation is not lost—the women are televising portions of their lives, yet attempting privacy in their social media commentary.

In several interviews, Tina disclosed that she would not have allowed the cameras into such a private life issue if she had known her husband was cheating prior to season 3. Yet, she said she allowed taping to continue so that her situation could help someone else. Tina's initial reluctance to reveal her issue signifies her adherence to the unwritten rules of black privacy, only breaking them to give counsel.

Despite the religious nature of the program, the characters still have a tendency to fall into a pattern of "messiness," which reveals the same stereotypes present in other reality shows. Thus, the atmosphere of faith that they work to build seems to diminish in the wake of some of their actions. According to the Center for Media Literacy (2005), "the values of mainstream media typically reinforce, and therefore, affirm, the existing social system," which is inclusive of perpetuating existing stereotypes.[75] For instance, the relationship between the sisters and their white manager, Mitchell, is often contentious. Both sides feel that they deliver their best, and each side feels the other is not up to par. On several episodes, Erica, Tina, and their sister/stylist GooGoo, engaged in heated exchanges with Mitchell. There were two separate occasions where male cast members (GooGoo's then boyfriend and Erica's husband) tried to "check" Mitchell after exchanges with the sisters. Both women presented their arguments in a loud and disruptive manner, consistent with the angry black woman stereotype. They also spoke to their significant others about the arguments, causing the men to confront Mitchell. This positioned both as menacing black men. Though each justified his actions under the guise of protecting his woman, it potentially reinforced a stereotype.

While the full details of what lead to the relationship meltdown between *Mary Mary* and Mitchell are not clear on the show, we see glimpses of possible problems. The fact that Tina frequently was late for performances and then justified it with an excuse or indifference, exemplifies another stereotype of a black cultural lack of regard for time, and also exacerbates the cultural differences between the women and Mitchell.

Some fans commenting on the WE TV website seem to uphold the same conclusion. Under Mitchell's cast photo, some are messages of support. For instance, one fan/follower tweets:

> I think it is very unprofessional the way that they fired you on national TV. You pushed them into mainstream and now they are treating you like crap because they are on TV. I am sorry that you got fired, but glad you no longer have to deal with them.

Another fan tweets:

> Mitch, I have been watching this show since the previews of the series. Now I don't know about editing but I have seen the girls treat you like something stuck on their shoes. My nine year old was watching with me and she says they are mean to Mitch. You shouldn't have to have husbands, boyfriends, stylists or even the people you work with treat you with so much disrespect. . . . I have seen them cancel tours so they can have babies, spend time with cheating husbands and you have to clear it all up for them. . . . I just don't like what I see in these women. . . . Good riddance to them Mitch.

Realizing that all involved are human, it seems that a key opportunity was missed to mesh religious principles with conflict resolution, and rise above the poor problem solving methods used on other reality shows. Though the show places a religious duo at the heart of its premise, it seems to focus more on sensational behaviors consistent with the perceived wants of reality TV viewers.

## CONCLUSION

Tina Campbell and Erica Campbell are undoubtedly women of faith. On the show, they display physical markers of religion by praying, singing, teaching and sharing personal testimony at their concerts. It is also shown on their social media in the form of established Christian prayers and doctrines. Their faith is expressed with decrees of knowing that God will pull them through the difficult situations they face, that their prayers will be answered. Though leaning more toward expressions, of religion and faith, their social media posts reveal a subtle spirituality, that their concept of God is also informed by self-knowledge.

The show is evidence that while faithful, the sisters are also flawed. In watching, there is a sense of performance that viewers may perceive as a function of director's prompts and creative editing. No network maintains a show that is not well-rated; one could postulate that a certain level of drama is what keeps viewers interested and advertisers happy. This juxtaposition of the sacred against the secular shows the influence that non-religious spaces have on the lives of the religious. They are human, and grapple with the same human problems. This analysis shows that religion does not preclude them from having the same feelings or approaches to hurdles that non-religious characters have, though it does inform their subsequent responses to the issues. This, however may also result from societal pressure to conform to religious norms.

Reality television is just that—a reality that will be around as long as the American public has the tolerance for it. The genre has given audiences a look into areas of life where there would otherwise be no access. This freedom of access has expanded the offerings and opportunities for black women, as there are currently in excess of twenty-five programs running or in development that feature black women. Of the current offerings, about one third of these shows are religious in nature. Questions for further research include: (1) what are the women featured doing, and (2) what roles do faith, religion and spirituality play for the cast when the cameras are off? These are important questions as the faith community wrestles with responding to the content of some religious reality shows.

*Mary Mary* does not purport to be a program that revolutionizes societal views on Christianity and black women, or Christianity and the black community as a whole. Neither does the show profess to have expertise on religion and conflict resolution, or to approach life's problems from an 'academic,' or even productive perspective. Erica and Tina assert that they wanted to give the world a glimpse into their own lives, but not necessarily serve as blanket examples of what Christians should be like. However, societal and Biblical Christian norms do dictate how a Christian look, think, speak and behave. This is an area where we see the sisters' struggle. When people in the public eye profess to be beacons of faith, the public then holds them to higher standards, some of which are unreasonable for a human being.

WE TV is not a religious channel, and it is probably safe to assume that they did not pick up *Mary Mary* for its intrinsic artistic value—it is, after all, entertainment. The network is a business, and hence only sticks with shows that make good business sense, i.e. the ones where advertisers will spend money.

At its core, *Mary Mary* is about faith, family and music. This is a family not unlike some others, except that their lives play out on national television and social media. There are positive aspects to the program, such as the dedication the sisters have to their families and their fans. The show also deals with negative themes; the infidelity and how the sisters deal with their former manager are examples. Thus, it cannot be argued that this show is good or bad, but a creation that is subject to the humanness of the characters, editing, ratings and advertising. Faith, religion and spirituality aside, the show is a commodified cultural product.

Shows like *Mary Mary* do have the propensity to engage segments of the society that have previously been ignored in television, such as the religious and African American communities. However, if such shows continue to demonstrate that they are little more than a *Real Housewives of Atlanta* with a dash of prayer thrown in, they could quickly be tossed aside and any possible social value will be ignored.

## NOTES

1. "*Washington Post*-Kaiser Family Foundation poll of black women in America," *Washington Post*, January 29, 2012, http://www.washingtonpost.com/wp-srv/special/nation/black-women-in-america/.

2. Robert Joseph Taylor, Jacqueline Mattis and Linda Chatters, "Subjective religiosity among African Americans: A synthesis of findings from five national samples," *Journal of Black Psychology*, 25 (1999): 524.

3. Richard. R Grinker, Stephen C. Lubkemann and Christopher B. Steiner, *Perspectives on Africa: A reader in culture, history, and representation*. Oxford, England: Blackwell, 2010.

4. Rosetta Ross, "Black Theology and the History of U.S. Black Religions: Post civil rights approaches to the study of African American religions." *Religion Compass*, 6, no. 4 (2012): 250.

5. Ibid.

6. Ibid. 251.

7. Ibid.

8. Fredrick C. Harris, "Something Within: Religion as a Mobilizer of African-American Political Activism," *The Journal of Politics*, 56, no. 1 (1994): 50.

9. "A Religious Portrait of African-Americans." *Pew Research Religion and Public Life Project*. 2009, http://www.pewforum.org/2009/01/30/a-religious-portrait-of-african-americans/.

10. "*Washington Post*-Kaiser Family Foundation poll of black women in America," *Washington Post*, January 29, 2012, http://www.washingtonpost.com/wp-srv/special/nation/black-women-in-america/.

11. Leopoldo Gomez and Clyde Wilcox, "Religion, group identification, and politics among American blacks," *Sociological Analysis*, 51, no. 3 (1990): 271.

12. Ibid., 272.

13. Joyce A. Baugh, "Religion and politics: Do black churches impermissibly mix them?" *The Journal of Religious Thought*, 50, no.1 (1993): 82.

14. Adolph Reed Jr., *The Jesse Jackson Phenomenon: The Crisis of Purpose in Afro-American Politics*, 57, New Haven: Yale University Press, 1986.

15. Dennis Cauchon, "Black churches conflicted about Obama's stance on gays," *USA Today*, May 14, 2012: 15.

16. Richard L. Allen and Richard P. Bagozzi, "Cohort Differences in the Structure and Outcomes of an African American Belief System," *Journal of Black Psychology*, 27 (2001): 377.

17. Ibid.

18. Ibid.

19. Linda M. Chatters, Jeffrey S. Levin, and Robert Joseph Taylor, "Subjective Religiosity among African Americans: A Synthesis of Findings from Five National Samples," *Journal of Black Psychology*, 25(1999): 529.

20. Ibid.

21. Ibid., 524.

22. Ibid., 533.

23. Nellie. Y McKay, "Nineteenth-century Black women's spiritual autobiographies: Religious faith and self-empowerment," *In Personal Narratives Group (Eds.), Interpreting women's lives: Feminist theory and personal narrative*, 141, Bloomington: Indiana University Press, 1989.

24. Hans Mol, *The Faith of Australians*, Sydney: George Allen and Unwin, 1985.

25. Leslie Francis, "The Psychology of Gender Differences in Religion: A Review of Empirical Research," *Religion*, 27, no. 1(1997): 82.

26. Ibid.

27. Linda M. Chatters, Jeffrey S. Levin, and Robert Joseph Taylor, "Subjective Religiosity among African Americans: A Synthesis of Findings from Five National Samples." *Journal of Black Psychology*, 25(1999): 529.

28. Tia Tyree, "African American Stereotypes in Reality Television," *Howard Journal of Communications* , 22, no. 4 (2011): 395.

29. Cary Darling, "Reality TV encourages racial stereotyping," in K. F. Balkin (Ed.), *Reality TV,* 42, San Diego, CA: Greenhaven Press, 2004.

30. Clint C. Wilson and Felix Gutierrez, *Race, multiculturalism, and the media: From mass to class communication* (2nd ed.), 42, Thousand Oaks, CA: Sage Publications, 1995.

31. Tia Tyree, "African American Stereotypes," 402.

32. Ibid.

33. Patricia G. Devine and Andrew J. Elliot, "Are racial stereotypes really fading? The Princeton trilogy revisited." *Personality and Social Psychological Bulletin,* 21, (1995): 1140.

34. *Within Our Gates*, VHS, directed by Oscar Micheaux (1920; USA: Micheaux Book & Film Company, 1920).

35. "Mega Churches: Large congregations spread across Black America." *Ebony*, December 2004, 157.

36. Robert Joseph Taylor and Linda M Chatters, "Religious Media Use Among African Americans, Black Caribbeans, and Non-Hispanic Whites," *Journal of African American Studies* 15, no. 4 (2011), 433–454.

37. Nielsen 2013.

38. Andrea Seikaly, "Religion Makes an Appearance on Reality TV Landscape," *Variety*, June 11, 2014, http://variety.com.

39. Ibid.

40. Rahiel Tesfamariam, "Pastors Gone Wild: The Church and Reality TV Don't Mix," *Washington Post*, September 26, 2013, http://www.washingtonpost.com/blogs/local/wp/2013/09/26/pastors-gone-wild-the-church-and-reality-tv-dont-mix/.

41. Ibid.

42. Hicks, Jonathan, "Black Pastors Denounce the Reality Show *The Preachers of LA*," *BET.com,* October 18, 2013, http://www.bet.com/news/.

43. Newsone.com, accessed January 2015, http://newsone.com/category/newsone-now/.

44. Oxygen.com, accessed January 2015, http://www.oxygen.com/preachers-of-la?sky=ps_cm_goo_PreachersOfLA.

45. Alan McKee, *Textual Analysis: A Beginner's Guide,* 1, London: Sage Publications, 2003.

46. Ibid.

47. Ibid. 5.

48. Leanne Lewis Newman, "Faith, spirituality, and religion: A model for understanding the differences," *College Student Affairs Journal,* 23, no. 2 (2004): 107.

49. Ibid. 106.

50. Ibid. 103.

51. Ibid. 106.

52. Ibid.

53. Ibid.

54. Linda M. Chatters, Jeffrey S. Levin, and Robert Joseph Taylor, "Antecedents and dimensions of religious involvement among older Black adults." *Journal of Gerontology Social Sciences*, 47, no.6 (1992): S272.

55. WeTV.com, accessed January 2015, http://www.wetv.com/shows/mary-mary.

56. Erica Campbell, interview by Tavis Smiley, *Tavis Smiley*, PBS, June 25, 2009.

57. Erica Campbell and Tina Campbell, interview by Arsenio Hall, *The Arsenio Hall Show*, CBS, March 3, 2014.

58. *Mary Mary*, Season 3, Episode 7, We TV, 2014.

59. The Sisterhood, Season 1, Episode 1, accessed January 2015, http://www.tlc.com/tv-shows/the-sisterhood/.

60. *Mary Mary*, Season 3, Episode 7, We TV, 2014.

61. Ibid.

62. *The Holy Bible*: King James Version, World Bible Publishers, Inc.

63. Ibid.

64. *Mary Mary*, Season 3, Episode 7, We TV, 2014.

65. Leanne Lewis Newman, "Faith, spirituality, and religion: A model for understanding the differences," *College Student Affairs Journal*, 23, no. 2 (2004): 107.

66. *Mary Mary*, Season 3, Episode 6, We TV, 2014.

67. Ibid.

68. Leslie Francis, "The Psychology of Gender Differences in Religion: A Review of Empirical Research," *Religion*, 27, no. 1(1997): 85.

69. Adam Harris, "Charleston shootings: Power of forgiveness in African-American church," *BBC News*, June 20, 2015, http://www.bbc.com/news/world-us-canada-33209801.

70. Stacy Patton, "Black America should stop forgiving white racists," *The Washington Post*, accessed January 2015, https://www.washingtonpost.com.

71. *Mary Mary*, Season 3, Episode 7, We TV, 2014.

72. *Mary Mary*, Season 3, http://www.wetv.com/.

73. Fred R. Shapiro, "Who Wrote the Serenity Prayer?" *The Chronicle of Higher Education*, April 28, 2014, http://chronicle.com/article/Who-Wrote-the-Serenity-Prayer-/146159/.

74. Evelyn M. Simien, *Black Feminist Voices in Politics*. Albany, New York: State University of New York Press, 2006.

75. Center for Media Literacy, *Five Key Questions That Can Change the World*. http://www.medialit.org/.

# THREE

# From 1990s Girl to Hip-Hop Wife

## *An Analysis of the Portrayal of Tiny as Black Mother in Reality Television*

## Ryessia D. Jones, Johnny Jones & Siobhan E. Smith

Although African-American women are still underrepresented in narrative television, reality television appears to be a site where one can find many portrayals of them. As other scholars have explained, the representations of African American women in reality television are usually negative, generally presenting them as loud, angry, and without "class."[1] However, there has been little research on the complicated relationships of black motherhood, black wifehood, and their portrayals on reality television. One black mother who illustrates this tense interaction is Tameka "Tiny" Harris, nee Cottle, formerly of the 1990s girl group Xscape, and star of two reality television programs—BET's *Tiny & Toya*, and VH1's *T.I. and Tiny: The Family Hustle*. Though both programs prominently feature Cottle, BET's program constructs Tiny as an emotionally strong and pragmatically capable business woman who maintains the emotional health and financial stability of her family while her relational partner/husband, rapper Tip "T.I." Harris, is serving time in prison. However, upon T.I.'s return home, *The Family Hustle* presents Tiny as having little business savvy and as overly permissive with their blended family. This is a dangerous portrayal, given that reality TV purports to disseminate some version of "reality" to its viewers.[2]

Central to this critical textual analysis of reality television is the history of black motherhood and black wifehood in television. From shows such as *Julia* (1968–1971) to *My Wife and Kids* (2001–2005), black women have been portrayed in various sociohistoric contexts. Reality television has only added to this complexity, providing audiences with supposedly authentic sites to view black women and their lived experiences. As Boylorn (2008) explains, "the danger [of reality TV] is embedded in the inability of some consumers to distinguish between reality and fiction on the television screen."[3]

Not only does this project fill a gap in the literature, given that there are few studies exploring the representations of black motherhood and black wifehood, but it also encourages readers/viewers to critically engage the performances of black reality television participants and to create a "redistribution of power" in which they recognize the intentional reproduction of oppressive images generated to perpetuate racial, gender, sexual, and class constructions.[4] Although these texts attempt to normalize these constructions, a rereading of these shows can empower blacks and women viewers to confront and resist these images. In other words, black reality television is more than just a site for entertainment.

Respecting the importance of the aforementioned issues, this chapter reveals the manner in which the media texts of *Tiny & Toya* and *The Family Hustle* contradict and correspond in constructing Tiny's role as a black mother and black wife in reality television, portraying her as the Stage Mother, the Hip-Hop Wife, and the Celeb-reality Wife.

## REALITY TELEVISION AND PORTRAYALS OF WIFE AND MOTHERHOOD

One subgenre of reality television, the situation comedy, is often regarded highly by critics and audiences; it was pioneered by MTV's *The Osbournes* (2002). Featuring rock star Ozzy, wife Sharon, and children Jack and Kelly, this show was overwhelmingly popular with audiences and established reality TV as a safe media outlet for celebrity participation.[5] Further, reality sitcoms are intriguing sites for scholars interrogating gender, particularly (white) wifehood and motherhood. According to Casper and Gilmour, "the growing celebrity status of reality television mothers is itself a double-edged sword: the 'reality' in reality television creates the expectation that the people we see on television are the same off camera and indeed in every aspect of their lives."[6] Furthermore, reality television mothers are expected to fit the mother trope.[7] Using the Freudian Madonna/whore dichotomy, Casper and Gilmour (2012) examine Kate Gosselin's portrayal of motherhood on *Kate Plus 8* (previously known as *Jon & Kate Plus 8*). They argue that appropriate motherhood is associated with morality. Through Kate's reality, the audiences see what happens to a woman when she desires to be more than a mother: she is punished or her parenting skills are questioned. After divorcing Jon, Kate was forced to take on more parenting responsibilities, which caused her persona to change on the show. Furthermore, when Kate became more invested in her personal appearance, touting hair transformations, cosmetic surgeries, and fitness regimes, she became more invested in her own personhood and presented herself as a sexual being. However, she was then criticized for exploiting her children and for being sexually loose, resulting in others questioning her motherhood. In essence, Kate illustrates that if a woman attempts to be more than a mother and (re)establish a career, then she will be penalized for neglecting her motherly duties and responsibilities.

## REALITY TELEVISION PORTRAYALS OF BLACK WIFEHOOD AND BLACK MOTHERHOOD

Current academic scholarship on reality TV has also focused on the construction of black womanhood,[8] the black family, and black fatherhood.[9] However, examinations of the black woman as wife and mother in reality television have been lacking. Boylorn's (2008) autoethnography questions the portrayals of African-American women in reality TV, examining how these representations converge and diverge from her own experiences as a black woman. Her study utilizes the oppositional gaze to "document how black women can assemble counterstereotypical experiences and relationships to resist the negative effects of what is seen on television."[10] In sum, Boylorn (2008) views reality television as repulsive, because it features black women as modern day Jezebels, yet appealing and relatable to her as a black woman. She states, "[p]aying attention to lives, experiences, and conversations of black women who watch reality television can expand current scholarship by recognizing that black women's lives are more than what is seen on TV."[11] Our study, though not (auto)ethnographic, does focus on two aspects of black women's lives: wifehood and motherhood.

Some argue that *The Cosby Show*'s ability to relate to most families, regardless of race, was responsible for its popularity.[12] In fact, Smith's (2008) exploration of the series declares that "*The Cosby Show* normalized the nuclear family."[13] Smith (2008) goes further, examining the relationship between *The Cosby Show* and reality television programs featuring black families. She states that like *The Cosby Show*, neither *Run's House* nor *Snoop Dogg's Father Hood* present black families in distress. In fact, the worlds presented in these programs are pretty carefree, emulating *The Cosby Show* and other television shows that present traditional nuclear families. However, Snoop's show seems to connect more with black audiences through the references to black cultural institutions.[14] *Run's House* and *Father Hood* present black fathers as present in the home and actively engaged with their families. These portrayals ultimately dispute many myths about absentee black fathers and broken black families.[15] *T.I. &*

*Tiny: The Family Hustle* is the latest reality television show to emulate *The Cosby Show* with the portrayal of black traditional nuclear family.

## TINY HARRIS: XSCAPE AND BEYOND

*Tameka "Tiny" Cottle: 90s Girl.*[16] The reality TV shows that feature Tiny inform viewers of a few known and unknown facts: she is a Georgia native; she is the child of the second interracially married couple in the state of Georgia; her father, Charles Pope, was a member of the R&B group The Tams and he died from Alzheimer's disease in 2013; she is a mother of six (three biological children and three stepchildren); and she is the wife of superstar rapper T.I. However, in order to fully understand our analysis of her performance on reality television, readers should consider a brief overview of Tiny and her career as a singer-songwriter with the R&B girl group Xscape of the hip-hop soul/divas era during the 1990s.

In 1993, Xscape, originally made up of sisters LaTocha Scott and Tamika Scott, and Kandi Burruss and Tameka "Tiny" Cottle, helped super-producer Jermaine Dupri launch his So So Def Recordings imprint with the release of the group's debut album, *Hummin Comin' at Cha*. Dupri's signature production style, which broke through with the national success of teen rap duo Kris Kross (Ruffhouse/Columbia Records), originates from his production of Southern hip-hop bass music that was highly popular in Atlanta at the time.[17] With *Hummin'*, Xscape gave Dupri a smoother, more mature, R&B approach to match the thumping 808 drum programming specific to Dupri's sound. The female quartet's vocal harmonies, soulful vocals from all of its four members, and affectionate lyrics about love and relationships, combined with Dupri's sound, made debut singles like "Just Kickin' It" and "Understanding" climb the hip-hop/R&B charts, as well as the Hot 100. *Hummin Comin' at Cha* went certified platinum within a year, selling over a million copies, peaking at number seventeen on the *Billboard* 200 and number three on the Top R&B Albums charts.[18]

Xscape's laid-back sound and urban image put them in the same playlist and video rotation as groups such as TLC, SWV, and soloist Mary J. Blige. These acts are all pioneers of the hip-hop soul era that transformed pop in the early 1990s with soulful vocals, baggy clothing, and sports bras to complement a b-girl swagger.[19] Although Blige is the undisputed queen of this era and TLC briefly became the most successful female group of all-time, the original Xscape quartet succeeded with two more albums after *Hummin'* (i.e., *Off the Hook*, 1995; *Traces of My Lipstick*, 1998). Xscape, however, went on hiatus after *Traces*, with both Tamika and La-Tocha Scott recording solo music. Burruss wrote several hits, including TLC's "No Scrubs" (1999), which was co-written with Cottle. In 2005,

Tiny and the Scott sisters reformed the group with Keisha Miles, who replaced Burruss for their album *Unchained*. The group, however, has not recorded since.

Tiny's diminutive stature and light complexion gave her an incidental visual presence, opposite her Xscape cohorts. She regularly sang soprano for the group and was the lead vocalist on their second single, "Understanding." For the song and video "Do You Want To" (1996), she provided lead vocals and was the focus for the video's narrative—showing Tiny regularly missing Xscape events because she spends time with her boyfriend "Zeboe," who is cheating on her in other scenes of the video. Still, Tiny sings passionately about this relationship. The Tiny–Zeboe drama was a common theme for the group's videos during this period—the previous single, "Who Can I Run To" (1995), features Zeboe with another woman at a nightclub where Xscape happens to be the surprise headliner for the night. This is an interesting choice for the group and for Tiny, particularly during this period, because she was either pregnant or had given birth to her first child, Zonnique Pullins (born 1996), whose father is Tiny's former boyfriend Zonnie "Zeboe" Pullins.[20] Although the "Zeboe" in the videos is an actor, this is significant because the presence of the name, combined with the reality of Tiny's situation, positioned her relationship as the group's dramatic centerpiece. What is more ironic is that Tiny's imitation-of-life via music video eventually returns to reality, as years later she admits that she abandoned her career to focus on her relationship with T.I., who was still an up-and-coming rapper; her career as a singer-songwriter flourished with the Grammy Award winning "No Scrubs," and the aforementioned Xscape album, *Unchained*. During this period, one can see Tiny as a more independent, self-sufficient "90s Girl" who respects herself as a strong-willed, sexy black woman. Today, after halting her career in the music industry during the hip-hop soul era, Tiny is mostly seen on reality TV shows, where she defers to her husband's career and works on getting her daughter, Zonnique, and sons Major and King into the music business.

*Tiny and reality television.* On June 28, 2009, *Tiny & Toya*, a reality television show that documents the friendship between Tameka "Tiny" Cottle and Antonia "Toya" Carter in Atlanta, Georgia, made its debut on Black Entertainment Television (BET). While balancing motherhood, family, and fame, Tiny and Toya (re)establish their careers. Wanting to be more than Lil Wayne's "babymama," Toya embarks on a journey to make a name for herself by establishing her career as a writer and also conquering her fear of water. Desiring to be more than a stay-at-home mother, Tiny prepares to open a nail salon, develops a production company, and starts two girl groups during T.I.'s incarceration. It is interesting to note that the show's ratings do not benefit from the usual hypervisibility of the two rap icons. The men's absence on the show is noticeable and peculiar: T.I. only appears via phone conversations and Lil Wayne is completely absent. Although the show focuses on the women's lives and goals, *Tiny & Toya* reveals some interesting dynamics about Tiny's agency as a career woman, mother, and companion to then-fiancé T.I. Despite having two successful seasons of *Tiny & Toya*, the show ended on June 22, 2010 and allowed Tiny and Toya to pursue other business opportunities.

With seventy-one episodes over four seasons, *T.I. & Tiny: The Family Hustle*, which first aired on December 5, 2011, is one of VH1's more recent "celeb-reality" TV projects by Abrego's 51 Minds Entertainment. This company also produced the controversial and popular show, *Flavor of Love*, starring hip-hop icon Flava Flav. *The Family Hustle* is about the work of Tip "T.I." Harris as he returns from a one-year federal prison stint to revive his music and acting career and to work on bringing his blended family of six children together with his wife, Tameka "Tiny" Harris. Although the show boasts similar or greater star power than VH1's current slate of reality TV shows (e.g., *Love & Hip Hop, Hollywood Exes, Basketball Wives*), "family is priority No. 1," stated T.I. in the show's supertrailer. *The Family Hustle*, therefore, avoids the typically scandalous melodrama of reality TV and functions as a family reality sitcom, much like *The Osbournes, Run's House, Fatherhood*, and of course fictional narrative *The Cosby Show*.

The history of black wives and mothers in television, in addition to Tiny's history as a successful black musician, a popular rapper's wife, mother of a blended family, and her appearance in two reality TV shows lead to the study's research questions: (1) How do *Tiny & Toya* and *T. I. & Tiny: The Family Hustle* construct Tiny as black mother and wife? And (2) how does reality television construct black mothers and black wives?

## METHOD

This study used critical textual analysis to understand the construction of black motherhood in RTV.

## SAMPLE

The first season of *Tiny and Toya* was downloaded from iTunes; the first season of *The Family Hustle* was viewed on VH1's website and/or downloaded from iTunes. *Tiny and Toya* consisted of eight episodes, and *The Family Hustle* included fourteen episodes. Each episode is approximately twenty minutes long.

## THEME DEVELOPMENT

Each episode was viewed three times; specific examples of Tiny's behaviors, particularly as they spoke to black wife- and motherhood, were recorded with both a time-code and a brief description of the situational context. This chapter supports the view that Tiny Harris can be analyzed in the tradition of American television's black mother and/or wife, primarily seen in sitcoms and today transferred into reality television. Like sitcom mothers such as Julia Baker, Florida Evans, Louise Jefferson, Claire Huxtable and Vivian Banks, Tiny's performance reflects "controlling images"[21] that perpetuate troubling scripts of black women, despite the positive reviews Tiny receives as a progressive, hard-working black woman.[22] Although the authors realize that Tiny receives praise as an authentic black mother and wife, we also recognize the contradictions in her character and the oppressive effects it can have on black women.

The researchers discussed and agreed on the themes only after they had all watched the show three times. There was consensus that the two shows portrayed Tiny differently, reflecting her attempt to negotiate her roles as both wife and mother. The researchers also noted how the shows presented other wives and mothers.

## FINDINGS

Critical textual analysis of the show revealed three themes that spoke directly to Tiny's multiple identities, which are portrayed on *Tiny & Toya* and *T.I. & Tiny: The Family Hustle*. These identity themes include that of the Fiancée and Stage Mother, and the Hip-Hop Wife. The third identity, the Celeb-reality Wife, represents the friction the shows display as Tiny attempts to negotiate between the two formerly mentioned identities.

## THE DEVOTED FIANCÉE AND
## COMPROMISED STAGE MOTHER

When Tiny is introduced to viewers in *Tiny & Toya*, she references her success as a singer-songwriter, but she also admits, "Tip doesn't really care for me to work," and has abandoned her career at her man's request. Several moments throughout the show, from her commentary on her relationship with T.I. and her oldest child's father, to the conversations with Toya and other girlfriends about not working, Tiny is depicted as a woman devoted to her man. For instance, during the opening commentary Tiny expresses her loyalty to the father of her first child (a "street dude") who got arrested and served ten years in the penitentiary. During his absence, Tiny says her songwriting career flourished for a short time before she met T.I. and quit, which is the decision that Tiny begins to question on the show. First, as she sits in her home studio doodling on paper, her mother walks in after dropping off Tiny's sons and tells her that she had just heard the Xscape hit, "Just Kickin' It," on the radio and it made her wonder if Tiny would ever return to singing: "Are you gonna just give it up? . . . That's your life. It's always been your life. Been your life since you were fourteen, thirteen years old." Amid the motherly en- couragement, Tiny—swiveling in the chair, blushing and wearing ear- rings with a picture of T.I. painted on them—silently ponders her moth- er's comments.

Later in the same episode, Tiny creates a small intervention for herself during a "ladies night" slumber party at the home of her girlfriend, Phae- dra Parks. Amid conversations about finding the right man and building a relationship, Tiny asks the other women if they would be willing to abandon their careers if their men asked them to and in return promised to provide for them. After some of the women advocate this choice, some make it clear that people have to develop their own identities in a rela- tionship because they "can't be complete to somebody else if you're not complete to yourself." Tiny sits and seems to ponder her identity as the show ends.

In Episode 2 ("Miami Forever"), Tiny seems to be responding actively to the questions about her identity as she pulls up (in a Lexus) to her nail salon, a stagnant business venture that she admits still has not opened in over a year since she started it. Nonetheless, she says that the nail salon will give her "something to do" while her fiancée is in prison. A career in music, however, is out of the question, because "it's totally against what my honey wants." Early in the series, Tiny's devotion to her man and willingness to forfeit her independence is emphasized for viewers. Her confessionals demonstrate her submissiveness to patriarchy for the show's audience, which is mostly made up of women. Viewers witness a fiancée who shows ideal wife-like devotion who "stages" independence as a businesswoman, but is actually an unmarried housewife who spends most of her time on the show discussing love and relationships with her girlfriends as she awaits her man's next move. This is further proven as Toya and Tiny sit in the salon chairs of her unopened nail shop and discuss being publicly recognized as their significant other's "babyma- ma" or "wife," even though they are unmarried. Although Tiny express- es some disgust with only being noticed as T.I.'s wife, she blows it off as typical Internet and social media gossip. This scene, along with the slum- ber party, is standard in women's reality TV shows in which the perpetu- ation of little work and materialistic living is regularly portrayed in ele- gant salons, restaurants, and homes. The relaxed response to her lack of agency, along with the presentation of the finer life, connects Tiny's per- formance to other portrayals of black women in reality television. This gives viewers a problematic portrayal of black womanhood, considering the fact that the show claims to provide "a true look" into the lives of two young black women.

Tiny as devoted fiancée, or "ride or die bitch" (as she refers to herself in the pilot episode of *T.I. & Tiny: Family Hustle*), evokes some of the same racial and sexual stereotypes prevalent throughout the history of patriarchal oppressive depictions of black women. She carries her stereotypical submissiveness and extends it into a reality TV portrayal that is in line with the history of black mothers in television who regularly deferred to their husbands. The primary proof of this development lies in her evolution into a "stage mother." As the show *Tiny & Toya* develops, we notice that Tiny's passion to record music is directed towards her oldest teenage daughter, Zonnique. During one scene of Episode 2, "Miami Forever," "Niq Niq" (as she is affectionately called) sits on her bed, combs her dog's hair, and sings "Amazing Grace." Tiny eavesdrops for a few seconds before she walks into her bedroom and says, "Yeah! You sound good girl!" Then, as she sits on the bed with her daughter, she asks her if she is ready to come downstairs into the studio with her and former Xscape member, Kiesha Miles. During the confessional, Tiny says, "I'm very proud of Zonnique. She would always tell me, 'I want to sing; I want to do this.' But now, it's different. And if I can help her with that, I would like to do that." She takes Niq Niq into the studio, and they rehearse a chorus of a song that Tiny and Kiesha wrote. Eventually, Tiny goes into the studio with her daughter to help her record the chorus. The young girl's inexperience is evident in the scene, but Tiny helps her with everything from breathing to wearing headphones. This pleases Tiny, because it gives her an opportunity to live her passion:

> Music in my life right now is just starting to try and work its way back in. Watching Zonnique sing, it's making me feel like I gotta take this further. . . . [Tiny and Toya's counselor] Dr. [Ron] Elmore was telling me I didn't have to cut my life off to make Tip happy. I love Tip. The last thing I wanna do is damage or tear my relationship up. But, I think I wanna do some more music in some kind of way. (Episode 2, "Booty Tag")

This solution for Tiny to do more music constitutes her motherly duties on the show. In Episode 5 of *Tiny and Toya*, "Vent-Elation," Tiny talks to Kiesha about creating a record label and a new girl group. Later in the confessional, Tiny says that she has had a longtime desire to be a businesswoman, so she is forming a record label with two girl groups. During this scene and other scenes on the show, it is noticeable that Tiny's "mother time" mostly takes place in the studio or during meetings with Zonnique and the other girls in the groups as they prepare for a showcase. For example, in the final episode of the season, Tiny refers to all the girls as her "babies." She says she listens to them, offers advice, and is "grooming them" for the music industry. Even though she appears with her toddler sons during the opening of the show, and also in a few lengthy scenes (like her son Major's birthday party), the baby boys spend a lot of time with Tiny's mother. Meanwhile, Tiny "mothers" in the studio. This depiction is one of the rare portrayals of normal black families that exploit the black family for commercial and/or entertainment purposes. Tiny could very well be a responsible, fit mother, but American television has little desire in portraying that, especially in reality TV.

The Stage Mother's displaced motherhood and misconception of agency does not seem apparent to Tiny as the show progresses. She justifies the music groups as her achieving independence as a businesswoman, but she does not realize the continuous references she makes to her own career and obvious desire to perform again. Meanwhile, as the *Tiny & Toya* series ends after two seasons, her business falls to just one girl group, the OMG Girlz, which still features Niq Niq. As we view the first season of *T.I. & Tiny: The Family Hustle*, viewers notice the growth of Tiny's work with the group, as they prepare for the acclaimed, teen-focused "Scream Tour" (Episode 103). When the girls go on tour, however, Tiny's focus on business is not taken as seriously as it was on *Tiny & Toya*, and she is often grouped in scenes with her girlfriend Shekinah for comic relief and loud, dramatic, petty arguments (described in depth, below). In fairness, *The Family Hustle* does feature more of Tiny interacting with her sons King and Major, as well as with T.I.'s other three children from previous relationships. However, her work with them is also eventually framed in the Stage Mother role when she visits Los Angeles and tries to enlist King and Major for acting and modeling auditions, respectively (Episode 113, "Can You Work?"). This effort does not really support Tiny as a businesswoman, but ultimately supports the focus of *The Family Hustle*, which is to highlight and showcase T.I.'s premise to rebuild his family by teaching them how to "hustle," or make money in the industry (Episode 101, "God, Family, Hustle"). Tiny is merely considered as a role player in this and is not particularly significant.

## THE DEFERENTIAL HIP-HOP WIFE

In addition to Tiny portraying the faithful fiancée and eventual Stage Mother, she also presents herself as the Hip-Hop Wife. This identity appears in contrast to the Stage Mother, and is characterized by Tiny being playful and lacking serious business ventures, being treated as one of the children by T.I., and being absent in moments of childrearing. This identity is most prevalent on *The Family Hustle*.

*The Family Hustle* regularly suggests that Tiny, and by extension, her business ventures, should not be taken seriously. The show most often relies on presenting business attempts outside of T.I.'s approval as ridiculous, silly, and poorly planned. The show makes light of Tiny's endeavors with her best friend, Shekinah Anderson, through the editing and the content itself. Tiny and Shekinah's interactions are usually framed as arguments, with both women loudly yelling at one another. Viewers first see this in Episode 5, "I Will Put My Foot on Your Back Pocket," in which Tiny, Shekinah, and Tamarra, their other girlfriend, go to a plastic surgeon for a consultation while T.I. is promoting his new book, *Power and Beauty*, in Los Angeles. The root of this argument is Shekinah's frustration over "being a friend at one time and a worker in another." T.I. walks in on their fight, quickly pivots and exits the room, mocking "girl fight!" as he leaves. The ladies do work through this tiff, but it foreshadows their explosive relationship. In Episode 12 ("Sixty Forty"), Tiny decides to fund the development of Shekinah's sitting hair dryer prototype. Tiny visits Shekinah's home-based salon, and is initially pleased with Shekinah's invention; the tensions begin when Tiny initiates a discussion of revenues, what she believes should be "sixty/forty" in her favor. Shekinah becomes enraged. This leads to an argument punctuated with beeped-out vulgarity. Ladies in Shekinah's salon watch aghast. The only thing the two do agree on is that they need a mediator's assistance. The narrative follows the ladies to mediation, where the ladies continue to argue. Tiny and Shekinah finally come to agree on dividing their revenues at "fifty-six/forty-four" in Tiny's favor.

Through editing, these techniques contrast greatly with T.I.'s studio session with R&B artist Usher, which shows them complimenting each other, singing and rapping their respective parts, and enjoying playing their track back. They speak quietly with each other, and in fact, the editing suggests that the entire session was over quickly and without issue. T.I. and Usher's partnership is the polar opposite of Tiny and Shekinah's. In fact, T.I.'s reference to their business and its issues as a "girl fight" reveals *The Family Hustle*'s inner workings: the show reduces Tiny's projects outside of T.I.'s approval as fleeting, childish, and poorly developed. This element of the Hip-Hop Wife is one who cannot be successful outside of what her husband desires. At the conclusion of *The Family Hustle*, T.I. deems Tiny's successes with the OMG Girlz as somehow "part of [his] plan for the girls." All of Tiny's work with the group, including her first steps with the girls when T.I. was incarcerated, as shown in *Tiny & Toya*, is suddenly attributed to him. This is because although a Stage Mother can be successful (through her children), she cannot be successful on her own, in those undertakings that do not have her hip-hop husband's blessing. Considering the trajectory of the black woman in television, a reversal is seen in *The Family Hustle*. Black wives have traditionally played the "straight men" to the comic schemes of their husbands (e.g., *The Cosby Show*). However, unlike Claire Huxtable, Tiny is made to be the comic buffoon through her association with Shekinah; T.I. spins the role often inhabited by Claire Huxtable: funny, yet ultimately calm and always wise.

In addition to being a failure at business opportunities, Tiny is also presented as one of the children. *The Family Hustle* often shows T.I. calling family meetings. In Episode 6, as T.I. is gathering the children together, he says to Tiny, "even you too." In another, he tells her, "no shoes in the white room!" which he often tells the children. In addition, during these family meetings, Tiny is shown laughing or rolling her eyes at her husband's lectures, similar to the manner in which their children respond to their father. It is also noticeable that these lectures are generated as a result of T.I.'s desire to put disciplinary regulations into place, as he speaks to the audience about them during his confessionals. He and Tiny do not sit together during these confessionals as a united front to rear their children, and this structure continues as he lectures his family— Tiny does not stand with him.

In this same episode, "Bad and Sneaky," T.I.'s daughter Deyjah confesses to him that she has a boyfriend. He is horrified to learn this, and even more frustrated to discover "the entire family has kept secrets from me." T.I. confronts Tiny with the information, and she insists that although she did know the secret, Deyjah came to her because she felt comfortable to confide in her. "I wasn't going to betray her trust," Tiny insists. She also points out that Messiah, T.I.'s oldest son, has a girlfriend. "That's besides the point!" T.I. quips. Tiny is frustrated with this double standard, and addresses it in her confessional to the audience. However, she does not bring this point up when she is gathered, with the children, for T.I.'s family secret-excising meeting.

The pattern of T.I. as "head" of the family meetings is also displayed in Episode 8, "Tip Clause," in which T.I. presents his family with the idea for doing a play based on Messiah's book. Once again, Tiny is regulated to a role as one of the children; she receives directions from him, as the children do. This is different from the portrayal of the Stage Mother, who can be an independent worker and thinker, if only because she has to be. By contrast, the Hip-Hop Wife's identity does not put her on equal footing with her husband in child rearing or goal development; she plays a subordinate and submissive role to her husband, like that of her children. Returning to the history of black women in television, although most black men were the heads of their households, their wives were a close second in terms of power and control (e.g., Claire Huxtable, Florida Evans). Tiny's representation on *The Family Hustle* breaks from this tradition and portrays T.I. as a patriarch who rules over his family subjects— including his wife.

Probably the most dangerous facet of the Hip-Hop Wife is its implication that Tiny is an absentee parent, especially when it comes to discipline. Many recaps of previous episodes and previews of upcoming *The Family Hustle* episodes are completely lacking Tiny's presence. For example, the previews to Episodes 10 and 14, and the recap of Episode 2, do not feature Tiny at all. Instead, in the first instance, T.I. is seen as a father concerned over his son's poor grades, and in the second, working through security issues at his fashion show (jokingly with comedian Kevin Hart), and in the third, T.I. is speaking with Niq Niq before she leaves for the Scream Tour. This is particularly ironic, as Niq Niq is *Tiny's* biological daughter. These teasers suggest that Tiny does not have a hand in child rearing. According to Casper and Gilmour (2012), the act of filming motherhood and female behavior regulates both by "normalizing" through examples of appropriate and inappropriate mothering;[23] these instances act as instructional "what not to do['s]" of mothering. Further, Episode 10, which focuses on T.I. trying to discipline Domani for his poor schoolwork, and T.I. attempting to motivate him with the promise of shooting his own video, barely includes Tiny at all. She only appears at the beginning of the episode, when she learns from T.I. that Domani is failing. "He sucks!" T.I. declares, only to have Tiny insist that "[Domani] does not suck!" Although it could be a result of family dynamics that Tiny does not seem to know what was happening with Domani (recall that Domani is T.I.'s son from a previous relationship, and not her biological son), Tiny appears oblivious to Domani's situation. Her lack of knowledge of the situation is odd, considering the large amount of time *The Family Hustle* suggests that the *whole* family spends together. The entirety of these images suggests that T.I. is the more "hands-on"—and perhaps more devoted and nurturing—parent.

Further, the show implies through the use of dialogue and selected footage that Tiny is an absentee parent. In Episode 7 ("King of the House"), King is disobedient and throws temper tantrums. During T.I.'s term in prison, T.I. declared his son the "King of the House." The narrative explains that while T.I. was gone, "Tiny needed help" in raising her children, and her mother was integral in assisting her; her mother kept King. (*Tiny & Toya* also showed Dianne keeping both of the youngest boys.) Tiny speaks with her mother, who insists that King is not a bad child, but "a loving child." Later in the episode, the Harris's are gathered at home, sitting around the dinner table, when King lets loose with curse words. T.I. decides to take his four sons down to his grandfather's house, hopefully so that they will see the impoverished roots from which their father came and be appreciative of their comfortable lifestyle. Although his eldest sons Messiah and Domani "get it," King—and Major—are too young to process the lesson. T.I.'s mother states that now that T.I. is home, it is "time for order to be restored," and tells her son that "until [he] change[s] it," nothing will change King's behavior, "because [she and the others] can't." The drama continues when Tiny attempts to have King complete his homework. She is unsuccessful until T.I. helps her. King is not yet fully reformed, however, as he resists going to sleep. Despite these struggles, T.I. gets him to bed, and manages to restore order in the home.

This narrative suggests that Tiny and her mother's child rearing leave a bit to be desired. It also suggests that T.I. has the power to produce obedient children, and his mother's quote only bolsters his paternal mastery. It is also T.I.'s idea to take his sons to his childhood home. Tiny makes no appearances here, and the editing suggests that she had no say in this decision. Further, this is the only time the show displays Tiny helping her children with their schoolwork, though T.I. declares that "he will put his foot on [his children's] back pockets" if they do not do well in school. Tiny does not make such threats. In addition, in two separate instances, Tiny appears more engrossed in her cell phone than parenting her children, and the duty to bring the family under control is left to T.I.

*The Family Hustle* suggests that Tiny is most nurturing in her role as Stage Mother as she provides the OMG Girlz with love, attention, and support. Although the Stage Mother's love does not appear particularly deep outside of the entertainment realm, the Hip-Hop Wife mothers her children very little. As a result, it is up to T.I. to parent the children. Tiny's love supplements, rather than complements, his love for their family. The Hip-Hop Wife is not an attentive parent. The Hip-Hop Wife appears to break away from images of black mothers put forth in previous decades of television. In series such as *Good Times*, *The Cosby Show*, and *Julia*, it was not uncommon to see the mother interact closely and lovingly with her children. Even if it was to discipline them with stringent choice words, Florida Evans style, mothers were intimate with their children. The Hip-Hop Wife is not a mother in this vein.

## IDENTITY CONFLICT: THE CELEB-REALITY WIFE

The Hip-Hop Wife identity supplements the Fiancée and Stage Mother role, yet also often contrasts with it. The resulting tension is representative of the Celeb-reality Wife. This term also recognizes that this role was produced from the brand created by 51 Minds Entertainment, "celeb-reality." In particular, in *Tiny & Toya*, the theme of black mothers, specifically Tiny, suffering from an identity clash is demonstrated in Episode 2 ("Miami Forever"), in which the audience sees Tiny's unfinished nail salon. While there, Tiny receives a phone call from T.I., asking her where she is and why she did not wake him up before she left. Although the audience is not able to hear T.I. on the phone, through Tiny's responses to him, she reveals that he is upset with her for not speaking with him before she left, despite her insistence that she did what she could to wake him. Casper and Gilmour (2012) state that "a good homemaker—a good-mother—was expected to enable her husband's and children's dreams, nurturing the young while often ignoring or postponing her personal aspirations to instead make real the dreams of her children."[24] Their conversation suggests that because Tiny has invested time in her nail salon, she has started to fail in her duties as a hip-hop wife who is always at her husband's (and by association, her children's) beck and call—if not at his side as he sleeps. Further, it is important to note that the nail salon represents Tiny's urge to be an entrepreneur. Tiny reveals that she plans to invest more time in the nail salon once T.I. is incarcerated, "to keep [her]self busy." Because T.I. will be away, she will have more time to work at her business projects, and will not have to negotiate between spending time with him or working at her businesses.

In the next episode, "A Tiny Pain," Tiny seeks relationship advice from Dr. Elmore. Their conversation reveals what audiences learned in the previous episode: T.I. financially supports her, but does not support her when she expresses an interest in continuing her career and developing new business opportunities. In fact, when she invested time in her career, "[they] split up while [she] was on the road." This situation illustrates Sachs's argument that mothers often find other facets of themselves subsumed by their identities as mothers.[25] At the end of the conversation, Tiny says that she does not want to be a stay-at-home mother and partner. Yet, Tiny is still hesitant to pursue her entrepreneurial goals because of fear that she will damage or ruin her relationship with her husband. This is representative of Casper and Gilmore's (2012) claim that "[s]ome contemporary women harbor a love-hate relationship with their roles. The duality of their lives [as persons and mothers]—two all-consuming set of responsibilities often in conflict with each other—is a never-ending frustration."[26] Tiny appears conflicted as she attempts to be faithful to her husband's desires . . . and her own wants and needs.

Only when T.I. is sent to prison does Tiny become more invested in her career and businesses. As discussed above, Tiny and former member of Xscape, Keisha, develop two girls groups, writing and producing the songs for Juice and the OMG Girlz. When discussing music, Tiny states that she is passionate about it "because it allows [her] to be artistic," but more importantly, "it allows [her] to be fulfilled." In Episode 6, Keisha states, "I think what's so cool about us doing the group is that we still get to express ourselves musically, but just through them." Keisha's statement perfectly captures why managing these girl groups makes Tiny happy. To ensure that her relationship with T.I. is not damaged because of her career in the music industry, Tiny chooses to remain behind the scenes. Though she does not sing herself, she is able to meet her own personal creative needs while mothering the groups.

Another example that illustrates Tiny's conflict with her Stage Mother and Hip-Hop Wife identities is in Episode 2 ("Booty Tag"), when she plans to have a girl's night out with her girlfriends. As Tiny and her friends gather at Phaedra's house to get dressed for the club, Tiny receives a phone call from T.I. Once again, the audience is not able to hear what he is saying, and must infer his comments from her responses. In the scene, Tiny informs T.I. that she is going clubbing only because it is a girls' night out. She attempts to reassure him with "there's no men here, there's nothing going on." Unhappy with her response, T.I. hangs up on her. Not wanting to cause problems between her and T.I., especially with his incarceration date approaching, Tiny decides to skip girls' night and go home to be with her family. "I stayed home to keep it calm," she states in the confessional. Though she maintains a brave face and her friends are supportive, viewers can feel the palatable awkwardness of the unhealthy situation as she leaves an event planned to cheer her up. In essence, for Tiny to maintain her Hip-Hop Wife Identity, she must withdraw from her friends to fulfill her wifely duties. As Tiny becomes more committed to T.I., she becomes less committed to herself and what fulfills her, which can be "disorienting and unhealthy."[27]

More of Tiny's identity conflict is revealed in Episode 11, "Baby Girl," of *The Family Hustle*. Tiny and the OMG Girlz's *Hype Hair* photo shoot is interrupted by T.I., or as Tiny refers to him, the "fun police." As T.I. observes the photo shoot, he critiques the OMG Girlz's make-up, informing the make-up artist that their daughter, Niq Niq, has too much make-up on her face. As T.I. confronts Tiny about the Girlz's make-up, he also starts to critique their wardrobe, specifically their wedged shoes. T.I. asks Tiny if she is aware of Niq Niq's make-up and she responds in the negative. As Tiny and T.I. continue to discuss if the Girlz will be allowed to wear the wedged shoes, the hair stylist grooms Tiny. Although Tiny is in the same room with the OMG Girlz, she is framed as being absent, so consumed with her own photo shoot with *Hype Hair*, that she is unable to manage the OMG Girlz. Tiny's failures of a mother-manger is illustrated when T.I. states: "I would and should assume that what we went through at the [previously shown] video shoot would be retained, and everyone would have a concise understanding as to what would be expected when it came to wardrobe. [He imitates a buzzer.] Wrong again." In an attempt to allow the OMG Girlz to dress, as Tiny says, "with the times" and in the style common to young people in the music industry, Tiny fails to "have a concise understanding" of T.I.'s wardrobe rules, which were established in a previous scene at the OMG Girlz's video shoot. In allowing the OMG Girlz to make their own decisions about their wardrobe and make-up, Tiny is accused of neither dressing the girls age-appropriately, nor properly mothering them. In particular, T.I. hints that because of Tiny's failure as a mother, the girls will likely engage in inappropriate behaviors.

## DISCUSSION

Our findings reveal three identities Tiny Harris embodied on *Tiny & Toya* and *The Family Hustle*: the Fiancée and Stage Mother, the Hip-Hop Wife, and the Celeb-reality Wife. In discerning these identities, the analysis also made the following inferences: (1) the portrayal of mothers other than Tiny in the two shows, (2) the contrast between reality television portrayals and their portrayals in social media, and (3) the tension regarding cast members' agency in constructing their own identities in reality television.

Further illustrating Tiny's failures as a good mother and wife, *Tiny & Toya* and *The Family Hustle* offer other representations of motherhood. According to Ladd-Taylor and Umansky (1998), "the definition of a 'bad' mother intertwines with that of a 'good mother.'"[28] In *Tiny and Toya*, both white and black, "good" and "bad," representations of motherhood are present. Tiny's mother, Dianne, represents a good mother and wife. Throughout the season of *Tiny & Toya*, Dianne assists Tiny with her motherly duties. (Also, recall that in *The Family Hustle* it was revealed that Tiny was unable to control King. For this particular reason, King would often stay at Dianne's house.) Furthermore, Dianne is portrayed as a good wife to Charles. Because Charles suffers from Alzheimer's disease, his health was deteriorating. To demonstrate her faithfulness to Charles, in Episode 7 ("A Musical Escape") Dianne renews her vows to him.

Additionally, in examining Toya's representation of motherhood, she is viewed as being attentive to Reginae, her only child. When Toya discovers her daughter is not doing well in her math class, Toya hires a tutor, because she admits she does not have the skills herself. Throughout the series, Toya seems to have an active role in Reginae's life. Ladd-Taylor and Umansky (1998) mention "'good' mothers remain self-abnegating, domestic, preternaturally attuned to her children's needs."[29] For instance, in Episode 7 of *Tiny and Toya*, "A Musical Escape," after Toya returns from a business trip, Toya picks up Reginae from school. In the car scene, Toya and Reginae have a dialogue about the importance of education and behaving in school. Then, in Episode 8, Toya and Reginae have a conversation about Toya dating. They agree that Toya can date when Reginae turns eighteen, and Reginae gives her mother permission to start dating.

In her interview, Toya expresses an interest in dating but mentions, "I'm just real careful about who I date because of my daughter." With Toya's hesitation to date, she is portrayed as a good mother because she is aware of her daughter's concerns about her dating. Toya's exclusive focus on her daughter suggests that she is a "good" mother.

Although there is little camera time for Toya's mother, Anita, she is portrayed as a bad mother. As Ladd-Taylor and Umansky (1998) note, a bad mother fails to subsume her goals and desires for family members; she is selfish.[30] In Episode 5, Toya travels to New Orleans to throw her brother, Rudy, a surprise birthday party because their mother failed to acknowledge Rudy's seventeenth birthday. In her interview, Toya mentions that she raised Ruby, hinting at their mother's failure of being a mother. This was a result of Anita's drug addiction. Rudy further confirms his mother's failures when he states, "[s]upposed to be there for your children, if you're gonna make a child, you're suppose[d] to be there for 'em, like, if I make a child, I'm gonna make sure that my child get what he want[s]." The contrast between Toya and Anita as mothers adds to the poignant feel of *Tiny & Toya.*

In Episode 1, viewers see Toya travel to New Orleans to find her mother, Anita. After looking for her mother in several crack houses, Toya finds her mother on the street corner. To help her mother with her drug problem, or as Toya says, "get [her] shit together," Toya offers to take her mother to Atlanta. Although Toya does not explicitly say her mother is a bad mother, she reveals that her mother is an absent mother when she states, "[y]ou've got to get your shit together so you can take care of your kids" (Episode 1). Despite Toya's efforts, Anita declines the offer to go to Atlanta. In Episode 6, before heading back to Atlanta, Toya goes to her aunt's house to discuss her mother's drug habits. Toya is hesitant to leave New Orleans without her mother because she is concerned about Anita's well-being. This particular scene reveals that Anita's drug lifestyle takes priority over her children's needs and desires.

Another caveat of this analysis that becomes apparent—and must be confronted as readings of celebrities in reality television continue—is the ongoing narrative beyond the highly constructed reality on shows such as *Tiny & Toya* and *The Family Hustle.* Although networks regularly entertain viewers by exploiting negative portrayals of marginalized groups, the goal of cast members is often to achieve fame and build brands for themselves. Thus, many black reality TV participants spend considerable time in the public to keep themselves "hot," or relevant to their fans. This makes research subjects like Tiny difficult to analyze. For example, during the summer of 2014, while completing this chapter, the authors were met with many significant events closely related to the subject. For several months, Tiny was at the center of a celebrity love triangle, or "beef," between her husband T.I. and boxing champion Floyd Mayweather. This led to an excess of gossip, tabloid fodder, and rumors via their own social media accounts, celebrity blogs, and entertainment "news" outlets such as TMZ. Following an altercation between T.I. and Mayweather, both parties issued statements, created confessional videos, and Tiny even wrote, performed, and recorded a video for her first solo R&B single in years. Her song, "What the Fuck You Gon' Do," seems to be a response to T.I.'s recently released single, "Stay," as both songs attempt to express some of the issues the couple recently faced. Scandalous subtext of songs between couples and current or former friends and lovers is commonly performed in R&B and hip-hop music. Furthermore, the "ghetto opera" genre pioneered by artists such as Gerald Levert and R. Kelly has provided plenty of entertainment for listeners and video viewers.

It is interesting to note that Tiny has been attached to the complicated subtext of her songs since her days with Xscape, when she starred in the group's videos and used the name of her oldest daughter's father as the male lead. The drama provided through the Internet and social media surrounding Tiny and T.I., however, troubles their reality TV portrayals. This is because the family values that are acclaimed on the show contradict with problems revealed to audiences via the Internet and other social media. This creates multiple intersecting layers of Tiny that not only confine her to controlling images, but further confirm the authors' hypothesis that she lacks true agency. Even her reality TV brand as a supportive wife and mother to her family "hustle" is called into question by the highly publicized spectacle. There is little escape for her.

In addition to the conflict between reality TV and celebrity lives, our study also encourages one to consider the issue of agency when it comes to identity/image construction in the reality TV context. As Orbe explains:

> For groups historically under- and/or mis-represented within television, like people of color, reality TV seemingly offers the opportunity for individuals to have a direct effect on revamping mass mediated portrayals that have been created through a top-down, centralized fashion . . . reality TV producers . . . have gone as far as to describe this genre of programming as one where the roles of the audience and producer are reversed.[31]

For example, one African American reality TV star, Omarosa Manigault-Stallworth, stated in an interview with *The Morning News*[32] that though she was not initially aware of how she would be portrayed while taping *The Apprentice*, after she was portrayed as a black bitch on the show,[33] she knew from that point on that she would have to act badly to get screen time.[34] It can be argued that Omarosa has used her brand as a villainess to promote her self-help book, *The Bitch Switch: Knowing How to Turn It On and Off,* and to parlay her appearance on *The Apprentice* into appearances on other reality TV shows such as *Celebrity Apprentice, I Love New York,* and *The Ultimate Merger,* a dating program with a *The Bachelorette*-like structure that centered around her.[35]

However, Orbe (2008) argues that rather than allowing a space for reality TV cast members to construct their own identities, the genre actually suggests that some stereotypes "are more 'real' than others,"[36] citing the negative portrayals of African-American men on *The Real World* as examples. In an interesting contrast from the quote provided above, Omarosa states in *Jet,* a magazine targeted at black Americans: "These [reality television] shows are constructed. They are constructed reality. . . . Historically, African Americans are portrayed negatively. . . . You've got to start looking and saying, 'Is that really how all African-Americans are?'"[37] In this interview, Omarosa seems to distance herself from her portrayal on *The Apprentice,* suggesting that she had little power to prevent the construction of her "aggressive" identity, and that this negative portrayal was just "consistent with what [reality television producers] have done in the past."[38] These tensions can prompt viewers to wonder how much power Tiny had in constructing her identity as black wife and mother in *Tiny & Toya* and *The Family Hustle*.

Also, recall that Casper and Gilmour (2012) argue that motherhood is associated with proper morals: a woman should be a mother first and foremost, or risk being criticized.[39] Tiny is certainly punished during episodes of *Tiny & Toya* when she attempts to negotiate her role as a wife; T.I.'s attempts to control her, including hanging up on her, forbidding her to participate in a girl's night, and leaving their relationship illustrate his passive-aggressive behaviors. It is often easier for viewers to sympathize with her than T.I. By contrast, Tiny is mocked on *The Family Hustle*: the show portrays her business ventures with Shekinah, her (mis)management of the OMG Girlz, and her children running amok under her watch, just for laughs. Icons of televised black motherhood, such as Claire Huxtable, were never treated this way. Even *The Osbournes*, the reality sitcom that paved the way for its descendants, treated the whole family, even the bumbling, fumbling, and grumbling Ozzy, with teasing affection. *Tiny & Toya* and *The Family Hustle* imply that when (reality television) mothers such as Tiny aren't falling in line, the construction of the programs must serve to put them in their places. Whether punished or mocked, these programs suggest the mediated sociopolitical landscape is not yet ready for an Independent Woman.

## LIMITATIONS AND IMPLICATIONS FOR FURTHER RESEARCH

First, though *Tiny & Toya* did air for two seasons before Tiny left the production to appear on *The Family Hustle*, we analyzed only the first season of *Tiny & Toya*. In addition, *The Family Hustle* is still in production, with the fifth season airing in the summer of 2015. However, only the first season of *The Family Hustle* was included in our analysis. Second, our analysis did not include explorations of Tiny's music. Our analysis did not examine the videos for or the lyrics to Xscape's songs in depth, many of which, as discussed above, were penned by Tiny. Lastly, a portion of the construction of Tiny as an individual, as well as that of her marriage, is produced on the Internet and social media, as discussed above. Future analyses of black motherhood on reality TV—in fact, those that engage in examinations of "celeb-reality"—should take these sources into account to present another facet of analysis.

## IMPLICATIONS FOR FUTURE RESEARCH

The real problem this chapter highlights is the easy acceptance of "dumbed down" portrayals of black women in reality television, including the depiction of Tiny in *Tiny & Toya* and *The Family Hustle*. Her shift from career-minded "90s Girl" to redirected "Fiancée and Stage Mother" to deferential "Hip-Hop Wife" and conflicted "Celeb-reality Wife" is not recognized by viewers as regressive, and it is never really indicated that she can equally perform her roles simultaneously. If Tiny's strength during her husband's incarceration was exclusively acknowledged on *Tiny & Toya*, and her career was presented to viewers as something she was genuinely pursuing, one would have seen a more complete, well-rounded woman. Instead, Tiny is included within the plethora of black women on reality TV who claim more progressive values (e.g., sisterhood, love, independence) and pursuits, but succumb to the production once the cameras roll and the "actors" begin to interact with one another. Even though our original hypothesis suggested that Tiny Harris represents a progressive image of black women on reality TV, it is obvious that more series presenting a range of portrayals need to be produced to confront the excessive, misguided constructions in reality TV as a whole.

The popularity of black women on reality TV demands a more critical lens to help viewers better understand the oppressive portrayals as they perform within the drama of the shows. Examining Tiny specifically through the reality TV shows she has participated in enables viewers to recognize controlling images underlying her performance. This analysis invites viewers to watch reality television programs critically and question their meanings. This is even more important for young, black, and female viewers because it enables them to decipher the constructed, scripted reality in the shows and not to be overly influenced by their more inauthentic aspects. This is a necessary step in the process towards understanding sociohistorical connections inherent in this entertainment form. Thus, more analyses of individual characters are suggested as black women continue to influence viewers' ideals about black womanhood, motherhood, wifehood, and relationships with men and other women. Furthermore, if reality television continues to produce limited images of black women, viewers should be more equipped to analyze these portrayals.

## NOTES

1. Robin M. Boylorn, "As Seen on TV: An Autoethnographic Reflection on Race and Reality Television," *Critical Studies in Media Communication* 25 (2008): 413–433; Rachel E. Dubrofsky and Antoine Hardy. "Performing Race in *Flavor of Love* and *The Bachelor*," *Critical Studies in Media Communication* 25 (2008): 373–392.

2. Ji Hoon Park, "The Uncomfortable Encounter between an Urban Black and a Rural White: The Ideological Implications of Racial Conflict on MTV's *The Real World*," *Journal of Communication* 59, no. 1 (2009): 152–171.

3. Boylorn, "As Seen on TV," 421.

4. Shannon B. S. Campbell, and Steven S. Giannino. "Flaaaavooor—Flav: Comic Relief or Super Coon?" in *Masculinity in the Black Imagination*, ed. Ronald L. Jackson II and Mark C. Hopson (New York: Peter Lang, 2011), 103–112.

5. Richard M. Huff, *Reality Television* (New York: Praeger, 2006).

6. Mary F. Casper and Deneen Gilmour. "The Reality of Televised Motherhood: The Personal Quest and Feminine Test of Kate Gosselin," in *Media Depictions of Brides, Wives, and Mothers,* ed. Alena Amato Ruggerio (Lanham, MD: Rowman & Littlefield, 2012), 27.

7. Ibid.

8. Boylorn, "As Seen on TV."

9. Debra C. Smith, "Critiquing Reality-Based Televisual Black Fatherhood: A Critical Analysis of *Run's House* and *Snoop Dogg's Father Hood,*" *Critical Studies in Media Communication* 25 (2008): 393–412.

10. Boylorn, "As Seen on TV," 415.

11. Ibid., 430.

12. Marco R. Della Cava, "Relatable Characters Help Fill Television's Generation Gap," *USA Today*.com, August 21, 2009, http://usatoday30.usatoday.com/life/television/news/2009-08-19-generationaltv-main_N.htm.

13. Smith, "Critiquing Reality-Based Televisual Black Fatherhood," 394.

14. Ibid.

15. Ibid.

16. The "90s Girl" colloquialism was popularized during the hip-hop soul era, as artists such as Xscape, Mary J. Blige, and TLC became more liberal with their image and sound, yet demanded respect from men as independent women. The song, "90s Girl" (1994), recorded by short-lived Atlanta-based group, BlackGirl, actually features lyrics about the politics of being a woman of a new era, and it suggests that to be a "90s Girl" is to be independent and strong.

17. Roni Sarig, *Third Coast: OutKast, Timbaland, and How Hip-Hop Became a Southern Thing* (New York: Da Capo Press, 2007).

18. *Billboard.* "Xscape: Chart history," accessed June 13, 2014, http://www.billboard.com/artist/431553/xscape/chart.

19. Elysa Gardner, "Hip Hop Soul," in *Vibe History of Hip Hop* (New York: Three Rivers Press, 1999), 307–317.

20. Tameka&Clifford Blog!! "RECENT PIC OF ZONNIQUE," (blog) April 27, 2007, http://tipharris-tameka.blogspot.com/2007/04/recnt-pic-of-zonnique.html.

21. Patricia Hill Collins, *Black Feminist Thought.* 2nd ed. (New York: Routledge, 2000), 69.

22. Pamela Berger, "What it takes to make good reality TV," CNN.com, October 27, 2011, http://www.cnn.com/2011/10/27/showbiz/tv/good-reality-tv-berger/.

23. Casper and Gilmour, "Reality of Televised Motherhood," 34.

24. Ibid., 28.

25. Wendy Sachs, "The Truth about Motherhood," *Huffington Post,* July 21, 2010, http://www.huffingtonpost.com/wendy-sachs/the-truth-about-motherhoo_b_654401.html.

26. Casper and Gilmore, "Reality of Televised Motherhood," 28.

27. Sachs, "Truth about Motherhood," para. 5.

28. Molly Ladd-Taylor and Lauri Umansky, eds., *"Bad" Mothers: The Politics of Blame in Twentieth-Century America* (New York: New York University Press, 1998), 6.

29. Ibid.

30. Ibid.

31. Mark P. Orbe, "Representations of Race in Reality TV: Watch and Discuss," *Critical Studies in Media Communication* 25 (2008): 349.

32. Keith Hollihan, "The Omarosa Experiment," *The Morning News,* July 17, 2006, http://www.themorningnews.org/archives/manufacturing_reality/the_omarosa_experiment.php.

33. Jennifer L. Pozner, *Reality Bites Back: The Troubling Truth about Guilty Pleasure TV* (Berkley, CA: Seal Press, 2010).

34. *Jet.* "Omarosa: 'The Apprentice' TV Show's Most Popular Contestant has the Nation Talking and Watching." April 2004, 60–61.

35. Omarosa Manigault-Stallworth, *The Bitch Switch: Knowing When to Turn It On and Off* (Beverly Hills, CA: Phoenix, 2008).

36. Orbe, "Representations of Race," 350.

37. *Jet*, "Omarosa," 60-61.

38. Ibid., 61.

39. Casper and Gilmour, "Reality of Televised Motherhood."

# FOUR

# Are Black Women Loud?

*Neoliberal and Postfeminist Protagonists in OWN's Televisual Sphere*

## Mia E. Briceño & Evene Estwick

In 2011, when *Newsweek* reporter Allison Samuels asked Star Jones about her relationship with *Celebrity Apprentice* cast-mate NeNe Leakes, Jones responded, "I really don't make a point of spending a lot of time with strippers."[1] In spite of this suggestion of interpersonal conflict between the two reality television stars, Jones remarked further on the rationale behind participating in a show that also featured Leakes. She stated:

> Pitting us against each other is good ratings. So we're the ones who had to be smart enough to know how to handle it. . . . From the moment I was cast in *Celebrity Apprentice* I knew exactly what I was there for. I was there to raise money for heart disease and to publicize my book. Look at every clip of me and you see my book or the symbol I wear for heart disease. Honey, I had a plan.[2]

Jones' comments reflect a general consensus among TV critics and viewers that: 1) the black women who command the most attention on reality television tend to portray stereotypical, Sapphire-like characters; 2) as audiences consume such portrayals, there is a consistent line of argument from producers that insists "pitting [black women] against each other" is expected or "what the people want;" and 3) black female reality TV stars are willing to indulge the Sapphire fantasy if it means they will be able to further a personal and/or professional agenda. These are important themes to interrogate, especially given the history of mass mediated representations of black Americans, as well as the present-day "evolution" of black characters and other characters of color on unscripted and scripted American television. However, because attention is primarily focused on arguably "negative" portrayals, there has not been much critical analysis of "alternative" or more nuanced portrayals of black women in the televisual sphere.

This chapter represents an attempt to fill in some of that blank space by focusing attention on an underexplored and relatively new consortium of reality television programming that features black women who are defined by their roles as mothers and entrepreneurs. Although such roles are not entirely new to the reality TV landscape, they take on new and more complex meanings as they are communicated via the medium of the *Oprah Winfrey Network* (OWN)—a channel whose figurehead is none other than media mogul Oprah Winfrey. Considering Winfrey's legacy as *the* successful, self-made, black American woman, it is no small feat to inhabit a similar subject position and to be a featured player on her network. The black female protagonists in *Welcome to Sweetie Pie's*, *Raising Whitley*, and *Mom's Got Game* simultaneously evoke the tokenized, arguably one-dimensional Oprah model of success *and* demonstrate the complex and arguably evolving nature of the black televisual sphere.[3] It is significant that, unlike Winfrey herself, the protagonists of OWN's reality programming are often identified by their roles as mothers and/or matriarchs of their families. In spite of that difference, however, Robbie Montgomery, Kym Whitley, and Pamela McGee are like Winfrey in that they are independent, career-focused, and representative of the "Horatio Alger" mythology that is often reinforced in mass mediated narratives of African Americans.[4] In this chapter, we analyze the Sapphiric representations of black women in reality programming on OWN, in order to demonstrate the symbolic impact of those neoliberal, postfeminist representations in and on the black televisual sphere.

## REPRESENTATION AND OPRAHFICATION

Communication studies and cultural studies scholarship focusing on the representation of black Americans in the media has a rich history. In addition, scholarly conversations about and interventions on the Habermasian notion of the public sphere have become increasingly considerate of mediated spheres of communication, especially television. A key theoretical component in this scholarship has been the Gramscian notion of hegemony, or as Dana Cloud (1996) explains it, the conception that "capitalist societies produce relations of power not only in structures of commodity production and exchange, but also through structures of ideas, or ideologies, that become the taken-for-granted common sense of the society."[5] Where mediated representations of black Americans are concerned, critical scholars must consider the role of visual rhetoric and mass media as hegemonic structures that produce and reify negative stereotypes of black culture in general and black women in particular.[6] As K. Sue Jewell (1993) argues, "[I]t is through ideological hegemony that those in power control not only the means of production but also the production of ideas."[7] Because mass media are a primary means through which ideology is communicated, it is via mass media content that our understanding of individuals and particular groups of people are shaped. By extension, the media plays a significant role in the shaping of cultural attitudes, public policy, and as demonstrated here, societal notions of what it is like to be and what the potential life paths might be for members of different identity groups.[8] If this is true—and we concede that it is—television in general, and reality television in particular, is a legitimate space for public debate and deliberation. As such, it offers its addressed publics certain political ideals. In this study, we analyze televisual representations of black women in that context. Thus, although stereotypical images of black women have transformed slightly over the years, the basic media molds in which those images are formed remain the Mammy, the Jezebel, and the Sapphire, as noted in previous chapters.[9] There is much room for expansion and adaptation of these portrayals, as Tia Tyree (2011) has argued. However, these arguably "new" stereotypes that reflect and "update" black women's roles in public life—as represented on reality television—including the freak, the welfare mother, the gangsta female, the Angry Black Woman (ABW), and the gold digger, remain largely "negative."[10]

There is no doubt that Tyree's list of types includes those representations that are most pervasive across reality television programming. However, there are some arguably "alternative" representations of black womanhood that challenge the ubiquity of this negativity. As this analysis will show, although reminiscent of the Sapphire model, the female protagonists of OWN's reality series present a more complex portrait of black womanhood, and while these representations cannot be fully extricated from the grips of black stereotypes in general—and the Sapphire figure in particular—their presence in the reality TV landscape potentially provides an alternative ideology, relative to black culture. This discussion also demonstrates the potential to shape cultural attitudes, and possibly, public policy differently.

Considering that Oprah Winfrey herself—and by extension, her brand—have been at the center of popular culture, as well as media studies and cultural criticism for at least twenty-five years, the products affiliated with her brand are backed by a "real" power to influence. There is scarcely an arena of contemporary American culture that has not been linked with Winfrey, or theorized, in light of her sweeping influence in mass media and popular culture. For example, in 2006, Baum and Jamison argued a correlation between voters' consumption of "entertainment-oriented soft news"—a la daytime talk shows—and their voting behavior, which they termed "The *Oprah* Effect." Billye N. Rhodes and Kristal Moore Clemons (2013) demonstrate that Winfrey is not only an imposing figure in the world of television, but also a cultural icon whose attitudes and opinions have the ability to shape discourses of race in the United States.[11] In Communication Studies literature specifically, Ted Striphas (2003) argues that women who relate to and participate in Winfrey's eponymous Book Club engage in a "dialectic with the everyday" that opens a space for those readers to engage in and with feminist cultural politics.[12] Perhaps most pertinent to this study is Cloud's (1996) critique of Winfrey's "rags-to-riches biography," stating that it has been coopted in order to:

> [C]onstruct an 'Oprah' persona whose life story . . . resonates with and reinforces the American Dream, implying the accessibility of this dream to Black Americans despite the structural economic and political obstacles to achievement and survival posed in a racist society.[13]

Cloud (1996) focuses on the biography that has been constructed around Winfrey, asserting that she "[does] not mean to indict Oprah Winfrey herself." However, she demonstrates that Winfrey's participation in the construction of her own persona is key. Moreover, the rhetorical construction of Winfrey's biography extends to her network and its programming. And although the televisual niche for career-oriented, successful representations of black women is small, if it is going to thrive anywhere it is arguably on the OWN network, as Winfrey's particular brand of success opens the door for more portrayals of women "like her."

A general acceptance of the American Dream narrative and of Winfrey's ascent to, in particular, imply a kind of collective cultural allegiance to the late twentieth and early twenty-first century economic and political philosophy of neoliberalism. Janice Peck (2008) argues that, in "the age of Oprah," it is important to situate Winfrey's "journey" from "mere talk show host to cultural icon" in the context of "the rise and triumph of neoliberalism."[14] Facilitated by mediated portrayals of Winfrey's success story and also by her own declaration,[15] Winfrey arguably reigns as the poster child for pulling oneself up by one's proverbial bootstraps. The female protagonists of OWN's reality programming thus exist in the shadow of Winfrey's biography and are expected and/or selected to reflect her brand of individual self-improvement and independent financial stability (if not wealth).

Keeping in mind the stereotypical nature of "minority" representation in mass media, as well as long shadow cast by Winfrey's public persona, we argue that the women at the center of this analysis exist in a kind of liminal space between deeply engrained stereotypes of black womanhood and another kind of "Oprah effect," in which the narratives of "successful" black women are more frequently produced and consumed. As a result, they offer updated—if not "better"—representations of Black women on reality television, and arguably evidence a black televisual sphere that, we will show, is not only counterpublic but also postfeminist.[16]

## "OPRAHFIED" TV TALK AND THE PUBLIC SPHERE

The concept of a black public sphere, or a multiplicity of black public spheres both inspires and facilitates the analysis in this chapter. Herman Gray (1995) argues, "[C]ommercial culture serves both as a *resource* and a *site* in which Blackness as a cultural sign is produced, circulated, and enacted."[17] As such, it is necessary to interrogate the portrayal of black female protagonists on television via a conversation of the black televisual public sphere and to approach our text from the perspective of communication studies, cultural studies, and feminist theory. Most central to our analysis is Catherine R. Squires theory of "an alternative vocabulary for multiple public spheres" that, we will show, supports our view of OWN programming as fitting the requirements of a televisual counterpublic.

For at least twenty years, scholars have argued that television plays a significant role in U.S. culture and politics, or what is broadly termed "the public sphere." Peter Dahlgren (1995) contends that television is "the major institution of the public sphere in modern society."[18] This is so because "the dynamics of democracy are intimately linked to the practices of communication, and societal communication increasingly takes place within the mass media."[19] Although television does not echo the Habermasian notion of the early bourgeois public sphere—which "[was] composed of narrow segments of the European population, mainly educated, propertied men . . . [who] conducted discourse not only exclusive of others but prejudicial to the interests of those excluded"[20]—it is a notable modern-day alternative to that idyllic notion. As critical challenges to the Habermasian conception of the public sphere have shown, while Habermas' theory is a helpful tool, it "stops short of developing a new, post-bourgeois model of the public sphere."[21] Through an examination of a selection of OWN programs—programs that feature historically marginalized or underrepresented subjects and that are disseminated via a contemporary and evolving mass medium—we seek to contribute to a multi-faceted, multi-dimensional conception of a "post-bourgeois public sphere."

In order to support our contention that OWN influences and is influenced by a televisual counterpublic, we must first articulate the interconnections among Black Public Sphere Theory, neoliberalism, and postfeminism. According to The Black Public Sphere Collective, "[The] black public sphere is [a] critical space where new democratic forms and emergent diasporic movements can enrich and question one another."[22] It is a "critical social imaginary" that is not limited to "intellectuals," but rather, includes "a wider sphere of critical practice and visionary politics, in which intellectuals can join with the energies of the street, the school, the church, and the city to constitute a challenge to the exclusionary violence of much public space in the United States."[23] Thomas C. Holt (1995) argues, "Between 1980 and 1992, the black public sphere expanded in reach and complexity, despite the fact that progressive black political agendas were being shattered and significant social programs gutted by the policies of the Reagan-Bush era."[24] As noted above, Peck (2014) contends that Oprah Winfrey is *the* "cultural icon" for this neoliberal era. Relatedly, Mary Douglas Vavrus (2012) defines postfeminism as being comprised of three "ideological fragments," which are as follows:

> (1) An 'individualistic focus' such that successes and failures are attributed to individual women rather than to a complex formula of individual work, group efforts, and structural influences; (2) a 'lifestyle character' in which praise of feminist politics also typically casts it as 'an avenue to a higher-status lifestyle, with consumption of high-status commodities;' and (3) a solipsistic perspective from which 'white, heterosexual, and middle-class women's issues [are] generalized to all women, including those whose identities include none of these traits.'[25]

Taken together, these claims reflect the ethos of Winfrey's media empire in general, as well as OWN reality programming in particular. The qualities of neoliberalism and postfeminism described by Peck and Vavrus are not lacking in the black televisual sphere that is represented by the protagonists of *Welcome to Sweetie Pie's*, *Raising Whitley*, and *Mom's Got Game*. We will demonstrate the ways in which these themes contribute to a changing view of the Sapphire stereotype and black female televisual types more broadly.

The daytime television talk show boom of the 1980s and 1990s prompted scholarly and political questions about the role of the talk show in public debate and deliberation. In 1994, Jane M. Shattuc argued, "[N]o other public forum replicates the town meeting's democratic sensibility better than the first generation of daytime TV talk shows born in the 1970s and 1980s."[26] Shattuc (1999) counts *The Oprah Winfrey Show* as the chief contributor, among these "first generation" talk shows, to a certain kind of late twentieth century public debate. However, this "Oprahfication," as she calls it, is not necessarily a beacon to the "bowling alone" era,[27] so much as it arguably "[trivializes] 'real' politics by promoting irrational, victimized, and anomalous individuals as representative of the citizenry."[28] Shattuc's (1999) observations reflect the often gendered, and in the case of Winfrey, racialized perceptions of the kind of "talk" that daytime television programming perpetuates. By labeling this talk "Oprahfied," it demonstrates the meanings associated with Winfrey's production efforts beyond her talk show. Although we do not attend to *The Oprah Winfrey Show* in particular or daytime talk shows in general here, it is nearly impossible to divorce Winfrey's legacy in the televisual public sphere from the artifacts we analyze. As products of OWN, the reality TV shows examined herein are inevitably linked with Winfrey's brand. Also, as we demonstrate below, the ideologies espoused in each program reflect the "Oprahfication" of the public sphere, as well as Winfrey's own personal, American Dream success story. Thus, while the trend toward reality television programming in general appears to remove the "public forum" aspect of the daytime talk show, it continues to engage "issues that are central to [average Americans'] political lives: racism, sexuality, welfare rights, and religious freedom."[29]

Today's black female television characters, "real" and fictive, are affected by a troubled and troubling history of stereotypic representations of black womanhood. As representations of black women on television have increased and become more nuanced, it has become more apparent that producers create—and audiences consume—those representations in the shadow of long-perpetuated stereotypes of black womanhood. Rebecca Wanzo (2013) contends:

> What is most interesting about black representation in the 21st century is not whether it is racist or not, or whether it evokes stereotype or not, but how the strands of a stereotype, fantasy, history, and experience all interact. Who knows when we will be free of the ghosts of Mammy, coons, and sapphires? If we simply begin our analysis with the presupposition that the shadows of these representations are always there, we can focus on the idea that in fictions, as in our lives, we are constantly dealing with fictions about race and gender that cannot do justice to the complexity of human experience. When we dwell in the space between hope and failed expectations, we see with more clarity the pain and possibilities inherent in negotiation.[30]

We agree with this contention, because stereotypical representations are so prominent in our collective cultural consciousness that the representations of black womanhood on OWN will likely be interpreted via the lens of stereotypical black womanhood. Winfrey herself has long been accused of embodying a mammy stereotype,[31] especially as she exudes a kind of "cross-racial appeal" that attracts white, middle class, female audiences.[32] Rather than condemning these representations as either typically derogatory or positively transgressive, however, audiences and critics must engage with televised black womanhood as a complex discourse that is, in part, inflected with a racialized history of popular culture imagery.

The stereotypes that cast the longest shadow over our chosen texts are that of the Mammy and the Sapphire. Of course "Mammy" is perhaps the most recognizable stereotypical portrayal of black womanhood in U.S.

popular culture, as previously noted. On the other hand, the "Sapphire" stereotype is constructed as a foil to a black male figure. That is, the female Sapphire and her black male counterpart are frequently engaged in conflict, evidenced by "an ongoing verbal duel" between the two.[33] Because our protagonists are both mothers and career-driven, professionally successful women, we are particularly attuned to the potential for them to be pigeon-holed as either the Mammy or the Sapphire, or both. In addition, given Winfrey's public persona and the mass media's tendency early in her career to describe her in the Mammy mold, then as a Sapphire—following her portrayal of the "brassy" character Sofia in the film adaptation of Alice Walker's novel *The Color Purple*—it would be easy to fall into the same sort of characterization of Robbie Montgomery, Kym Whitley, and Pamela McGee.

Acknowledging the potential power of such stereotypes to overtake this analysis, we keep Wanzo's (2013) insight in mind and sharpen our focus to closely interrogate two major themes that are prominent in each of our chosen texts.[34] Those themes—which have an explicit relationship with the Mammy or Sapphire concepts—are motherhood and family, and work/entrepreneurship. In addition to these major themes, we consider the communicative significance of two subthemes that are woven throughout the texts—class and conflict. We purport that these subthemes can contribute mightily to our contention that OWN's programming contributes substantially to a neoliberal, postfeminist conversation within the black televisual sphere.

## THE REAL (COUNTERPUBLIC) MATRIARCHS OF OWN

The programs on which we focus our analysis are *Welcome to Sweetie Pie's*, *Raising Whitley*, and *Mom's Got Game*. We selected these three shows because they are similar in structure and—as we will demonstrate—ideology. Each of these programs features a mature female protagonist who simultaneously inhabits the roles of family matriarch and businesswoman. Moreover, the structure and marketing of these shows position the female protagonists as mothers primarily. Hence, their relationships with their families are at the center of the shows' concepts, and also the pivot around which individual episodes revolve.

Because family and female entrepreneurship are the main foci of these shows, yet there is little explicit discussion of issues of race, gender, or class, we argue that they are exemplary of a counterpublic and postfeminist televisual sphere. Catherine Squires (2002) argues for three types of "marginal publics" within the broader African American public sphere, which she names "enclave," "counterpublic," and "satellite."[35] We are most concerned with the "counterpublic" category of marginal publics in this analysis. Nancy Fraser (1990) defines counterpublics as "parallel discursive arenas where members of subordinated social groups invent and circulate counter-discourses, which in turn permit them to formulate oppositional interpretations of their identities, interests, and needs."[36] This oft-cited definition is an important starting point for understanding counterpublics, but Squires (2002) contends that the generic term "counterpublic" does not "help us understand the heterogeneity of marginalized groups."[37] Assuming that the reality programming of OWN is a part of the broader black (counter) public sphere, it is fallacious to assume that all "subgroups within [that] counterpublic" share "the same counter ideologies."[38] For this reason, Squires (2002) contends that instead, "one should speak of multiple black public spheres constituted by groups that share a common racial makeup but perhaps do not share the same class, gender, ethnic, or ideological standpoints."[39] Of the three types of public spheres in Squires' typology—enclave, counterpublic, and satellite—we demonstrate that OWN's reality programming tends toward the counterpublic category. It qualifies as such because it arguably "[emerged] in response to a decrease in oppression . . . [and] an increase in resources" and is also facilitated by a mass medium that "increased public communication between the marginal [read: black] and dominant [read: white] spheres."[40] This kind of counter-publicity, Squires (2002) contends, "Is facilitated by greater independent media resources and distribution channels."[41] Winfrey's brand, although frequently accused of catering to White audiences,[42] has arguably found a more independent channel of distribution in OWN, where reality shows in particular feature black female protagonists, and Winfrey seems to be offering a "leveling field in the land of television."[43] Additionally, the fact that the protagonists in the shows analyzed herein engage in a kind of collectivist management of their respective business enterprises is counter to the assumption of the individual accumulation of wealth, which is the trademark of a capitalist system. In spite of these arguably positive challenges to the bourgeoisie public sphere, OWN's reality programming is also subject to one of Squires' caveats regarding counterpublics. She states, "Although counterpublics create more opportunities for intersphere discussions, the members of dominant publics may monopolize these opportunities."[44] Relatedly, "even if marginal groups utilize the speech norms and rules manufactured by dominant publics, they may not succeed because of adverse reaction to their embodied speech."[45] As the analysis below demonstrates, while each of the artifacts in question features black-bodied cast members, their proximity to the Oprah Winfrey television empire suggests a drive to demonstrate "broader" appeal, which may come across as the "whitewashing" of black characters and storylines for the sake of staying "true" to the brand.

In addition, and broadly related to the cooptation of black counterpublics, OWN's reality programming is vulnerable to accusations made against the "Oprah" persona and the Oprah Winfrey brand for roughly

thirty years. That is, the reality shows of OWN and their respective protagonists privilege the "Horatio Alger myth," or "the success myth" perpetuated, in part, in the nineteenth century juvenile novels of Horatio
Alger, Jr.[46] Alger's stories, Richard Weiss (1969) argues, reflect the *mythos*
of the self-made millionaire of the Gilded Age of U.S. history. In his
critique of "the American myth of success," Weiss (1969) describes Alger's fiction as "[idealizing] the certainties of a past time when wealth
was regarded as 'the direct consequence of honesty, thrift, self-reliance,
industry, a cheerful whistle and an open, manly face.'"[47] Although Alger's tales are rarely read today, their message is perpetuated in the arguably "rags-to-riches" stories that are the focus of much reality television
programming. In our contemporary, neoliberal context, OWN's tendency
to emphasize narratives that affirm "the success myth" strongly implies
that the measure of success is the individual accumulation of material
wealth. By extension, and as a further reflection of the broader Oprah
Winfrey persona and brand, a postfeminist *ethos* of individualism, consumption, and colorblindness is also implicitly espoused.[48] In order to
understand how elements of counter-publicity and postfeminism are embodied in the protagonists of our chosen artifacts—and perhaps, conten-
tiously so—we turn now to a brief description of *Welcome to Sweetie Pie's,
Raising Whitley*, and *Mom's Got Game*, respectively.

The *Oprah Winfrey Network* launched on January 1, 2011, in order to
"entertain, inform and inspire people to live their best lives."[49] *Welcome to
Sweetie Pie's* premiered in October of that same year and has become a
relative constant on the once-struggling network. Robbie Montgomery,
"a 1960s backup singer and former 'Ikette'" is the titular Sweetie Pie, and
she is the matriarch of the family and the boss of the family business.[50]
The description of the show positions Miss Robbie as a mother, entrepreneur, and breadwinner. Considerable amounts of "hilarity and drama" are provided by Miss Robbie's son and business partner Tim, as well
as Tim's ex-fiancée Jenae, and Miss Robbie's nephew Lil' Charles. While
the family is not "nuclear," it is relatively "traditional," in that all members are blood relations, or married into the family, and there are clear
generational distinctions. Montgomery's family, as portrayed in *Welcome
to Sweetie Pie's*, also reflects "traditional" characteristics of black families
in the United States, including single parenthood and close-knit extended
family.[51] In structure and in terms of seniority, *Sweetie Pie's* is the "flag-
ship" reality program on OWN, and thus a kind of model for the reality
series that followed on the network.

The premise of *Raising Whitley*, which premiered on OWN in April
2013, varies slightly from the more "traditional" familial foundations of
*Sweetie Pie's* and—as we will show—*Mom's Got Game*. As a successful
Hollywood actor and comedian, Kym Whitley had no plans to start a
traditional family. However, those plans changed abruptly when a girl
she had previously mentored delivered a baby and chose Whitley to be

the baby's legal guardian. The show's storylines revolve around Whitley's utilization of her close circle of friends—The Village—to support her in her new role as a mother to baby Joshua, as well as in her career and personal life. The members of Whitley's "Village" include—Rodney, her longtime friend and the more "traditional" father figure to Joshua; Wendell, Whitley's flamboyant "Hollywood Husband;" and Samantha, her personal trainer.[52] As this description illustrates, Whitley's family is distinctly non-traditional, relative to U.S. cultural standards. And in spite of its arguably transgressive structure, *Raising Whitley* emphasizes roles and themes that are indeed "traditional" to televisual representations of black womanhood, which are central to the present analysis.

Premiering in January 2014, *Mom's Got Game* is the newest among the shows we examined. The program primarily follows the lives of Pamela McGee and her son JaVale McGee. The elder McGee is a former WNBA star and presently works as her son's manager. JaVale is continuing in the "family business," as he has been playing in the NBA for six years—currently with the Denver Nuggets. In fact, JaVale has the honor of being the first NBA player whose mother played in the WNBA. As Pamela McGee notes during one of her individual interviews, "The Kennedys do politics, the McGees, we do basketball."[53] The show revolves primarily around Pamela McGee's "career and her big life," so the cast/family is less extended than those of *Sweetie Pie's* and *Raising Whitley*. In addition to mother Pam and son JaVale, Jay—Pam's personal assistant—is featured prominently, and tertiary characters include several members of Pam's group of single, female friends. Moreover, the "single-mother" storyline is critical to *Mom's Got Game*, which acts as a response to the myth of the state-dependent, Black, single mother embedded in our collective cultural consciousness.[54] We turn our attention now to an analysis of selected instances of the themes and subthemes present across these three shows.

## WELCOME TO SWEETIE PIE'S

Miss Robbie's role as mother is essential to the ongoing plot and structure of *Welcome to Sweetie Pie's*, but it is difficult to divorce entirely from her role as businesswoman and entrepreneur. Miss Robbie is a mother and a grandmother, and her relationship with her son, Tim, figures prominently in the show. It is relatively infrequent, however, that Miss Robbie is shown interacting with her family outside the confines of the restaurant, or outside the broader context of the family business. The "mama drama" that Miss Robbie serves up is usually connected to managing her son and business partner, Tim, as well as keeping her nephew Charles in line, and managing the employees.

A recurring plot-point involving Tim, revolves around Tim's relationship with Jenae, his former fiancée and the mother of his child. When Jenae breaks off the engagement, she leaves her ring with Miss Robbie, and Miss Robbie is charged with the task of returning the ring to Tim. "Hey Tim," she says, "now I'm not trying to be in your business, I'm just your mother, and I know I got a place, *but*, I still got this ring and you and Jenae need to decide, because I'm tired of being responsible for it."[55] In that scene, Miss Robbie gently asserts herself with Tim, demonstrating her savvy as a mother and mediator. Her concern is significant, and like any involved mother, her link to their relationship is inextricable. Miss Robbie's nephew Charles, works for her and he is habitually late and generally irresponsible in both his personal and work life. Although he is Miss Robbie's employee, she regularly interacts with Charles as a family member. In a sequence in which she contemplates firing Charles for his repeated ineptitude, she states, "Even if I have to watch him fall, I can no longer be his safety net."[56] This statement echoes the sentiment that a mother must let her child "leave the nest" and fend for him/herself. Charles may not be Miss Robbie's son, but her interactions with him are undoubtedly maternal.

Miss Robbie's motherly/matriarchal obligations extend beyond her wrangling of Tim and Charles' personal and professional lives. In an interview segment regarding Miss Robbie's style of "tough love," Tim states, "I can't say who gets Miss Robbie's tough love worse, us, the family, or the employees, I mean, she kinda dishes it out evenly."[57] In the sequence that follows, Miss Robbie threatens to fire a group of employees and disapprovingly inspects the work of a kitchen employee. The sequence ends with Jenae's declaration that all employees are usually given a second or even third chance, demonstrating that Miss Robbie's nurturing instincts always win out over her "tough love" façade.

Another storyline that involves Miss Robbie's brother emphasizes her role as mother and matriarch. George is set to undergo open-heart surgery, and as Miss Robbie explains her connection with her brother, she recalls, "I promised my mom that I would look out for George, and if anything happened to George, I would be devastated. I'd rather it happen to me than George because he does not understand."[58] Not only does Miss Robbie literally take the place of her own mother as George's caretaker, but she also emphasizes the need to act as a guardian to her brother, even as they are peers and mature, older adults. She takes on this responsibility due to his intellectual disability.

Due to the overlap in her personal and professional identities, it is difficult to identify a "pure" moment of her role as businesswoman and boss. For example, in the aforementioned "tough love" sequence, Jenae states, "Robbie's probably the toughest on Tim, but the reason that she's toughest on Tim is probably because she sees the most potential in him to be able to take care of the business."[59] A clear connection is made here between Miss Robbie's style of mothering and her entrepreneurial spirit. Despite this blending of identities, it is clear that the *Sweetie Pie's* protagonist is independent and career-oriented, in the mold of the network's founder, Oprah Winfrey. On the occasion of Winfrey's first visit to the restaurant, Miss Robbie revealed to an off-camera interviewer, "I admire Oprah because she's a Black woman that struggled, and she made it, and when I grow up, I wanna be like Oprah."[60] Miss Robbie's declaration is a confirmation of the link between her and Winfrey, as members of the Harpo family. It also suggests that Black women, irrespective of their professions or socio-economic standing, may aspire to following in the legendary footsteps of one of the most powerful women in the world.[61]

## RAISING WHITLEY

Kym Whitley's *de facto* motherhood is the very basis for *Raising Whitley*. She did not plan or expect to become a mother. Thus, Whitley is portrayed—not as a sage, experienced matriarch—but as a bumbling and excited, learn-as-you-go parent. "I had no idea how to take care of a baby," she says in the first season, as well as, "He was a gift . . . that I never asked for."[62] In order to give baby Joshua a stable and supportive upbringing, Whitley decided to "build Joshua a village" by "[rallying] up the good people in [her] life," which she sees as mirroring the family structure in which she grew up.[63]

As the title implies, this show revolves around Whitley's coming of age as a parent. So as baby Joshua grows up, Whitley herself grows as a mother. Audiences watch as Whitley struggles to make independent decisions about the best way to raise Joshua, and also as she deals with the multiple influences of members of "The Village." There is an especially significant dynamic between Whitley and Rodney, Joshua's "more traditional" father. Whitley and Rodney's relationship is platonic, but she refers to him as a co-parent and she and Joshua call him Da-da. However, Rodney's parenting beliefs and behaviors are a constant source of frustration for Whitley. When Whitley takes Joshua for his first haircut at the barbershop, she asks for Rodney to meet them there—in order to calm Joshua's fears and perhaps coax him to stop crying. Whitley does not want the barber to cut all of Joshua's hair; however, once Rodney arrives, her wishes are ignored and the barber does away with Joshua's "Mohawk," which Whitley explains has always been the pattern in which Joshua's hair grew. Rodney is pleased to see Joshua looking "like a man," but Whitley is visibly upset that the Mohawk—which, for her, represented a bond between mother and child—is gone. Despite her disappointment, Whitley calmly celebrated Joshua's new haircut with him, so as not to associate the clippers or the act of the haircut with anything negative.[64]

Whitley's waffling in her co-parenting with Rodney is further evidenced in a sequence in which Wendell, her "Hollywood husband," arrives at her home while Rodney is also present. Wendell presents Joshua with a gift of a baby doll. As soon as Whitley sees the gift, and before Rodney does, she predicts aloud, "Rodney's going to . . . he's gonna be *mad*." She is correct in her prediction, and her discomfort is visible as Wendell encourages Joshua to play with the doll and Rodney exclaims, "Are you out of your mind? It's a girl doll. . . . Why couldn't you give him a boy doll?" Whitley appears to chalk the mild conflict up to the fact that Rodney and Wendell have different "lifestyles" and that they are "constantly butting heads." In the end, she is not particularly clear on her own opinion of the gift, or the situation overall.[65]

As Whitley is learning to parent and also to assert herself as a parent, she is also busy maintaining her career as an actor and comedian. Unlike *Welcome to Sweetie Pie's, Raising Whitley* does not often portray Whitley at work, but it is tacitly understood that she is busy providing for Joshua and herself. One of the ways that this understanding is communicated is through Whitley's struggle to decide whether or not to hire a nanny for Joshua. After Whitley loses her steady job on a canceled NBC television show, Joshua leaves daycare and Whitley has a conversation with a friend—fellow actor and comedian Caroline Rhea—about the struggles of raising a child. Rhea validates Whitley's feelings about parenthood, and Whitley asks, "So, nanny . . . is OK?" This conversation is especially pertinent to this analysis considering the history of the Mammy stereotype and the kind of role reversal that a single, black mother employing a "domestic worker" implies. This is a clear indication of how Whitley's class status enables her to be the employer of a nanny, but her question, "So, nanny . . . is OK?" is telling, relative to historical and current cultural context surrounding the employer/nanny/Mammy relationship.[66]

## MOM'S GOT GAME

She is a mom and a manager, but she insists that she is not a "momager." However, because Pamela McGee is both mother and manager to her son—like Robbie Montgomery—it is sometimes difficult to discern when and where one role is more prominent than the other. In the premiere episode of *Mom's Got Game*, the first two words out of Pamela McGee's mouth in the initial interview segment were, "My son," a phrase that identifies her primarily as a mother. That interview footage was edited with footage of Pam and her assistant, Jay, driving across the country with JaVale's dogs in tow. She provides a kind of confessional to the off-camera interviewer, saying, "JaVale wants his dogs in L.A., so my assistant and I . . . we got to bring 'em from Denver to L.A. Sucker mother. I'll bring him the dogs." Immediately following this sequence, however,

Pam switches gears from mother to manager. "I'm here to make sure he stays on point. . . . All my job is to make sure everything off the court is tight, and all he gotta do is concentrate on playing ball."[67] Further evidence of this blending of roles is clear when JaVale goes car shopping and sets his sights on purchasing a $400,000 Maybach. Pam is quick to halt the sale, citing that it is a financially unsound decision, but also noting that "JaVale would like a Maybach because he sees other players drive Maybachs." The financial advice is solid, but the rationale that Pam provides suggests that she is attempting to prevent her son from giving in to a kind of peer pressure.[68]

## SAPPHIRIC EVOLUTION AND THE PUBLIC SPHERE

A critical view of the black female protagonists on OWN's reality programming reveals that today's representations of black culture on television are inextricably linked with representations of the past. Thus, as audiences watch Robbie Montgomery, Kym Whitley, and Pamela McGee assert themselves in their roles as mothers/matriarchs and career-driven professionals, there is a strong inclination to see their identities as a reflection of the Mammy and Sapphire stereotypes embedded in our cultural consciousness. It is important to consider, then, whether present-day representations are "true" incarnations of those stereotypes, or if they represent some kind of Mammy/Sapphire hybrid. In addition, how are these representations influencing and being influenced by a counterpublic, postfeminist conception of the contemporary black televisual sphere?

As the analysis above demonstrates, each of these female protagonists is assertive, opinionated, and relatively independent. The fact that they are primarily positioned as mothers underscores the potential for them to be read through as pervasively negative over-generalizations of black womanhood—including the no-nonsense, yet docile, Mammy, and the outspoken and neutering Sapphire. However, although we must acknowledge the lingering specters of those figures as well as the new crop of black female caricatures on reality TV—the women of OWN cannot simply be boiled down to those stereotypes. All three of our protagonists represent the complexity of Black female experiences in the United States today, especially as it concerns motherhood and career. None of the portraits of these women seems to be sensationalized, or exploited for one particularly unsavory characteristic or another. However, it is arguably because their successes echo those of Winfrey's and other tokenized Black public figures—i.e. they fit the Horatio Alger myth and demonstrate achievement outside of the structural inequalities that continue to plague historically marginalized populations in the United States—that they have been "selected and appropriated"[69] to reify the collective assumption that "if Oprah can do it, so can you."[70] It appears that OWN's reality programming simply reifies old myths about American meritocracy, but it is perhaps more productive to consider how it contributes to an evolving conception of Black womanhood and thus represents and/or reflects a Black counterpublic.

> Analyzing Sapphire from a black female perspective, bell hooks (1993) contends: Grown black women had a different response to Sapphire. They identified with her frustrations and her woes. They resented the way she was mocked. They resented the way these screen images could assault black womanhood, could name us bitches, nags. And in opposition they claimed Sapphire as their own, as the symbol of that angry part of themselves white folks and black men could not even begin to understand.[71]

It is possible that the reality characters of Robbie Montgomery, Kym Whitley, and Pamela McGee are examples of the potential of the oppositional gaze that black female viewers engage in and with. As single, black, female, mothers from middle-class to wealthy, all three simultaneously embody and reject the traditional characteristics of black female caricatures, as well as the contexts in which they arose.

Limiting the conception of an evolving or adapted black female "type," represented in a televisual space, is the question of audience. Who consumes OWN programming in general, and these three shows in particular? It is safe to assume that OWN's viewers are the same viewers—or at least similar to the viewers—of the now defunct *Oprah Winfrey Show*, and the research suggests as much. In April 2014, OWN gained the momentum it had been lagging in its first two years on the air. The first three months of 2014 represented the network's most-watched quarter ever, delivering "double digit growth across all key [demographics]."[72] In addition, OWN ranked 24th among women 25–54 and 4th among African American women 25–54. On Tuesday and Wednesday nights in particular, it was the number one cable network for African American women.[73] Notably, the prime time slots on Tuesdays and Wednesdays offered scripted series produced by none other than Tyler Perry—a black auteur who is often derided by critics who say that he explicitly perpetuates the long-standing, gendered and racialized oppressive stereotypes that black film and television should seek to challenge.[74] The very presence of Perry in Winfrey's brand empire, and the success of his shows on the OWN network, raise questions about the complex and arguably conflicting representations of black womanhood in the OWN universe and whether some "evolving" portrayals might reshape a shared cultural consciousness about or among black women in the United States.

However, while not as highly ranked overall, in terms of ratings, *Welcome to Sweetie Pie's* and *Raising Whitley* aired during OWN's "popular Saturday night lineup"—reaching a smaller audience, but still showing strong viewing trends among black women.[75] This trend is significant considering the potential for developing a new understanding of, or perspective on, the black televisual sphere. Certainly OWN is a "mainstream" network that draws audiences of mixed racial demographics, but with strong numbers of black women viewing these "alternative" portrayals of black womanhood, this confluence of viewer and viewed opens up the possibility of engaging differently with mediated representations of black women, thus disseminating a more nuanced view of the black public sphere, one that clarifies the term "counterpublic" and recognizes black women's equal potential to espouse a postfeminist ethos.

Hence, the days of pitting black female characters against one another, on reality television shows, as Star Jones and NeNe Leakes were on *Celebrity Apprentice*, are not likely to end anytime soon. However, as this analysis demonstrates, there are alternatives to the pervasive negative representations of black womanhood on reality and scripted television. In addition, these alternatives add nuance to assumptions that arguably prevail about a homogenous, non-intersectional black public sphere. Still, our alternatives are not entirely unproblematic, nor are they divorced from the tainted history of popular culture's stereotyping of black individuals and black culture. Yet, in spite of their imperfections, they open up a space for engaging in counterhegemonic discourse about the complexity of black womanhood and the evolving nature of counterpublic discourse as it arises from changing lived experiences within diverse marginalized publics.

## NOTES

1. Allison Samuels, "Reality TV Trashes Black Women," *Newsweek*, last modified May 1, 2011, http://www.newsweek.com/reality-tv-trashes-black-women-67641.

2. Ibid.

3. Dana Cloud, "Hegemony or Concordance?: The Rhetoric of Tokenism in 'Oprah' Winfrey's Rags-to-Riches Biography," *Critical Studies in Mass Communication* 13 (1996).

4. Ibid.

5. Ibid. 118.

6. See Cloud, and K. Sue Jewell, *From Mammy to Miss America and Beyond: Cultural Images and the Shaping of U.S. Social Policy* (NY: Routledge, 1993).

7. Jewell, 9.

8. Ibid.

9. Sonja M. Brown Givens and Jennifer L. Monahan, "Priming Mammies, Jezebels, and Other Controlling Images: An Examination of the Influence of Mediated Stereotypes on Perceptions of an African American Woman," *Media Psychology* 7, no. 1 (2005): 87–106; bell hooks, "The Oppositional Gaze: Black Female Spectators," in *The Feminism and Visual Culture Reader*, ed. Amelia Jones (NY: Routledge, 1993), 94–105.

10. Tia Tyree, "African American Stereotypes in Reality Television," *The Howard Journal of Communications* 22 (2011): 394–413.

11. Billye N. Rhodes and Kristal Moore Clemons, "The Queen of Television: Oprah Winfrey in Relation to Self and as Cultural Icon," in *African Americans on Television: Race-ing for Ratings*, eds. David J. Leonard and Lisa A. Guerrero (Santa Barbara, CA: Praeger, 2013), 263–281.

12. Ted Striphas, "A Dialectic with the Everyday: Communication and Cultural Politics on Oprah Winfrey's Book Club," *Critical Studies in Media Communication* 20, no. 3 (2003): 295–316.

13. Cloud, 116.

14. Janice Peck, *The Age of Oprah: Cultural Icon for the Neoliberal Era* (Boulder, CO: Paradigm Publishers, 2008), v.

15. Ibid. iv.

16. Catherine Squires, "Rethinking the Black Public Sphere: An Alternative Vocabulary for Multiple Public Spheres," *Communication Theory* 12, no. 4 (2002): 446–468; Mary Douglas Vavrus, "Postfeminist Redux?" *Review of Communication* 12, no. 3 (2012): 224–236.

17. Herman Gray, Watching Race: Television and the Struggle for "Blackness" (Minneapolis, MN: University of Minnesota Press, 1995), 2.

18. Peter Dahlgren, *Television and the Public Sphere: Citizenship, Democracy and the Media* (London: SAGE Publications Ltd., 1995), x.

19. Ibid. 2.

20. Craig Calhoun, "Introduction: Habermas and the Public Sphere," in *Habermas and the Public Sphere*, ed. Craig Calhoun (Cambridge: The MIT Press, 1992), 3.

21. Nancy Fraser, "Rethinking the Public Sphere: A Contribution to the Critique of Actually Existing Democracy," *Social Text* 25/26 (1990): 58.

22. The Black Public Sphere Collective, "Preface," in *The Black Public Sphere: A Public Culture Book*, ed. The Black Public Sphere Collective (Chicago: The University of Chicago Press, 1995), 1.

23. Ibid. 3.

24. Thomas C. Holt, "Afterword: Mapping the Black Public Sphere," in *The Black Public Sphere: A Public Culture Book*, ed. The Black Public Sphere Collective (Chicago: The University of Chicago Press, 1995), 325.

25. Vavrus, 226.

26. Jane M. Shattuc, "The Oprahfication of America: Talk Shows and the Public Sphere," in *Television, History, and American Culture: Feminist Critical Essays*, eds. Mary Beth Haralovich and Lauren Rabinovitz (Durham, NC: Duke University Press, 1999), 168.

27. Robert Putnam, *Bowling Alone: The Collapse and Revival of American Community* (New York: Simon and Schuster, 2001).

28. Shattuc, 169.

29. Ibid. 168–169.

30. Rebecca Wanzo, "Can the Black Woman Shout?: A Meditation on Real and Utopian Depictions of African American Women on Scripted Television," in *African Americans on Television: Race-ing for Ratings*, eds. David J. Leonard and Lisa A. Guerrero (Santa Barbara, CA: Praeger, 2013), 373–389.

31. Mark Anthony Neal, "Post-Modern Mammy: The Oprah Legacy," *NewBlackMan (in Exile): The Digital Home for Mark Anthony Neal*, last modified November 22, 2009, http://newblackman.blogspot.com/2009/11/post-modern-mammy-oprah-legacy.html.

32. See Janice Peck, "Oprah Winfrey: Cultural Icon of Mainstream (White) America," in *The Colorblind Screen: Television in Post-Racial America*, eds. Sarah Nilsen and Sarah E. Turner (NY: New York University Press, 2014), 85–86, and Aswini Anburajan, "Breaking Down Oprah's Numbers," *NBCNews*, last modified December 7, 2007, http://firstread.nbcnews.com/_news/2007/12/07/4425062-breaking-down-oprahs-numbers?lite.

33. Jewell, 45.

34. Wanzo, "Can the Black Woman Shout?"

35. Squires, 446–448.

36. Fraser, 67.

37. Squires, 447.

38. Ibid.

39. Ibid. 447 and 452.

40. Ibid. 460.

41. Ibid. 461.

42. See Peck, "Oprah Winfrey: Cultural Icon of Mainstream (White) America."

43. See Kate Dries, "Oprah Makes Shows for Black Woman and Finally Finds Success with OWN," *Jezebel*, last modified June 13, 2013, http://jezebel.com/oprahs-makes-shows-for-black-women-and-finally-finds-s-513093780, and Allison Samuels, "Why Oprah Winfrey's New Shows are Working for OWN," *The Daily Beast*, last modified June 13, 2013, http://www.thedailybeast.com/articles/2013/06/13/why-oprah-winfrey-s-new-shows-are-working-for-own.html.

44. Squires, 461.

45. Ibid. 462.

46. Richard Weiss, *The American Myth of Success: From Horatio Alger to Norman Vincent Peale* (New York: Basic Books, 1969), 48–49.

47. Ibid, 49.

48. Vavrus, 226.

49. "Home," *OWN TV*, accessed June 24, 2015, http://www.oprah.com/app/own-tv.html.

50. "Welcome to Sweetie Pie's," *OWN TV*, accessed June 24, 2015, http://www.oprah.com/app/sweetie-pies.html.

51. Steven Ruggles, "The Origins of African American Family Structure," *American Sociological Review* 59 (1994): 136–151.

52. "Raising Whitley," *OWN TV*, accessed June 24, 2015, http://www.oprah.com/app/raising-whitley.html.

53. "Sneak Peek: Watch the First 5 Minutes of Mom's Got Game—Mom's Got Game," *YouTube*, accessed June 24, 2015, https://www.youtube.com/watch?v=IJ7a_rsDrc8.

54. We find it notable that seemingly all of OWN's reality shows have storylines that revolve around nuclear and extended African American families. In addition to the shows highlighted in this analysis, OWN airs or has aired family-centric programs like *Deion's Family Playbook*, *Six Little McGhees*, *Beverly's Full House*, and *Flex & Shanice*. Whereas other highly rated reality television focuses on "friend" groups, romantic relationships, or competitions, OWN focuses on family relationships, both traditional and non-traditional.

55. "Is There a Future Together for Tim and Jenae?—Welcome to Sweetie Pie's," *YouTube*, accessed June 24, 2015, https://www.youtube.com/watch?v=o26QZtETy8U.

56. "Is Miss Robbie as Tough as She Seems?—Welcome to Sweetie Pie's," *YouTube*, accessed June 24, 2015, https://www.youtube.com/watch?v=LGSLm1Tue8I.

57. Ibid.

58. "Miss Robbie Takes Care of Her Sick Brother—Welcome to Sweetie Pie's," *YouTube*, accessed June 24, 2015, https://www.youtube.com/watch?v=Xxl5lr-pn4c.

59. "Is Miss Robbie as Tough as She Seems?"

60. "Oprah Visits Sweetie Pie's—Welcome to Sweetie Pie's," *YouTube*, accessed June 24, 2015, http://www.youtube.com/watch?v=sc4Z1zVrljU.

61. "The World's 100 Most Powerful Women: #12 Oprah Winfrey," *Forbes.com*, accessed June 24, 2015, http://www.forbes.com/profile/oprah-winfrey/?list=power-women.

62. "Sneak Peek: Watch the First 5 Minutes of Raising Whitley—Raising Whitley," *YouTube*, accessed June 24, 2015, https://www.youtube.com/watch?v=dEaGagxE6bQ.

63. Ibid.

64. "Joshua's First Haircut: Not the Mohawk!—Raising Whitley," *YouTube*, accessed June 24, 2015, https://www.youtube.com/watch?v=pSFQUbbu0Xo.

65. "Sneak Peek: Meet Kym Whitley's Hollywood Husband—Raising Whitley," *YouTube*, accessed June 24, 3015, https://www.youtube.com/watch?v=sg29KQmQlI0.

66. "Preview: Caroline Rhea and Kym Whitley: Is it OK to Get a Nanny?—Raising Whitley," *YouTube*, accessed June 24, 2015, https://www.youtube.com/watch?v=CTW-ZdAkcsA.

67. "Sneak Peek: Watch the First 5 Minutes of Mom's Got Game—Mom's Got Game."

68. "A Car Fit for a Basketball Star—Mom's Got Game," *YouTube*, accessed June 24, 2015, https://www.youtube.com/watch?v=ikqzdeSNPvk.

69. Cloud, 116.

70. Ibid.

71. hooks, 97.

72. Sara Bibel, "OWN Delivers Most Watched Quarter in Network History," *TV by the Numbers*, accessed June 24, 2015, http://tvbythenumbers.zap2it.com/2014/04/01/own-delivers-most-watched-quarter-in-network-history/250080/.

73. Ibid.

74. Robert J. Patterson, "Woman Thou Art Bound: Critical Spectatorship, Black Masculine Gazes, and Gender Problems in Tyler Perry's Movies," *Black Camera* 3, no. 1 (2011): 9–30.

75. Bibel.

# FIVE

# Can't Have It All

*An Analysis of Black Motherhood on Reality Television*

## Allison M. Alford, Madeline M. Maxwell, Ryessia D. Jones & Angelica N. Morris

In this chapter we analyze three reality TV (RTV) shows whose main characters do not fit the old movie stereotypes of dark-skinned maternal Mammies, bossy, brown Sapphires or light-skinned sexy Jezebels.[1] Many RTV shows with black cast members are falling back on such stereotypical representations.[2] In contrast, the female characters we analyze are smart and sophisticated, and they live in multi-racial environments. Hence, the primary media-related question we address concerns how one slice of black motherhood is represented. The social question we address concerns the extent to which the character presentations actually point to social progress, with diverse symbols and meaning making of real life, or are they as artificial and stereotypical—perhaps in new ways—as the old portrayals?

Black women are tuning in to the television in large numbers and looking for entertainment that matches their lifestyle. According to a 2014 Nielsen Cross-Platform report, the average black American spends more than six hours per day watching television, more than any other race/ethnicity measured.[3] America's favorite pastime is watching television, and the images onscreen become part of our national consciousness. Consequently, the black women on TV have social value beyond their entertainment value.

The three TV series we have chosen establish at least some social progress just in their synoptic descriptions: *Dance Moms,*[4] *Tia & Tamera,*[5] and *Run's House*[6] are capturing audiences interested in the privileged reality of rich, light-skinned, black mothers. Specifically, we look at the presentations of Holly in *Dance Moms* (the mother of three, including the only African American girl in a dance class); adult twins in *Tia & Tamera*, married to black and white husbands, respectively, and each mother to one child; and Justine Simmons in *Run's House*, who is married to a member of the popular 1980's hip hop trio Run-D.M.C. She is a mother of two, stepmother of three, and adopted mother of one. All of these women, by their personal appearance and their living situations, break the stereotypes of poor African Americans featured in many earlier depictions on television and in film.

We use a combination of Critical Discourse Analysis (henceforth, CDA)[7] and rhetorical analysis[8] to understand the positive and negative valence of the presentations of these RTV characters. CDA is a transdisciplinary method of analysis that allows the researcher to identify and probe networks of social practices, including possibly economic, class, political, cultural, family, etc.; so that the analysis can shift between social structures and social action, especially discourse practices.[9] Social practices are interpretable within a social group and indicate or articulate diverse social elements within relatively habituated structures. While there are several differences in how researchers use CDA, communicative and social practices include: activities, social relations, instruments, objects, situated time and place, forms of consciousness, values, and discourse.

## WHAT'S REAL(LY) HAPPENING ON TV?

### Wives and Mothers

Multiple studies have analyzed the imagery of wives and mothers on reality television.[10] When discussing shows like *Nanny 911* and *Supernanny*, Green argues these shows are educational and problematic.[11] The educational value concerns "helpful tips for parenting," but such shows are problematic in casting a sense of judgmental need to regulate and surveil parents, particularly mothers.[12] Shows like *Wife Swap, Trading Spouses, Supernanny*, and *Nanny 911* were all created to allow cameras to document the unscripted, yet spontaneous interactions of middle class families,[13] leading to a sense that the middle class suburban family is the normal model.[14]

In these shows, "motherhood is inextricably linked to successful and happy femininity," and the mothers are thus held to a higher standard than the fathers.[15] They are framed as incapable of successfully managing the duties of feminine wife, managing and nurturing mother, and competent employee,[16] especially overwhelmed by their children's disobedient behavior.

Nathanson (2007) points out that the mothers often solicit help from their nannies because the family environment is in chaos.[17] As a result, mothers often feel inadequate and appear incompetent. The nanny, who often has less formal education, is younger, is of a less sophisticated class than the mother, and is unmarried, takes the role of the wife's instructor on balancing her wifely and professional duties to bring order to the home. She tells the wives not to expect their husbands to take on extra caretaking responsibilities, but instead to better balance working full-time and the familial duties. Pozner argues "Reality TV has very clear, archaic notions about what a 'woman's place' is and what it isn't: The personal sphere is singularly female, the public sphere predominantly male."[18]

*Black Women*

According to Charlton (2013), portrayals of "respectable black motherhood are so rare as to be revolutionary."[19] The preponderance of the Mammy, Sapphire, and Jezebel stereotypes over decades may actually make it difficult for viewers to interpret more realistic characters. Furthermore, women who are married and/or have children are commonly presented through a lens of their marriage or children, which hooks (2003) says is a reification of the American patriarchy.[20] Hooks (2003) is so concerned about the negative impact of these images that she calls for black females to view all media with a critical eye: "Critical black female spectatorship emerges as a site of resistance only when individual black women actively resist the imposition of dominant ways of knowing and looking."[21] The three shows we analyze do not follow the dominant images, so are they a site of resistance? Do these glittery lifestyles do any justice to the cast members and viewers who are forming opinions through spectatorship?

Wallace (2013) argues, for example, that while presenting light-skinned black females who are not "Jezebels" breaks the stereotypes, it continues to perpetuate the hierarchy that lighter is better than darker.[22] Lighter skin tones are historically seen as more desirable and, thus idealized.[23] This colorism—perpetuated when Hollywood casts wealthy, light-skinned black women—confirms viewers' beliefs that light-skin is associated with wealth, comfort, and desirability. This reifies existing stereotypes and forces black women into a have or have-not position. According to Wallace (2013), even being in the idealized light-skinned group comes with its own pressures and limitations.[24] Shows like *Dance Moms, Tia & Tamera,* and *Run's House* are capturing audiences interested in the privileged reality of rich, light-skinned, black mothers, but is there a cost to the community if we privilege this group?

These three RTV shows create meaning for the audience through the genre of RTV, the discourse and narrative storylines of the participants, and the style of its presentation—including the negative, punishing events the black mothers suffer. If only one aspect of meaning was to be examined for any given RTV show with a black mother, one might conclude that a simple persona is being presented. However, the interplay of the multiple meanings present in the texts for these three RTV shows demonstrates the overall, distressing effect of portraying black mothers as incapable of properly balancing their multiple pursuits to their own detriment, and a privileging of light-skinned, upper-class black women. This ultimately leads the viewer to comprehend a simplistic attitude toward the black woman, which does little to promote her overall social position.

## WHAT WE'RE WATCHING AND THINKING

Any text, including reality television episodes, can be read as a presentation of the ideological values of the participants, directors, networks, and/ or viewers. Multiple implications are present in texts,[25] and an episode of reality television is jointly constructed by many forces from idea creation to filming, editing, and finally its air time.[26] A sub-plot or scene can be read as a unit within an episode, which can be read as a unit within the larger organization of the season, the season as a unit of the series, and the series as a unit of American society. While the people onscreen may use real names, jobs, and situations, the camera does not simply follow and present people as they pass before it. Narrative arcs are played out onscreen with the "real people" directed and edited to appear in a manner that garners ratings for the network and earns revenue.

Each episode-text can be analyzed along three aspects of meaning:[27] action, representation, and identification. Fairclough (2003) describes the action of a text as its genre, the representation as its discourse, and identification as its style.[28] These are not only creations of the authors/directors of the text, but are actually effects perceived by the audience. "Focusing analysis of texts on the interplay of action, representation, and identification brings a social perspective into the heart and fine detail of the text."[29] By dissecting popular RTV shows, we can learn more about how our society is currently comprehending black womanhood and motherhood.

Brummett (1994)[30] similarly proposes that texts are composed of a collection of signs that help individuals make meaning of the world. In Brummett's (1994) view, the ideology precedes and drives a text as a vehicle for presenting ideological viewpoints.[31] In this case, we can understand that RTV is more than reality. What may seem like a window opened to reveal the lifestyles of a unique group of average people is actually a heavily manipulated version of the wide scope of lifestyles found among black mothers. Sorting through how much ideology is constructed by and within the text[32] or conveyed by the text[33] is beyond the scope of this analysis. What they have in common is the discoverable ideology which allows us to address the question of the extent to which the character presentations actually point to social progress, with diverse symbols and meaning making of real life, or are as artificial and stereotypical—perhaps in new ways—as the old stereotypes. So we start with a small step toward a conclusion, because watching the shows puts us on edge with concern for the perpetuated bias and over-simplified connection to skin color. We acknowledge this bias and refine our question away from determining the effect of the presentations to a search for the cause of the queasiness that we (black and white) authors discovered we shared—that there is still something lacking and something disturbing in the way that these light-skinned, wealthy black mothers are presented.

### Black Mother #1: Dr. Holly

Black Mother #1, Holly, is a married mother of three with a PhD, and she is part of an ensemble cast of characters on her show. The show is *Dance Moms*, about the complex relationships between the director of a Pittsburgh dance studio and the mothers of her young female dancers. The environment is upscale and "respectable,"[34] as evidenced by the clothing and appearance of the individuals and the studio. In one episode we learn that annual tuition is $16,000.

The original cast included eight girls and six mothers with only one Black family—Holly and her daughter, Nia. Holly holds a doctoral degree in education and is often referred to simply as Dr. Holly. The director, Abby, and the dance moms often engage in arguments and physical altercations about treatment of the young dancers, the provocative costumes, and stereotypical cast roles. The young dancers travel to weekly dance competitions, with the hopes of earning first place there and on Abby's pyramid, which visually demonstrates the dancers' hierarchy within the company. The girls' positions on the pyramid depend on their performance, effort in rehearsals, attitudes, attendance, and their mothers' behavior. If the child or mother fails to meet the expectations of Abby, the dancer's dance privileges are revoked, placed on probation, and/or suspended.

*The Bad Mother.* Abby tells Nia—in front of the entire dance class— that she is replaceable because her mother is late (incapable of managing her duties as mother and job holder) in Season 2, Episode 1, titled "Everyone's Replaceable." She regularly criticizes Holly to her daughter, saying things like, "She needs to leave work, leave the job, forget it, and be here with you. That is what's important, yes? You want this, I know you want. I know you love it. She has to love it for you." When Holly confronts

Abby over this behavior, Abby questions Holly's ability to be a dance mom because she did not attend a required meeting. She claims that she herself cares more about Nia's success and future than her own mother. In a heated conversation with Holly, Abby insinuates that stay-at-home moms are better mothers than working mothers and implies that Holly is selfish and neglectful. When Holly is forced to send Nia alone on the bus to a dance recital because she cannot take off work, we see her crying, suggesting the emotional cost of her inability to fulfill both roles perfectly.

Thus Holly is like other RTV mothers who work—according to Pozner, RTV "generally portrays women as bad wives and mothers if they pursue professional or political interests outside the home."[35] A light-skinned elite black woman is normalized, but normalized to a negative, damaging stereotype of all mothers. Black mothers may, in fact, be more likely to suffer this stereotype because they may be more likely to have to work in order to maintain their economic status;[36] black mothers, then, are less likely to be able to choose the role of stay-at-home mom, making them more vulnerable to the critical portrayal.

In Season 2, Episode 11, Holly is once again absent from a crucial meeting. The other dance moms seem to join Abby in insinuating that Holly's absence is indicative of her bad mothering. Holly must agree, at least at some level, because when she arrives, she announces that she has chosen to take a leave of absence from work. With the leave of absence, Holly reveals that she is incapable of properly balancing work and family without giving up one for the other. Holly confesses that she has sacrificed time with her children and her husband for the advancement of her professional career. Holly's decision to become a stay-at-home mother can be directly tied to the advancement of her daughter at the dance studio. The apparent reward for her sacrifice comes in Season 2, Episode 23, when Nia wins an award for Most Improved Scholarship.

The action of the text is to make Holly look like other RTV working mothers—neglectful, selfish, and suffering until she gives up her work for the sake of her child. This representation does normalize Holly as a light-skinned black woman, but it normalizes her to a vulnerable, suffering, bad mother (and probably bad worker) who fails to support her daughter (husband, and other children) until she gives up her job. Her identification with mothers and with working women is thus problematized, as the two roles cancel each other out. Holly's ability to quit her job identifies her as someone whose family can afford to live without her income. This is not an accurate reflection of the average woman in America, 74 million of whom work to support their families.[37]

The Professional Woman

Unlike shows such as *Flavor of Love* and *Bad Girls Club*, Holly does not have cornrows, miniskirts, or plunging necklines.[38] In most of the episodes, Holly wears a skirt or dress that reveals her femininity, but covers up with a blazer to illustrate that her sexuality is contained by her professionalism. According to Brummett (2008), style is a way of "marking class and expressing values related to class positions."[39] He further adds that how one carries, grooms, and clothes herself indicates class value. Holly's style is tasteful and discreet.

In the first episode, Holly is briefly shown in her office as a school principal. We learn that she has finished a Master's Degree at Carnegie-Mellon University and is working on a PhD at the University of Pennsylvania. Thus Holly has not only achieved a high level of education but she has done so in prestigious institutions.

The action of the texts is to show Holly acting in the capacity and style of a professional woman. The representation does normalize Holly as a light-skinned Black woman, and the identification is with other professional women. The counterweight comes from comments about her in the dance studio and from her leave of absence rather than from some internal contradiction.

Blackness and Class

Holly displays middle class attitudes in parenting and communicating. For instance, in Season 4, Episode 7, when a fight breaks out between Abby and another mother, it was Holly who decorously and quickly rushed the young dancers out of the dressing room. Brummett (2008) argues, "one's tone of voice and choice of vocabulary, issues, of style, may also express values of class."[40] In essence, through her articulation, word choice and interactions, Holly reveals her upper-middle class status. According to Sciullo (2012), Holly is the "voice of reason" on the show.[41] In the world of RTV, this self-described "boring" woman in pearls was chosen for exactly that reason; she is the antithesis of other black women frequently portrayed on RTV.

Holly's class is also revealed through her ability to take a leave of absence from her job. Holly's decision to stop working, especially since she never says that her employment status alters her family's current way of life—her husband works in non-profits (according to Melissa in Season 1), and presumably she earns income from the TV show.

Sometimes upper/middle class values and style are seen at odds with blackness. In Season 1 Episode 7, Holly objects to Nia's frequent assignment to ethnic roles, specifically in this episode to the role of Laquifa, a black drag queen. Nia is given a leopard costume and Holly is instructed to purchase her an afro wig. As Simon (2011) writes in a blogpost, this is the point in the show where one might expect Holly to eloquently correct Abby for mocking African heritage and type-casting her daughter.[42] Instead, Holly turns her ire on the song and its culture. She repeatedly derides the afro hairstyle, privileging the processed style she prefers[43] and says that "we [Black people] are past that." Holly does not want Nia to dance to the music, which is simply "not her black experience." Holly feels that the performance highlights her daughter's blackness, while she insists that Nia is "a dancer first, not an ethnicity."

The action of the text makes a claim that blackness *is* the stereotype. Holly's claims rejects the stereotype. She claims to have a "black experience" but not that stereotypical black experience. She claims that Nia should be able to be perceived from actions (dancing makes her a dancer) rather than essence (skin color determines her experiences). This representation problematizes both the old stereotypes and efforts to appreciate aspects of blackness. When Holly derides the purchase of an afro wig, is she buying into the value that belittles natural African American hair, or is she objecting to the exaggerated metonymy of an afro style as the *only true* black experience? Is Holly trying to hide Nia's blackness? Is she a conformist minority repressing her blackness or is she a mother outraged that her ten-year-old daughter is expected to portray a drag queen? A variety of positions on interpreting Holly's words is represented in a blogpost and commentary by viewers[44]—demonstrating the complex issues that evoke stereotypes even while people are objecting to and rejecting stereotypes. Holly's identification is most assuredly not with Laquifa, big afros or drag queens. Yet she seems to imply that her own black experience is and should be perceived as legitimate. With the social history of repression,[45] Holly's claim of identification with a different black experience presents a dilemma. It does not seem reasonable at all to allow black Americans only one authentic identification; on the other hand, how is someone to experience authenticity when it has been engineered and colonized by a majority culture? This is a dilemma that doubly penalizes black participants in RTV and viewers seeking to expand their understanding of reality. By embracing a new perspective on blackness, are viewers negatively impacting the identities of black women by further narrowing the acceptable identities that one can claim into whitewashed categories of blackness?

*Black Mothers #2 and #3: Tia & Tamera*

Black mothers #2 and #3 are Tia Mowry-Hardrict and Tamera Mowry-Housley, stars of *Tia & Tamera,* a reality television program about their lives as mothers and wives. The show premiered April 8, 2011 on the *Style Network* and ran for three seasons until September 2013. The show followed twin sisters Tia Mowry-Hardrict and Tamera Mowry-Housley, best known for their childhood roles on the hit sitcom *Sister, Sister*. Storylines follow the sisters as they auditioned, posed for magazine covers, and acted in new roles. It is one of the first RTV shows starring biracial sisters, and featuring their interracial romantic relationships. These discussions of racial identity come on the heels of a show that treats the topic in a perfunctory manner, giving weighty topics little attention and focusing more on the twins' style and acting chops. Essentially, viewers are hooked by the constant break-up/make-up performances of the sisters and the drama of the events occurring in their lives.

*Marrying a Black or White Man.* Tia is married to Corey Hardrict, a light-skinned black man; and they have a son, Cree, who also has light black skin with black curly hair and dark eyes. Tamera is married to Adam Housley, a fair-skinned white man; and they have a son, Aden, who has very light skin, brown wavy hair and blue eyes. Essentially, Tia's family appears phenotypically and monoracially black; while Tamera's family has varying phenotypes and presents as interracial. Tamera seemed shocked by some of the public response upon posting her family's photo on Twitter in the Season 2, episode titled, "*Twinventors.*" Discussions of race and motherhood are still hot topics for the American public, and while RTV leaps into this area, exposing a variety of lifestyles and relationships, there is an injustice done when the tough conversations stop short of actual depth and progress. [46]

Both agree that they self-identify as black, though they are bi-racial, with a black mother and white father. Later, Tamera and her husband Adam, who is white, discuss the racial identity of their son, Aden. Tamera describes to Adam the "one drop rule" which, she explains, is an antiquated view of race wherein anyone with even one drop of black blood is considered black. Only a few minutes of an occasional episode were dedicated to these conversations, while alternate storylines focused on Tia learning a striptease dance to keep her sex-life spicy or Tamera redecorating her house. These discussions of racial identity are valid topics for these cast members to discuss, but the television portrayal of these conversations does not do justice to the weight of racial issues and the language of colorism, a form of prejudice based on skin color. [47]

The action of the text makes it clear that while both women identify as black, the public backlash against their interracial marriages and the skin color of their children expose that neither twin seems to be black *enough.* Thus again, blackness becomes the stereotype that this text struggles against as the women resist traditional presentations of blackness but suffer from their identification with whiteness. This highlights the point that racial topics are challenging to understand and discuss for many viewers of RTV shows who wish to pin down and categorize racial roles and behaviors into specific categories. Colorism includes bias from those outside or within one's own racioethnic group. [48] Like the criticism against Holly for her resistance to the Afro wig, there is resistance against Tia and Tamara for not representing enough of their blackness.

Upper-Class Lifestyle

The cast of *Tia & Tamera* appear to live an upper-class lifestyle in a high socio-economic position. It is clear that Tia and Cory are affluent based upon their home and surroundings. Their Los Angeles home, featured on the premiere episode of Season 2, "Sister Secrets," is large and has luxurious features throughout. Both Tia and Cory work, as actors, intermittently, revealing that they have adequate savings and income to afford such a work schedule. In Season 1, Episode 6 "Acting the Part," Tia hires the upscale and expensive design studio Petit Trésor to decorate Cree's nursery, which features twenty-two karat gold-leaf décor on the crib and dresser. However, in Season 2, episode 3 "Are you Jealous?" Tia does indicate that she must keep working to afford her lifestyle, while Tamera really does not need to. After her marriage to Adam, Tamera shares two houses with him—one in Napa and one in Los Angeles, California. Later, Tamera hires a designer for her son's nurseries, in both locations—featured on Season 2, episode 18 "Tussle and Flow." The pictures later appeared in *People* magazine.

Aside from income and lifestyle, Tia and Tamera portray other elements of upper-class status, like their diction and speech patterns, which have almost no accent and perfect grammar. Both women dress in fashionable designer clothes; and they very rarely wear the same outfit twice on the show. In the confessional scenes on the show, Tia and Tamera have what appears to be professional hair and make-up treatments, like an actor might have for a scripted television show. Both ladies graduated from Pepperdine University, a private institution in Malibu, CA, with degrees in Psychology.

It is clear from these examples that Tia and Tamera live a more extravagant lifestyle than the average black American woman. According to a 2012 U.S. Census Bureau report the median income for an African American is just $33,321 per household, with more than 28 percent of African-Americans living at the poverty level.[49] So why do we tune in? It's entertaining to watch those with vast wealth live their lives, but it's certainly not reality for most of the viewers.

The action of the text is to demonstrate the extraordinary qualities of the lives of Tia and Tamera, but in the attempt to sell this to viewers as a unique black lifestyle, the text instead sets these women apart as characters, not real people. The lifestyle shown is so extraordinarily different than those of the average black female viewer that the text serves to narrow the definition of black financial success and portray an example too far out of reach, so as to be a spectacle of wealth and riches.

## Mediocre Mothers

Tia has written a book, *Oh baby! Pregnancy Tales and Advice from One Hot Mama to Another*, featured in the Season 2, episode 11, "Are you pregnant?" which has a chapter on Hot Mama style, giving tips for shoes and outfits to wear that make you feel sexy during your pregnancy. Apparently that's what most moms are doing during their pregnancy, right? Buying sexy clothes! On the heels of her book, Tia and Tamera capitalized on their pregnancies, launching a maternity line called *Need*, with stretch mark cream called *Stretchy* and a lactation drink called *Milky*, all of which were featured on Season 2 Episode 20 "Twinventors." Both women and their families are vegan and created products that are all-natural and vegan because they could not find such products on the market. This dietary choice is another striking example of how different these ladies' lives are than other American black moms, more than two million of whom are currently enrolled in the Women Infants and Children (WIC) national food assistance program, struggling to feed their children.[50] The action of the text is to place these women as an example outside of the average black mother's life, not portray how black women, in general, provide for their children.

It's clear to see that Hollywood's version of reality is unreal for the American population. This divide, while seen as an entertaining look into the lives of these women, contributes to a shallow understanding of a real black American. Additionally, Tia and Tamera are frequently observed in situations which serve to marginalize them as women and mothers. For example, in the Season 2, Episode 4 titled "The Cree-Cree Crawl," Tia misses the first time her son crawls because she is working. She receives a text-message video of Cree crawling sent by the nanny. She is devastated that she missed it and the audience is left to presume that she is incapable of balancing her work and home life, making poor mothering decisions to the detriment of her son. Tia tells Tamera on a video chat about the situation, and Tamera asks her if she's okay with missing these moments because she's working a lot. As the conversation gets heated, Tia says, "Basically what you're implying is I need to stop working right now so that I can spend some more time with my son, correct?" Tamera replies, "It's okay to work. But when are you gonna be able to say no?" Tia tells her in a staccato voice, "I completely understand where you're coming from, but you're not in my situation. The reality of the situation is that I have to work." Tamera's response is cutting as she says, "First of all if you wanna do that, go ahead. But with the life that you're gonna lead, you are going to miss milestones. Now that I know that's the life you wanna live and you're living, fine." To this, Tia puts down the laptop screen and leaves the room, cutting the conversation short.

The action of the text is to show a black mother making a selfish choice because she wants to enhance her career instead of mothering her children. Never mind that Tia makes it clear her lifestyle depends upon the income from working. Her sister, Tamera, who has the luxury of not needing an acting income to maintain her lavish lifestyle, is shown judging—bullying, even—to make her point that working moms aren't adequate mothers. Besides the stay-at-home/work-outside-the-home debate, the action of the text is also to show two black mothers fighting, continuing a troubling depiction of black women as argumentative. When attempting to manage the difficult choices that so many mothers must make, Tia is punished on the show and portrayed as an inadequate, selfish mother. As she tells Cory, "It's just kinda hard finding that balance."

The Black Body

The final crime against black women is committed when they are portrayed as objects for men's gratification. Tia, particularly, was featured voicing concerns over her physical appearance and attempts to please Cory with her body. In the episode "You, Me & Baby Makes 3," Tia feels pressure to lose the baby weight just weeks after the birth of Cree so that she can be of adequate size to perform on her television show, *The Game*. She takes pole dancing lessons in Season 2 because she wants to put "the fire back in her relationship with Cory" after four years of marriage. Tia later performs in a Burlesque show in Season 3, saying, "I needed this to feel sexy." She also does a bikini photo shoot, makes a yoga fitness DVD, and signs up for a boot camp fitness course, because she is concerned about unflattering photos that make her feel fat. Tia repeatedly mentions her husband as her motivation to feel sexy and be slim. "Oh my god. My husband is going to freak," Tia says as she practices for her burlesque performance. In the Season 3, episode "V-steam my what?" the sisters go to a spa and get a special steam treatment for their vaginas. Tamera asks whether the V-steam treatment will help make sex with her husband better.

The action of the text is to bring viewer attention to the bodies of these black women and give viewers permission to evaluate them. Portrayals like these center the black female as an object for the male gaze, which ultimately marginalizes her position in society.[51] The action of the text is to show that as a light-skinned black female, Tia is open for evaluation as a sexy Jezebel rather than as a businesswoman. Rather than providing a modern example of black motherhood, old stereotypes are revived and devoured by the viewers. Tia Mowry-Hardrict and Tamera Mowry-Housley are talented, accomplished businesswomen who lead, what appear to be, extraordinary lives. Watching the show and enjoying the unique lives they lead, viewers must be aware that the show, while entertaining, cannot encapsulate an ideal version of black womanhood and motherhood for others.

*Black Mother #4: Justine Simmons*

The final black mother is Justine Simmons, the matriarch of the Simmons clan on her show, *Run's House*. This reality television series premiered on the MTV network in 2005. The show centers on the family of Joseph, "Rev Run" Simmons, Sr., a member of the popular 1980's hip-hop trio Run-D.M.C. The family resides in Saddle Ridge, New Jersey, a wealthy community just outside of New York City. Along with Rev Run, the show features his wife, Justine. Justine, who married Rev Run in 1994, is originally from Long Island, New York. In addition to being a wife and a mother, she is an author, who successfully published *God Can You Hear Me?* in 2007; and she co-authored *Take Back Your Family*, with her husband, in 2008. She also works as a motivational speaker and designs her own jewelry line, Brown Sugar.

Also on the show are daughters Vanessa, Angela, and Miley, and sons Joseph ("Jojo") Jr., Daniel ("Diggy"), and Russell ("Russy"). Vanessa Angela, and Jojo, are Rev Run's children from a previous marriage, while Miley, the youngest, was adopted shortly after the death of Rev Run and Justine's infant daughter, Victoria.

Reminiscent of light-hearted family sitcoms such as *The Brady Bunch*, and *The Cosby Show*, episodes of *Run's House* typically center on a problem, experience, or project concerning a family member or members. By the close of each episode, each issue is resolved under the guidance of Rev Run and the occasional help of Justine. The series reveals these resolutions to viewers through a final discussion Rev Run and Justine have in bed, and through Rev Run's "Words of Wisdom," a text he sends to friends and family at each episode's conclusion.

*Balanced (S)Mother.* In order to keep her chaotic blended family under control, Justine has to use some tactics that show a negative side to mothering. A notable example of this is seen in the Season 6, Episode 7, titled "Mother Smother." As suggested by the title, the major plot line of this episode focuses on the suggested "smothering" nature of Justine's parenting, a reoccurring theme throughout the series. Her alleged tendency to smother is typically evidenced in two ways: the way she disciplines her children, and the strategies she employs in becoming more knowledgeable on the personal aspects of her children's lives.

In this particular episode, Justine receives a school report from Diggy's gym and Spanish teachers, informing her that Diggy's academic performance is inconsistent, and that he is displaying insubordinate behavior. When Rev Run asks Justine how she plans to handle the situation, Justine replies that she will take away his laptop computer, as he spends more time on it than on his school work. After confiscating the laptop, Justine utilizes it for personal use. While working, she intercepts a video call from Pharrell Williams, a popular music artist and producer, and also mentor to son Diggy. During this call, she informs Pharrell of Diggy's problems with school. Additionally, in exchange for allowing Diggy to speak to him about business via his laptop, Justine asks Pharrell to speak to Diggy about the importance of doing well in school, hoping that as his mentor, he may offer effective encouragement.

Although restricting electronics is a common punishment for teens, and is considered a good parenting strategy by many, Rev Run's reaction to Justine's disciplinary actions frame her parental efforts as excessive and ineffective. Although Rev Run tells Justine that he agrees that taking Diggy's laptop "will probably get him to focus more," he points out that Diggy's activity on the computer is positive, as it is related to a business he is attempting to launch, and that restricting his access to his laptop will anger him. Rev Run's response suggests that although confiscating the laptop may help Diggy to focus more on school, he criticizes Justine's parenting and thinks she did not make the best disciplinary choice, thus undermining her mothering.

Additionally, after Justine informs Rev Run about the conversation with Pharrell, Rev Run chastises her, suggesting that instead of utilizing a smarter parenting strategy, her behavior was "a little invasive" and "a little smothering." Similarly, Rev Run also states that although he knew Justine planned to confiscate the laptop, he did not expect her to use the computer or intercept Diggy's "private" video calls, including the one in which she spoke to Pharrell.

In addition to being a smothering mother through disciplinary practices, the "Mother Smother" episode also frames Justine as an overbearing and ineffective mother in the strategies she employs to learn more about the personal lives of her children. For example, after Rev Run informs Justine that son Russy may have a crush on a female classmate, Justine simply asks Russy directly about the crush during a mother-son card game. She says to him, "I'm the only one you have eyes for, right?" Justine's comment is immediately followed by the sound effect of a scratching record, accompanied by Russy's response of "Mom! Oh my God," as he puts his head in his hands. Apparently hurt by Russy's refusal to share private information, Justine tells Russy that she feels that he tells Jojo and Rev Run information that he does not share with her. As he storms out of the bedroom with Justine in pursuit, Russy exclaims, "Mom! I don't want anything from you. . . . I'm not playing anymore."

Although it can be argued that Justine's motherly desire to know more about her son's life is not uncommon, Rev Run's responses to Justine's interest frames her parental efforts as excessive and ineffective. For example, when Justine expresses her desire to know more about Russy's crush—as she believes Russy shares more information with Rev Run than with her—Rev Run tells her, "Don't mess with him . . . leave him alone . . . it might embarrass him . . . with me . . . it's funny. With you it's a smothering thing." Not only does this comment suggest that the strategies Justine uses to bond with her children are overbearing and ineffective, but they are also subpar compared to his.

To further emphasize this point, Rev Run abruptly follows Justine's story with his day's experience with their son Jojo. With pride, he tells Justine how Jojo initiated an outing to the city in which he helped Rev Run select new, modern clothing. He states that despite his blessing, Jojo repeatedly ignored his friends' phone calls, so as to not disrupt quality time with his father. Rev Run expresses pride and happiness as he feels he naturally bonded with Jojo. Rev Run's story juxtaposed with Justine's, not only brings light to his parental successes with Jojo, but highlights her failures as a mother in her similar attempts to bond with Russy. Thus, Justine's mothering is framed through a lens of patriarchy and marginalized by her own husband.

The action of the text is to frame Justine's mothering style as negative and, her behaviors are excessive and over-the-top, causing her kids to distance themselves from her and turn toward their dad, Rev Run. Additionally, Justine's behaviors are framed through a lens of patriarchy. Her every behavior is analyzed from Rev Run's perspective and this pairing leaves her as the clear loser in parenting skills. Though Justine is presented at the outset of the show as a matriarch of this group, she is diminished in her power and standing by the storylines, her children, and her husband. This conversation highlights one way in which mothers on RTV are punished or criticized, emphasizing their inability to be caring, loving mothers because they are too busy smothering their loved ones.

## Big Spender

Run's House has received criticism for not providing an accurate representation of American family life, including the lives of black families.[52] It has been argued that Run's House offers a distorted representation of family life, while praising the extravagant consumption practices of the "hyper-rich" upper class.[53] Despite this criticism, however, Rev Run is depicted as the one cast member who attempts to keep the family grounded, frequently pointing out and attempting to correct the extravagant expectations and spending practices of the family. Conversely, Justine is frequently depicted as a wasteful, frivolous spender.

One example of this is seen in the Season 6, Episode 3 titled, "The Secret of my Excess." In this particular episode, Rev Run shows deep concern for the wasteful behaviors of Diggy and Russy, after the sons request their father purchase more basketballs instead of retrieving old balls that have rolled into the backyard creek. Rev instructs his sons to retrieve and clean the lost balls, as purchasing new balls would be a waste of money. Rev Run also addresses this issue of waste after witnessing Russy pouring out a glass of water and disposing of the cup after one use.

Rev Run brings the waste problem to Justine's attention in Miley's room. After Rev Run recaps the basketball and water cup occurrences, he looks around Miley's room and notices the amount of Elmo toys the young child owns. He says, "I'm noticing that there's Elmo's every-where. . . . I'm giving two of her Elmo's away to charity." He then ex-presses concern that in the instance of Miley losing one of her Elmo toys, Justine will simply purchase a new one instead of attempting to find the misplaced toy. Justine points out that the majority of the Elmo toys were gifts from friends, and responds with, "You're comparing me to the boys. Every time something comes up . . . you make it seem like the whole house is in disorder." To this comment, Rev Run responds with, "I don't think the whole house is in disorder. I think we have several balls and several Elmo's." At the episode's conclusion, however, Rev Run express-es to Justine that the family's issue with wastefulness has not being ade-quately resolved, stating that he "did the best [he] could around here," before providing her with strategies to effectively address his concerns.

The action of the text is to blame Justine for a concerning behavior amongst the whole family, because she is the mother/woman and there-fore the genesis of this behavior. Justine is framed as wasteful and irre-sponsible, while Rev Run is the sole relatable and sensible cast member. Rev Run's statement establishing that he did the best that he could in eliminating the family's wasteful practices not only further supports this view, but also calls into question Justine's parenting. He insinuates that she has failed in her parental duty to teach her children responsible con-sumption practices; and she instead is modeling poor choices. In her denial, Justine is framed as whiny and defensive, though clearly guilty of the crimes Rev Run listed. This RTV show, primarily produced to show-case an affluent black family, turns the tables and portrays the Simmons as wasteful, hyper-rich, and out of touch with average families. The text leads the viewer to agree with patriarch Rev Run, condemn the wasteful-ness and blame Justine for the entire issue.

## Light Skinned Lady

A common trend on *Run's House* is the depiction of Justine in a subor-dinate role. Despite her successful business and musical ventures de-picted throughout the series in numerous episodes—like Season 4, Epi-sode 5 titled "Rapper's Retreat"—Justine is shown responding to her children's requests with "Well, we'll have to ask Daddy. You know he's in charge." Similarly, in the episodes "Family Portraits" and "When the Cat's Away" which followed, Justine's pursuit of a music career and development of a jewelry line, Rev Run's role in her success is heavily emphasized to the point of crediting him for her achievement. What is particularly interesting about this portrayal is that it deviates from the common popular stereotype of black women as loud, dominant and emasculating. This particular portrayal of Justine's character may possibly be attributed to her lighter-skin complexion and the role skin tones are now playing in RTV character portrayals.

Due to the historical distinction between lighter and darker skinned blacks, rooted in slavery, different attributes and privileges are frequently attributed to light-skinned blacks versus dark-skinned blacks.[54] Colorism, proposes that lighter-skinned blacks are considered "closer to white" and privileged with higher social, political and economic status than their darker-skinned brothers and sisters.[55] Additionally, as lighter-skinned blacks are viewed as being "closer to white" on the racial spectrum, they are often perceived as being less ethnically authentic than darker-skinned blacks.[56]

The action of the text is to once again question the blackness of the Justine's body. Like Holly, Tia, and Tamara, Justine's representation of blackness is made problematic. Her light complexion is a pointer to her lacks as a mother and frivolous spender, someone who is out of touch with the average black woman and the typical mother. Additionally, her complexion aids in the effective framing of her character as a submissive wife, as her lighter skin distances her from the domineering and emasculating stereotype often considered to be a more authentic representation of black women. In sum, Justine's framing on *Run's House* undercuts the perceived authority of a black woman and potentially degrades her quest for equality in America.

## CONCLUSION: GIVE MOM A BREAK

The examples provided in this chapter serve to acknowledge the incomplete and vapid representations of black women and black motherhood present today on RTV, and also show the power of the old stereotypes that persist. Treating episodes of popular RTV shows as sites of struggle over race, colorism, and criticisms of effective mothering,[57] reveals a system of meaning which reifies existing stereotypes for black mothers.[58] These efforts to show other women's lives, other appearances and other classes are limited in success because they seem to betray and reject blackness. Instead of showing blackness in all of its richness and variety, results from textual analysis show that these programs seem to actually narrow the meaning of blackness while setting these representations outside of blackness.

The first step to change this pattern is an awareness that the entertainment viewers are devouring is a new breed of stereotyping and is ultimately harmful to the black female's struggle for equality in America. *Dance Moms, Tia & Tamera, Run's House* and similar RTV shows are certainly a more reasonable and enjoyable representation of black women than other shows that cast black women as angry, classless, and uneducated. But, in an effort to distance oneself from these old stereotypical views of *those* Bad Black Mothers, it is important not to turn too quickly toward securing the place of white patriarchy which tells us that Good Mothers cannot exist in certain bodies.[59] Accepting this new brand of rich, light-skinned black mothers as ideal is equally disempowering for the general black American population whose phenotype and socio-economic position are not represented by the cast portrayals seen on television today. Instead, let's strive toward, "a world where respect is seen as inherent in humanity itself and therefore the rights of all mothers, and all people, are universally respected. A world where no litmus test is required for us to see worth and dignity in the beautiful mess of complexities and singularities that we are."[60]

## NOTES

1. Gloria Ladson-Billings, "'Who you callin' nappy-headed?': A critical race theory look at the construction of black women." *Race Ethnicity and Education* 12, no. 1 (2009): 87–99; Lawanda Wallace, *Double Dutching in My Own Skin: An Autoethnography on Colorism* (PhD Dissertation, University of North Carolina Greensboro, 2013). Permalink:                                                                         http://libres
.uncg.edu/ir/uncg/f/Wallace_uncg_0154D_11127.pdf.

2. Elizabeth Ault, "'You can help yourself/but don't take too much': African American motherhood on The Wire." *Television & News Media* (2013): 386–401; Lorraine Fuller, "Are we seeing things?: The Pinesol Lady and the ghost of Aunt Jemima." *Journal of Black Studies* (2001): 120–131; Jennifer Pozner, *Reality bites back: The troubling truth about guilty pleasure TV* (Berkeley, CA: Seal Press, 2010).

3. "An Era of Growth: The Cross-Platform Report" *Nielsen Consumer Report,* (2014): 10.

4. *Dance Moms,* Television Series, Lifetime Network, debuted 2011.

5. *Tia & Tamera,* Television Series, Style Network, debuted 2011.

6. *Run's House,* Television Series, MTV, debuted 2005.

7. Norman Fairclough. *Language and Power* (London: Longman, 1989); Norman Fairclough. *Analysing disource: textual analysis for social research* (London: Routledge, 2003); Norman Fairclough, "Critical discourse analysis." In *The Routledge Handbook of Discourse Analysis,* edited by James Paul Gee and Michael Handford, 1st ed. (London: Routledge, 2012): 9–20. Permalink: https://www.academia.edu/3791325/Critical_discourse_analysis_2012_.

8. Barry Brummett *Rhetoric in popular culture* (New York: St. Martin's Press, 1994).

9. Lillie Chouliaraki and Norman Fairclough. *Discourse in Late Modernity: Rethinking Critical Discourse Analysis* (Edinburgh: Edinburgh University Press, 1999).

10. Jim Brancato, "Domesticating politics: The representation of wives and mothers in American reality television." *Film & History: An Interdisciplinary Journal of Film and Television Studies* 37, no. 2 (2007): 49–56; Fiona Green, "Supernanny: Disciplining Mothers through a Narrative of Domesticity." *Storytelling: A Critical Journal of Popular Narrative* 6, no. 2 (2007): 99–107; Elizabeth Nathanson. *Television and Postfeminism Housekeeping: No Time for Mother* (New York: Routledge, 2013).

11. Green, 99–107.

12. Ibid. 100.

13. Brancato, 49–56.

14. Nathanson. *Television and Postfeminism.*

15. Ibid. 162.

16. Brancato, 49–56.

17. Nathanson. *Television and Postfeminism.*

18. Pozner, *Reality bites back,* 118.

19. Tope Fadiron Charlton, "The impossibility of the Good Black Mother." In *The Good Mother Myth: Redefining Motherhood to Fit Reality,* edited by Avital Norman Nathan, 1st ed. (Berkeley: Seal Press, 2013): 196.

20. bell hooks. "The oppositional gaze: Black female spectators." In *The Feminism and visual culture reader,* edited by Amelia Jones, 1st ed. (New York: Routledge, 2003): 94–104.

21. Ibid. 112.

22. Wallace, *Double Dutching in My Own Skin.*

23. Tiwi Marira and Priyanka Mitra. "Colorism: Ubiquitous but understudied." *Industrial and Organizational Psychology,* 6, no. 1 (2013): 103–107.

24. Wallace, *Double Dutching in My Own Skin.*

25. John Fiske. "Television: Polysemy and popularity." *Critical Studies in Mass Communication,* 3, no. 4 (1986): 391–408.

26. Pozner, *Reality bites back.*

27. Fairclough. *Analysing disource,* 27.

28. Ibid.

29. Ibid. 28.

30. Brummett, *Rhetoric in popular culture.*

31. Ibid.

32. Fairclough. *Analysing disource,* 27.

33. Brummett, *Rhetoric in popular culture.*

34. Patricia Hill Collins. *Black sexual politics: African Americans, gender, and the new racism* (London: Routledge, 2004): 71.

35. Pozner, *Reality bites back,* 241.

36. Collins, *Black sexual politics.*

37. U.S. Census Bureau. *Income, poverty, and health insurance coverage in the United States,* 2012. Permalink: http://minorityhealth.hhs.gov/templates/browse.aspx?lvl=2&lvlID=51.

38. Pozner, *Reality bites back;* Beretta Smith-Shomade, *Watching While Black: Centering the Television of Black Audiences* (New Brunswick: NJ: Rutgers University Press, 2013).

39. Barry Brummett. *A rhetoric of style* (Carbondale, IL: Southern Illinois University Press, 2008): 52.

40. Ibid. 53.

41. Maria Sciullo, "Holly Hatcher-Frazier is a voice of reason on Dance Moms," *Pittsburgh Post-Gazette,* January 10, 2012. Permalink: http://www.post-gazette.com/local/east/2012/01/08/Holly-Hatcher-Frazier-is-a-voice-of-reason-on-Dance-Moms/stories/201201080179.

42. Alicia Simon, "What did Laquisha ever do to you?" *Eternally Summer* (blog), August 26, 2011, http://eternallysummer.wordpress.com/2011/08/26/lifetime-dance-moms/.

43. Candice Rigdon "I object! A natural attack on afros?" *Curly Nikki* (blog). August 28, 2011, http://curlynikki.com/2011/08/i-object-natural-attack-on-afros.html.

44. Simon, *Eternally Summer.*

45. See, for example, Byrd and Tharp's comprehensive book on hair, *Hair Story: Untangling the Roots of Black Hair in America* (2002).

46. Sassyism, "Tia & Tamera: What about the next generation of mixed folks?" *Sassyism* (blog), January 2013, http://sassyism.blogspot.com/2013/01/tia-tamera-what-about-next-generation.html.

47. Margaret Hunter, "'If you're light you're alright': Light skin color as social capital for women of color." *Gender & Society* 16, no. 2 (2002): 175–193; Margaret Hunter, "The persistent problem of colorism: Skin tone, status, and inequality." *Sociology Compass* 1, no. 1, (2007): 237–254; Wallace, *Double Dutching in My Own Skin.*

48. Marira and Mitra, 103.

49. U.S. Census Bureau.

50. United States Department of Agriculture (USDA). *Women, Infants, and Children (WIC) Participant and Program Characteristics 2012: Summary,* 2012. Permalink: http://www.fns.usda.gov/sites/default/files/WICPC2012_Summary.pdf.

51. hooks, 94–104.

52. Melanie McFarland, "Without wack jobs, 'Run's House' may not fly," *Seattle Post-Intelligencer,* October 12, 2005. Permalink: http://www.seattlepi.com/ae/tv/article/Without-wack-jobs-Run-s-House-may-not-fly-1184917.php.

53. Ibid.

54. Hunter, 237–254.

55. Ibid.

56. Ibid.

57. Brummett, *Rhetoric in popular culture.*

58. Fairclough, *Analysing disource.*

59. Charlton, 196.

60. Ibid. 199.

*II*

# Portrayals of the Angry Black Woman

# SIX

## Is She Strong or Just a b!@*#?

*Discussions of Black Women's Anger in the Reality Show* Bad Girls Club

### Adria Y. Goldman

It is near impossible to have a discussion of black women in reality television without mentioning the infamous Angry Black Woman (ABW). In fact, some critiques have argued reality television is damaging for black women since many shows focus heavily on this character.[1] This stereotypical characterization of black women is long-standing, due largely to its constant inclusion in media messages. As noted in chapter one, audiences were first officially introduced to her in the 1920s as Sapphire Stevens from the *Amos 'n' Andy Show*; and her character continued to resurface throughout the years, across several different genres. Despite the many time periods through which this image has traveled, the key characteristic of the Sapphire—her unexplainable anger and aggression—seem to resonate in many modern day images of black women.

But what if her anger could be explained? Although anger is primarily described as an unattractive and negative character trait in black women, some scholars acknowledge the group's ability to use anger purposefully. What Sheri Parks (2010) refers to as the "strong, (sometimes angry) black woman"[2] and Patricia Hill Collins (2005) labels the "Black Bitch,"[3] are additional examples of a black woman who uses her anger strategically, in order to benefit herself and others. Her anger is only part of her strength, for which she is celebrated. Hence a dichotomy exists when it comes to black women's display of anger—the good, purposeful anger versus the bad, unexplainable anger. Yet, such an "either-or" mentality can be troubling and can create fear for black women, as they cannot always predict how others will perceive their use of the emotion. In addition, these conflicting messages could create pressure for black women who are only trying to express an organic emotion.

Images featuring these positive and negative expressions of anger have been found in media programming that predates reality television (e.g. television sitcoms and movies). Researchers have also found the ABW to be a common role in reality television.[4] Knowing that this stereotypical character does exist within reality television, I offer an analysis inspired—in part—by the social interaction theory of emotion, focusing on the *purpose* of black female reality show participants' anger and how it relates to the dichotomy that exists between good and bad expressions of anger for black women. This involves looking at the expression of anger as well as responses to anger.

One reality television show, in particular, that uses anger as a major theme is Oxygen's *Bad Girls Club*. Each season of the docusoap has featured at least one black female, and the show seems to be a hit among viewers. Because of the show's popularity, in addition to its promise for "bad" girls, examining the show can contribute to the current discussion of black women and anger. In order to continue the conversation on the ABW, I offer an examination of black women's use of anger within *Bad Girls Club*. More specifically, I discuss the *purpose* for the women's anger and how it correlates with negative and/or positive characterizations of black women's anger—such as the "Sapphire/Bitch/Angry Black Woman" or the "Strong Black Woman/Black Bitch" (respectively).

The goal of this chapter is to go beyond looking at how black women display anger in reality television, and also look at how the reasons for their anger are presented and treated. Of course, reality television has a hand in how these situations are framed and presented to viewers through its editing processes and strategic casting; however, analyzing these presentations helps illustrate how the reasons for anger are presented as *reality* to viewers. The social interaction theory of emotion seeks a more subjective understanding of a person's feelings. According to this theory, "emotions are feeling states resulting from social interaction; they are interrelated with cognition; they are not universally experienced or expressed; and they have subjective meaning."[5]

Using the social interaction theory of emotion requires that I consider elements such as social factors, reasons, and reactions to anger.[6] In an effort to truly deconstruct the women's displays of anger, I also use past research on black women's reasons for anger. Then, I conclude the chapter with a discussion of the underlying messages communicated about black women and the implications that such reality television presentations have on society and black women's future displays of anger.

## THE MEANING OF BLACK WOMEN'S ANGER

In order to gain a subjective understanding of emotion more aligned with the social interaction theory of emotion and "[t]o understand the extent to which gestures correspond with feelings, one must know something of the persons involved and the conventions of the situation in which the gesture and emotion are presumably linked."[7] When examining anger of Black female reality television participants, understanding 'the person and conventions of the situation' should involve research on uses of anger, as well as existing media representations of the group.

Although anger is a natural emotion expressed by all types of individuals, differences among genders, ethnicities, and age groups are often stressed.[8] Research has found that women's expressions of anger are complex and serve many purposes.[9] Sandra Thomas argues that women use anger in response to stress, injustice, and others' irresponsibility.[10] However, anger is often seen as the default emotion for black women. Given this expectation of anger, the reasons behind the emotion are not always considered. In addition, there are certain stereotypes born out of this expectation of anger that also help to keep this belief alive.

J. Celeste Walley-Jean (2009) writes, ". . . evidence suggests that African American women's experience of anger is multifaceted, triggered by numerous factors, and can have negative behavioral effects."[11] For example, research shows how some black women use anger in response to feelings of powerlessness and injustice.[12] In Audre Lorde's keynote address on *The Uses of Anger*, at the National Women's Studies Association (NWSA) Convention, she explained, "My anger is a response to racist attitudes, to the actions and presumptions that arise out of those attitudes."[13] She goes on to explain how this anger should not be suppressed or ignored, but rather acknowledged and discussed. In fact, unexpressed anger is more dangerous and serves as an "undetonated device."[14]

Aside from using anger as a natural response to certain situations and feelings, researchers have also discussed how black women can use anger in order to serve specific purposes. Lorde (1981) explains, "Every woman has a well-stocked arsenal of anger potentially useful against those oppressions, personal and institutional, which brought that anger into being. Focused with precision it can become a powerful source of energy serving progress and change."[15] Anger can be used to create change and to empower; if people choose to learn from it. Other researchers have echoed this sentiment that anger can be used as a way to heal from and respond to oppression.[16]

Two images of black women that highlight this use of strategic and purposeful anger are the Black Bitch and the Strong Black Woman (SBW). Black Bitches—both words intentionally spelled with a capital B—are "super-tough, super strong women who are often celebrated."[17] For example, "[Pam Grier's character in the 1975 film *Sheba, Baby*] becomes a 'Bad Bitch' (e.g. a good Black woman), when she puts her looks, sexuality, intellect, and/or aggression in service to African American communities."[18] However, despite its more positive meaning, Collins (2005) argues that the Black Bitch is rarely seen within media messages.

Parks (2010) discusses the strategic anger exhibited by the SBW. She explains how, like the Sacred Dark Feminine, the SBW ". . . [doesn't] start fights, but she does finish them. Her anger is not out of control; it is strategic."[19] Within this image, anger is celebrated because it is used positively to serve a purpose and to protect others. However, she can sometimes be labeled as being angry, in a negative sense, because of her strength. Melissa Harris-Perry (2011) explains how the SBW incorporates elements of the Mammy, Jezebel, and Sapphire. For the latter, "the strong black woman looks like a way to channel the angry Sapphire in a socially acceptable direction."[20]

Although on surface level, the image of the SBW is more positive than the ABW, this characterization can still be problematic for black women. Scholars have argued that the expectation for women to be strong can be a burden and a difficult standard for black women to uphold. The images of the SBW also come with the expectation that the women should endure hard times and sacrifice for others, all while wearing a brave face and suppressing her own emotions.[21] Because of this image, "black women may believe that their anger must always be in service of others and rarely used in their own defense."[22] Such expectations can be quite stressful and may also lead black women to stray away from expressing their own anger and other "unpleasant" emotions, so that it will not tarnish the strong woman image.[23] Hence, black women are faced with quite the dilemma. While there are positive expressions of anger—because it is in service to others—it can limit their own healthy expression of anger in service to self.

Like others, black women do not always use anger in positive and constructive ways. Research shows that some black (and white) women recognize their use of "out-of-control anger."[24] However, black women are most often associated with this negative display of anger, rather than the more functional and strategic uses. This negative image translates into a stereotype, such as the ABW.[25] Parks (2010) argues that some individuals use the ABW stereotype as an insulting image ". . . that seeks to rob black women of emotional nuance and intelligence. It does not admit that anger could very well be a reasonable response to certain conditions."[26]

This negative and—so called—"illogical" use of anger is found in several stereotypical images of black women, such as the Sapphire, bitch, and ABW. As previously noted, Sapphire was initially introduced as a character                    on                    the *Amos 'n' Andy Show*. She was "sassy, verbose, and known for telling people off in a loud and animated manner."[27] Historically, she had a dark complexion and was intended to be unattractive, according to traditional Eurocentric beauty standards.[28] Although not identical to Sapphire, researchers have identified other recurring images of black women that share the unnecessary anger and aggression of the Sapphire.

In comparing the modern-day ABW to historical depictions, Phillip Kretsedemas explains, ". . . this stereotype is no longer being used to portray a particular type of black woman. Instead, it is increasingly being used as a standard template for portraying all black women, regardless of social class, skin tone and body type."[29] Collins (2005) also describes a newer image of black women and their anger. What she identifies as the "bitch" is a "controlling image . . . that depicts women as aggressive, loud, rude, and pushy."[30] This "confrontational and actively aggressive" role is most often assigned to working class and/or poor black women who are considered to be ugly and loud.[31] Collins (2005) clarifies that the term bitch can be assigned to women of all ethnicities, but she stresses how often it is used in labeling black women. She writes, ". . . presenting black women as bitches is designed to defeminize and demonize them."[32] With some variations of this image, hypersexuality is another element intertwined with the women's anger.[33] What the Sapphire, bitch, and ABW have in common is their negative, yet constant display of anger. Their anger is coupled with other unflattering qualities.

These images of black women are communicated, and continue to survive, with the help of mass media; and black women have long struggled with issues of media representations. Even with an increased amount of inclusion over the years, these images still manage to reflect stereotypical views. One reason why increased representations remain stereotypical and harmful is because these images and messages no longer overtly express racist ideas. Instead, the images have been re-packaged and watered down—racism is not absent from media, but it is being presented more subtly.[34] Thus, stereotypical images can continue to exist in media—particularly on reality television.

## THE ANGRY BLACK WOMAN ON REALITY TELEVISION

Like scripted television, research has revealed that some portrayals of black women on reality television are stereotypical.[35] The debate may still exist about the authenticity of reality television, but research has shown that this type of programming—whether fictional or nonfictional—has ideological power.[36] David Croteau and Wiliam Hoynes (2014) argue that media content, regardless of the genre, has social significance. Audience members look at media and walk away with some information about the world.[37] Reality television is no exception to the rule, and it carries the same risk of communicating ideas to its audience members.

Hans H. Gerth (1964) argues, "Various gestures have differing prestige values attached to them, and insofar as inner feelings may develop from the repeated use of gestures in recurring [media] roles, the emotions as well as the gestures of members of various status groups may be stereotyped."[38] When applying this concept to reality television images, the way in which a black woman's anger is consistently featured may impact the way others feel it is appropriate to use—or not to use—specific verbal and nonverbal cues to express this emotion. In addition, these recurring presentations have the potential to impact the way viewers perceive black women.

The ABW is one of those images to reappear in media, including reality television. One of the most infamous examples—as noted in Chapter One—is Omarosa Manigault Stallworth. Omarosa has been labeled one of the greatest reality television villains, following her appearance on Donald Trump's NBC reality show, *The Apprentice*. As Saira Anees wrote in an *ABC News* article on April 24, 2008, that one of Omarosa's co-stars labeled her as a "bitch" because of her attitude and treatment of others. In terms of the dichotomy, Omarosa's anger is framed in a more unflattering light.[39]

According to an April 3, 2013 article by Amanda Anderson-Niles in *Urban Belle Magazine*, Omarosa explains that her reality television persona is not a representation of who she is as a real person.[40] Instead, it is an act that she performed as part of her job in entertainment. Her explanation helps support what both researchers and many viewers have already acknowledged—reality television is not always real. Omarosa has been featured in additional reality shows, including a celebrity edition of *The Apprentice*, where she continued to fulfill her infamous role. Robin Boylorn (2008) argues that more outrageous behavior in reality television results in more airtime.[41] Perhaps this is the reason for Omarosa's continued callbacks for reality television casting calls. It also hints to the profitability associated with being the ABW. It appears that Omarosa reclaimed the stereotypical image in order to further her career; and she acknowledged her purpose for using anger on the show—to make a profit.

Hence, regardless of the motivation behind participating in reality television, the images found in the programming can still impact the way in which viewers construct meaning. For example, although Omarosa acknowledged her "acting" on reality television, some still feel that her portrayal as the ABW was authentic. Following Omarosa's appearance on Bethenny Frankel's day time talk show, Brande Victorian of the web publication *Madame Noire* reported in an October 30, 2013 article: ". . . the fact that nastiness, and quite frankly bitchiness, seem to follow her wherever she goes is not exactly a coincidence. That's why, although in other situations some might chalk her angry black woman labeling up to racial stereotyping, a lot of folks have figured out that title is actually sort of accurate."[42]

Research on representations of black women on reality television has revealed that the ABW has been featured on other shows, as well.[43] Boylorn (2008) argues that most of the black women on reality television ". . . are voluptuous, loud, brown-skinned with weave down their backs and wide eyes made for rolling, fake nails and an attitude for days."[44] In fact, researchers have found portrayals of the ABW on various reality shows, including MTV's *Road Rules*,[45] VH-1's *Flavor of Love*,[46] and VH-1's *I Love New York*.[47] Moreover, analyses of representations within numerous talent contests[48] as well as within the popular subgenre of docusoaps,[49] also revealed that anger is a common theme among black female participants.

While these findings illustrate the use of the ABW on reality television, I use the following analysis to take a deeper look at these presentations. As previously mentioned, the reasons behind a woman's anger are rarely considered. Since anger has been linked to both negative and positive images of black women, it is important to examine reality television in order to determine which way black women's anger is being represented.

## REALITY TELEVISION'S BAD GIRL

In December 2006, Oxygen debuted its show *Bad Girls Club*, an American reality television show that follows (approximately) seven, self-proclaimed "bad girls," as they live together and interact. According to the show's information page in 2011, the women ". . . recognize that their outrageous behavior had hindered their relationships, careers, and lives." In addition, the Oxygen media website reports the series (the original show and its spinoff) has resulted in record-breaking numbers for the network. The series is known for featuring both white women and women of color. Further, Rachel Dubrofsky (2011) notes how reality television sometimes uses racially ambiguous characters that may be perceived by viewers as any number of different races.[50] Each season of *Bad Girls Club* has featured women of color—many of whom could be perceived as black women.

This show serves as a good subject of analysis for the current study given that anger has often linked to *bad* girls. As the name implies, the characters on the show, and their behaviors, are *bad*. Thus, one may assume that their display of anger is negative. In addition, critics have discussed the inappropriate behaviors of the women. In a December 1, 2008 article of the *NY Daily News*, David Hinckley referred to the show as a "low-rent girlfight" featuring women who are "angry, vain, [and] insecure."[51] Further, Peggy Drexler discussed the potential impact of shows like *Bad Girls Club* in her February 1, 2011 article for *The Huffington Post*.

She argued that the "foul-mouthed swagger and mean-tempered aggression could, over time and with enough promotion, become an acceptable model of feminine behavior."[52]

Critics have also argued that the show is one of several guilty of presenting (and reinforcing) the stereotype of the ABW.[53] Research on *Bad Girls Club: New Orleans* (season 7) also revealed the presence of the ABW stereotype.[54] However, critics and researchers have not fully examined how the *reasons* for their anger are presented. Given that some women have begun to embrace the image of the black women as angry, because of the strategic use of the emotion, it is also possible that the black bad girl could portray "strength" rather than "anger." A closer examination of the show helps unpack the dichotomy associated with black women's anger by looking to see if their use of the emotion is displayed negatively—as is the case with images of Sapphire, the bitch, and ABW—or positively—like images such as the Black Bitch or the Strong (Angry) Black Woman.

I examine the first season of the *Bad Girls Club* in order to see how the show initially presented the black bad girl—a formula that seems to work for the successful docusoap. While all of the seasons should eventually be examined, this analysis initiates the process by focusing in on the first season of the show. Season one set the stage for the show, in the world of reality television programming. The first season initially featured two black female cast members—Leslie, a 24-year-old stripper from Atlanta, Georgia with dreams of modeling and completing a college education; and Ty, a 25-year-old from Atlanta, Georgia who was often depicted in reference to her sexuality, as an openly bi-sexual female. A third black female cast member, 26-year-old Andrea from High Point, NC, was introduced much later in the season (episode 17) as a replacement for one of the girls who left the house early.

Using a textual analysis, the three black female cast members were examined to see how they use their anger and if those reasons align more with the positive or negative images. The entire first season was initially examined to identify which episodes included the black female cast members exhibiting anger. A note-taking sheet was created and used while viewing the episodes. The questions and prompts on this collection form were inspired by the social interaction theory of emotion, as well as past research on black women's use of anger and media representations of such.

Since black women's anger is sometimes tied to aggression and violent behavior, the note-taking sheet inquired about any conflict in which the women were involved. This included if the conflict was verbal or physical and if the black female participant initiated the incident. To help identify possible reasons for anger, I also paid attention to the purpose of the conflict. The social interaction theory of emotion is also considered with interactions and responses to emotion.[55] Gerth writes, "We know our emotion by observations of our gestures and actions, and more importantly perhaps, by what other people observe and report to us, directly or indirectly by their responses and gestures to the gestures we have made."[56] Thus, the note-taking sheet also included prompts and questions related to how other cast members responded to and discussed the black female participants' behaviors related to conflict and anger. Additionally, notes were taken on whether the use of anger was criticized or celebrated. Consequences for exhibiting anger were also recorded. This information could assist the women in understanding their own anger, as well as helping viewers understand if the anger was framed positively or negatively. These additional areas on the note-taking sheet helped look out for some qualities that may be related to the positive and negative expressions of anger inherent in the other images of black women discussed earlier.

In addition to others' discussions of women's use of anger, notes were also taken on if and how the black female participants discussed their own anger. As mentioned earlier, discussions of this emotion can be beneficial. Such information could assist with understanding the reasons behind anger. In addition, the women's discussions (or lack thereof) could hint to comfort levels with discussing anger, especially when it is of service to self. Other questions on the note-taking sheet assessed whether the women exhibited anger related to the images discussed earlier—the Sapphire, bitch, Angry Black Woman, strong black (sometimes angry) woman, and the Black Bitch. For example, I looked to see if the women were presented as nagging, aggressive, or critical of others—like the negative representations of black women's anger—or if anger was used strategically to protect others, promote change, or combined with other positive characteristics such as humor and kindness—like the more positive representations.

Being descriptive on the sheets was especially important so that the context of the situation could be considered. For example, ". . . proponents of [the social interaction theory of emotion] are also interested in how people interact in social situations before, during and after the experience of emotion. In this way, the theory adds social factors, like interactions with others, to the biological basis for explaining emotions."[57] I conducted an initial review of the show, using the note taking sheet, then revisited the sheet afterwards and to make any necessary changes (e.g. combining synonymous terms). After two rounds of viewing, the findings were categorized by character. Next, the findings of each character were compared in order to look for differences and similarities, or rather, dominant themes.

It is important to note that both of the original black female cast members (Leslie and Ty) left before the show ended. However, their reasons for leaving are also examined to see if they are tied to their expression of anger. There were twenty-one half-hour episodes that aired in season 1.

This excludes the reunion special (that only featured the original cast members) and the end-of-the-season special, which aired unseen footage not chosen for the original episodes. Hence, the analysis only focused on the twenty-one regular episodes that presented audiences with a narrative about the women.

## EXAMPLES OF ANGER IN *BAD GIRLS CLUB*

Of the 21 episodes, Leslie appeared in 15; Ty appeared in 10; and Andrea appeared in 5 episodes. Leslie and Ty's reasons for leaving were tied to their anger. Ty was forced to leave after she got into a physical altercation with a fellow cast member. Leslie voluntarily left because she was angry that—as she proclaimed—she was in a house full of women who were not trying to make positive changes in their lives. Both of their reasons for leaving are discussed in more detail later in this analysis. Leslie exhibited anger in 5 of the 15 episodes, Ty in 8 of her 10 episodes and Andrea in 2 of her 5 episodes. Thus, only one of the black women used anger in the majority of her episodes. On the other hand, Leslie and Andrea's portrayals help communicate that the default emotion for black women does not have to be anger. Both women were often shown interacting with their cast-mates, while exhibiting other emotions. However, conclusions cannot be safely drawn from these numbers alone, as the analysis seeks to reveal the reasons for and reactions to their anger. The ladies expression of anger, and reasons for such, fit into the following categories: unexplainable anger, anger for protection, anger as a result of disappointment, and anger as a result of disrespect (which was also linked at times to disloyalty).

### Inexplicable Anger

As discussed earlier, one of the most common characteristics of black women's negative expressions of anger is that the emotion is unexplained and therefore, unjustified. Throughout the series, however, the women's use of anger is explained—except for in two occasions. Ty has one instance of anger and rude behavior in the first episode when she introduces herself to her fellow cast members, via a message on the answering machine. Because of her message warning roommates of her arrival and bragging about her assault charges, one of the cast members says they are expecting "big nasty women." This comment hints to the unattractive features that were historically expected of angry, threatening characters. The roommates are relieved to meet Ty and see that this was not the case. In fact, Ty is a tall, slender woman with a light complexion. After arriving, Ty smiles as she asks the women if they were frightened by her voicemail. She then assures them she is not going to hurt anyone. Although not explicitly discussed, it appears that Ty uses anger as a defense mechanism as she prepares to enter into a new environment. Upon arrival, she lets her anger and her guard down however, because she does not explain her reasons for anger, leaving the audience to assume. Here Ty uses her anger in service to herself, yet boasting about her past assault chargers and ability to harm others frames her use of anger negatively.

In another scene, Andrea is involved in an altercation with her roommate, Zara, over a cell phone. Zara expressed how she does not understand the reasons behind their disagreement. Andrea aggressively let her know that she does not need to understand. However, upon watching the rest of the scene, as well as the private confessionals of her fellow cast mates, it becomes clearer to viewers why Andrea was involved in the argument. She was waiting for a phone call at the time and she was annoyed by Zara's drunken behavior. So, while her anger is not explained to the person involved in the argument, viewers were offered an explanation. Aside from Zara's confusion, Andrea's anger is neither celebrated nor criticized. Yet the scene does illustrate the difference that exists when a person understands the reasons for anger. Moreover, all of the other roommates understand Andrea's anger; although they do not agree or disagree with her reasons, they do not critique her for displaying the emotion. Zara, on the other hand, did not feel as if Andrea's anger was necessary, yet she was also portrayed as oblivious to the situation. Once again, the (partially) unexplained use of anger was used in service to the Black female displaying the emotion.

*Anger for Protection*

Both Ty and Leslie are shown using their anger in service to others. Three of the instances of anger (two for Leslie; one for Ty) were the result of the ladies trying to protect a fellow cast member, not themselves. In the first episode of the season, Leslie takes it upon herself to defend her fellow cast mate, Jodie, from an aggressive male in a dance club. Leslie becomes aggressive with the male, causing her to get kicked out of the club. Although this strategic use of anger to protect others is mostly tied with more positive expressions of anger (e.g. the SBW), the protected roommate expresses her disapproval of Leslie's anger. In addition, the male in the club calls Leslie a "bitch" and the bouncers forcefully put her out for causing a scene. Apparently, neither feels as if Leslie's desire to protect her roommate was warranted and her use of anger is criticized.

Leslie is criticized again when she uses her anger to protect another cast mate. In this particular incident, Leslie is taking care of her drunken roommate, Ty. Another roommate, Aimee, complains about the noise they are making. Leslie, who is also intoxicated, is upset that Aimee does not have more compassion for Ty. In this scene, Leslie uses her anger to defend her drunk/sick roommate. Aimee negatively critiques Leslie's anger, saying that she is being rude and hypocritical (because if Leslie's sleep was interrupted, she would be upset too). Leslie's anger is used for protection, even when she is intoxicated. However, her attitude is described more negatively—as with the bitch or the ABW—by the other person involved in the conflict.

The only instance where "anger is used for protection of others" and it is not labeled as negative is when Ty expresses anger with her roommate, Ripsi, for attacking one of their other roommates. Not only does Ty get angry and argumentative with Ripsi, she also makes the danger of her rage known. She demands that Ripsi leave the room and warns her not to attempt to lash out. This use of anger aligns with the image of the Black Bitch and SBW, as Ty used her anger to protect others and she also explained how her anger can be dangerous, if provoked. No one on the show explicitly labeled her anger as good or bad, so viewers are left to make their own evaluation. Yet, the fact that she is protecting another roommate from being physically harmed could help present a more flattering frame of her anger.

*Anger from Disappointment*

Both Leslie and Andrea display anger as a result of their disappointment over another person's actions. Leslie exhibits anger towards Ty after she gets into a physical altercation that forces her to leave the show. In this example, Leslie was angry because Ty made a bad decision. Leslie's anger was never celebrated, nor was it critiqued as being negative. However, her desire for someone else to do well and her use of anger in response to that, could have been perceived in a more positive way. It appears that the source of her rage was actually her care and concern for Ty.

Similarly, Leslie expressed her anger before explaining that she was voluntarily leaving the *Bad Girls Club* house early. She discussed with the roommates that she was upset that no one in the house, besides her, was trying to make a change in their lives. She used anger to express her disappointment and to explain why they should want to take advantage of the opportunity to change. Again, this use of anger was not celebrated, nor was it critiqued as being negative by any of the roommates. She was using her anger to express disappointment in the women's lack of motivation and drive, but her expression of this emotion could have been evaluated positively. In this instance, Leslie's anger is used to explain her choices.

Conversely, Andrea's anger from disappointment was revealed during her confessional. She aggressively asked, "what the f***" when expressing her disappointment in her roommates for not being more excited about her arrival. In that instance, her anger was not critiqued as being positive or negative, because it was not discussed in front of her house-mates.

## Anger from Disrespect

The primary trigger for the display of anger on season 1 of *Bad Girls Club* was disrespect. Ty engages in a physical altercation with her fellow roommate, Aimee, over an issue of disrespect. She was also angry be-cause, in her opinion, Aimee was not being courteous of the other room-mates. This hints to the protective function of anger. However, she is also using anger in service to herself. Ty is kicked off the show for fighting with her roommate, which helps communicate that her expression of anger is inappropriate. Yet, Ty explained that she was happy she "beat up" Aimee as punishment for disrespecting her. Furthermore, before leaving the show, Ty explained in her confessional that she was disap-pointed with herself for messing up her opportunity to change, but she was still happy that she won the fight.

Although a feeling of disrespect caused Ty's anger, reactions to the fight seemed to align more with a negative expression of anger. For in-stance, when Aimee spoke of Ty's actions, she explains how she went "crazy" and "got so angry" because people would not do what she said. Aimee's comments suggest that Ty's actions were unnecessary. In addi-tion, Leslie's disappointment in Ty's actions (as discussed earlier) helps characterize this display of anger as negative. Furthermore, because Ty caused physical harm to another person (with no remorse), viewers may also classify her use of anger as inappropriate. Ty is the only person who seems to celebrate her own use of anger.

In yet another incident, both Leslie and Ty exhibit anger when they feel disrespected by a roommate who made a racially insensitive com-ment. When one of their white roommates, Zara, explained that she did not want to go to a "black club," the two ladies interpreted her words and actions as racist and disrespectful. Where they differ is that Leslie ex-pressed her anger more with other roommates and in her confessionals, while Ty actually confronted Zara and explained why she was upset by her comments. Nonetheless, both used anger to combat against what they consider to be a racial issue. This use of anger aligns with what past research has found on women using their anger to respond to racism; however, this use of anger was not labeled as positive or negative. In fact, Leslie became upset with Ty for interacting with Zara and allowing her anger to subside. According to Leslie, for Ty not to show anger after such disrespect and racist thinking was unacceptable and disloyal. This could also tie in to what Leslie considers to be an expectation for black women and their use of anger.

*Anger from Disloyalty (and Disrespect)*

Leslie confronted Ty after her reconciliation with Zara. To Leslie, Ty was a traitor for quickly forgiving the act and for engaging in friendly conversation with Zara. Hence, the two became involved in a verbal altercation. Leslie's use of anger was critiqued as being negative, since Ty called her a "bitch" for acting out and being upset. Although the two quickly reconciled, both used anger—Leslie's was in response to her perception of Ty's disloyalty, while Ty's appeared to be a defense mechanism, as well as a response to disrespect. She was unhappy that Leslie questioned her authenticity.

Leslie also responded to a feeling of disloyalty during the scene where she protected Jodie, as noted earlier. She, and some of her roommates, felt that Jodie's failure to protect Leslie was wrong. Despite explanations of why Jodie should "have Leslie's back," Jodie still felt that she behaved appropriately and that Leslie was out of line. As the debate continued, and insults were exchanged, Leslie grabbed Jodie and warned her to 'sleep with one eye open.' She also mocked Jodie about her image ("Playboy bunny wannabe") in order to disrespect her in the same way she felt disrespected. In this instance, some roommates understood Leslie's anger, but it was still labeled as unnecessary by Jodie. She also threatened bodily harm.

## DECONSTRUCTING THE BLACK BAD GIRL'S ANGER

Leslie, Ty, and Andrea's representations on the *Bad Girls Club* reality show reveal underlying messages about the reasons black women display anger. These representations and messages have potential implications for viewers, as well as for Black women who contemplate the way in which they may express their own anger. Below I briefly discuss some of the underlying messages found within the show's presentations.

*Misunderstanding my Anger*

The women's use of anger, as compared to others,' hints to the subjectivity associated with emotion. What one may consider unexplainable anger may be considered purposeful to others. For example, when Leslie decided to use her anger to protect her roommate, Jodie, she considered it to be a worthy cause. Although she just met her roommates, Leslie was willing to use her emotion to guard Jodie from a disrespectful man. Her anger intensified when Jodie did not seem to understand her use of anger. While other roommates understood Leslie's point of view, the individuals who did not understand her actions were quick to label her use of anger as inappropriate. Viewers of the show will also attach their own meaning to the women's expression of anger. Yet, the responses of others as well as other media representations impact those constructions of meaning. Even when Leslie uses anger to protect her roommate, this purposeful use may be overshadowed by the fact that she uses aggression and threatens violence, while also being labeled a "bitch"—all of which are consistent with negative expressions of anger.

Although Leslie's display of anger is aggressive at times, her reasons for using the emotion do have a purpose. Negative responses to the women's anger, even when it was used to defend others, may reinforce the fear associated with black women's expressions of anger. For example, Leslie's mother was featured encouraging her daughter not to use anger anymore, even if it was to defend others—since her first attempt to protect her roommate ended so terribly. Hence, these women may be unwilling to express their emotions out of fear that others will misunderstand it and label them in an unflattering light. Such fear of expressing oneself may have deeper implications, given that holding in one's emotions can lead to deeper aggression later down the line. This fear could also add to the pressure placed on the SBW. While she is expected to use anger in service to others, she must do so in a way that is accepted by others and not misconstrued. Adding additional stress to this role could lead to less willingness to naturally express anger.

*Learning the Deeper Meaning; Communicating about Anger*

Throughout the season, we see Leslie and Ty discussing their anger. In fact, Leslie made reference to these interactions during one of her confessionals. During some discussions, Leslie often encouraged Ty not to display anger that is negative. Ty was also shown discussing her anger with others. During these confessionals or in her conversations with different cast mates, Ty explained that she was not a mean person unless people "bring it out of her." She also made connections between her anger and her feelings of loneliness, which date back to her childhood and her experience in foster care. Of course these connections were not acknowledged when the anger was actually exhibited.

Ty's explanation helped to illustrate how she was not just an angry and aggressive person without reason, like a Sapphire, bitch, or ABW. Instead, she explained that her anger was tied to psychological issues. This also helps communicate the importance of understanding a woman's use of anger. For example, the most common trigger for anger, within the series, was a feeling of disrespect. Unpacking this issue could further help to explain whether feelings of disrespect are linked to larger issues for the women. Such an explanation could provide a better understanding of their use of anger overall.

Failure to communicate about anger only leads to misunderstandings of the emotion, which can lead to the default conclusion that the anger these women display is unexplainable or inappropriate. For example, when Andrea is upset with Zara because of her drunken behavior, the other roommates seem to understand her frustrations. Zara, on the other hand, considered her display of anger to be without purpose and unnecessary, because she did not understand the true meaning associated with Andrea's feelings. This helped to illustrate the importance of learning to communicate and understand the reasons behind a display of anger. Lorde (1981) explained that anger should not be feared, but instead it should be discussed. However, black women must feel as if they are able to explain their anger and be understood.[58] We see an example of how anger can intensify if a woman feels she is misunderstood. After Leslie's attempts to defend Jodie, her anger turned to violent threats when she felt as if Jodie did not understand her use of anger.

### Does Positive Anger Exist?

Although the majority of the instances of anger were purposeful and explainable, the women's anger was not portrayed positively. For example, their anger was never linked to qualities such as strength or empowerment, but it was often explicitly labeled in a negative way (e.g. Leslie being referred to as a bitch or being called crazy). Moreover, negative consequences and backlash were attached to anger when it was used, even when the emotion was used to help others. For example, Ty was kicked off of the show for using anger and becoming violent with others. However, Leslie also received backlash when she used anger to respond to racist statements and to protect her roommates. In the end, anger was a detriment to both Ty and Leslie as it led to their departures from the show. Although Leslie left willingly, it was her anger with her roommates that motivated her to leave. One might wonder if Leslie would have decided to stay and work on herself if she was able to discuss that anger openly at an earlier point. In addition, the fact that she left because of others lack of motivation could also tie in to the pressure that may be felt by black women who are expected to be strong. Not only was Leslie concerned with her own well-being, she also carried the burden of worrying about her roommates' success.

In instances where the women's use of anger was neither critiqued nor celebrated, active audience members had to decide how the women were portrayed. While viewers certainly are free to draw positive conclusions, we must also acknowledge the troubling nature of such presentations. At first glance, the women's use of anger does come across as being aggressive, frightening, or unnecessary. Moreover, when discussing the differences between positive and negative portrayals of anger, researchers acknowledge that the negative representation is more common in media. In fact, some viewers may not even be aware that more positive expressions of anger exist. Thus, when given additional examples of anger without assistance on how to unpack such images, viewers might automatically label the women negatively. Without actively discussing and acknowledging the black women's use of anger as a source of strength, to help others, or to protect themselves, the negative portrayal of anger cannot be fully discredited.

## IMPLICATIONS AND CONCLUSION

Anger is an emotion regularly expressed by the black female participants on *Bad Girls Club*; however, Leslie, Ty, and Andrea were not portrayed as nasty, aggressive, nagging, or rude at all times. This is not to say that their rage was considered appropriate when exhibited, but the women were not shown acting in this manner on a regular basis. For two of the three women, they did not express anger in the majority of the episodes they appeared in. When these qualities were exhibited, they were combined with anger that was used to protect others or in response to disrespect and other uncomfortable situations. In this sense, the "Black Bad Girls" were not portrayed completely as Sapphires, bitches, or the ABWs.

Although the majority of their anger was for a purpose, both Leslie and Ty were critiqued negatively for their anger and they were sometimes labeled as "bitches." Even when their rage was used in more positive ways, such as to protect others or to motivate others to change, their roommates rarely celebrated the women's expressions of anger—as is often the case with the Black Bitch and SBW. Instead, there were instances when the show implied that their use of anger was understood; however, viewers were left to draw their own conclusions.

It appears as though Leslie and Ty were presented as being a combination of the Sapphire/bitch/ABW and the Black Bitch/SBW; while Andrea's anger, on the other hand, was not a primary focus. Overall, the characteristics of the Sapphire/bitch were more explicit, while the characteristics of the Black Bitch/SBW were more implicit. As such, viewers who are not familiar with positive and more strategic uses of anger by black women may only perceive demonstrations of anger as negative. This carries several implications for society and their expectations and treatment of black women. Not only would this image continue to communicate to black women that their expressions of anger are unhealthy and automatically negative, but it also continues to communicate to society that black women are naturally angry.

This is not to say that the messages about the women's anger do not communicate any moral value. Ty's discussion of her anger helped to illustrate how the emotion could be tied to psychological issues. In addition, both Ty and Leslie are often shown encouraging other housemates and giving them advice on how to handle various situations. Thus, the bad girls are also portrayed as having some positive traits. The mix of anger with other positive characteristics also helps to illustrate that black women are not one-dimensional, angry beings. However, in the majority of instances, the anger exhibited is critiqued negatively and/or not openly acknowledged as being purposeful and even strategic. More discussion and education on the use of anger by black women in more positive ways is required in order to begin to combat images such as the ABW.

The representations within *Bad Girls Club* also shine a light on the issue of healthy expressions of anger. On the other hand, two of the three cast members were involved in physical altercations; and despite their reasons (protection for Leslie and to demand respect by Ty), the act of causing bodily harm to another is certainly inappropriate. What is especially interesting is that even in an instance where Ty tried to discuss her anger (over the racist comments), she was criticized by her fellow black female cast member. Yet Ty was also reprimanded for using physical violence to unleash her anger. This has the potential to speak volumes to viewers, who are left to decide the appropriate way to respond to anger. Especially considering that Leslie and Andrea were also criticized for their use of anger, some black women may be left asking: so how *can* I express my anger without being criticized? The Sapphire, bitch, and ABW stereotypes all help to paint black women as being angry for no reason. Some of the instances within *Bad Girls Club* help to show that there *are reasons* for displays of anger. Thus, instead of assuming that all black women are constantly angry, consideration should be given to why these women are angry and how improvements can be made in their expressions of that anger. Most importantly, the show illustrates how black women are not angry at all times—and that all black women are not the same, including when they express anger. Although Leslie, Ty, and Andrea share similarities, their behaviors on the show did, in fact, differ.

Furthermore, the portrayals on the show add to the discussion on the pressures associated with the SBW image. Again, even when the women would use anger to help others, it was not always well received. This may increase black women's hesitancy to express anger, not only in service to others, but for the sake of themselves. In addition, this may cause some black women to suppress this emotion, which can have detrimental psychological effects, as discussed earlier.

The cast members from *Bad Girls Club* do demonstrate that black women are not perpetually angry. Like all human beings, they sometimes use anger as an emotion in response to an uncomfortable feeling or situation. Leslie, Ty, and Andrea, each used their anger in response to situations. However, despite their use of explainable anger, the women were more often critiqued negatively for their emotional outbursts. In addition, there were instances where the expression (and not the purpose) of the anger was unhealthy. Thus, the positive and strategic use of anger was not the dominant theme of the show. Instead, the message was still communicated that black women were often angry—and wrongfully so. Hence, the ABW and bitch both live on to see another series.

# NOTES

1. For examples of such criticisms, see: EUR, "Reality Shows Designed to Maintain Angry, Black Woman Stereotype," *EUR This N That,* May 5, 2011, accessed January 12, 2012, http://www.eurthisnthat.com/2011/05/05/reality-shows-designed-to-maintain-angry-Black-woman-stereotype/; Jarrah Hodge, "Finding the Balance: Portrayals of Black Women," *Gender Focus,* May 25, 2011, accessed January 7, 2012, http://www.gender-focus.com/2011/05/25/finding-the-balance-portrayals-of-Black-women-on-tv/; Allison Samuels, "Reality TV Trashes Black Women," *Newsweek,* May 1, 2011, accessed January 7, 2012, http://www.newsweek.com/reality-tv-trashes-black-women-67641; Terry Shropshire, "Is This the Black Reality," *Rolling Out,* July 12, 2012, accessed March 3, 2014, http://rollingout.com/covers/is-this-the-black-reality/#_.

2. Sheri Parks, *Fierce Angels: The Strong Black Woman in American Life and Culture* (New York: One World, 2010).

3. Patricia Hill Collins, *Black Sexual Politics: African Americans, Gender, and the New Racism* (New York: Routledge, 2005), 123–124.

4. Mark Andrejevic and Dean Colby, "Racism and Reality TV: The Case of MTV's Road Rules," in *How Real is Reality TV?: Essays on Representation and Truth,* ed. David S. Escoffery (Jefferson: McFarland & Company, 2006); Shannon B. Campbell et al., "I Love New York: Does New York Love Me?," *Journal of International Women's Studies* 10, no. 2 (2008); Adria Goldman and Damion Waymer, *African American Women Depictions in Television Docusoaps* (New York: Peter Lang Publishing, 2015); Jennifer L. Pozner, *Reality Bites Back: The Troubling Truth About Guilty Pleasure TV* (Berkley: Seal Press, 2010); Tia Tyree, "African American Stereotypes in Reality Television," *The Howard Journal of Communications* 22, no. 2 (2011).

5. Richard West and Lynn H. Turner, *IPC2: Interpersonal Communication* (Boston: Cengage Learning, 2016), 136.

6. Ibid. Hans H. Gerth, *Character and Social Structures: The Psychology of Social Institutions* (New York: Harcourt, 1953); Hans H. Gerth and C. Wright Mills, *Character and Social Structures: The Psychology of Social Institutions* (New York: Harcourt, 1964).

7. Gerth, *Character and Social Structures,* 67.

8. Shirley A. Thomas and A. Antonio Gonzalez-Prendes, "Powerlessness, Anger, and Stress in African American Women: Implications for Physical and Emotional Health," *Health Care for Women International,* 30, (2009).

9. Deborah L. Cox, Patricia Van Velsor, and Joseph F. Hulgus, "Who Me, Angry? Patterns of Anger Diversion in Women," *Health Care for Women International,* 25 (2004).

10. Sandra Thomas, "Women's Anger, Aggression, and Violence," *Health Center for Women International,* 26 (2005).

11. J. Celeste Walley-Jean, "Debunking the Myth of the 'Angry Black Woman': An Exploration of Anger in Young African American Women," *Gender & Families* 3, no. 2 (2009): 74.

12. Becky Fields et al., "Anger in African American Women in the South," *Issues in Mental Health Nursing,* 19 (1998); Thomas, "Women's Anger"; Thomas and Gonzalez-Prendes, "Powerlessness."

13. Audre Lorde, "The Uses of Anger," *Women's Studies Quarterly* 9, no. 3 (1981): 7.

14. Ibid. 8.

15. Ibid.

16. Fields, et. al., "Anger in African American Women"; Dalia Rodriquez and Afua Boahene, "The Politics of Rage: Empowering Women of Color in the Academy," *Cultural Studies, Critical Methodologies,* 12, no. 5; Thomas, "Women's Anger."

17. Collins, *Black Sexual Politics,* 124.

18. Ibid.

19. Parks, *Fierce Angels,* 110.

20. Melissa V. Harris-Perry, *Sister Citizen: Shame, Stereotypes, and Black Women in America* (New Haven: Yale University Press, 2011), 187.

21. A. Antonio Gonzalez-Prendes and Shirley A. Thomas, "Powerlessness and Anger in African American Women: The Intersection of Race and Gender," *International Journal of Humanities and Social Science* 1, no. 7 (2011): 4–6; Harris-Perry, *Sister Citizen*; Joan Morgan, *When Chickenheads Come Home to Roost: A Hip Hop Feminist Breaks it Down* (New York: Touchstone, 1999).

22. Harris-Perry, *Sister Citizen*, 187.

23. Harris-Perry, *Sister Citizen*, 187; Gonzalez-Prendes and Thomas, "Powerlessness and Anger in African American Women," 4–6.

24. Thomas, "Women's Anger," 511.

25. Walley-Jean, "Debunking the Myth."

26. Parks, *Fierce Angels*, 87.

27. Shawna V. Hudson, "Re-creational Television: The Paradox of Change and Continuity within Stereotypical Iconography," *Sociological Inquiry* 68, no. 2 (1998): 247.

28. Hudson, "Re-creational Television," 247; Carolyn West, "Mammy, Sapphire, and Jezebel: Historical Images of Black Women and Their Implications for Psychotherapy," *Psychotherapy*, 32, no. 3 (1995): 461–462.

29. Phillilp Kretsedemas, "But She's Not Black! Viewer Interpretations of 'Angry Black Women' on Prime Time TV," *Journal of African American Studies* 14 (2010): 150.

30. Collins, *Black Sexual Politics*, 123.

31. Ibid.

32. Ibid.

33. Ibid. For example, review images such as the sexualized bitch, discussed by Collins.

34. David Croteau and Williams Hoynes, *Media/Society: Industries, Images, and Audiences*, 5th ed. (Los Angeles: Sage, 2014), 199–200; Robert Entman and Andrew Rojecki, *The Black Image in the White Mind* (Chicago: University of Chicago Press, 2000).

35. Examples of such findings can be found in the following research studies: Andrejevic and Colby, "Racism and Reality TV"; Robin M. Boylorn, "As Seen on TV: An Autoethnographic Reflection on Race and Reality Television," *Critical Studies of Media Communication* 24, no. 4 (2008); Campbell et al., "I Love New York"; Pozner, *Reality Bites Back*.

36. For examples of the ideological power of reality television, see the following: Sarah Banet-Weiser and Laura Portwood-Stacer, "I Just Want to Be Me Again! Beauty Pageants, Reality Television, and Post-Feminism," *Feminist Theory* 7 (2006); Erika Engstrom, "Creation of a New 'Empowered' Female Identity in WEtv's Bridezillas,"*Media Report to Women* 37, no. 1 (2009); Jon Kraszewski, "Country Hicks and Urban Cliques: Mediating Race, Reality, and Liberalism on MTV's 'The Real World,'" in *Reality TV: Remaking Television Culture, 2nd edition*, eds. Susan Murray and Laurie Ouellete (New York: New York University Press, 2009); Rebecca Stephens, "Socially soothing stories? Gender, race and class in TLC's A Wedding Story and A Baby Story," in *Understanding Reality Television*, eds. Susan Holmes and Deborah Jermyn (New York: Routledge, 2004).

37. Croteau and Hoynes, *Media/Society*, 152–185.

38. Gerth, *Character and Social Structures*, 68–69.

39. Saira Anees, "The 15 Meanest Reality TV Villains," *ABC News*, April 24, 2008, accessed December 1, 2010, http://abcnews.go.com/Entertainment/15-meanest-reality-tv-villains/story?id=4694189.

40. Amanda Anderson-Niles, "Omarosa Says Her Villain Image is Just for Reality TV," *Urban Belle Magazine*, April 3, 2013, accessed August 1, 2013, http://urbanbelle-mag.com/2013/04/omarosa-says-her-villain-image-is-just-for-reality-tv.html.

41. Boylorn, "As Seen on TV."

42. Brande Victorian, "Omarosa to Bethenny: You Get Rewarded for Being Mediocre Cause You're White," *Madame Noire*, October 30, 2013, accessed December 1, 2013, http://madamenoire.com/317604/omarosa-to-bethenny/.

43. For examples of the Angry Black Woman (or uses of anger) in other reality shows, see: Andrejevic and Colby, "Racism and Reality TV"; Campbell et al., "I Love

New York"; Goldman and Waymer, *Black Women in Reality Television Docusoaps*; Pozner, *Reality Bites Back*; Tyree, "African American Stereotypes."

44. Boylorn, "As Seen on TV," 419.

45. Andrejevic and Colby, "Racism and Reality TV."

46. Pozner, *Reality Bites Back*.

47. Campbell et al., "I Love New York."

48. Tyree, "African American Stereotypes."

49. Goldman and Waymer, *Black Women in Reality Television Docusoaps*; Tyree, "African American Stereotypes."

50. Rachel E. Dubrofsky, *The Surveillance of Women on Reality Television: Watching The Bachelor and The Bachelorette* (Lanham: Lexington Books, 2011), 29–32.

51. David Hinckley, "'Bad Girls Club' are Back in Real-Life Fright Club," *NY Daily News*, December 2, 2008, accessed December 10, 2012, http://www.nydailynews.com/entertainment/tv-movies/bad-girls-club-back-real-life-fright-club-article-1.355083.

52. Peggy Drexler, "Mean Girls and Media: The Teenage Fists of Feminism," *Huffington Post*, February 1, 2011, accessed December 10, 2012, http://www.huffingtonpost.com/peggy-drexler/mean-girls-and-media-the_b_816941.html.

53. As mentioned in note 1, for examples of such criticisms, see: EUR, "Reality Shows Designed to Maintain Angry, Black Woman Stereotype," *EUR This N That*, May 5, 2011, accessed January 12, 2012, http://www.eurthisnthat.com/2011/05/05/reality-shows-designed-to-maintain-angry-Black-woman-stereotype/; Jarrah Hodge, "Finding the Balance: Portrayals of Black Women," *Gender Focus*, May 25, 2011, accessed January 7, 2012, http://www.gender-focus.com/2011/05/25/finding-the-balance-portrayals-of-Black-women-on-tv/; Allison Samuels, "Reality TV Trashes Black Women," *Newsweek*, May 1, 2011, accessed January 7, 2012, http://www.newsweek.com/reality-tv-trashes-black-women-67641; Terry Shropshire, "Is This the Black Reality," *Rolling Out*, July 12, 2012, accessed March 3, 2014, http://rollingout.com/covers/is-this-the-black-reality/#_.

54. Goldman and Waymer, *Black Women in Reality Television Docusoaps*.

55. West and Turner, *IPC2*, 135.

56. Gerth, *Character and Social Structures*, 64.

57. West and Turner, *IPC2*, 135.

58. Lorde, "The Uses of Anger."

# SEVEN

# The "Tyra Tyrade"

*Reinforcing the Sapphire Through Online Parody* [1]

## Tracey Owens Patton & Julie Snyder-Yuly

Tyra Banks, supermodel and producer, is the creator of the reality show *America's Next Top Model* (*ANTM*), which is now in its twenty-second cycle, and features contestants who present themselves to a panel of judges for modeling critique. *ANTM* has been nominated for twenty-nine awards, including the GLAAD Media Award and Image Award, and the show has received five awards in 2009 from the Teen Choice Award and the Director's Guild of America Award. [2] Further, *ANTM* is currently shown in over 120 countries. The winner of each cycle receives a featured spread in a magazine, a modeling contract with a prominent agency, and a $100,000 modeling contract from a cosmetics company. In 2005, however, there was an infamous episode—dubbed the "Tyra Tyrade," [3]—where Tyra Banks yelled at a contestant whom she had just eliminated from the show. This episode was parodied more than any other *ANTM* episode, with the penultimate parody shown on a 2007 episode of *Family Guy* (a primetime cartoon television show with millions of viewers each week), [4] where Tyra turns into a lizard and eats the model. [5] While this episode is now nine years old, parodies from as recently as 2014 continue to live on and, as we argue, perpetuate negative stereotypes of black womanhood, particularly as related to the Sapphire mediated stereotype—loud, bossy, angry black woman. From the various interpretations of the "Tyra Tyrade," it is clear that those who created the parodies covertly and overtly ventured into maintaining white supremacist stereotypes of black womanhood—where one is supposed to be beautiful, a jezebel, or a mammy,

127

but not a Sapphire.[6] Continuing the marginalizing mediated tradition, in almost every parody, the Tyra character becomes the object of ridicule for being "excessively black" and outside the parameters of her hegemonically prescribed role, because she demonstrated negative emotions resulting in an assertion of her power as the expert.

The purpose of this chapter is to examine the "Tyra Tyrade" incident and its various parodies to illustrate how a Bakhtinian Carnivalesque moment, designed to challenge hegemony, was recreated—which subsequently reinforce the Sapphire stereotype through the continuance of racism, sexism, and power. While numerous critical feminist and womanist, and media scholars have written about mediated representations of African Americans, few scholars have analyzed the too often naturalized stereotype of the quintessential Sapphire. Additionally, given that *YouTube* parodies have become a popular expression of online creativity, there is limited research on these mediated effects. Therefore, we ask: Do the parodies of Tyra Banks as they relate to her "Tyra Tyrade" on *America's Next Top Model* reify the stereotype of Sapphire, and if so, how does this happen?

## STEREOTYPES OF AFRICAN AMERICAN WOMEN AND REALITY TELEVISION

While media scholars, like Tia Tyree correctly argue that "creators of reality television should work to ensure a more balanced portrayal of African Americans by not manufacturing situations that solicit or accentuate stereotypical behaviors and do not select African Americans simply because they embody stereotypical characteristics,"[7] the problem is this will likely never happen because stereotypes sell. Stereotypes can be defined as generalizations about a group of people that are used to explain or predict behavior. Over time, the repetitive representation not only becomes the "truth," but also undergirds and perpetuates a hegemonic hierarchy that can actively contribute to marginalization and an imbalance of power (see Stuart Hall 1997).[8] Media of any kind, but particularly reality television, relies on the exploitation of stereotypes. Stereotypes are profitable, money-making enterprises for wealthy media conglomerates and are unlikely to disappear anytime soon. While scripted television and NFL programming continue to top the most viewed broadcast shows, reality shows consistently rank among the most-watched shows of the season.[9] Moreover, daily ratings of both broadcast and cable television illustrate that reality television shows are frequently the most viewed shows of the day.[10] Therefore, given that there are no paid actors who command a large salary, and the shows generate a ratings pull and profits for media companies, reality television will continue to be a media force, particularly since the shows are supposedly about "regular peo-ple."

Smith and Wood find (2003) that reality television "involves placing 'ordinary' people before the camera and deriving some entertainment value from the perception of their activities being unscripted."[11] Godard believes that "the edited footage of unscripted interactions, broadcast as a television series about participants' naturally occurring social life," is the attractive or sellable aspect about reality television.[12] Dowd, on the other hand, argues that not only does the aspect of "real television" prove to be exciting in terms of content that makes these shows appealing to millions of viewers, but also "the key characteristic of this genre is that it asks its audience to view the individuals on the program as real, i.e., not ac-tors."[13] However, it is the absence of reality and the reliance upon anti-quated stereotypes—in addition to the fact that there is little focus on the post-editing productions that take place behind the scenes—that make the reality television the antithesis of "reality." Many scholars address the impact of reality television in terms of "reality," along with societal issues and stereotypes like racism, sexism, socioeconomic status, and surveil-lance.[14]

Despite the fact that reality shows generally, and shows like *ANTM* specifically, have more ethnic and racial diversity, more LGBTQ repre-sentation, and more women featured on their shows, critical cultural scholar, Mark Orbe notes "that the inclusion of reality-based program-ming has strengthened such stereotypical portrayals given that such im-ages are perceived to be 'real' than others."[15] Media becomes the major vehicle in which stereotypes are conveyed, simply because it is accessible by the masses through the televisual realm—as well as through online content, where one can watch television shows via computer and mobile devices. Through these technologies, visual media have been horrifyingly effective in the perpetuation of stereotypes that now reach a worldwide audience.

Far from being two dimensional representations, the tropes that real-ity television use and the characters they employ appear to be "regular Jane's and Joe's." Mark Orbe—in echoing Escoffery's 2006 claim—claims that "by understanding how producers and consumers of reality TV negotiate issues of representation and truth we can generate insight into a multiple of personal, cultural, economic, and political issues that con-tinue to have great saliency to life in the US."[16] For example, Walter Ong talks about a "second orality" where electronic media reintroduce certain characteristics of oral culture/storytelling.[17] However, because the story told by reality television is grounded in the replication of harmful stereo-types—in this case racist stereotypes—what results is a secondary orality that eats the other.

Cultural critic and scholar bell hooks introduced the concept of "eat-ing the other," and no clearer is this concept demonstrated than in reality television and its parodies (the second orality).[18] "Eating the other" is a critique of consumer culture as it related to mediated consumption of people of color, in this case, African American women. As hooks notes:

> The commodification of Otherness has been so successful because it is offered a new delight, more intense, more satisfying than normal ways of doing and feeling. Within commodity culture, ethnicity becomes spice, seasoning that can liven up the dull dish that is mainstream white culture.[19]

While the dish may be dull in white mainstream culture, mediated misrepresentation of people of color has become standard fare. Media scholars have long established that there are few people of color on television, but when they are on television, they are often portrayed in stereotypical roles. "The bodies of individuals can be seen as constituting an alternative playground where members of dominating races, genders, sexual practices affirm their power-over in intimate relations with the Other."[20] As articulated by media scholars such as Stuart Hall and Herman Gray, media is one way—and the most popular way—in which we come to understand the dynamic state of the world, and race is one of those mediated concepts.[21] Televisual media (and this includes reality TV) creates a racial Xanadu—a paradise where there are no hegemonic hierarchies and all things are possible if one works hard enough to overcome personal failings not related to race, gender, or institutional and structural forms of discrimination and racism. In the mediated duality of the Horatio Alger Myth coupled with the Wizard of Oz—if you believe it, it will come true—the visual fantasy of equality bursts from the screen and onto the internet with parodies and blogs replete with stereotypes in tow.

## SAPPHIRE EVOLVES INTO ANGRY BLACK WOMAN

Black people rarely see themselves positively represented in media, as has been well documented by scholars like Donald Bogle. Far from the great equalizer, blacks have had to fight to have a seat at the mediated table. According to Feagin and Vera:

> These stereotypes exist because stereotyped portrayals of African Americans and the unrealistic sanguine views of contemporary racial relations often presented in the mainstream media help perpetuate the racist myths held by ordinary white Americans. Leonard Berkowitz [year unknown], among many others, has argued that the mass media play an important role in reinforcing antisocial images and behavior. The U.S. media are overwhelmingly white-oriented and white-controlled. White control of powerful institutions—from mass media to corporate workplaces to universities to police departments—signals white dominance to all members of the society.[22]

With reference to African American women, the mediated representation is paltry and replete with stereotypes, as noted in Chapter One. Media capitalizes on the long-held stereotypes about black women which run the gamut from mammy (obese, sexless, overbearing), to jezebel (seductress, scheming, evil), to tragic mulatto (bi-racial, self-hatred, desire to pass for white). What these stereotypes allow the viewer to do is to further categorize, disempower, and marginalize a constituency that is barely represented in visual realms. Black women become commodified sideshows in represented categories that do not even mirror their own lived experiences. According to Hudson, "Television . . . provides a space which continually updates and re-creates Mammy and Jezebel stereotypes, and in turn, presents them as icons of what black womanhood is today."[23] One icon that has so long been naturalized that it is nearly forgotten is the Sapphire. According to Black feminist scholars Morgan and Bennett:

> The stereotype of the angry, mean Black woman goes unnamed not because it is insignificant, but because it is considered an essential characteristic of Black femininity regardless of the other stereotypical roles a Black woman may be accused of occupying. These stereotypes are more than representations; they are representations that shape realities.[24]

Often parodied in television, online spoofs, and rap music/videos—and as noted in previous chapters—a Sapphire is a caricature of a black woman who is "rude, loud, malicious, stubborn, and overbearing" and angry.[25] The Sapphire must have a character to play against, and that is usually the coon (lazy, scheming, loud, money hungry) or the nagged spouse or sibling. Unlike the predecessor stereotypes, the Sapphire emerged more than a hundred years after slavery ended, during the technological age.[26] As further noted in previous chapters, the term Sapphire and her character—coined during the popular radio show, *Amos'n' Andy* (1928–1960)—evolved into what today we might identify as the "Angry Black Woman (ABW)." On *ANTM*, the Sapphire or ABW is created by playing against almost any other competitor on the show. As Mary Thompson finds in her research on *ANTM*, there is a more contemporary version of the Sapphire whose character consistently engages in dramatic confrontation with other contestants.[27] Finding its permanent spot in the media landscape, the Sapphire character was particularly popular in 1970s, as outlined in chapter one; and she was recently with popular comedians Keegan Michael-Key and Jordan Peele's popular sketch comedy show *Key and Peele* on Comedy Central (2012–present). Their season 1, episode 1 "I Said Biiitch . . ." sketch introduced 2.1 million viewers to the Sapphire stereotype and parodied the fear black women bring to their emasculated, meek husbands.[28] While some women in comedy and female rap artists have contested the term bitch and tried to reclaim it as a term of resistance (e.g., Missy Elliot, Lauryn Hill, Queen Latifah, Salt N' Pepa, Wanda Sykes), feminist scholar Patricia Hill Collins notes that black male comedians have been using the Sapphire as angry-black-woman bit in their sketches as standard fare for many years:

> Contemporary Black popular culture's willingness to embrace patriar-chy has left the "Black bitch" as a contested representation. Ironically, Black male comedians have often led the pack in reproducing derisive images of Black women as being ugly, loud "bitches." Resembling Mar-lon Riggs' protestations about the "sissy" and "punk" jokes targeted toward Black gay men, "bitches" are routinely mocked within contem-porary Black popular culture. For example, ridiculing African American women as being like men (also, a common representation of Black lesbians) has long been a prominent subtext in the routines of Redd Foxx, Eddie Murphy, Martin Lawrence, and other African American comedians.[29]

Outside of the realm of comedy, First Lady Michelle Obama was visu-ally stereotyped when the 2008 *New Yorker Magazine* cover created a char-acterization of her in military fatigues, a large 1970s afro, and a fist bump. Further, conservative television hosts on *Fox News* in 2008 tried to imply that the First Lady was a Sapphire (presumably since she does not fit any of the other more common stereotypes—e.g., jezebel, mammy, tragic mu-latto) when she was referred to as a "butt-shaking Hoochie [sic] Mama"…and "Senator Obama's 'Baby Mama.'"[30] Based on its complete enmeshment with U.S. culture and media, any black woman with an opinion (particularly one that challenges the hegemonic hierarchy) is at risk of being labelled a Sapphire. What makes the Sapphire one of the most dangerous stereotypes and caricatures for black women is that it makes black women responsible for power they do not truly have, when in reality it is being used by other social groups.[31] It is this stereotype that has become naturalized into the media landscape and is readily used, absorbed, and parodied in media.

## BAKHTIN'S CARNIVALESQUE AND PARODY

Parody is a particularly powerful tool to challenge hegemonic hierarchies and one that puts the power back in the hands of the viewer, and away from the hegemonic structure (in this case the media industry). For this study, we employ Russian philosopher Mikhail Bakhtin's concepts of the carnival and carnivalesque. The concept of the carnival gained popularity from Bakhtin, with his acclaimed work, *Rabelais and His World.*[32] Through the concept of the carnival, Bakhtin reconstructs a type of folk humor that challenges the hegemonic hierarchy through humor, laughter, masks, masquerades, and performance. According to Arthur Lindley, "Carnival, for Bakhtin, is an embodiment of the liberated communality of the people in perennially renewed rebellion against the social and spiritual restrictions of the official order."[33] This celebration is for a marked period of time "where the commonly held values of a given cultural milieu are reversed, where new 'heads of state' are elected to 'govern' the ungovernable, and where the generally accepted rules of polite behavior are overruled in favor of the temporarily reigning spirit of Carnival."[34] During this temporary centering of the carnival, "players" such as the "fool, madman, or clown" may emerge to serve as "regent" and people become participants and spectators, a spectacle (of theater, music, and dance), in which they may (un)ceremoniously partake"[35] and where they ridicule traditional society for all of its hegemonic hierarchies, rules, and oppressive structures.

Carnival works through parody. As Simon Dentith (2000) explains:

> For the notion of the 'carnivalesque' can be extended to include all those cultural situations where the authority of a single language of authority is called into question, notably by the simultaneous co-presence of other languages which can challenge it. One principal method by which such challenges are mounted is parody. In this extended Bakhtinian view, then, parody is both a symptom and a weapon in the battle between popular cultural energies and the forces of authority which seek to control them.[36]

For Bakhtin, parody was the method used to unmask the official power. Bakhtin recognized that parody could be a double edged sword: "Thus it is that in parody two languages are crossed with each other, as well as two styles, two linguistic points of view, and in the final analysis two speaking subjects."[37] Through parody, "high" or official discourse is parodied by low discourse or that of the people resulting in a double-voiced discourse. Bakhtin states double-voiced discourse "serves two speakers at the same time and expresses simultaneously two different intentions: the direct intention of the character who is speaking, and the refracted intention of the author."[38] Today, parody is viewed as a process of recontextualizing text in such a way to create a new text,[39] a cultural practice providing a polemic allusive imitation of another cultural practice,[40] and as a form of imitation characterized by ironic inversion, not always at the expense of the original text.[41] As Bakhtin's idea of double-voiced discourse seems to be at the root of each of these (and other) definitions, the authors chose not to follow one particular definition of parody, but rather utilize the multivocality present to illustrate the ways in which parody can function.

Because of the ability to post, respond, spoof, and/or be a silent voyeur, dichotomous ideas can be contested but so too can traditional stereotypes, marginalizations, and racisms be reified. Just because temporary power is in the hands of the viewer does not necessarily mean there is equality in the performativity of response to or even a parody of popular media. We argue that the "Tyra Tyrade" is an ironic form of parody that relies heavily on racist Sapphire stereotypes to challenge the carnivalesque performance. *ANTM* parodies are not unique in this, because generally it can be argued that reality television and the production of parodies are prime examples of the carnival in action. Participants, both on reality television and in the subsequent parodies produced, perform in ways that would not be tolerable on a daily basis. However, parody today enacts different types of double edged swords: through these mediated productions, participants show a current way to temporarily alter the hegemonic hierarchy (who is speaking), but at the same time the parodies reify the very hierarchy they seek to challenge through the reinscription of marginalization, racism, and, in this case, the use of the Sapphire stereotype. As critical cultural scholars Tracey Owens Patton and Julie Snyder-Yuly illustrate in their work on the imaged carnivalesque, through reality television the carnival can occur "in the sanctioned space of television where it can be witnessed but not experienced"[42] resulting in the moment being over when the episode is turned off. Through online parodies, this carnivelesque moment can be continually relived, yet at the expense of whom? This study adds to research on race, reality television, parody and womanhood because we examine how concepts of the carnival are used to further marginalize black womanhood through the continued use of the Sapphire stereotype.

## METHOD

Founded in 2005, *YouTube* was created to enable users to house, share, and watch originally created videos.[43] According to the website, there are more than 1 billion unique users who visit YouTube each month, more than 6 billion hours of video are viewed monthly, and more than 100 hours of video are uploaded hourly. Additionally, they note that 80 percent of their traffic comes from outside the United States and they are localized in sixty-one countries with sixty-one languages. Nielsen ratings found that *YouTube* subscribers reach more United States adults ages 18–34 than any cable network,[44] and Gutelle finds that 41 percent of YouTube users are under 34.[45]

In order to identify videos directly relating to the specific scene from the 2005 episode of *ANTM*, a targeted sampling approach was used. A combination of the words/phrases "Tyra" and "Tyra Banks" with "tyrade," "tirade," "spoof," "parody," "yells at girl," "yells at contestant," "goes crazy," and "crazy," as well "America's Next Top Model," "spoof" and "parody" were searched on YouTube, Google video, and Bing video.[46] From the results of these searches, additional videos were examined based on recommended videos or links to similar videos. Because of the sheer volume of results, videos not directly related to the "Tyra Tyrade" episode, videos with fewer than 1,500 views, and videos created or uploaded prior to the original airdate of the episode were eliminated from the sample. The remaining videos were reviewed for content indicative of the original scene, which included one or more of the following: a multiple elimination of contestants, the Tyra character calling back the eliminated contestants to talk to them, the Tyra character yelling at the contestant who was eliminated, direct or paraphrased quotes from the scene (see the "Tyra Tyrade" for the text of the original scene), actual footage from the original scene, the Tyra character comparing the contestant's situation or problem with her past situation or problem, and/or a general tirade berating all the contestants.

Three styles of parodies emerged from the remaining twenty videos. The first was a more traditional form of parody that recreates the original text. Both live performance and cartoon creations were used to re-create a version of the original scene. According to Dentith (2000) "one of the typical ways in which parody works is to seize on particular aspects of a manner or a style and exaggerate it to ludicrous effect."[47] Some examples of this style of parody include: the Tyra character's behavior resulting in her turning into a lizard or werewolf as a result of her tirade, focusing on herself rather than the character, and throwing a temper tantrum. There were eight of these types of parodies with views ranging from 8,511 to more than 1 million.[48]

The second style of parody we identified included fusions/video splicing. In fusions, clips from the original scene were spliced with video clips or images of other well-known individuals such as Britney Spears, Miley Cyrus, Lindsay Lohan, President Obama, Justin Bieber, and Jessie Slaughter. These types of parodies were frequently titled "Tyra yells at . . ." Instead of Tyra yelling at contestant Tiffany, other individuals were shown, giving the impression that Tyra was yelling at them. There were fifteen parodies that had more than 1,500 views and many more with fewer views. Of particular interest is that the majority of this type of parody—and those with the most views—focused on her yelling at other women. For example, almost one million individuals viewed Tyra yelling at Miley Cyrus, and over 700,000 viewed her yelling at Britney Spears in two separate but similar parodies;[49,50] whereas there are only slightly more than 8,000 views of Tyra yelling at President Obama[51] and just more than 15,000 where she yells at Justin Bieber.[52]

In video alerting, the original scene was used but the audio speed was changed and/or visual editing was used to draw attention specifically to Tyra's words and actions. Similar to the traditional parody, the fusion and alerting exaggerates the situation. However, this type of parody is focused on ridiculing the subject. In terms of parody and the perpetuation of the Sapphire stereotype, Hutcheon (1985) notes that this "is one of the major modes of formal and thematic construction of texts"[53] and functions in a way that seems to invoke ideological beliefs regarding how women, especially black women in this case, are seen and heard.

The final style of parody identified is that of a lip-sync or word for word reenactment. This type of parody was specifically done by men and frequently associated with the gay or drag community. Hutcheon (1985) explains, "Parody is normative in its identification with the Other, but it is contesting its Oedipal need to distinguish itself from the prior Other."[54] Just as the Sapphire is perceived as exaggerated, sassy, verbose, and often not taken seriously, the same may be true of the gay and drag community. As such, this type of parody seemed to be paying homage more than mocking—illustrating a kinship between the carnivalesque moments within the fashion and drag communities.

## TYRA TYRADE: A DISCUSSION

The ANTM episode began with an acting challenge, requiring the contestants to perform a scene where they had to memorize a script and perform it in a Cockney accent.[55] Contestant Tiffany struggled with learning the lines and performing. Prior to the elimination, the contestants had to read a fashion news story from a teleprompter, in which Tiffany quit after a few lines, noting that she "couldn't do it." Following a reprimand from Tyra, Tiffany tried again and then stormed away stating, "This is humiliating more and more each week." It was during the final elimination when the Tyra Tyrade took place. Two women who stood before Tyra, a white woman (Rebecca) and a black woman (Tiffany).[56] In the original episode, both women were eliminated; and the eliminated contestants went over to the remaining contestants to say their goodbyes. While Rebecca had tears in her eyes, demonstrating her disappointment as she hugged the other contestants, Tiffany laughed and joked, wishing the other young women good luck. As a result, Tyra called both women back in front of her. Tyra expressed admiration toward Rebecca and complimented her show of emotion; but for Tiffany, she expressed disappointment.

> *Tyra* (speaking in an accusing tone): Tiffany, I'm extremely disappointed in you. This is a joke to you. You've been through anger management. You've been through your grandmother getting her lights turned off to buy you a swimsuit for this competition. And you go over there and you joke and you laugh? . . . This should be serious to you.

> *Tiffany* (speaking with a saddened tone): Looks can be deceiving. I'm hurt, I am, but I can't change it Tyra. . . . I'm sick of crying about stuff I cannot change. I am sick of being disappointed. I'm sick of all of it.

*Tyra* (speaking sternly): You're not. If you were sick of being disappointed, you would stand up and you would take control of your destiny. Do you know you had a possibility to win? . . . And then you come in here and you treat this like a joke? . . .

*Tiffany* (speaking slightly more assertively): I don't have a bad attitude! Maybe I am angry inside. I've been through stuff. I'm angry!

*Tyra* (cutting off Tiffany and yelling): Be quiet Tiffany, be quiet! What is wrong with you? STOP IT! I have never in my life yelled at a girl like this! When my mother yells like this it's because she loves me! I was rooting for you! We were all rooting for you! [pointing at the judges on the panel]. How dare you! Learn something from this! When you go to bed at night you take responsibility for yourself! Because nobody is going to take responsibility for you. You're rolling your eyes and you act like you've heard it all before. You don't know where the hell I come from! You have no idea what I've been through! But I'm not a victim I grow from it and I learn. Take responsibility for yourself![57]

Typically, of all the judges on the show, Tyra has been the least harsh when directly dealing with the contestants. Tyra makes an effort to come across as a confidant and someone to emulate. She attempts to construct a safe environment, have heart-to-heart talks with the women, and wants each woman to succeed in the modeling industry. While the other judges on the show may have more caustic humor, Tyra provides constructive criticism mixed with humor and/or disappointment, until this infamous episode. Prior to this berating, one may question the believability of the reprimand Tiffany received, particularly when Janice Dickinson—one of the other judges on the show—stated that the women had "plateaued." And Nigel Barker, another judge, said the women needed a "wake up call," something that will "really get the competition going again."[58]

Owens Patton and Snyder-Yuly question, "Was this a wakeup call or was this a publicity stunt? Was this an imaged-carnival moment that failed? Was it a coincidence that the contestant who was reprimanded was the poor black woman who Tyra had been empathic with from the beginning of the cycle? Here, the imaged-carnivalesque moment crossed back into white hegemonic reality; there can be no angry, negative critique of a white woman by a black woman."[59] Questions of authenticity abound and are apt when it comes to reality television, as Elizabeth Schroeder notes, reality television is "the manipulated portrayal of unscripted actions to create a politically and ideologically scripted viewer response."[60] In trying to create a humorous parody on par with the carnivalesque moment, the manipulated reviewer relies upon racist Sapphire caricatures; thus, re-centering whiteness and marginalizing black-ness.

Two significant themes emerged from the three types of parodies re-lating to the Sapphire stereotype. The first focused on the extreme exag-geration of the actual behavior presented. The second theme was the transformation from an intra-racial exchange to an inter-racial exchange; thus decontextualizing a situation that may have truly demonstrated a black mentor's frustration with her black protégé. Collectively, these par-odies showed Tyra evolving from an initial angry outburst to a crazed individual—yelling at any and every one. The following sections further explicate these themes.

THEME 1 SAPPHIRE GONE WILD!:
BLACK WOMEN CAN'T BE ANGRY

The U.S. media has been treated to caricatures about Black women that involve the mammy figure. The U.S. media likes happy mammy figures as role models, but not the Sapphire. According to Sue Jewel, the Sap-phire is noted for her sassiness and verbosity. "She is also noted for telling people off, and spouting her opinion in an animated loud manner. Because of her intense expressiveness and hands-on hip, finger-pointing style, Sapphire is viewed as comedic and is never taken seriously."[61] Tyra Banks, in her moment of anger, violated the tenuous trust she had with her viewers who allowed her and her show to temporarily invert the hegemonic hierarchy. It can be argued that viewers loved and love the show with all of its carnivalesque escapades and over-the-top photo shoots. However, in the minds of the viewers and subsequent parodies, Tyra is not allowed to be angry. Tyra's emotion reveals that she suffers from the twin oppressions so many feminist scholars refer to—the dou-ble-bind. Tyra is virtually smacked in the face by the parodies, which show that she cannot operate in both binary worlds.

Two fusion videos are excellent examples that illustrate the Sapphire character's sassiness, verbosity, opinionated attitude and telling people off. In the case of Miley Cyrus, Tyra appears to be reprimanding her for some personally and professionally scandalous photos.[62] And, in the case of the Britney Spears parodies, Tyra is depicted as yelling at Britney following her appearance on the 2007 *Video Music Awards*.[63] In each video, it appears as if the celebrity is in dialogue with Tyra, and reacting to her words. The creator of one of the Britney Spears videos goes so far as to superimpose a shot of Brittany in the actual scene where Tyra was yelling at Tiffany.[64] These clips function as parody, as they critically illus-trate what many people would like to say to these young women, but do not have the ability to do so. In these examples, the parodies reify the Sapphire putting a couple of young divas in their place.

Whereas the Britney and Miley videos were fairly well created and thought out, many of the other fusion parodies seemed to be spliced together with images and video that did not work as well—simply to create the feeling of discourse. Additionally, the Miley and one of the Britney parodies were timelier in their creation, within one to two years following the original episode. Many of the others, however, were created between 2010 and 2014. And because so many other events have happened since the original episode, the parody no longer has much relevance. As Dentith explains, the more distant you get from the original act being parodied, the more difficult it is for the reader/viewer to understand.[65] Even within the Britney and Miley videos, there was clearly a lack of understanding that this was a parody. There were multiple comments suggesting viewers thought these videos were real, didn't get it, or implied that Tyra needed to leave them alone. As both Dentith (2000)[66] and Hutcheon (1985)[67] elucidate, the reader/viewer needs to understand parody in order for its intention to be recognized. Finally, the quantity and repetitive nature of the fusion videos reinforces the stereotype of the angry black woman always having the last word, no matter the individual or situation.

It is not just the idea of a black woman always having the last word, it is about the situation and her behavior that reinforces the Sapphire stereotype. One parody created by the Los Angeles sketch comedy troupe Frog Island Flicks is an excellent example of the extreme portrayal of Tyra.[68] The parody begins with her description of the judges and crediting herself for single handedly starting the 1950s/1960s civil rights movement; yet, within less than a minute she is already referring to the contestants as "bitches." Shortly after that, she has the contestants bowing down to her and saying that she is their "collective master and we are your filthy servants," while she snaps her fingers at them. The "models" have a photo shoot on death row in San Quentin Penitentiary, at which time one woman complains that she was sodomized during the photo shoot. Later, this same woman apologizes for her poor picture and said she would have done better if she hadn't been "gang raped between shots." The poor image and the excuse of being raped sends the Tyra character into a rage yelling, "bitch, I been raped by more niggas than you have ever seen in your life!" She further noted that her agent told her she would only make it in the business if she let him and his friends "fuck me in every orifice I have." She goes on to say they "fucked me in my eye, did you think this eye was real?!" Then she pulls out her fake eye and throws it at the contestant, eventually eliminating her in a dismissive manner. This video is so extreme that its actual purpose becomes questionable, particularly as it relates to the issue of rape and race. Unfortunately, this is not the only parody that invokes rape. In another parody, the Tyra character equates one contestant being raped with Tyra having to ride the bus, and the other two contestants suddenly assert that they have been raped, as well as experiencing other misfortunes.[69] While Tyra's behavior and commentary are often over the top on the *ANTM*, she has never once joked about rape. In fact, she even dedicated an episode of her talk show to rape prevention. These parodies miss the mark in their attempt to poke fun at Tyra or make a statement about the show or fashion industry. Instead they belittle a history filled with violence against black people—and black women in particular.

Finally, several parodies go to the extreme of dehumanizing Tyra. In the *Family Guy* parody,[70] Tyra gets so angry that she turns into a giant lizard and eats the contestant; in the parody titled "YTP—Tiger Banks" her face is superimposed on a tiger;[71] and in the "America's Next Top Monster" parody, Tyra turns into a werewolf.[72] However, while the other parody videos seemingly give Tyra the last word, this parody ends with Tyra about to be crushed by a giant monster named Tiffany. Hutcheon (1985) notes that "Parody is a form of imitation, but imitation characterized by ironic inversion, not always at the expense of the parodied text."[73] Although some parodies seem less offensive and more humorous than those just mentioned, the question becomes: why was this one moment on a show hosted by an African American woman the one chosen to parody, especially since Tyra is known for her often outrageous behavior?

This *ANTM* episode of "angry" Tyra presented an image that viewers did not like. However, yelling hosts seem to be a staple of reality television—when Simon Cowell, Piers Morgan, or Chef Ramsey go off on a tirade it is an allowed, expected, and even anticipated behavior. But what is allowable for a white male clearly is not for a black female. When Tyra demonstrates quite possibly genuine emotions and asserts her power as the expert, she becomes the one mocked and ridiculed by the audience because she did not stay within the allowable boundaries of her role. Even in a carnivalesque moment, she was ultimately reinforcing the Sapphire or ABW stereotype. As Hutcheon explains ". . . parody's transgressions ultimately remain authorized—authorized by the very norm it seeks to subvert. Even in mocking, parody reinforces; in formal terms, it inscribes the mocked conventions onto itself, thereby guaranteeing their continued existence."[74]

## THEME 2 ERASURE: HOW A BLACK WOMAN TURNS WHITE

While the contestant Tyra yells at was African American, in all but two parodies and on the animated television show, *The Family Guy*, the young woman she yells at magically changed from being African American to being Caucasian. For example, one parody titled, "Cleveland's Next Top Model—Ep 3 'Acting Lesson'" is particularly interesting in that it mirrors the behaviors of Tiffany—portrayed by a black woman—from the actual episode; but ultimately Tyra eliminates the white contestant for her bad attitude and for reading a legal deposition during the photo shoot.[75] Not only is the contestant eliminated a white woman, she is portrayed as more intelligent and educated than the black woman. The Sapphire is invoked because Tyra yells at a white woman who clearly is not invested in modeling, rather than eliminating the lower performing contestant. In another parody, "America's Next Top Model: Celebrity Edition" all the characters are played by a white male, including Tyra and Nicki Minaj.[76] Although at the end of the video Tyra yells at Nicki, it becomes a white on white elimination—effectively disregarding racial difference altogether. A final parody titled, "America's Next Top Miser" racially portrays the judges accurately, but the contestants are all white males, resulting in Tyra yelling at a white male.[77]

These parody productions leave us with a larger question: Why does the victim have to be white? Perhaps the answer to this question comes from Amy Hasinoff who invokes the concept of neoliberalism that reinvokes the power and privilege of whiteness.[78] "Top Model imagines race in a uniquely neoliberal way it transcends race by denying institutional racism and embraces race by transforming racial difference and the process of imagining racial difference into lucrative marketable commodities. Top Model capitalizes on its racial diversity to promote itself to a wide audience."[79] By denying race as a commodity, and thereby racism as its output, those who parody have deftly avoided any arguments about their portrayals being racist. After all, the incident involving the tirade was between two African American individuals, not a racially mixed—one-up (Tyra Banks–African American), one-down (the model–white) relationship. However, in their desire to preempt any conversations about race through the erasure of blackness, the parodists in their carnivalesque moment reinscribe whiteness and power back onto not only them, but the media in general. It becomes crucial to the parodies in their narrative of reclamation of power (sans race and racism) to make Tiffany white. Without Tiffany being afforded the white privilege of invisibility, there is no identification the viewer or the parodist can make to Tyra's tirade, particularly since there is no understanding of why Tyra may be angry in the first place. All they see is a Sapphire or "angry black woman" yelling at a white person.

*ANTM* sells whiteness as its exported commodity, not blackness. As Hasinoff notes, "Top Model offers the valuable commodity of superficial racial diversity while centering whiteness as the default unmarked race for U.S. citizens. While models of color are praised for their exotic look, blonde-haired white models are referred to as 'all-American.'"[80] In crafting the show, anger from the judges is not an attribute that "sells," even if it is for a valid reason, ratings, or to shake up a dull show; anger from the contestants, however, does sell.

In her berating of Tiffany, Tyra uses classic U.S. patriotic myths as the foundation for why she is angry, where she herself not only makes the U.S. "white," but herself as well. She yells, "Take responsibility for yourself! Because nobody is going to take responsibility for you." All that is missing is Tyra's overt valorization of the Horatio Alger myth, the "work hard and you will succeed" mantra, and the singing of the national anthem. According to Hasinoff:

> The invisibility of whiteness and white privilege intensifies with the belief that race no longer matters and that achievement is equally obtainable to all who seek it. Success—in such a worldview blind to structural inequalities and hidden privileges—is a matter of making good choices. On *ANTM*, contestants of color struggle to make such "good choices," through their strategic performances and downplaying of markers of difference.[81]

Tiffany, however, being a poor black single mother, with a low-class southern accent, challenges this myth. Tiffany says she is "sick of crying about stuff that I can't change, I'm sick of being disappointed, I'm sick of all of it" because she knows the Horatio Alger myth has not worked for her. "In neoliberal fashion, however, Banks interprets her lack of the necessary cultural capital as a self-defeatist attitude and lack of desire to succeed. Tiffany . . . came to stand in for the ghetto welfare queen, who, as the antithesis of neoliberal values, is presumed unable or unwilling to appreciate opportunities to 'improve' herself."[82] This may be a more positive view for Tyra, who can stand there and say the so-called American Dream in the white male-dominated fashion industry worked for her. Because Tyra created a show in which whiteness is valorized and visible ethnic minorities are exoticized, it is crucial that she herself remain as white as possible—the loving mentor. She cannot let her "blackness" show. With the confrontation with Tiffany, and according to white hegemonic standards, there could only be one black winner who remains white, and that is Tyra. However, this hubris ultimately comes back to get her through the various spoofs, because as "white" as Tyra made herself in juxtaposition to "blackness," viewers only saw a Sapphire in that episode—an angry black woman.

## CONCLUSION

As Bakhtin explains, "In carnival, parodying was employed very widely, in diverse forms and degrees: various images (for example, carnival pairs of various sorts) parodied one another variously and from various points of view; it was like an entire system of crooked mirrors, elongating, diminishing, distorting in various directions and to various degrees."[83] As such, parody is not simply about imitating, recreating a text, or randomly splicing one text with another. Carnival, with its use of parody, was a mechanism used to challenge and critique power or monologic cultures with humor. If this is the case, it begs the questions what power does Tyra have and what cultures are being critiqued? Or, the more important question may be how is the function of parody changing in contemporary times?

Dentith notes that Bakhtin's carnival describes the particular cultural dynamics of a society in transition, where prolific parodic energies were directed towards specific authoritative targets. [84] Today, he conveys that our "sacred world' is constantly in flux resulting in a continual disruption and reinvention of what social order considers sacred and pathetic. Just as parody can be transgressive in challenging power, it can also be authoritative by keeping languages of out-groups, marking the different/strange, the new, or challenging in check. [85] In this case, an African American woman with her own television show becomes parodied as Sapphire, thus reinscribing the roles where black women are traditionally found. Along with this, Dentith discusses the role of popular culture and parody, noting the penetration of the culture industry through technical innovation has caused a significant transformation in the presence of parody. "Some of this parody is sharply directed at deflating self-importance, and is politically and socially pointed and telling. Other parody, meanwhile, is done simply for the fun of it." [86] Just as the carnival and parody invert the hegemonic hierarchy, these same tools are now being used by some to reinvert it, wresting temporary power from an African American woman and putting it back in the hands of whiteness.

According to hooks, "television does not hold white people responsible for white supremacy; it socializes them to believe that subjugation and subordination of black people [and other people of color] by any means necessary is essential for the maintenance of law and order." [87] This idea may not only be because of white supremacy, but also due to the way people of color are socially constructed in general, and visually caricatured in mediated forms. Parody is often about a counterculture movement. We do not truly understand what real parody is. The viewer must be able to decode something as a parody for the intention to be realized. In order to do this, they must know the text or conventions being parodied if it is to be understood as something separate from a non-parodic literature.

What power does Tyra have? Yes, she is rich and famous, but what does that mean for a black woman in the United States? As a black woman, she is examined through racial stereotypes (in this case Sapphire) rather than celebrity. Apparently, this one African American woman's temporary power to invert the hegemonic hierarchy—so whiteness is decentered once a week for one hour—is so threatening to some that Tyra needs to be sanctioned through racist, sexist caricature. Parody, in this case, must be about the preservation of white centeredness since Tyra interrupted the acceptable temporary paradigm shift. She was supposed to remain in her role as confidant—an Oprah protégée or even "model mom"—dispensing advice and wisdom about the modeling industry, not showing any human emotion or opinion beyond what whiteness allows through the stereotypes of black womanhood.

Richard Alba aptly notes:

> Whites are largely free to identify themselves as they will and to make these identities as important as they like. This is especially true of the emerging majority of white Americans who come from mixed ethnic backgrounds, who can present and think of themselves in terms of a hybrid identity, or emphasize one ethnic component while recognizing the other (or others), or simplify their background by dropping all but one of its components, or deny altogether the relevance of their ethnic background.[88]

Tyra cannot deny her racial background (even if she could be racially ambiguous), because she has already been defined through mediated stereotypes about black women and black womanhood, whose tropes are comprised of racist and sexist characterizations. In the same way in which *ANTM* rewards models for not being "too ethnic," the show and its viewers can punish someone for being "*too ethnic*"; for operating outside of the expected characterization. Tyra and her anger are caught up in the double-bind—be African American so long as you do not disrupt the white hegemonic mediated norms of black womanhood. Tyra interrupted those mediated expectations, and, as a result, she and her temporary carnival power were high-jacked through parody for the reinscription of white hegemonic norms.

## NOTES

1. Acknowledgements: The authors wish to thank Dr. Marcus Watson and Amanda Stow for their suggestions regarding this manuscript.

2. IMDb 2014, http://www.imdb.com/.

3. The word "Tyrade" has been used in several of the parodies, online media, and in at least one academic article (see Thompson, 2010). Although both authors dislike the use of "Tyrade" we chose to use it as a reminder of one of the ways the Sapphire stereotype is perpetuated. Following this incident, some individuals began confusing Tyra Banks and Naomi Campbell, both African American supermodels from the same era. Campbell gained notoriety on several occasions being accused of assault charges, most notable throwing her cell phone at her maid.

4. Seth MacFarlane and David Zuckerman (creators), "No Meals on Wheels" *Family Guy* (March 25, 2007). http://www.fox.com/family-guy.

5. We recognize that we are violating traditional journalistic standards by listing Tyra Banks by her first name instead of her last name. We do this not to demean her, but to refer to her in how she refers to herself. Tyra Banks has become a first-name household name and, similar to Oprah and Cher, is commonly referred to as simply Tyra.

6. The authors recognize that historically and today, Black individuals have been involved in the creation and maintenance of racial stereotypes. However, this discussion is beyond the scope of this chapter.

7. Tia Tyree, "African American Stereotypes in Reality Television." *The Howard Journal of Communications* 22, (2011): 409.

8. Stuart Hall, "The Spectacle of the 'Other,'" In *Representation: Cultural Representations and Signifying Practices,* edited by Stuart Hall (London, UK: Sage Publications, 1997).

9. Lynette Rice, Top 50 broadcast TV shows of 2013–2014, May 20, 2014. *Entertainment Weekly,* http://insidetv.ew.com/2014/05/20/top-50-broadcast-tv-shows-of-2013-14/
.

10. Zap2it.com, TV by the numbers, July 2, 2014, from http://tvbythenumbers.zap2it.com/.

11. Matthew J. Smith and Andrew F. Wood, eds., *Survivor Lessons: Essays on Communication and Reality Television* (Jefferson, NC: McFarland & Company, 2003), 2.

12. Ellis Godard, "Reel Life: The Social Geometry of Reality Shows," in *Survivor Lessons: Essays on Communication and Reality Television* (Jefferson, NC: McFarland & Company, 2003), 73.

13. John Dowd, "Telling it like it is:" Subject positions on reality television. "Kaleidoscope: A Grade" *Journal of Qualitative Communication Research,* 5, no. 17 (2006): 17–33.

14. See Mark Andrejevic, *Reality TV: The Work of Being Watched* (New York, NY: Rowman & Littlefield, 2003); Mark Andrejevic and Dean Colby, Racism and Reality TV: The Case of MTV's Road Rules," in *How Real is Reality TV?: Essays on Representation and Truth,* ed. David S. Escoffery (Jefferson, NC: McFarland & Company, 2006), 195–211; Anita Biressi and Heather Nunn, *Reality TV: Realism and Revelation* (London, United Kingdom: Wallflower Press, 2004); Rachel E. Dubrofsky, "The Bachelor: Whiteness in the Harem," *Critical Studies in Media Communication,* 23, no. 1 (2006): 39–56; Adele A. Hasinoff, "Fashioning Race for the Free Market on *America's Next Top Model,*" *Critical Studies in Media Communication,* 25 no. 3 (2008): 324–343; Mark P. Orbe (1998). "Constructions of Reality of MTV's *The Real World*: An Analysis of the Restrictive Coding of Black Masculinity," *Southern Communication Journal,* 64 no. 1 (1998): 32–47; Mark P. Orbe, M. "Representation of Race in Reality TV: Watch and Discuss" *Critical Studies in Media Communication,* 24 no. 4 (2008): 345–352; Laurie Ouellette and James Hay (2008). *Better living through reality TV* (Malden, MA: Blackwell, 2008).

15. Mark Orbe, "Representation of Race in Reality TV: Watch and Discuss," *Critical Studies in Media Communication* 24, no. 4 (2008): 350.

16. Ibid., 349.

17. Walter Ong, *Orality and literacy,* 2nd ed. (New York: Routledge, 2002).

18. bell hooks, *Black Looks: Race and Representation* (Boston, MA: South End Press, 1992).

19. Ibid., 21.

20. Ibid., 23.

21. See Stuart Hall, "The Whites of their Eyes: Racist Ideologies and the Media," in *The Media Reader,* eds. Manuel Alvarado and John O. Thompson (London: BFI Publishing, 2006), 723; Herman Gray, *Watching Race: Television and the Struggle for "Blackness"* (Minneapolis: University of Minnesota Press, 1995).

22. Joe R. Feagin and Hernán Vera, *White Racism: The Basics* (New York: Routledge, 1995), 12.

23. Shawna V. Hudson 1998, "Re-creational Television: The Paradox of Change and Continuity within Stereotypical Iconography," *Sociological Inquiry,* 68 (1998): 245.

24. Marcyliena Morgan and Dionne Bennett, "Getting off of Black Women's Backs: Love Her or Leave Her Alone," *Du Bois Review,* 3 no. 2 (2006): 490.

25. Jim Crow Museum of Racist Memorabilia (n.d.). Sapphire caricature (para. 1). http://www.ferris.edu/jimcrow/sapphire/.

26. Shawna V. Hudson, 1998, "Re-creational Television: The Paradox of Change and Continuity within Stereotypical Iconography," *Sociological Inquiry,* 68 (1998): 242–257.

27. Mary Thompson, "Learn Something from This: The Problem of Option Ethnicity on *America's Next Top Model,*" *Feminist Media Studies* 10, no. 3 (2010): 335–352.

28. Key and Peele, January 31, 2012, https://www.youtube.com/watch?v=5LGEiIL1__s.

29. Patricia Hill Collins, *Black sexual politics: African Americans, Gender, and the New Racism* (New York, NY: Routledge, 2005), 54–55.

30. Jim Crow Museum of Racist Memorabilia (n.d.). Sapphire caricature (para. 23). http://www.ferris.edu/jimcrow/sapphire/

31. Marcyliena Morgan and Dionne Bennett, "Getting off of Black Women's Backs: Love Her or Leave Her Alone," *Du Bois Review*, 3 no. 2 (2006): 485–502.

32. Mikhail Bakhtin, *Rabelais and his World*, 2nd ed. Translated by Helene Iswolsky. (Cambridge, MA: M.I.T. Press, 1984).

33. Arthur Lindley, *Hyperion and the Hobbyhorse* (Newark, NJ: University of Delaware Press, 1996), 17.

34. David K. Danow, *The Spirit of Carnival: Magical Realism and the Grotesque* (Lexington, KY: The University Press of Kentucky, 1995), 3.

35. Ibid., 4.

36. Simon Dentith, *Parody* (New York, NY. Routledge, 2000), 23.

37. Mikhail Bakhtin, *The Dialogic Imagination*. Edited by Michael Holquist. Translated by Caryl Emerson and Michael Holquist (Austin, TX: University of Texas Press, 1981), 76.

38. Ibid., 324.

39. Dan Harries, *Film Parody* (London: British Film Institute, 2000); Margaret A. Rose, *Parody: Ancient, Modern, and Post-modern* (Cambridge, UK: Cambridge University Press, 1993).

40. Dentith, *Parody*, 9.

41. Linda Hutcheon, *A Theory of Parody* (New York, NY: Methuen, 1985), 6.

42. Tracey Owens Patton and Julie Snyder-Yuly, "Roles, Rules and Rebellions: Creating the Carnivalesque through Judges Behaviors on *America's Next Top Model*," Communication Studies, 63, no. 3 (July, 2012), 381.

43. YouTube, Statistics, July 3, 2014, https://www.youtube.com/yt/press/statistics.html.

44. Ibid., July 3, 2014.

45. Sam Gutelle, As early adopters group up, will YouTube's audience age in place? April, 2013. http://www.tubefilter.com/2013/04/02/youtube-age-in-place-audience-demographics/.

46. Each video identified was on YouTube; however, because YouTube reports its results by views the same videos kept coming up. By utilizing Google and Bing video searches, the algorithms and search functions brought up differing sets of videos to review.

47. Dentith, *Parody*, 32.

48. *The Family Guy* parody had more than 500,000 views throughout YouTube, however, because it was shown as part of a television show that number increases greatly with the viewership of the show.

49. BasiComedy, "Tyra Banks yells at Miley about her NEWEST Scandal Pictures" (August 12, 2008), https://www.youtube.com/watch?v=BqRbPwXJtH0.

50. Cakm 93's, 2007, https://www.youtube.com/watch?v=lFtE5jlx4Wc; Princ Ali, "All New! Brittany Spears on Tyra Banks!" (December 12, 2014), https://www.youtube.com/watch?v=0HSBZVFxF6o.

51. Jesus Christ is Lord!, "Tyra Banks yells at Obama" (September 5, 2011), https://www.youtube.com/watch?v=3jsrUMnl2Z4.

52. RaheemDTV, "Tyra Banks Yells at Justin Bieber after Arrest" (January 24, 2014), https://www.youtube.com/watch?v=Y8cJfNHclx0.

53. Hutcheon, *A Theory of Parody*, 2.

54. Ibid. 77.

55. *America's Next Top Model*. Episode no. 7, "The Girl that Pushes Tyra Over the Edge," Executive producer Tyra Banks (UPN television), April 13, 2005.

56. Every week before elimination, the models stand before Tyra to hear their critique. This performance is another example of Tyra as mentor; she frequently seems to use this as an opportunity to show her compassion, give advice/critique, and tell the contestants to be strong, etc.; Tiffany Richardson was originally selected to Cycle 3 of ANTM but was disqualified as she had an altercation with another contestant. Following this, she chose to attend anger management to learn to control her temper (see ANTM411.com/tiffany-richardson, n.d.).

57. *America's Next Top Model*, cycle 4, episode 7 (2006).

58. Ibid.

59. Tracey Owens Patton and Julie Snyder-Yuly, "Roles, Rules and Rebellions: Creating the Carnivalesque through Judges Behaviors on *America's Next Top Model*," *Communication Studies*, 63, no. 3 (July, 2012), 378.

60. Elizabeth R. Schroeder, "Sexual Racism" and Reality Television: Privileging the White Male Prerogative on MTV's *The Real World*" in *How Real is Reality TV?: Essays on Representation and Truth*, ed. David S. Escoffery (Jefferson, NC: McFarland & Company, 2006): 181.

61. Sue K. Jewell, *From Mammy to Miss America and Beyond: Cultural Images and the Shaping of US social policy* (London: Routledge, 1993): 45.

62. BasiComedy, "Tyra Banks yells at Miley about her NEWEST Scandal Pictures" (August 12, 2008), https://www.youtube.com/watch?v=BqRbPwXJtH0.

63. Cakm 93's, 2007, https://www.youtube.com/watch?v=lFtE5jlx4Wc; Princ ali, "All New! Brittany Spears on Tyra Banks!" (December 12, 2014), https://www.youtube.com/watch?v=0HSBZVFxF6o.

64. Princ Ali, "All New! Brittany Spears on Tyra Banks!" (December 12, 2014), https://www.youtube.com/watch?v=0HSBZVFxF6o.

65. Dentith, *Parody*.

66. Dentith, *Parody*.

67. Hutcheon, *A Theory of Parody*.

68. Frog Island Flicks. The sketch comedy troupe notes on their YouTube page they make "people laugh while addressing socially relevant issues, such as politics, racism, the environment, Muppets, and dick jokes" (Frog Island Flicks, 2006).

69. Carly Rhodes, *America's Next Top Model Spoof (Tyra Banks Parody)*, YouTube video, 3:45. (May 6, 2008), https://www.youtube.com/watch?v=lFtE5jlx4Wc.

70. Seth MacFarlane and David Zuckerman (creators), "No Meals on Wheels" *Family Guy* (March 25, 2007), http://www.fox.com/family-guy.

71. Suss Jaj (September 24, 2014), https://www.youtube.com/watch?v=LnR1CZiNb58.

72. Galacticfemme, "America's Next Top Monster" (October 30, 2007), https://www.youtube.com/watch?v=guXVuqRG1Yk.

73. Hutcheon, *A Theory of Parody*, 26.

74. Ibid. 75.

75. Atomic Wedgie, "Cleveland's next Top Model" (December 3, 2009), https://www.youtube.com/watch?v=TRtimkX2Ok0.

76. Timato, "America's Next Top Model: Celebrity Edition" (February 19, 2012), https://www.youtube.com/watch?v=NSej330RpOQ.

77. Salvador Sepúlveda Guajardo, 2009 "America's Next Top Miser" (November 30, 2009), https://www.youtube.com/watch?v=WabYuNVDbA8.

78. Amy Hasinoff, "Fashioning Race for the Free Market on *America's Next Top Model*" *Critical Studies in Media Communication* 25, no. 3 (2008).

79. Ibid. 332.

80. Ibid. 333.

81. Ibid. 344.

82. Ibid. 346.

83. Mikhail Bakhtin, *Problems of Dostoevsky's Poetics* (Minneapolis: University of Minnesota Press, 1984): 127.

84. Dentith, *Parody*, 187.

85. Dentith, *Parody* and Hutcheon, *A Theory of Parody.*

86. Dentith, *Parody,* 185.

87. bell hooks, *Killing Rage* (New York: H. Holt & Company, 1995): 112.

88. Richard Alba, *Ethnic Identity: The Transformation of White America* (New Haven, CT: Yale University Publishers, 1990): 295.

# EIGHT

# A Critical Analysis of Black Womanhood in NBC's *The Apprentice*

## Donyale R. Griffin Padgett & Donnetrice C. Allison

Reality programs rose to prominence based on claims that the shows depicted "real life," but in recent years many shows have come under fire for being anything but "reality." Orbe (1998) suggests viewers are drawn to such programs based on the notion that they show "real people in everyday interactions," and there is a certain level of "unpredictability that comes with reality."[1] However, what has become predictable and potentially problematic, over the past two decades, are the negative stereotypes associated with African American women on these programs. This skewing of reality is particularly significant when we consider the limited opportunities these shows provide viewers to witness the many facets of black womanhood. From the head-bobbing and finger-waving of Alicia Calaway on season two of the hit show *Survivor* to the on-and-off-air mudslinging between Kenya Moore and NeNe Leakes of *Real Housewives of Atlanta* fame, black women are portrayed as disloyal, bitchy, lazy, difficult to work with, and a threat to others.[2]

In several interviews after hearing "You're Fired," by Donald Trump on NBC's *The Apprentice*, Omarosa Manigault, who was a contestant on the first season of the show, contends that much of the program was edited to make her appear as a villain. For instance, in an interview with radio host, Donnie Simpson,[3] she noted that she was never shown smiling on the show or interacting with any of her roommates; yet, in that two or three month period, she maintained that she made several good friends. These manipulations of reality on "reality" TV may be particularly problematic for those groups subject to stereotypical portrayals.

149

Through the use of Black Feminist Theory, this chapter analyzes the depiction of the African American female contestants on seven seasons of Donald Trump's original installment of *The Apprentice*. We only focus on those seasons where the contestants were not celebrities, so as to avoid the presumption that *The Celebrity Apprentice* is inevitably dramatized by virtue of the contestants "celebrity" status. Therefore, we chose to focus on portrayals of women who were never before in the public eye.

As such, the questions that guide this analysis include:

1. What are the images of black women portrayed on *The Apprentice*?
2. What do these images indicate about the ways in which black womanhood is constructed on the show?
3. What are some possibilities for shifting "realities" to represent more accurate portrayals of African American women on television?

As this book extensively demonstrates, black women have always had to contend with stereotypes, which Chapman, Kaatz and Carnes (2013) call "well-learned sets of associations between some trait and a social group."[4] These associations are dangerous because they do not allow for variance at the individual level of a group. Research on the stereotypes associated with black women is vast; and much work has called attention to the demeaning characterizations of black women on television and in film: from the black Barbie doll trying to look and act like a white woman of the 1980s, to the booty-poppin' video vixens of the 1990s, to the self-centered—educated, but disloyal—black woman of the twenty-first century.[5] These negative depictions are reinforced over time through discourse about black women, and become particularly harmful because they become commonplace—i.e., socially acceptable. And, as previously noted, portrayals of black women on reality TV may be especially powerful because of their very position[ing] as "real." It is this current portrayal of black women that we believe to be most harmful today, as illustrated in the popular reality show, *The Apprentice*.

## FROM FEMINISM TO WOMANISM

Foss (2004) describes the purpose of feminist criticism as exploring what an artifact suggests about the construction of gender; how male domination is constructed and maintained; and finally, how such constructs can be challenged.[6] Feminist criticism is rooted in a critical tradition, which seeks to interpret the acts and symbols of society in order to understand the unique ways in which various social groups are oppressed. Using this approach, researchers examine power structures and hegemonic systems in order to bring often hidden structures to light. As a methodology, feminism helps to shed light on the "social organization and social relations" that produce knowledge bases that are used as "objective" measures of particular groups of people.[7] Because of privilege and power status, the dominant culture generally has a view of society that reflects the hegemonic perceptions about how society functions. In contrast, marginalized groups, who are usually denied access to power, bring more insight to the way that society functions, particularly within power systems.[8]

Early feminists were concerned with proving that men and women are equal. More contemporary notions of feminism seek to provide a social space for the lived experiences of women, demonstrate the centrality of the feminine perspective in making knowledge claims, and "critique dominant knowledge claims" that most often parallel a white male perspective.[9] Thalos (1994) describes feminism as a theory which emphasizes "the strengths and qualities that have been associated with the feminine" and thus devalued in society.[10] According to Wanca-Thibault and Tompkins (1998), the responsibility of feminist thought extends beyond simply making room for the feminine voice and critiquing patriarchy, to "creating opportunities to transform or balance the status quo."[11] The latter has been the source of much criticism.

Perhaps more than any other contemporary social or critical theory, feminism is the victim of a love/hate relationship with the academy.[12] Scholars have both praised it and cursed it. In the decades since women have won economic, political, and social advancements, many scholars have rendered feminism limiting and void of a unified epistemology, pointing to still rampant inequality—not only among women, but other marginalized groups as well (ethnic groups, handicapped persons, the elderly, etc.). Calas and Smircich (1996) suggest that some critics claim feminism has gone too far, while others claim that it has not gone far enough. Many contend that the different genres of feminist thought are "white, western, and middle class," and speak to the privileged instead of bringing liberation to marginalized men, women and groups around the world.[13]

Hamer and Neville (1998) reject the notion of feminism as a "monolithic approach to the liberation of women against [patriarchy]."[14] Instead, they describe this approach as an "umbrella term covering myriad theories and positions."[15] A broad concern within feminism is whether women should be viewed as a group; and whether all women share the same experience of oppression. Hallstein (2000) notes that the end of the 1980s and the beginning of the 1990s were characterized by a discussion of difference "led by women of color . . ."[16] She continues,

> At the center of the difference discussion, which is often informed by postmodern theory, is the idea that women are diverse and occupy different positions or standpoints based on elements of race, class, and sexuality.[17]

A major proponent during this time was Patricia Hill Collins, who "artic-ulated a specifically black feminist standpoint."[18] Similarly, in an article exploring the challenges and consequences of being an African American in academia, Allen (1998) writes, "being black and woman engenders complex ways of knowing and being"[19] and can often lead to what Col-lins calls a "dialectic of identity" among women of color who negotiate "dual membership" within the dominant culture.[20]

This understanding creates a space for black feminist or "womanist" ideology, which according to Dill (1987), "criticizes the value of imagin-ing a racially and culturally homogenous woman . . . who is really a bourgeois, white, western woman."[21] Since Alice Walker coined the phrase "womanist" in her 1983 book, *In Search of Our Mothers' Gardens*, black feminism has "emerged as a response to feminist theories and white (bourgeois) women's movements that omitted serious examination of racism, and the general concerns of black women and other women of color."[22] Additionally, Clenora Hudson-Weems coined the term "Africana Womanism"—first called Black Womanism in the mid-1980s, then re-named in the 1990s to Africana Womanism.[23] According to Hud-son-Weems (2004):

> Africana Womanism, emerged from the acknowledgement of a long-standing authentic agenda for that group of women of African descent who need only to be properly named and officially defined according to their own unique historical and cultural matrix, one that would re-flect the co-existence of men and women in a concerted struggle for the survival of their entire family/community.[24]

Nonetheless, womanist ideology differs from Africana Womanism in that it brings into focus the uniqueness of black women's oppression in the realm of a patriarchal sphere. This parallels more traditional notions of feminism. One of the foundational differences between womanism and feminism is that while feminist epistemology mainly "ranked different systems of oppression and thus prioritized the liberation agendas of cer-tain groups [over other]," womanist epistemology projects race, class, gender, and sexuality as "codependent variables that cannot readily be separated and ranked in scholarship, in political practice, or in lived ex-perience."[25] Womanism also allows for the exploration of Collins' (1991) concept of the dialectic of identity between race and gender that black women must reconcile; a phenomenon that further separates it from white feminist thought.[26] In Allen's (1998) article on black womanhood, she chronicles the lived experiences of women of color, many of whom are forced to choose between their blackness and womanhood. This not only complicates the perspective black women have on the dominant social structure, but affects the way they must negotiate this "two-ness" in the same social contexts as white women.[27]

## CONSTRUCTING BLACK
## WOMANHOOD ON *THE APPRENTICE*

In this chapter, we ask "How is black womanhood constructed within the framework of a patriarchal and Eurocentric context on the hit NBC reality show, *The Apprentice*?" Through a critical analysis, we take an in-depth look at the images that are constructed and projected each season for the show's "non celebrity" black women—a total of nine women spread over seven seasons—by writers and producers and by the women themselves.

*The Apprentice* joined NBC's primetime lineup in January 2004 and quickly became a hit with viewers. The premise of the show—created by the "King of Reality Television," Mark Burnett, also known for the *Survivor* series and the short lived *Restaurant*—is a 13-week interview, whereby 16–18 candidates (8–9 men and 8–9 women) are selected to perform various business tasks for real estate mogul, Donald Trump. The candidates are separated into two teams and each week the losing team has to face Donald Trump in the boardroom, where he fires one of the candidates from the losing team. The final remaining candidate is hired to become Donald Trump's apprentice in a one-year position, at a salary of $250,000.

Omarosa Manigault was among the candidates selected for the first installment of *The Apprentice*. She was the only black female in the group and in her self-description on the first episode, she stated: "I grew up in the projects, but I am now a PhD candidate and work as a political consultant. Four years ago I worked at the White House for the president of the United States."[28] With an equally impressive resume, Stacie J., the only black female cast member on the show's second season, has a bachelor's degree from Emory University and an MBA from Mercer University. After pursuing a modeling career, she owned and operated a Subway Sandwich Shop franchise in Harlem, New York at the time she was selected for the show.[29] Season three offered viewers the rare opportunity to see two black women on the same program—Verna and Tara. Verna, in addition to being a wife and mother, earned an MBA in business communication and climbed the corporate ladder in sales and marketing. Tara, on the other hand, did not earn a college degree, but she too excelled in marketing and public relations as the first African American, and the youngest person ever to serve as Director of Appointments in the Office of the New Jersey Governor, where she managed the process of gubernatorial appointments to over 500 boards and commissions.[30] The seasons that followed included equally impressive and accomplished black women that will be further discussed in the Analysis section of this chapter.

In looking at black womanhood on *The Apprentice*, a black feminist perspective is necessary to explain the framework within which black female identity is constructed. In order to answer the question of how these images are constructed, we point to the patriarchal ideologies of white supremacy, devised during slavery to sustain subjugation. These same ideologies followed black women out of slavery and are reified in popular culture through their continual reproduction on television, in film, and other mediums.[31] "The constructions," asserts Mullings (1994), "seek to define the categories through which reality is to be understood . . ."[32] This limits the array of images of black female identity to those images that were manufactured to suppress black womanhood. The detriment, Mullings (1994) explains further, is "they are not fully articulated, which makes them difficult to confront and contest."[33] In a study of portrayals of racial minorities on prime time television, Mastro and Greenberg (2000) found African Americans were more negatively portrayed than Whites and Latinos. Findings indicated African Americans were "judged as the laziest and the least respected."[34]

Another significant factor in the construction of black womanhood on television, in general, and reality television specifically, is the dismal representation of African American talent behind the camera. From casting directors and writers to show creators and producers, the television industry continues to be predominantly white.[35] Although, as this book indicates, we have made some gains with the likes of Shonda Rhimes, Mara Brock Ali and Lee Daniels, black talent behind the camera is marginal. *The Apprentice* is no different from the long list of television shows produced and directed by majority white males. In directing the production of images, this hegemonic sphere of influence is responsible for defining and directing the performance of "cultural forms and expressions" that "reflect women's experiences, perspectives, and meanings."[36] Foss (2004) contends that because "culture features men's perspectives and devalues and silences those of women" it is a foregone conclusion that the "various manifestations" we witness on television are portrayed from a male point of view.[37] In the case of *The Apprentice*, the nine black women featured on seasons 1–6 and season 10 had to contend with both a male and white-dominated framework from which they were forced to carve out notions of black womanhood for the masses of pop culture fans who witnessed their stints on the reality show—some more controversial than others.

Carr (2004) describes the process of whittling 250,000 candidates down to sixteen as one in which casting directors seek individuals who are "believable, interesting and unpredictable" (A1).[38] Yet, in the past two decades of reality television, the same stereotypical characters seem to appear, such as the infamous SWA, previously discussed. And more recently, in many cases the SWA has been college educated; she is articulate and attractive; yet she is harsh and condescending to her fellow castmates, who eventually grow to despise her.

According to Orbe (1998), creators, producers, and casting directors for reality programs, who tend to be predominantly white, seek to cast members who have the greatest potential for cultural clash and the ability to create tension.[39] Presumably, this is what creator Mark Burnett, and casting director, Rob LaPlante saw in the contestants they selected for the show—particularly Omarosa Manigault. As noted in chapter one, Omarosa made it clear in her audition video, that she knew what it took to be a winner. And while she didn't actually "win," the apprenticeship on the show, she forged quite a relationship with Donald Trump, such that he brought her back for season 7—the first installment of *Celebrity Apprentice*—and he built an entire dating show around her quest to find love again, called *The Ultimate Merger*.

On *The Apprentice*, the construction of black womanhood struggles against two paradigms: 1) a white male patriarchal context within which black women must struggle to project a true self-image and image of black womanhood, and 2) a white patriarchal ideology that reproduces the same negative images of black women that have become markers of black female identity. Through the design of roles, and editing led by the show's producers in the former context, it is difficult for the two to "move from external, societal definitions of [black] womanhood to an internal, personally salient definition of [black] womanhood."[40] In fact, in Omarosa's controversial post-*Apprentice* interviews she accused the show's producers of editing her "personality," and she discussed the pressure to conform to societal views of black women. She did, however, continue to participate in an additional two seasons of the show and numerous other reality programs where she continued to "perform" as the infamous SWA. So while these institutionalized images maintain a system where black womanhood continues to exist on the margins, it appears that some black women have knowingly entered into this arena and conformed to these characterizations.

## ANALYSIS

Employing a critical analysis, we examined a total of 65 episodes of *The Apprentice*—seasons 1–6 and season 10. Seasons 1–6 feature the original format of the show, whereby contestants were selected from the workforce, in various fields, to win a one-year position with Donald Trump's organization. Season 7, however, switched the format to *The Celebrity Apprentice*, whereby celebrities—actors, musicians, athletes and other performers—were selected to compete in various business tasks and ultimately win money for their favorite charity if they were the last surviving contestant. This format continued in seasons 8 and 9, but season 10 returned to the original format, in response to the U.S. recession that put many talented individuals out of work.[41] As such, show producers recruited 16 contestants who were all struggling financially and professionally, to varying degrees.

For this chapter, we examined each of the above-mentioned seasons, focusing only on those episodes that included black women. Some were "fired" by Trump sooner than others, so the number of episodes examined varied each season. We examined 10 episodes of season 1, as Omarosa was fired in episode 9, but returned to assist Kwame—an African American male who was among the final two contestants—in his task for the season finale. In season 2, Stacie J. was fired in episode 3; and in season 3, Verna was fired in episode 3 and Tara was fired in episode 6. In season 4, Marshawn Evans—a sports and entertainment lawyer—was fired in episode 8, but returned in the final episode to assist Randall (the African American male who ultimately won the apprenticeship that season) in his task. In season 5, Roxanne—also a lawyer—lasted the entire season, all 15 episodes. She was among the final four contestants; then, she was selected by one of the final two contestants to assist in the final task. In season 6, Jamaican-born Muna—another lawyer—was fired in episode 9. Finally, in season 10, which featured contestants hit by the recession, show producers selected several women of color. There were two women of African descent—Kelly, a public relations professional and Kenyan-born Liza, business owner and professional golfer. There was also an Iranian woman and a Latina selected that season. Kelly was fired in episode 6; and Liza lasted the entire season—13 episodes—and she was among the final three contestants.

Upon reviewing all 65 episodes and taking detailed notes, we looked for themes and the following emerged: black woman as bitch, black woman as lazy and incompetent and black woman as invisible.

## BLACK WOMAN AS BITCH/SWA

Of all nine black women we examined for this analysis, Omarosa was overwhelmingly portrayed as the bitch of season 1. In fact, she was referred to as a "bitch" seven times in 10 episodes—either to her face or during a confessional scene featuring one of the other contestants. The first time Omarosa was called a "bitch" was by Erika in the airport. The second time was by a young woman named Katrina, who had become close friends with Erika. In that scene, Katrina was yelling and screaming at Omarosa and even grabbed Omarosa's arm when Omarosa tried to leave the room. Without raising her voice, Omarosa said, "Don't touch me," and Katrina, while vigorously pointing her finger, yelled, "Life's too short to be a bitch!"[42]

The third time Omarosa was called a bitch was by Amy, who had been portrayed as the heroine in the group, because she would volunteer to "deal with" or "tolerate" Omarosa on certain tasks. Nonetheless, Amy called Omarosa "a scheming, conniving, bitch" during her confessional scene.[43] Heidi, who was also initially portrayed as being able to "tolerate" Omarosa, called Omarosa a bitch four times in a row. First she called Omarosa "an absolute lunatic bitch." Then she went on to yell out at Omarosa, "I can't fucking stand you. All you do is whine and complain. Bitch . . . Bitch . . . Bitch . . ."[44]

As noted in previous chapters, the characterization of black woman as bitch, or SWA is nothing new. It goes back to Sapphire and notions of black women as inherently evil.[45] From the nagging Sapphire of the 1950s, we moved to the wealthy diva—played by Diahann Carroll—in *Dynasty* in the 1980s. In the 1990s, as noted in chapter 1, MTV introduced the SWA—sistah with an attitude—on *The Real World* and reality television producers have continued to portray her more outrageously with each passing decade. It began with young women like Tami, Cynthia and Kameelah on early seasons of *The Real World*, who were always ready to curse out a fellow cast member; to Omarosa of the early 2000s, who was poised and well educated but condescending and bitchy; to the wealthy Housewives of Atlanta ready to kick ass even if they are wearing an evening gown and fine jewelry.

On numerous occasions during season 1, the white women spoke very negatively about Omarosa, with comments like: "Seven out of eight of these girls are phenomenal. We do not need her [Omarosa]," and "What can we do to get rid of her? It might be worth losing to get rid of Omarosa and move on so that we'd make more progress." Another young woman commented, "Omarosa creates such negative energy all around her. . . . I think it would be best for the team if Omarosa was fired." Omarosa, on the other hand, seemed fully aware of the other women's disdain for her and she appeared to be unconcerned—and in some cases she even appeared amused. In one scene she told another contestant, "I'm not here to make friends. I said that from day one"[46] Then, in a confessional scene after she'd overheard some of the women talking about her, she said with a smile, "They're strategizing to get me out, and I'm strategizing to stay in."[47] The interesting question is—To what extent does Omarosa's intelligence and strategic communication get perceived as bitchiness? Is she an SWA, or is she simply a business savvy young women, doing whatever she has to do to survive as Other? It is important to note that she is the *only* contestant from the original *Apprentice* format to be called back to participate in the *Celebrity Apprentice*. Additionally, she is the only contestant from the original format that Trump built another show around.

## BLACK WOMAN AS LAZY AND INCOMPETENT

The characterization of black women as lazy and incompetent was the most common characterization assigned to the black women of *The Apprentice*. While Omarosa was primarily portrayed as the bitch of the show, she was also accused of being a lazy drama queen. In episode 7, teams were tasked with renovating an apartment. During the opening scene, a piece of plaster fell out of the ceiling on to Omarosa's head, as they stood in an unfinished building. Once her team selected which apartment they'd renovate and the others began working on the project—painting, cleaning and fixing up—she was shown primarily sitting down, taking notes, and giving orders. Then later in the episode, she was shown playing ball with some neighborhood children. Katrina commented, "Omarosa got a bump on the head and created a drama series out of it, whereas Heidi found out that her mom was diagnosed with cancer and was so incredibly classy about it." Amy later added, "it really disgusts me to see Omarosa elevating this minor injury into something that she thinks is making her look like this poor victim, when in fact we're all laughing at her behind her back."

Omarosa was also brought back on the show's season finale to assist one of the final two contestants: entrepreneur, Bill Rancic and Wall Street investment manager, Kwame Jackson—the only black male on the show. During this episode Omarosa was also depicted as lazy and incompetent. It was implied that she lied about whether or not she had received an important phone call, and she was often shown fooling around on the job. She was selected to work for Kwame, who was assigned to manage a major concert at one of Trump's casinos. Ultimately, Kwame did not win the apprenticeship position with Donald Trump's, and it was implied that that was partly due to his inability to control Omarosa's behavior. In the end, Kwame said, "I would never hire Omarosa. She's intelligent, but she's a space cadet."

Similarly, in a mere three episodes of season 2, Stacie J. was accused of not contributing to the team at the same level as her counterparts, being a loose cannon and not being able to handle pressure—though in her "real" life she was a successful business owner. In fact, in the first episode she is accused by another contestant of "buckling under the pressure" in a scene where she appeared to be trying to make her teammates laugh by playing with a magic 8-ball. After that, several of her teammates tried to insinuate that she was emotionally unstable, though none of them were clinical psychologists; and some even suggested that they were in fear for their lives. Comments included:

- "Her whole demeanor changed. I've never seen anything like it."
- "It was borderline schizophrenic."
- "She flipped out. I was so scared I had to hide in a corner."
- "I feel sad for this, because I'm not sure if this is something clinical and I'm sensitive to that, but it was one of the most scary moments of my life."
- "I was absolutely horrified."[48]

In season three, Trump separated teams by college educated versus non-college educated contestants. It was touted as Book Smarts versus

Street Smarts. The two black women on the show were therefore divided, as one was "book smart" and one was "street smart." Verna, who was a member of the 'book smart" team, was depicted as having a meltdown, whereby she stormed off of the project (to renovate a motel) and wandered the streets aimlessly as Carolyn—one of Trump's colleagues—followed her trying to bring her back. In the end, her teammates called her "dead weight." The next episode, rather than be fired, she quit. She was the first contestant to ever do so.

In season 4, Marshawn, who was a young lawyer, had the opportunity to lead the team in episode 2, but she was largely portrayed as laissez-faire leader; and her team members complained that she was doing more "watching" than leading. Then, in episode 8—where she was ultimately fired—she was accused of "dropping the ball," on a task because she backed out of doing the presentation at the last minute. She implied that she thought she was being set-up to take the fall for the team if they lost, but nevertheless Trump fired her. Again, it's a question of strategy and business savvy versus laziness or incompetence.

In season 5, Roxanne, also a young lawyer, became the project manager for the task in episode 5, and she was immediately accused of being too inexperienced and disorganized to affectively lead the task. However, she stood up for herself by confronting two of her teammates, stating, "When you all were PMs I gave you all the respect in the world . . . didn't mean I agreed with everything you said but I did give you respect. The only thing I am asking for is respect!"[49] Then in episode 13, right before she was fired, her teammate—with whom she had previously been very close—accused her of having an attitude and being difficult to work with. The irony of her statement is that for the entire season she—a white female—and Roxanne were depicted as close allies and friends, but in the end, she fell back on old stereotypes of black women to convince Trump to fire Roxanne. Trump easily took the bait and asked Roxanne during a boardroom scene, "You don't get along with many people do you," which was a rather odd question given that he noted—in previous episodes—the alliance she'd formed with two white female contestants. Nonetheless, she was fired and accused of not being able to handle a position within the Trump organization.

In season 6, Muna received very little camera time. She was neither praised nor criticized very much. The only real criticism she faced during the season was for being too religious—when she was shown reading her bible before going into the boardroom to face possible elimination—and for being difficult to understand due to her Jamaican accent. Liza, of season 10, on the other hand, was criticized in nearly every episode, by nearly every member of her team, for not contributing to a task and for being incompetent—though she too was a business owner in her "real" life. As early as the second episode of the season she was touted as the weakest player on the team, even though up to that point she was shown on camera actively participating in whatever task the team was assigned. In each subsequent episode she continued to be named the weakest player, but her team continued to win tasks, so she was never fired. Then in episodes 5 and 6, Liza was pitted against the other black female on the show—Kelly, who was of lighter complexion than Liza and to that point had been portrayed more positively. Kelly accused Liza of "throwing her under the bus" in the boardroom, regarding a task that Kelly made a decision that Liza didn't agree with. An upset Kelly stated that she would no longer defend Liza, even though Liza had tried to apologize to her. Kelly was fired in episode 6 and Liza remained, though still constantly criticized. Some of the negative comments included: "Liza has no brain," and she's "incompetent." In fact, one of her greatest critics, a white woman named Stephanie—a very arrogant and vocal woman, who would likely have been characterized an SWA had she been black—referred to Liza as her "secretary," when the two had to work together on a task. Nonetheless, even with all of the criticism she faced, Liza remained on the show until the very end, and she was among the final three; and while she did not win, Trump called her "outstanding in every way," though also asserting that she needed to learn to get along better with others.

It is important to note here that to date, after 14 seasons of *The Apprentice* and *Celebrity Apprentice*, no black woman has even won an apprenticeship with Donald Trump. In the book, *Presumed Incompetent: The Intersections of Race and Class for Women in Academia*, several authors speak to the challenges that black women faculty face trying to overcome established stereotypes held by their peers, students and administrators.[50] And while we are both black women in the academy facing similar challenges, we assert here that the academy is not the only institution where black women face these challenges. We believe that black women face the presumption of incompetence in nearly every professional field, due in large part to the long-standing negative stereotypes that have been portrayed in media. No matter the accomplishments of the women on *The Apprentice*—lawyer, business-owner, doctoral candidate, PR specialist— they still faced this presumption, so much so that none were deemed worthy of a position within the Trump organization. Though Omarosa was apparently deemed so good at fulfilling the bitch/SWA stereotype that Trump continues to cast her over and over again as "reality" television fodder.

## BLACK WOMAN AS INVISIBLE

While Omarosa, of season 1, experienced a great deal of camera time and attention, many of the other black women in seasons that followed, were rendered virtually invisible. In season 2, Stacie J. was often ignored and disregarded by her teammates. Aside from casting her as "unstable," they otherwise cast her aside. Conversations would often cease when she walked into a room and her teammates would often disperse when she'd try to join in on the discussion. It was fairly blatant and obvious during her brief stint on the show. In the seasons that followed, black women saw very little camera time. They were often shown as background or ancillary to the task at hand; yet, when they were featured it was often only to question their contribution to the group. This falls in line with a recent article in *Fortune Magazine*, which purported that black women are treated as virtually invisible in corporate America. In the article, Valerie Purdie-Vaughns (2015), a psychology professor at Columbia University, offered the following contention:

> I've examined how people's brains are biased to ignore black women. When many think about "black executives," they visualize *black men*. When they think about "female executives," they visualize *white women*. Because black women are not seen as typical of the categories "black" or "woman," people's brains fail to include them in both categories. Black women suffer from a "now you see them now you don't" effect in the workplace.[51]

This holds true for *The Apprentice*, given that in the seven seasons we viewed the three "women" that won were white women and the one "black" person that won was a black man.

Another example of invisibility includes Omarosa's attempt to bring all the women together to randomly decide who to select for the first project manager of the first task in episode one of season one. She suggested that all the women put their names in a bowl to pick the project manager. The other women—all white women—decided to choose Amy with no discussion. They did not consider or even acknowledge the suggestion offered by Omarosa. Similarly Stacie J's suggestions were always ignored or disregarded because she was deemed "unstable" early on by her peers. In season 3, Verna quit the show in episode 3 and Tara was rarely shown on camera until episode 6 when she took on the project manager position and was ultimately fired. In season 4, Marshawn received little camera time, but her brief interactions were mostly positive; and although she was fired in episode 8, Randall—the African American male who ultimately won the apprenticeship—chose her to return for the season finale to be a part of his team on the final task. In season 5, Roxanne was shown as the black woman most integrated with the rest of her teammates, and she lasted the entire season, though in the end when she was fired, Trump claimed that she didn't get along well with others, which was never portrayed. She was never shown in a verbal altercation; in fact, she never even raised her voice, even when she demanded respect from her teammates. In season 6, Muna was once again virtually ignored. She was rarely shown speaking and when she did speak—a few times in the boardroom—she was very proper and polite. The most camera time she received was in episode 9 when she took on the acting role in her team's task to create a commercial. She was then criticized for her heavy Jamaican accent, and ultimately fired. In season 10, like Roxanne, Liza lasted the entire season and Liza did receive more camera time, but it was typically to feature her as a background, ancillary participant on her team. In other words, she was typically shown performing a minor task that was not important to her team's victory, to prove that she was a weak link. Nonetheless, even given her presumed incompetence, she lasted the entire season.

While we chose to only focus on the original format of *The Apprentice*, it is important to note that the more in-line with commonly held stereotypes black female cast members behaved, the more camera time they received. This was most noticeable in the *Celebrity Apprentice*, whereby the bitch/SWA was featured heavily: from Omarosa's return in the first installment of *Celebrity Apprentice* and her antagonistic relationship with British television personality Piers Morgan, to the constant cat fights between Star Jones and NeNe Leakes in season 11 and Vivica A. Fox and Kenya Moore in season 14. Moreover, Trump would often add fuel to the fire during those arguments. He would ask, "Is that true," and he would allow the camera to continue to roll. Rarely would he ask these women to stop the arguing, and he would say things like, "Why are you so nasty to everyone," or "Why can't you get along with anyone?" In fact, he allowed the argument between Vivica A. Fox and Kenya Moore to go on for nearly twelve minutes in episode six of season 14.[52] Apparently, that made for great television—watching two black women hurl insults back and forth as three white men egged them on.

## SHIFTING REALITIES:
## DISCUSSION AND INTERPRETATIONS

Overall, in our analysis, we found that black women were cast as bitchy, incompetent and invisible. These images indicate a manufactured reality of black womanhood that confirms the need to explore the multiple tensions black women negotiate between gender, race and class.[53] Both Omarosa and Stacie J., when interviewed on NBC's *Today Show*, said that they were mischaracterized, and much of the literature on reality television asserts that such shows are far from "reality." On the other hand, Heather B., from the first season of MTV's *Real World* argued that a show can only broadcast what you give them.[54] In other words, regardless of the context, cast members behaved that way [at some point] and were simply caught on camera acting out their true personalities. This kind of limited portrayal favors those behaviors that confirm the stereotyped image being created each week on the show. Hence, through a patriarchal mainstream lens, one might argue that Omarosa did, in fact, act like a bitch and a snob during the taping of *The Apprentice*, and Stacie J. did behave in an unstable manner during the first episode of the second season, which caused others to question her sanity. In addition, Verna was a quitter and Liza did not perform as a highly competent potential executive. This is the implication.

However, extending this lens, we might also interpret Omarosa and Roxanne's behavior as responding to a hegemonic structure that sought to render them voiceless, powerless and place them in the position of an outsider. We might interpret Stacie J. and Verna's behavior as acting out the frustration of their failed relationship with the same hegemonic power that rendered them equally voiceless. We might further assert that Marshawn, Muna, and Liza were rendered invisible and voiceless given that they did not "perform" the desired stereotypical role of the loud, brash black woman.

What is reality here is that whether these women were selected because of their likelihood to cause drama or whether they were depicted as causing drama in the editing room, continued negative portrayals of black women in media are harmful because they are likely to affect viewers' perceptions—particularly viewers who have little direct contact with black women in their everyday lives. Parallel to this, the notion that these programs are "reality" may suggest to some that black women are as they are depicted on these programs. This is the danger of stereotypes, which reinforce the generalizations made by "socially dominant groups about socially oppressed groups" and are all too prevalent in the media.[55]

The true reality is, black women range from assertive to aggressive, from generous to snobbish, from selfless to selfish, from conniving to nurturing, and everything in between. In addition to limiting portrayals to a few identities, these depictions fail to provide opportunities for authenticity. Perhaps the real question this analysis generates is: What are the possibilities for shifting realities to represent more accurate portrayals?

An expanded dialogue on black feminism/womanism is central to answering this question. Proponents of this framework encourage a "serious examination of racism, and the general concerns of black women and other women of color."[56] Failure to recognize the politicized portrayals of black womanhood as an outpost of patriarchy and oppression continues to render these women voiceless.

What is clear from this analysis is a need to extend research in the area of black feminist ideology into being true to the critical tradition, which asserts that once individuals understand oppression, they can become empowered to act against the oppression. In her analysis of Standpoint Theory, Collins (1986) asserts that black women must not allow themselves to be defined by others' stereotypical views of them and they must not submit to these stereotypes themselves.[57] Additionally, Collins (1986) notes that black women must define and validate themselves, and bring their standpoint into various forms of discourse and contexts.[58] This has begun to happen in television formats outside of reality TV and in film, with more black women leading the charge to create shows and media content that depicts more authentic portrayals.[59]

It becomes imperative that future research in this area fuse theory with practically demonstrated strategies that black women can use to create instances of liberation from mainstream stereotypes and more "realistic" notions of black womanhood. From a theoretical standpoint this involves contesting the structure and ideology that generates negative portrayals. On a more practical level, it involves taking up the charge to "eradicate oppression" by creating opportunities to present more authentic manifestations of black womanhood for a new generation of mass media consumers. Gorham (1999) supports this assertion. He suggests fostering "critical and active reading in the next generation . . . so that they may be less likely to develop automatic stereotype-congruent interpretations."[60] Finally, this analysis contributes to the dialogue on strategies for black women's liberation from politicized media portrayals by calling for an examination of the interwoven tensions of oppression these women face and a validation of their lived experiences.

## NOTES

1. Mark P. Orbe, "Constructions of Reality on MTV's *The Real World*: An Analysis of the Restrictive Coding of Black Masculinity," *The Southern Communication Journal* 64 (1998), 44.

2. Tamara Winfrey Harris, *The Sisters are Alright: Changing the broken narrative of black women in America* (Oakland, CA: Berrett-Koehler Publishers, 2015); and Kimberly C. Roberts, "Reality TV still beaming black and white," *The Philadelphia Tribune* online (February 15, 2005), accessed August 2015, http://www.phillytrib.com/.

3. Omarosa Manigualt on *The Donnie Simpson Morning Show*, WPGC-FM radio, Washington, DC, 2004.

4. Elizabeth N. Chapman, Anna Kaatz & Molly Carnes, "Physicians and Implicit Bias: How Doctors May Unwittingly Perpetuate Health Care Disparities," *Journal of General Internal Medicine* 28, no.11 (2013), accessed August 2015, http://www.ncbi.nlm.nih.gov/pmc/articles/PMC3797360/.

5. Donald Bogle, *Toms, Coons, Mulattoes, Mammies & Bucks: An Interpretive History of Blacks in American Films*, 4th Edition (New York: NY: Continuum, 2001); Erica Chito Childs, "Looking behind the stereotypes of the 'Angry Black Woman': An exploration of Black women's responses to interracial relationships," *Gender & Society* 19, no. 4 (2005); Winfrey Harris, *The Sisters are Alright*.

6. Sonja K. Foss, *Rhetorical Criticism: Exploration and Practice*, 3rd Edition (Chicago, IL: Waveland Press, Inc., 2004), 158.

7. Susan A. Mann & and Lori R. Kelley, "Standing at the Crossroads of Modernist Thoughts: Collins, Smith, and the New Feminist Epistemologies," *Gender and Society* 11 (1997).

8. Mark P. Orbe, "From the Standpoint(s) of Traditionally Muted Groups: Explicating a Co-cultural Communication Theoretical Model," *Communication Theory* 8 (1998), 3; and Dorothy L. Pennington, "Black-White Communication: An Assessment of Research" in *Handbook of Intercultural Communication*, eds. Molefi K. Asante, Eileen Newmark & Cecil A. Blake (Los Angeles, CA: Sage Publications, 1979), 392.

9. Brenda J. Allen, "Black womanhood and feminist standpoints," *Management Communication Quarterly* 11 (1998), 575.

10. Mariam Thalos, "The Common Need for Classical Epistemological Foundations: Against a Feminist Alternative," *Monist* 77 (1994), 545.

11. Maryanne Wanca-Thibault and Phillip K. Thompkins, "Speaking Like a Man (and a Woman) About Organizational Communication," *Management Communication Quarterly* 11 (1998), 607.

12. Judi Marshall, "Viewing Organizational Communication from a Feminist Perspective: A Critique and Some Offerings," *Communication Yearbook* 16 (1993).

13. Marta B. Calas & Linda Smircich, "From 'the woman's' point of view: Feminist approaches to organizational studies," *Handbook of Organizational Studies*, eds. Stewart R. Clegg, Cynthia Harding & Walter R. Nord (London: Sage, 1996), 219.

14. Jennifer Hamer & Helen Neville, "Revolutionary Black Feminism: Toward a Theory of Unity and Liberation," *The Black Scholar* 28 (1998), 23.

15. Ibid.

16. Lynn Hallstein, "Where Standpoint Stands Now: An Introduction and Commentary," *Women's Studies in Communication* 23 (2000), 3.

17. Ibid.

18. Susan Heckman, "Truth and Method: Feminist Standpoint Theory Revisited," *Signs* 22 (1997), 341.

19. Allen, "Black womanhood and feminist standpoints," 577.

20. Ibid.

21. Bonnie T. Dill, "The Dialectics of Black Womanhood," in *Feminism and Methodology: Social Science Issues*, ed. Sandra Harding (Indiana: Indiana University Press, 1987), 97.

22. Hamer & Neville, "Revolutionary Black Feminism," 23.

23. Clenora Hudson-Weems, *Africana Womanist Literary Theory* (Trenton, NJ: Africa World Press, Inc.), 1.

24. Ibid.

25. Barbara Ransby, "Black Feminism at Twenty-one: Reflections on the Evolution of a National Community," *Signs* 25 (2000), 1218.

26. Patricia Hill Collins, *Black feminist thought: Knowledge, consciousness, and the politics of empowerment* (New York: Routledge, 1991).

27. Allen, "Black womanhood and feminist standpoints."

28. *The Apprentice*, "Meet the Billionaire," NBC, premiere episode aired January 8, 2004, created by Mark Burnett.

29. *The Apprentice*, "Toying with Disaster," NBC, season 2 premiere episode aired September 9, 2004, created by Mark Burnett.

30. *The Apprentice*, "Whopper 101," NBC, season 3 premiere episode aired January 20, 2005, created by Mark Burnett.

31. Dana E. Mastro & Bradley S. Greenberg, "The Portrayal of Racial Minorities on Prime Time Television," *Journal of Broadcasting & Electronic Media* 44 (2000): 690–703.

32. Leith Mullings, "Images, Ideology, and Women of Color," in *Women of Color in U.S. Society*, eds. Maxine Baca Zinn & Bonnie Thornton Dill (Philadelphia: Temple University Press, 1994), 275.

33. Ibid.

34. Dana E. Mastro & Bradley S. Greenberg, "The Portrayal of Racial Minorities on Prime Time Television, 700.

35. "The Status of Women in U.S. Media," Report of the Women's Media Center (2004), accessed August 2015, http://wmc.3cdn.net/6dd3de8ca65852dbd4_fjm6yck9o.pdf.

36. Foss, *Rhetorical Criticism,* 159–160.

37. Ibid. 160.

38. David Carr, "Casting Reality TV, No Longer a Hunch, Becomes a Science," *The New York Times* (March 28, 2004): A1.

39. Orbe, "Constructions of Reality on MTV's *The Real World,* 43.

40. Alicia D. Boisnier, "Race and Women's Identity Development: Distinguishing Between Feminism and Womanism Among Black and White Women," *Sex Roles* 49 (2003), 212.

41. *The Apprentice,* Episode 1, NBC, season 10 premiere episode aired September 16, 2010, created by Mark Burnett.

42. *The Apprentice,* "Respect," NBC, episode 3, season 1, air date January 21, 2004, created by Mark Burnett.

43. *The Apprentice,* "Ice Escapades," NBC, episode 8, season 1, air date February 26, 2004, created by Mark Burnett.

44. *The Apprentice,* "DNA, Heads and the Undead Kitty," NBC, episode 9, season 1, air date March 4, 2004, created by Mark Burnett.

45. bell hooks, *Ain't I a Woman: Black Women and Feminism* (Boston, MA: South End Press, 1981), 85.

46. *The Apprentice,* "Respect," episode 3.

47. *The Apprentice,* "Sex, Lies and Altitude," NBC, episode 2, season 1, air date January 15, 2004, created by Mark Burnett.

48. *The Apprentice,* "Send in the Clowns," NBC, episode 3, season 2, air date September 23, 2004, created by Mark Burnett.

49. *The Apprentice,* "Cruise Control," NBC, episode 5, season 5, air date March 27, 2006, created by Mark Burnett.

50. Gabriella Gutierrez y Muhs, Yolanda Flores Niemann, Carmen G. Gonzalez and Angela P. Harris (editors), *Presumed Incompetent: The Intersections of Race and Class for Women in Academia* (Boulder, CO: The University of Colorado Press, 2012).

51. Valerie Purdie-Vaughns, "Why so few black women are senior managers in 2015," *Fortune Magazine* online (April 22, 2015), accessed August 2015, http://fortune.com/2015/04/22/black-women-leadership-study/.

52. *Celebrity Apprentice,* "Who Stole My Phone?" NBC, episode 6, season 14, air date February 2, 2015, created by Mark Burnett.

53. Mullings, "Images, Ideology, and Women of Color;" and Brenda J. Allen, "Gender, Race, and Communication in Professional Environments," in *Women and Men Communicating: Challenges and Changes,* eds. Laurie P. Arliss and Deborah J. Borisoff (Prospect Heights, IL: Waveland Press, 2000).

54. *MTV.com,* accessed November 2014, http://www.mtv.com/.

55. Carolyn A. Stroman, Bishetta D. Merritt and Paula W. Matabane, "Twenty Years After Kerner: The Portrayal of African Americans on Prime-Time Television." *The Howard Journal of Communications* 2 (1989); Bradley W. Gorham, "Stereotypes in the Media: So What?" *The Howard Journal of Communications* 10 (1999).

56. Hamer & Neville, "Revolutionary Black Feminism," 23.

57. Patricia Hill Collins, "Learning from the outsider within: The sociological significance of Black feminist thought," *Social Problems* 33 (1986), S28.

58. Ibid. S15.

59. "The Status of Women in U.S. Media," Report of the Women's Media Center.

60. Gorham, "Stereotypes in the Media: So What?," 244.

# III

# Portrayals of Black Women as Spouses, Girlfriends and Lovers

# NINE

## Dehumanized and Empowered?

*Black Women, Reality Television, and*
Love and Hip Hop Atlanta

### Patrick Bennett and Rachel Alicia Griffin

In recent years, scripted television has been joined by a more "realistic" look into peoples' lives—reality television. Reality television claims to give viewers an unmediated glimpse into how real people live. The "real-ness" of reality television invokes controversy by providing a voyeuristic and potentially exploitive look into people's lives.[1] As the genre has matured, shows that offer insight into communities that are systemically underrepresented have become common. Indicative of this trend are shows that depict the lives of African Americans and opportunistically exploit representations of black culture for drama, ratings, and profit. One network that has taken considerable advantage of this is VH1—first, with the success of *Flavor of Love*[2] and its spinoffs, then more recently with shows such as *Basketball Wives*[3] and *Love and Hip Hop*.[4] In fact, the excessive amount of fighting among Black women on *Basketball Wives* led to a boycott of the show, which prompted creator Shaunie O'Neal to promise less violence in its next season.[5] Akin to *Basketball Wives*, *Love and Hip Hop Atlanta*[6] exemplifies the trend of exploiting black culture. As members of the black community, we find ourselves both intrigued and troubled by the implications of the show. Capturing the essence of our paradoxical interpretation of *Love and Hip Hop Atlanta*—as one of many reality television shows that simultaneously reproduces and challenges negative stereotypes about blackness—are contradictory headlines such as "The 21 Most Ratchet Women of Black Reality TV,"[7] "How Reality TV has Changed our Daughters,"[8] and "Wealthy Reality Stars Humanize Black Women."[9]

Indicative of its mass popularity, *Love and Hip Hop Atlanta* garners an average rating of 3.3 million viewers per episode compared to the 2.2 million viewers of its predecessor *Love and Hip Hop*.[10] *Love and Hip Hop Atlanta* is especially important to deconstruct because of its popularity and nuanced focus on representations of black femininity, black masculinity, and black relationships under the umbrella of Hip Hop. Each cast member is either an aspiring Hip Hop or R&B artist, an established veteran of the Hip Hop industry, or a key person that influences the lives of the main characters. The significance of Hip Hop to the show cannot be underestimated, since Hip Hop has become one of the central means to deconstruct a wide range of socio-political issues in black America including poverty, violence, imprisonment, and social protest.[11] However, within both Communication and Hip Hop studies, there has been little critical examination of the merger between Hip Hop and reality television, or the implications of these merged representations of black identity, relationships, and culture.

This chapter furthers discourse on Hip Hop, media representation, and how Hip Hop paradoxically represents, influences, and transforms black culture—for better and for worse. To compel a rich analysis, we use Hip Hop Feminism[12] as our theoretical frame, and textual analysis[13] as our method. Embracing the transparency that Hip Hop Feminism calls for, below we offer individual statements on our respective postionalities to contextualize our forthcoming analysis:

*Patrick*: As a viewer of *Love and Hip Hop Atlanta*, I am complicit in the success and continuation of the negative stereotypes of the black community trumpeted on the show and find such imagery troubling. I am interested in critiquing the show because of its popularity within the black community, but I also want to understand my own enjoyment. As a black man, what *Love and Hip Atlanta* represents concerns me in regards to how the show portrays black femininity and black relationships. As a black male Hip Hop fan, Hip Hop Feminism exposes my complicity in the objectification of black females and offers a theoretical means to explore how Hip Hop shapes representations of black culture. Moreover, this chapter is also a personal endeavor to examine myself as a complicit viewer and a political endeavor to explore how black females can access agency in the realm of Hip Hop, despite its considerable inaccessibility to them. Accordingly, I align my views with Peoples[14] and Morgan[15] who discuss how Hip Hop can be a political, social, and cultural tool to reclaim black women's and men's voices.

*Rachel*: As a biracial (black and white) black feminist, my relationship to *Love and Hip Hop Atlanta* is quite different than Patrick's—in fact, it was Patrick who introduced me to the show. To prepare myself to advise his research on the show, I read reviews and watched a few episodes to familiarize myself with his text. While watching the show, my black feminist sensibilities were shocked and offended at the ease with which negative stereotypes about black identity and culture were being reproduced. To be fair, I did see hints of resistance but those hints, to me, were overshadowed by stereotypical inscriptions that "reconstituted and redefined" [16] black femininity and black masculinity in accordance with the dominant imagination. When Patrick asked me to help him reconstruct his research for this important collection, I was hesitant . . . unsure of how much *Love and Hip Hop Atlanta* I could ingest. However, I opted to accept his invitation not only to honor Patrick's commitment to learn how to publish as a young scholar but also because I too have been complicit as a consumer of popular culture that perhaps does more harm than good with regard to how the black community is represented and understood. I also genuinely believe that deconstructing popular culture using marginalized frameworks such as black feminism and Hip Hop Feminism *matters*. Like Patrick, for me, this chapter is both personal and political. Personally, this chapter necessitates reflection on my feeling implicated in the realm of reality television. Politically, this chapter demands—via Hip Hop Feminism in particular—that I, as a black feminist, reflexively acknowledge the potential of Hip Hop to empower black women.

Together, we employ Hip Hop Feminism (HHF) to deconstruct how *Love and Hip Atlanta* paradoxically reinforces misogynistic and stereotypical understandings of women of color. To do so, we first examine the historical and contemporary representations of black women in television. Next, we summarize the plotline of season one and introduce the characters. Then, we define HHF as theory, in relation to black feminist thought and situate textual analysis as our method. Utilizing HHF and textual analysis, we deconstruct *Love and Hip Hop Atlanta* to expose how the show reinforces stereotypical caricatures of black women, while simultaneously depicting agency for black women in Hip Hop. Finally, we offer suggestions for progressive representations of blackness in Hip Hop reality television shows and end our chapter with an articulation of what we learned about ourselves personally and politically in the aftermath of our analysis.

## CRITICAL MEDIA STUDIES &
## REPRESENTATIONS OF BLACK FEMININITY

In the last decade, media scholarship has become increasingly critical by focusing on the mediated reproduction of dominant racial ideologies. Critical media scholars have examined media, specifically film and television, to expose how representations reaffirm whiteness and "post-racial" ideology at the expense of people of color.[17] For example, Joseph (2009)[18] discusses colorblindness in *America's Next Top Model* and argues that Tyra Banks' use of a colorblind philosophy fosters her success as a black female in a white-dominated industry. Similarly attuned to black femininity, Griffin (2014)[19] argues that *Precious: Based on the Novel "Push" by Sapphire* represents black culture through an oppressive white gaze that endorses "post-racial" ideology despite the film's black female protagonist. These examples illustrate how mainstream media's privileging of whiteness and reproduction of racist ideology are masked by the appeal of "post-racialism."

In alignment with the arguments made by Joseph (2009)[20] and Griffin (2014),[21] Black females in media—both the characters and actors who play them—have often been ignored, relegated to the background, and/or confined to the dominant imagination.[22] Historically—as discussed in previous chapters—Black females have been scripted in media as the Mammy, Tragic Mulatto, or Jezebel.[23] More contemporary scripts such as the welfare mother, freak, gold digger, diva, and dyke also negatively permeate representations of Black women's lives.[24] Defined by Stephens and Phillips[25] the welfare mother has children for economic gain; the freak is hypersexual and has little, if any, emotional attachment to her sexual partners; the gold digger uses sex to gain material wealth and social status; the diva is a high maintenance and has a dramatic attitude; and the dyke dislikes men and competes with men for power. Both historical and contemporary scripts dominate representations of black womanhood and are readily found in media today.[26]

The scripted objectification of black womanhood normalized by mainstream media mutes black female voices and undermines black female agency.[27] Boylorn (2008)[28] describes current representations of black femininity as binary in nature meaning that black women are highly educated or uneducated, sexy or ugly, and ambitious or listless. Equally problematic is that negative scripts (e.g., jezebels, gold diggers, mammies, etc.) are more visible in contemporary media and popular culture than positive representations, such as community heroines.[29] Unfortunately, very few television producers have made room for complex black female characters on television, and the overwhelming white and/or male controlled industry has resulted in black women being confined to mostly stereotypical scripts that have, unfortunately, proven to be profitable.[30]

From this vantage point, the commodification of black women on reality television is driven by dominant ideologies steeped in racism and sexism coupled with the exploitive undercurrent of capitalism. More specifically, black females are dehumanized in reality television for ratings and profit, and such representations circulate and strengthen negative perceptions of black femininity. For example, by swapping contestants' real names for fake names, *Flavor of Love*[31] robs black females of the chance to fully express their personhood, forever associating them with nicknames such as Bootz and New York.[32] The removal and replacement of names also signifies the powerlessness that women have on the show and reflects a site of oppressive objectification.[33] Overall, the lack of competing positive representations offered via reality television leaves little space to examine the complexities of black women's lives. As such, the critique of *Love and Hip Hop* and its multiple spinoffs is essential as a means to challenge the prevailing negative imagery. Moving forward, in the next section, the characters and plotline of Season One of *Love and Hip Hop Atlanta* are summarized to center the paradoxical nature of this particular show.

## VIEWING *LOVE AND HIP ATLANTA*

Set in Atlanta, Georgia, *Love and Hip Hop Atlanta* revolves around women of color who are connected to the Hip Hop industry through an affiliation with artists and singers. The executive producer and creator of the show is Mona Scott-Young, a black woman who owns Monami Entertainment. The main characters of the show are Mimi, Stevie J, Joseline, K. Michelle, Karlie, Benzino, Erica, Lil' Scrappy, Rasheeda, and Kirk. All of these main characters identify as black American—with the exception of Joseline, who is Puerto Rican, though often read as black. Mimi is the mother of one of Stevie J's children, and sometimes his girlfriend. Stevie J is a Grammy-award-winning record producer for Bad Boy Records, and is arguably the main antagonist throughout the season. Joseline, a former exotic dancer, aspires to be a Reggaeton rapper and has asked Stevie J to produce her music. Joseline is also Stevie J's mistress. K. Michele is an R & B singer searching for a new record deal with a major record label and dealing with the effects of an abusive relationship. Karlie is an aspiring rapper/singer who is trying to get a record deal and is in a relationship with Benzino. Benzino is a rapper, Hip Hop editor, and former owner of *The Source* magazine. Erica is the former fiancée of Atlanta rapper, Lil' Scrappy, and is the mother of his daughter. Lil' Scrappy appears throughout the season as he and Erica try to mend their relationship, despite his mother's (Mama Dee) objections, and the distracting presence of his friend Shay. Finally Rasheeda, an independent rap artist, appears on the show with her husband Kirk, as they deal with being partners in life and business.

Season One begins with Mimi's discovery of Stevie J's infidelity with Joseline, as Stevie J. attempts to have both women as sexual and life partners. During the season, Joseline becomes pregnant and has an abortion at Stevie J's request, despite her misgivings. After Joseline's abortion and her continued threats toward Mimi, Stevie J, Joseline, and Mimi all go to therapy, which leads to Joseline slapping Stevie J. for lying to her about continuing to live with Mimi. By the end of the season, their love triangle remains unsettled.

Meanwhile, Erica and Lil' Scrappy continue to try to rebuild their relationship, but are conflicted about past issues and the negative influence of Mama Dee on their relationship. Mama Dee thinks Erica is bad for her son and she prefers that he have a relationship with Shay. K. Michelle is trying to restart her career, but becomes upset with Rasheeda when she questions the validity of the abuse K. Michelle suffered in a previous relationship. Karlie leaves her boyfriend Antonio and starts dating Benzino. For the majority of the season Karlie and Benzino's relationship goes well, until she finds out he cheated and ends their relationship.

By comparison to the other couples on the show, Rasheeda and Kirk appear to be the quintessential couple. However, Rasheeda's status as an independent artist, with Kirk as her manager, wears on their marriage. Rasheeda considers leaving Kirk's management for a mainstream management company, to further her career, but decides the business and her marriage are more important than being managed by a label. Then they decide to renew their marriage vows which makes Rasheeda and Kirk the only couple with a happy ending at the conclusion of the first season. The next section examines the origins and commitments of Hip Hop Feminism (HHF) followed by an explanation of how we use HHF to theorize *Love and Hip Hop Atlanta*.

## HIP HOP FEMINISM: A THEORETICAL FRAMEWORK

Hip Hop Feminism can be situated in the trajectory of Third Wave Feminism and Black Feminist Thought (BFT). Situating BFT in relation to the metaphoric waves of feminism, BFT emerged during the second wave and remains relevant to third wave conversations concerning identity politics, power, privilege, oppression, and media representation. BFT was created by Collins (1986)[34] as a response to her perception that black women were largely missing among the theorizations of second wave feminists. Generally speaking, black feminist scholarship is committed to: 1) theorizing black women's unique experiences and perceptions as individuals and members of a marginalized (e.g., via race and gender at minimum) collective, 2) accounting for intersectionality and the matrices of domination, 3) increasing agency and securing empowerment for black women, and 4) creating coalitions among black women and other marginalized groups.[35] Overall, the critical impetus of black feminist scholarship is to center black women's voices and raise critical consciousness about the experiences of black women.[36]

Though BFT importantly places black women's experiences at the forefront, this framework does not often speak to the lives of contemporary black women and their paradoxical love/hate relationships with institutions and cultural phenomenon, such as media, Hip Hop, and reality television. Writers and activists such as Rebecca Walker, Kristal Brent Zook, and Joan Morgan (among others) have troubled the rigid either/or dichotomy that often frames contemporary black women's engagement with feminism. This dichotomy does not typically work when black women engage with and enjoy paradoxical popular culture such as Hip Hop.

Differently from BFT, Hip Hop Feminism (HHF) is concerned with how Hip Hop represents black femininity, deploys black female bodies, and serves as a tool to empower black women.[37] A survey of key HHF works—including Morgan[38] (1999), Pough et. al (2007),[39] and Peoples (2008)[40]—reveals four defining commitments of HHF that include: 1) critiquing misogyny and black female exploitation in the Hip Hop industry, 2) increasing self-definition and agency among black women, 3) providing room for black men in feminist conversations, and 4) leveraging Hip Hop's potential to address contemporary social issues such as Black sexual politics, heterosexism, and classism.[41] Taken together, these commitments underscore the plausibility of Hip Hop serving as a site and source of liberation for black women despite the well-documented problematics of Hip Hop as a site and source of oppression.[42]

Hip Hop Feminism is a more fitting framework to critique *Love and Hip Hop Atlanta* because it underscores the transformative and paradoxical presence of black people in Hip Hop whereas BFT does not as readily embrace the transformative presence of Hip Hop in the lives of Black women in particular. The two HHF commitments that we rely heavily upon are the framework's focus on the misogyny toward and exploitation of black women and its' insistence on increasing self-definition and agency for black women. However, HHF's remaining commitments related to black men and feminism and social justice, albeit to a lesser degree, will also be drawn upon to closely examine *Love and Hip Hop Atlanta*. The research questions guiding our analysis are:

1. What does HHF reveal about Hip Hop in relation to representations of black females and males on reality television?
2. How do black women subvert male privilege in the Hip Hop reality television sphere?

3. Having discussed our theoretical framework, we now turn to textual analysis as the method we employ to deconstruct *Love and Hip
   Hop Atlanta.*

## TEXTUAL ANALYSIS

Drawing upon analytical traditions in multiple disciplines including literature, art, rhetoric, cultural studies, journalism, and cinema,[43] scholars
generally describe textual analysis as a qualitative means to explore sense
making.[44] Offering more refined descriptions, Fürsich (2009)[45] articulates
textual analysis as "a type of qualitative analysis that . . . focuses on the
underlying ideology and cultural assumptions of the text"[46] and McKee
(2003)[47] says "we interpret texts in order to try and obtain a sense of the
ways in which, in particular cultures at particular times, people make
sense of the world around them."[48] Taken together, these descriptions
articulate textual analysis as a method used to deconstruct texts to evaluate how they signify culture and pedagogically influence perceptions. As
such, textual analysis is concerned with both implicit and explicit meaning in popular culture texts such as reality television shows. Guided
closely by Hip Hop Feminism, we employ textual analysis to deconstruct
representations of Black culture in *Love and Hip Hop Atlanta.*

Our analysis[49] of *Love and Hip Hop Atlanta* began with an initial viewing of six of the ten episodes from Season One—episodes four through
nine. These episodes were chosen because they are past the introductory
phase of the series and offer rich content. The initial viewing of these
episodes entailed watching the show to get acquainted with the characters and storylines opposed to taking notes. Guided by HHF, the second
viewing entailed watching to record explicit themes that appeared on the
show. Broadly, these themes included: dysfunctional black relationships,
black dis/empowerment, verbal and emotional abuse, and violence. The
third viewing entailed watching more closely for how black femininity
was represented. Then, each episode was viewed three times in a row—
with 10-minute intermissions between each viewing. This process was
repeated until all of the episodes had been viewed multiple times and
refined themes emerged to narrate the implicit and explicit implications
of the show in accordance with HHF. To shape our analysis, we focus on
our refined themes which included the: (1) misogynistic exploitation of
black women, (2) enactment of black male patriarchy, (3) empowerment
of black women, and (4) use of Hip Hop in alignment with social justice.
To highlight examples of each aforementioned theme, we focused on the
characters' interactions and their confessional spaces. During confessionals, cast members speak directly to the camera about their perceptions of
experiences with other cast members. Overall, the characters' interac-

tions, relationships, and confessions are key to theorizing *Love and Hip Hop Atlanta*'s representation of black culture.

The analysis of black women in reality television that follows is located at the intersections of race, gender, and class. At times, the characters reinforce historical caricatures, scripts, and stereotypes that have problematically confined black people to the dominant imagination throughout the history. In contrast, the characters also reveal the power of love among black women and the potential of Hip Hop to serve as a site and source of empowerment.

### *Analyzing* Love and Hip Hop Atlanta

This section examines *Love and Hip Hop Atlanta* through an HHF lens to critique representations of blackness on reality television. First, we examine misogyny and male privilege in Hip Hop, through the character of Stevie J. in his business and personal relationships with Joseline; as well as the reproduction of male privilege via the character of Mama Dee. Next, we examine Mimi, Joseline, and K. Michelle and their negative reinforcement of black female scripts coupled with an exploration of their agency in relation to sexuality and language. Finally, the overlap between Hip Hop and social justice work is explored via K. Michelle's character.

*"Chalk it Up to Business": Men Up, Women Down*

*Stevie J. and Joseline:* The relationship between Stevie J. and Joseline is characterized by sexual, physical, and emotional control, which is reminiscent of Jackson's (2006)[50] description of the pimp-whore complex. The pimp-whore complex refers to black males controlling black females' minds and bodies for economic gain.[51] Exemplifying this complex, Stevie J. mentions that he will take Joseline back to where he found her—meaning, the strip club. Stevie J. explains, in his response to Joseline threatening not to have sex:

> I'm cool with that. I'm not thirsty for no pussy. I'm thirsty for that bread, know what I'm saying. I'm thirsty for her to make a way for herself, so she ain't gotta hit the club no more and can have her own million dollars. So at the end of the day she'll respect me more and I'm sure I can do whatever I like after that bread come through.[52]

His comments not only objectify Joseline by reducing her to body parts, but also exemplify his belief that she will willingly do whatever he pleases after she reaps the financial benefits of working with Stevie J. In response, Joseline remarks that Stevie J. has no concern for her body or how she feels, but is only concerned with business.

From an HHF perspective, this scene illustrates the commodification of women of color's bodies for industry purposes and also signifies male gain. It is an equation in which money, plus power, equals access to and control over the bodies of women of color. Albeit an incredibly different circumstance, this logic is shockingly similar to slavery ideology and white male slave owners' emphasis on power, respect, and profit.[53] In contemporary society, Stevie J's focus on money—at the sacrifice of Joseline's needs—demonstrates how Hip Hop can be a destructive space that robs agency from women of color. Similar to Fitts's (2008)[54] examination of black women in music videos, women of color are dehumanized and commodified on *Love and Hip Hop Atlanta*.

Later in Season One, as Karlie positions herself to work with Stevie J, the dynamic between Joseline and Stevie J. continues to reflect the pimp-whore complex. Stevie J. wants Karlie and Joseline to work together because it is good for business. Karlie wants Stevie J. to produce her music because she needs a hit single and wants studio time with Stevie J. Stevie J says he can do that for her and makes her perform on the stage to prove her worth and talent. Stevie J. wants Joseline and Karlie to record together, but Joseline does not want them to record together. When she refuses, he stands, looks at her with a serious grin, and tells her "I need you to do this."[55] Joseline responds by saying "No, I work too hard to get where I'm at to just do a song with her."[56] Stevie J. continues to insist that Joseline perform with Karlie for him by saying, "This is about a business, so you put your emotions to the side."[57] Then, Joseline gives in saying, "I'll do a song with her because of you, but only one song . . . (speaking to Karlie) because I respect him and I'm loyal to him."[58] Despite her decision, Joseline continues to protest to Stevie J.; in response to her tears, he tells her to "chalk it up as business, let's do what fuck we got to do, and keep it moving."[59]

Stevie J's embodiment of black masculinity in this scene aligns with Miller-Young's (2008)[60] discussion of black males performing a pimp-masculinity and Jackson's (2006)[61] script of Black males embodying the pimp-whore complex—both of which dehumanize black women from a HHF perspective. Stevie J's insistence on business first reinforces the pimp-whore dynamic that they share and not only mutes Joseline's voice and agency but also negates her emotional needs. In this context, Stevie J. draws upon sexist ideology, male privilege, and his patriarchal status in the industry to control Joseline's career and body. The relationship between Stevie J. and Joseline highlights the hostility and exploitation that women of color can and do experience in Hip Hop. Therefore, Stevie J.'s embodiment of black masculinity can be understood as a conduit for the racist and sexist oppression of women of color that mirrors oppressive ideologies espoused by white men for similar purposes.

*Mama Dee:* Although black women do not systemically benefit from the reproduction of male privilege and misogyny, they can reproduce patriarchal and misogynistic ideologies via Hip Hop reality television. A black woman serving as an agent of sexist ideology can be seen in the character of Mama Dee. As the mother of Lil' Scrappy, Mama Dee is protective of her son's emotions and relationships. For instance, Lil'

Scrappy asks Mama Dee about his situation with Erica and Shay after an emotional meeting with Erica the previous day. Lil' Scrappy explains the possibility that he and Erica will reunite, and Mama Dee responds with "No the hell you didn't. . . . You really think I'm feeling that bitch?"[62] In a confessional, Mama Dee says Lil' Scrappy needs a new woman and spells out "bitch" to explain how she feels about Erica. Mama Dee tells Lil' Scrappy "You ain't ready for a relationship. Keep it real with them. Let them come in and out. Let them know you only in and out, in and out. Do what players do. How do players play? All day, every day."[63]

Watching this particular scene, we were struck by Mama Dee's reinforcement of black males as hypersexual, emotionally uninvolved players. A hip hop feminist perspective exposes Mama Dee's reproduction of the masculine, promiscuous gaze in Hip Hop and dehumanizes black females as objects in the process. This reproduction of sexist ideology limits black women's agency and conceptualizations of black femininity, and confines black men to negative stereotypes. In essence, Mama Dee reduces black women, Erica and Shay in particular, to interchangeable objects for male consumption and pleasure. In the next section, we discuss how self-definition and agency emerge for black women in Hip Hop from an HHF perspective.

## "I'M A BITCH, SO WHAT!": AGENCY, SELF-DEFINITION, AND VOICE IN *LOVE AND HIP HOP ATLANTA*

In Hip Hop, black women have been relentlessly marginalized by black males on multiple fronts ranging from lyrics to music videos to management and ownership.[64] Fostering resistance and empowerment, HHF interrogates Hip Hop to explore the agency that black women can access via Hip Hop to counter their marginalization.[65] This section highlights Mimi and Joseline from *Love and Hip Hop Atlanta* to reveal their paradoxical relationships to Hip Hop and explore how they define themselves apart from the imposition of dominant discourses in the lives of black women. This section also highlights K. Michelle's reinforcement of the Jezebel script and how she, in opposition to the Jezebel, advocates for social justice via Hip Hop.

*Mimi:* Mimi functions paradoxically throughout the first season as an embodiment of the Sapphire script[66] and, on the contrary, as an empowered black woman. Mimi embodies the Sapphire by commonly yelling, using profanity, and expressing anger in her interactions with Stevie J. For example, after discovering Joseline's pregnancy, Mimi lashes out at him. Then, Mimi explicitly refers to Joseline as a "bitch" and emphasizes Stevie J.'s promiscuous irresponsibility referring to his decision to have sex without being mindful of the consequences of his actions. In this scene, she embodies a loud, aggressive posture with her hands moving rapidly, while Stevie J. remains calm with a knowing smirk on his face that communicates disrespect and indifference in response to Mimi. Examining this scene, Mimi can be understood as the Sapphire described by Pough[67] — a Black woman who draws upon abusive language and has the potential for violence.

The antics of Stevie J. cause Mimi great anger and also great anguish. She has been emotionally abused and lied to by him repeatedly. After Stevie J. performs a song for Mimi, he asks her to meet him outside to talk. Mimi begins to cry saying, "I don't think you know how much you hurt me . . . as you managing this one and that one and I'm at home with a baby by myself. You hurt me to the core. I don't think you understand that."[68] Even after this emotional scene, and despite the fact that she did not come with Stevie J., Mimi leaves with him. This scene underscores the emotional pain that black men can inflict on black women and the agency that black women have in their relationships, regarding their decision to leave or stay. To be fair, Mimi does not have complete agency to leave her relationship with Stevie J., since she is still invested emotionally; however, Mimi is financially independent (i.e., she owns a cleaning service) which highlights her access to agency.

Although Mimi embodies the Sapphire, she simultaneously represents a unique embodiment of agency and self-definition. Likewise, although Mimi is manipulated by Stevie J., she also displays self-empowerment. For instance, Mimi drops Stevie J's belongings off at his house, so she could rid herself of his presence. Communicating her anger and anguish, she remarks "You spend more time with that bitch, more than me and your daughter. I don't want to be with a man that's with a bitch every day."[69] Through an HHF lens, Mimi is using her agency to cleanse herself of Stevie J's control and to protect herself and her daughter from his philandering ways. Problematically, her comments reproduce sexism toward Joseline and arguably blame Joseline more so than Stevie J.; however, revealing the complexity of black womanhood that HHF calls for, this scene also exemplifies Mimi's embodiment of strong black womanhood. She is not fully reduced to a Sapphire; rather, she is a strong black woman who stands up for herself and her daughter. Necessitating an even more complex understanding of black womanhood, her strength is also consequential — reaping both benefits and costs. For example, Mimi's repeated usage of the word "bitch" in reference to Joseline, and her breakdown driving away from Stevie J's house indicates the emotional burden of her strength. Morgan (1999)[70] and Pough and Carpenter (2006)[71] situate the strong black woman in relation to Hip Hop and helps us understand how Mimi functions paradoxically. Both Pough and Carpenter state, in reference to provocative Hip Hop artists Lil Kim and Foxy Brown, that their sexual image though not wholly positive, "represent a space of freedom for whatever reason we (Black women) haven't had."[72] Thus, Mimi functions as the simultaneous embodiment of multiple controlling images used to oppress black women such as the Sapphire and liberation. Inspired by Morgan[73] and Carpenter and Pough,[74] Mimi's strength behind her words and direct demeanor demonstrate black women having agency in Hip Hop reality television.

Joseline

Throughout the episodes, the woman who is the most mentally and emotionally abused by Stevie J. is Joseline. Joseline, like Mimi, serves as an example of the paradoxical space that HHF allows women of color to occupy. As previously mentioned, Joseline had an abortion after being pressured by Stevie J. After the abortion, Joseline exerts her sexual agency while talking to Stevie J. by explaining, "If we gon' to be together, we gon' be together. If we not gon' be together we not having no sex, we not doing this, we not doing that."[75] By articulating her sexual agency, Joseline is situated alongside women of color and Hip Hop artists, such as Nicki Minaj and Missy Elliot,[76] who refuse to be sexually defined and/or controlled by men. Like these women, Joseline creates a space where women of color in Hip Hop can express their sexuality and define what they are and are not comfortable with despite the imposition of patriarchal ideology. In response, Stevie J. jokily says, "I'm celibate."[77] To us, his willingness to joke about such a serious matter underscores his disrespect toward, and dehumanization of women of color. This serves as an additional instance in which Stevie J.'s embodiment of black masculinity reproduces and co-signs the racist and sexist oppression of women of color.

Beyond the aforementioned scene, Joseline continues to embody and underscore the complexities of womanhood in Hip Hop. For example, Stevie J. confronts Joseline for texting Mimi vulgar messages and tells her not to ever text her. Joseline responds, "She is a bitch"[78] and Stevie J. says "So what are you?"[79] Joseline explains "I'm a bitch too. I ain't tripping about me being a bitch."[80] Reading this scene through an HHF lens, this statement is both empowering and problematic. First, her use of the word "bitch" as a term of self-definition, reclaims the word from its traditional negative connotation. In this sense, Joseline is creating a space for women of color to use the word in an empowering rather than dehumanizing manner, in that the label does not negatively define her. This is not to say that the usage of "bitch" is unproblematic toward women of color, or women of any color. The freedom to use "bitch," when women of color historically have not had the space to express themselves, is an important issue.[81] Yet, by referring to Mimi as a "bitch," Joseline reinforces an underlying patriarchal ideology that polices all women by, as Collins (2005) explains, "putting women in their place."[82] Thus, on one hand, calling Mimi a "bitch" situates the term in its historical and contemporary oppressive connotation. However, by calling herself a bitch without concern for the patriarchal legacy, Joseline draws upon her agency to self-define. In this context, Joseline depicts herself as a liberated woman who controls her voice and enacts self-definition. Also rendering black womanhood more complex than dominant ideologies allow for.

K. Michelle

Similar to Joseline, examining K. Michelle from an HHF perspective also reveals controlling imagery and the liberating potential of Hip Hop. K. Michelle's embodiment of black femininity often aligns with perceiving black women as Jezebels, defined by Collins as "sexually aggressive women with large sexual appetites."[83] For example, K. Michelle goes on a blind date with an NFL player, where their interaction is dominated by sexual conversation. For example, K. Michelle says "I don't like a lot of drama. A lot of drama is good if it leads to hot sex. . . . I think you're pretty hot and tempting."[84] In this scene, her embodiment of Black femininity aligns with the Jezebel because she is hypersexual in her pursuit of a man and uses sexual innuendo. After additional sexualized conversation, we leave them as they kiss and K. Michelle jumps onto his lap leaving the audience with the interpretation that sex will likely occur.

Despite embodying the Jezebel at times, K. Michelle also illuminates the potential of Hip Hop to function as a vehicle for social justice, which is often a possibility emphasized by Hip Hop feminists.[85] K. Michelle embodies social justice outreach via Hip Hop when she performs for the organization Saving Our Daughters. In a confession directly presented to the audience, K. Michelle explains that Saving Our Daughters is an organization that educates young women about domestic violence. K. Michelle begins her performance in a wedding dress, with a bruised eye and cuts on her lip. Tears flowing throughout the performance, she articulates that the relationship she idealized came in the form of a dream record deal from an industry executive, who also gave her love and affection. Then, she explains the change in their relationship by saying, "The arms that use to wrap me with love, were now bruising, crushing me, and threatening me."[86] K. Michelle concludes her performance with, "As a girl I dreamed of this moment right here, when I would be okay with me, with who I am, and accepting my flaws and everything about me. For all of you, I wish this such moment."[87] This scene ends with K. Michelle during a confessional telling the viewing audience that a burden has been lifted because the performance for Saving Our Daughters helped in her own healing process.

HHF scholars, such as Morgan,[88] Pough,[89] and Durham,[90] view Hip Hop as a revolutionary vehicle to conceptualize black female identity and provide avenues for social justice within the black community. This above-mentioned scene at Saving Our Daughters mirrors the goals of HHF in two ways. First, K. Michele's decision to publicly narrate her story as an R & B singer connected to the realm of Hip Hop potentially helps other young women in similar situations. Exemplifying this possibility in the episode, we see the emotional reactions from audience members, indicating the possible positive effect of her performance. K. Michelle embodies social justice through her performance teaching young black women about domestic violence via her own lived experiences. Secondly, K. Michele implicitly critiques male privilege in the Hip Hop community. Thus, the fact that her abuser is still working in the industry speaks to the power that males continue to have in Hip Hop. Her abuser's ability to maintain his status in the Hip Hop community, despite his abuse of K. Michelle, reflects sexism and the systemically ingrained power of males in Hip Hop. By speaking truth to power, K. Michelle troubles and "talks back"[91] to male privilege in Hip Hop through her mediated performance.

*Friendships and Bonding*: Another progressive aspect of *Love and Hip Hop Atlanta* that surfaces in most episodes is the communal love that the black women share with each other. Despite the arguments on the show, strong black female friendships present an alternative to the stereotypical portrayals that typically center black women in reality television. Two specific examples highlight progressive representations of black female friendships. First, after discovering that Joseline is pregnant by Stevie J., Mimi, K. Michelle, and Mimi's friend Arianne meet over drinks to discuss the news. As Mimi begins to cry and explain the emotional stress that Stevie J. causes her, K. Michelle sheds tears and consoles Mimi. While offering advice, K. Michelle explains "If you want to hurt, you can hurt with me . . . cuz' I've been there and I still have hurt days. You got to hold on being strong. And my heart goes out to you because I'm a single mama just like you."[92] The mutual understanding exchanged between K. Michelle and Mimi highlights how black women love and empathize with each other. Secondly, Erica meets with K. Michelle and Rasheeda to discuss her situation with Lil' Scrappy. Erica explains her break up with Lil' Scrappy after he felt she was not there for him during an asthma attack. Their discussion is characterized by bonding and mutual understanding as well, rather than the vulgar language exchanged between and among black women that is often depicted on the show. For example Rasheeda, in response to the breakup says, "I don't understand it [the break-up] and I know that's got to be killing you."[93]

Conceptualizing the empowering relationships between Black women on the show, Cooper (2012)[94] offers "ratchet feminism" which aligns with HHF. Although the word "ratchet" is primarily associated with black women who are loud, unintelligent and usually hypersexual,[95] Ratchet Feminism refers to speaking against systemic oppression via "ratchtness" through what may be considered loud or ghetto language.[96] Cooper (2012)[97] articulates that although black women, like those featured in *Love and Hip Hop Atlanta*, may be considered ratchet, they provide important insight that exposes sexism in Hip Hop. As such, both Ratchet Feminism and HHF create avenues for the women of *Love and Hip Hop Atlanta* to embody and further feminist ideals through language that is relatable to everyday black women.

## CONCLUSION

This chapter has examined representations of black femininity, and to a lesser degree black masculinity, in *Love and Hip Hop Atlanta* utilizing HHF as a theoretical framework. We used textual analysis to expose dominant scripts and negative stereotypes that are present in this popular reality television show. This chapter extends scholarship focused on representations of blackness and black culture by addressing the unique crossroads between reality television and Hip Hop. Additionally, using HHF allows for more complex representations of black femininity to emerge from the realm of reality television.

Overall, the representations of black females on *Love and Hip Hop Atlanta* reveal the continuing presence of negative imagery that plagues black people on television in general, and in reality TV specifically. Females such as Mimi and K. Michelle embody the Sapphire and the Jezebel. Yet, despite these dominant scripts, *Love and Hip Hop Atlanta* also presents more holistic, positive representations of black females. Viewing *Love and Hip Hop Atlanta* through a HHF lens reveals black women as caring mothers, compassionate friends, and strong, independent women. Secondly, we accounted for black men exerting their male privilege in Hip Hop reality television and how black women subvert male privilege. HHF renders it clear that black males continue to control the careers of black female artists. These personal and professional relationships were characterized by female acquiescence—whether they agreed or not—to male managers and producers. The considerable absence of female management in the industry highlights how Hip Hop remains a male-dominated space that marginalizes women. Centering black women in Hip Hop reality television reveals that black women can, if their individual circumstances allow them to, subvert male privilege through two main avenues. First, black women can exert control over their sexual agency and the means by which they define themselves. Secondly, black women can "talk back"[98] to black men by challenging sexism and demanding control over their bodies and artistry. Reading black women, such as Mimi and K. Michelle, through HHF provides nuanced insight into how black females embody agency in Hip Hop reality television.

As a result of our analysis, we have each contemplated our personal and political growth in different ways and for different reasons:

*Patrick*: As an avid viewer of the show, examining *Love and Hip Hop Atlanta* from an HHF perspective has offered great insight into my enjoyment of the show. As a black male, I enjoy the show because of the dramatic storylines that are presented on screen. Storylines situated around black female drama, instigated by black men, is entertaining to me because of the fighting that occurs among the cast members. However, taking pleasure in black women's drama and fighting troubles me, because in some sense it situates the black female body as abnormal, different, and Other, which further marginalizes their bodies and voices. As a black man, with male privilege, I have the luxury to enjoy black women's drama, without losing anything of consequence. Yet, the mistreatment of black women does implicate black men—including myself—because if black women can be dehumanized then black men, just as easily, can be as well. If black women are being objectified and oppressed, then black males are too. From my perspective, we cannot escape that we are brothers and sisters and that each of us plays a part in our culture. Thus, my enjoyment of the show implicates me in the continued oppression of black women.

Recognizing my complicity has made me question my future viewing of the show, and has also made me contemplate my relationship with feminism, and Hip Hop Feminism in particular. For example, I find myself asking: have I become a feminist? And how does HHF resonate in my own life and practice? This complexity or "intriguing shades of gray"[99] is where I find myself in relation to Hip Hop reality television, feminism, and Hip Hop Feminism. Embracing transparency, I still watch *Love and Hip Hop Atlanta*. Yet my relationship with the show is more of a love/hate relationship, rather than a pure form of escapism. The drama attracts me, but the objectification of women calls me to critique and pulls me out of an entertainment-only stance.

*Rachel:* As a black feminist who too quickly dismisses the progressive potential of reality television, Hip Hop, and Hip Hop reality television, I have learned a great deal by co-authoring this chapter with Patrick and following his lead to allow new knowledge to emerge from unexpected spaces. While I am not an avid viewer of *Love and Hip Hop Atlanta* or any other reality television show, I do fully align with Hip Hop Feminism's insistence on opening up space for black womanhood to be theorized as complex/paradoxical/contradictory. As a black feminist, I believe that doing so for all black women is key—and perhaps even more important are dialogues that do so for highly visible black women to ensure that they are not reduced to stereotypical scripts as if the purpose of their personhood is only to be entertaining. Rather, I believe that all women and all women of color benefit when black women are understood on a spectrum (i.e., beyond binary logics) as compassionate, intellectual, ambitious, *and* entertaining. Yes, a black woman can be angry, ignorant, and lazy—we can breathe truth into stereotypical scripts—and yet it must be understood any black woman, including the characters on the show, is too multi-faceted to be dehumanized and consumed by stereotypical scripts designed to undermine our confidence and potential.

Jointly, we believe that the utilization of HHF as the primary theory for this chapter offers more complex theorizations of representations of blackness in Hip Hop reality television. Since black women are most often presented via stereotypical scripts, they have limited agency to express their voices. This is problematic because black women need representations that underscore the diverse experiences of black women in society. Future directions for analysis of Hip Hop reality television could explore representations of black males, classism, "authentic" blackness, and female beauty in relation to Hip Hop culture. For example, the cast of *Love and Hip Hop Atlanta* were rarely shown working, but they drove expensive cars and lived in large homes, indicating upper-class privilege. This perception, in relation to black culture, is an area for further analysis. We also recommend examining the entire first season of *Love and Hip Hop Atlanta*, coupled with Season Two, to further analyze how privilege and marginalization continue to inform the representations of the characters on the show. Another possibility for future research is to cross-compare representations of blackness among the multiple locations of the show (e.g., New York, Atlanta, Hollywood).

Reality television needs more diverse depictions of black femininity and black relationships that do not solely position black women as loud, violent, or rude. Reality television also needs representations of black relationships as loving and affectionate, rather than manipulative and dysfunctional. From our perspective, a dialogue needs to occur not only among the black community, but within society at large, to address how people of color are explicitly and implicitly damaged via our representations on reality television programs. However, this dialogue should certainly be informed by how such shows simultaneously depict favorable representations that can positively impact our community. A dialogic space that allows for both the critique and celebration of black culture is where we believe there is the most progressive potential for more inclusive and complex representations of blackness.

## NOTES

1. Susan Murray and Laurie Ouellette, *Reality TV: Remaking television culture* (New York, NY: New York University Press, 2009).

2. Abrego, "Flavor of Love."

3. Emerson and O'Neal, "Basketball Wives."

4. Abrahamson and Scott-Young, "Love and Hip Hop Atlanta."

5. Eben Gregory, "Shaunie O'Neal promises less fighting on Basketball Wives," *Hip Hop Weekly*, May 14, 2012, http://www.hiphopweekly.com/2012/05/14/shaunie-

oneal-promises-less-fighting-on-basketball-wives-video; McCorquodale, A. "Basketball Wives gets Massive Boycott against Evelyn Lozada and a movie deal," *Huffington Post*, May 4, 2012, http://www.huffingtonpost.com/2012/05/03/basketball-wives-received_n_1475136.html.

6. Abrahamson and Scott-Young, "Love and Hip Hop Atlanta."

7. Tracy Garraud, "The 21 Most Ratchet women of Black Reality TV," *Vibe*, June 27, 2012, http://www.vibe.com/2012/06/21-most-ratchet-women-black-reality-tv/.

8. Janelle Harris, "How Reality TV has changed our daughters," *The Root*, February 5, 2015, http://www.theroot.com/articles/culture/2015/02/how_reality_tv_has_changed_our_daughters.html.

9. Evette Dionne, "Wealthy Reality Stars Humanize Black Women," *The New York Times*, January 28, 2015, http://www.nytimes.com/roomfordebate/2014/01/16/why-we-like-to-watch-rich-people/wealthy-reality-stars-humanize-black-women.

10. Jonathan Landrum Jr. "Scott Young's 'Love and Hip Hop overcomes backlash,'" *Associated Press*, April 22, 2013, http://tv.yahoo.com/news/scott-youngs-love-and-hip-hop-overcomes-backlash-195627656.html.

11. Michael Eric Dyson, *Know What I Mean?: Reflections on Hip-Hop* (New York, NY: Basic Civitas Books, 2007); Murray Foreman and Michael Anthony Neal, *That's the Joint! The Hip Hop Studies Reader* (New York, NY: Routledge, 2012).

12. Joan Morgan, *When Chickenheads Come Home to Roost: A Hip-Hop Feminist Breaks it Down* (New York, NY: Simon and Schuster, 1999); Gwendolyn D. Pough, "Do the Ladies Run This . . . ?: Some Thoughts on Hip-Hop Feminism," in *Catching a Wave: Reclaiming Feminism for the 21st Century*, eds. Rory Dicker and Alison Piepmeier, 232–243 (Boston, MA: Northeastern University Press, 2003).

13. Bonnie Brennen, *Qualitative Research Methods for Media Studies* (New York, NY: Taylor & Francis, 2012); Alan McKee, *Textual Analysis: A Beginner's Guide* (Thousand Oaks, CA: Sage Publications, 2003).

14. Whitney A. Peoples, "'Under Construction': Identifying Foundations of Hip-Hop Feminism and Exploring Bridges between Black Second-Wave and Hip-Hop Feminisms," *Meridians: Feminism, Race, and Transnationalism* 8 (2008).

15. Morgan, *Home to Roost*.

16. Ronald L. Jackson, *Scripting the Black Masculine Body: Identity, Discourse, and Racial Politics in Popular Media* (New York, NY: State University of New York Press, 2006).

17. Phil Chidester, 2008, "May the Circle Stay Unbroken: Friends, the Presence of Absence, and the Rhetorical Reinforcement of Whiteness," *Critical Studies in Media Communication* 25, no. 2 (2008): 157–174; Jennifer Esposito, What Does Race have to do with Ugly Betty? An Analysis of Privilege and Postracial (?) representations on a Television Sitcom. *Television & New Media, 10,* 521–535; Rachel Alicia Griffin, "Push Ing into Precious: Black Women, Media Representation, and the Glare of the White Supremacist Capitalist Patriarchal Gaze," *Critical Studies in Media Communication* 31, no. 3 (2014): 182–197; Rachel Alicia Griffin, "Problematic Representations of Strategic Whiteness and "Post-Racial" Pedagogy: A Critical Intercultural Reading of The Help," *Journal of International and Intercultural Communication* 8, no. 2 (2015): 147–166; Ralina L. Joseph, "Tyra Banks Is Fat": Reading (Post-)Racism and (Post-)Feminism in the New Millennium," *Critical Studies in Media Communication* 26, no. 3 (2009): 237–254; Davi Johnson Thornton "Psych's Comedic Tale of Black–White Friendship and the Lighthearted Affect of "Post-Race" America," *Critical Studies in Media Communication* 28, no. 5 (2011): 424–149.

18. Joseph, "Tyra Banks."

19. Griffin, "Push Ing into Precious."

20. Joseph, "Tyra Banks."

21. Griffin, "Problematic Representations."

22. Beretta Smith-Shomade, *SHADED LIVES: African-American women and television* (New Brunswick, NJ: Rutgers University Press, 2002); Keli Goff, "There is racism in

reality TV, but not on The Bachelor." *Huffington Post,* June 24, 2012. http://www.huffingtonpost.com/keli-goff/the-bachelor-racism_b_1447859.html.

23. Donald Bogle, *Toms, Coons, Mulattoes, Mammies, and Bucks: An Interpretive History of Blacks in American Films* (New York, NY: Continuum International Publishing Group, 2001); Patricia Hill Collins, *Black Feminist Thought: Knowledge, Consciousness, and the Politics of Empowerment,* 3rd ed. (New York, NY: Routledge, 2009).

24. Collins, *Black Feminist Thought;* Dionne P. Stephens and Layli D. Phillips. "Freaks, Gold Diggers, Divas, and Dykes: The Sociohistorical Development of Adolescent African American Women's Sexual Scripts," *Sexuality and Culture* 7, no. 1 (2003). 3–49.

25. Stephens and Phillips, "Freaks, Gold Diggers."

26. Robin M. Boylorn, "As Seen On TV: An Autoethnographic Reflection on Race and Reality Television," *Critical Studies in Media Communication* 25, no. 4 (2008), 413–433; Collins, *Black Feminist Thought;* Griffin, "Push Ing into Precious"; Griffin, "Problematic Representations."

27. Patricia Hill Collins, *Black Sexual Politics: African Americans, Gender, and the New Racism* (New York, NY: Routledge, 2004); Smith-Shomade, *SHADED LIVES.*

28. Boylorn, "As Seen on TV."

29. Dawnie Walton "Essence image study: Bonus insights," *Essence,* October 7, 2013.http://www.essence.com/2013/10/07/essence-images-study-bonus-insights.

30. Smith-Shomade, *SHADED LIVES.*

31. Abrego, "Flavor of Love."

32. Boylorn, "As Seen on TV."

33. Shannon Campbell and Steve Giannino, "Flaaaavooor-flav: Comic Relief or Super-Coon?" in *Masculinity in the Black Imagination,* edited by Ronald Jackson and Mark Hopson, 103–112 (New York, NY: Peter Lang Publishing, 2011).

34. Patricia Hill Collins, "Learning from the Outsider Within: The Sociological Significance of Black Feminist Thought," *Social Problems* 33, no. 6 (1986): 14–32.

35. Collins, "Learning from the Outsider"; Patricia Hill Collins, "The Social Construction of Black Feminist Thought," *Signs: Journal of Women in Culture and Society* 14, no. 4. (1989): 745–733; Collins, *Black Feminist Thought;* Kimberlè W. Crenshaw "Mapping the Margins: Intersectionality, Identity Politics, and Violence against Women of Color" in *After Identity: A Reader in Law and Culture,* eds. Dan Danielson & Karen Engle, 332–354. (New York, NY: Routledge, 1995); Audre Lorde, *Sister Outsider: Essays and Speeches* (Freedom, CA: Crossing Press, 1984); Kristin Waters, "Some Core Themes of Nineteenth-Century Black Feminism," in *Black Women's Intellectual Traditions: Speaking Their Minds,* eds. Kirsten Waters and Carol Conway, 365–392 (Burlington, VT: University of Vermont Press, 2007).

36. Collins, *Black Feminist Thought.*

37. Aisha Durham, Brittney C. Cooper, and Susana M. Morris, "The Stage Hip-Hop Feminism Built: A New Directions Essay," *Signs: Journal of Women in Culture and Society* 38 (2013); Peoples, "Under Construction"; Gwendolyn D. Pough, *Check It While I Wreck It: Black Womanhood, Hip-Hop Culture, and the Public Sphere* (Boston, MA: Northeastern University Press, 2004).

38. Morgan, *Home to Roost.*

39. Gwendolyn Pough, Elaine Richardson, Aisha Durham, and Rachel Raimist. 2007. *Home Girls Make Some Noise!: Hip Hop Feminism Anthology.* Edited by Gwendolyn D Pough, Elaine Richardson, and Aisha Durham (Mira Loma, CA: Parker Publishing, 2007).

40. Peoples, "Under Construction."

41. Durham, Cooper, and Morris, "The Stage"; Morgan, *Home to Roost*; Peoples, "'Under Construction"; Pough, Richardson, Durham, and Raimist, *Home Girls.*

42. Tricia Rose, *Black Noise: Rap Music and Black Culture in Contemporary America* (Hanover, NH: University Press of New England, 1994); Tricia Rose, *The Hip Hop Wars: What We Talk about When We Talk about Hip Hop—And Why It Matters* (New York, NY: Basic Civitas Books, 2008).

43. Elfriede Fürsich, "In defense of textual analysis: Restoring a challenged method for journalism and media studies." *Journalism Studies, 10*, no. 2 (2009): 238–252; Stuart Hall, "Introduction" in Paper Voices: *The Popular Press and Social Change, 1935–1965,* ed. Anthony Charles H. Smith, 11–24 (London, EN: Chatto and Windus, 1975), Peter Larsen, "Mediated Fiction," in *A Handbook of Media and Communication Research: Qualitative and Quantitative Methodologies,* ed. Klaus Bruhn Jensen, 117–137 (London, EN: Routledge, 2002); Stephen E. Lucas, 1988. "The Renaissance of American Public Address: Text and Context in Rhetorical Criticism," *Quarterly Journal of Speech,* 74 no. 2 (1988): 241–260.

44. Bonnie Brennen, *Qualitative Research Methods for Media Studies* (New York, NY: Taylor & Francis, 2012); McKee, *Textual Analysis.*

45. Fürsich, "In defense of textual analysis."

46. Ibid., 240.

47. McKee, *Textual Analysis.*

48. Ibid. 1.

49. Since this chapter is derived from the first author's culminating research report for his Master's Degree program, our analysis is largely based upon his original analysis of the show.

50. Jackson, *Scripting Black Masculinity.*

51. Ibid.

52. *Love and Hip Hop Atlanta.* "Scrappin." Produced by Brad Abramson and Mona-Scott Young. VH1 Television, July 9, 2012.

53. hooks, bell. *Ain't I a Woman: Black Women and* Feminism (Boston, MA: South End Press). This is not to imply that black men and white men are privileged equally. Rather, it is to illuminate how black men can draw upon their male privilege and reproduce patriarchal ideology at the expense of black women. Doing so of course strengthens racist ideologies that marginalize black women and black men. See Mutua (2006) for a discussion of gendered racism.

54. Mako Fitts. "'Drop It like It's Hot': Culture Industry Laborers and Their Perspectives on Rap Music Video Production." *Meridians: Feminism, Race, Transnationalism* 8, no. 1 (2008): 211–235.

55. *Love and Hip Hop Atlanta.* "No Receipts." Produced by Brad Abramson and Mona-Scott Young. VH1 Television, July 16, 2012.

56. Ibid.

57. Ibid.

58. Ibid.

59. Ibid.

60. Mireille Miller-Young "Hip-Hop Honeys and Da Hustlaz: Black Sexualities in the New Hip-Hop Pornography." *Meridians: Feminism, Race, Transnationalism* 8 no. 1 (2008): 261–292.

61. Jackson, *Scripting Black Masculinity.*

62. *Love and Hip Hop Atlanta.* "Loyalty Card." Produced by Brad Abramson and Mona-Scott Young. VH1 Television, August 6, 2012.

63. Ibid.

64. Pough, "Do the Ladies"; Aisha Durham. "Hip Hop Feminist Studies," *International Journal of Africana Studies, 16*, no. 1 (2010). 117–140.

65. Morgan, *Home to Roost*; Pough, *Check It While I Wreck It.*

66. Collins, *Black Feminist Thought*; Jackson, *Scripting Black Masculinity.*

67. Pough, *Check It While I Wreck It.*

68. *Love and Hip Hop Atlanta.* "Therapy." Produced by Brad Abramson and Mona-Scott Young. VH1 Television, July 30, 2012.

69. *Love and Hip Hop Atlanta,* "No Receipts."

70. Morgan, *Home to Roost.*

71. Faedea Chatard Carpenter and Gwendolyn Pough: An Interview with Gwendolyn Pough. *Callaloo, 29*, no. 3 (2006). 808–814.

72. Ibid., 808.

73. Morgan, *Home to Roost.*

74. Carpenter and Pough, "Gwendolyn Pough."

75. *Love and Hip Hop Atlanta*, "Scrappin."

76. Theresa Renee White, "Missy "Misdemeanor," Elliott and Nicki Minaj: Fashion-istin' Black Female Sexuality in Hip-Hop Culture—Girl Power or Overpowered?" *Journal of Black Studies* 44, no. 6 (2013): 607–626.

77. *Love and Hip Hop Atlanta*, "Scrappin."

78. *Love and Hip Hop Atlanta.* "No Apologies." Produced by Brad Abramson and Mona-Scott Young. VH1 Television, July 23, 2012.

79. Ibid.

80. Ibid.

81. Carpenter and Pough, "Gwendolyn Pough."

82. Collins, *Black Sexual Politics*, 121.

83. Collins, *Black Feminist Thought*, 88.

84. *Love and Hip Hop Atlanta*, "Therapy."

85. Durham, "Hip Hop Feminist Studies"; Peoples, "Under Construction"; Pough, *Check It While I Wreck It.*

86. *Love and Hip Hop Atlanta*, "Loyalty Card."

87. Ibid.

88. Morgan, *Home to Roost.*

89. Pough, *Check It While I Wreck It.*

90. Durham, "Hip Hop Feminist Studies."

91. hooks, *Talking Back*, 9.

92. *Love and Hip Hop Atlanta*, "Scrappin."

93. *Love and Hip Hop Atlanta*, "No Receipts."

94. Brittany Cooper "Ratchet Feminism," *Crunk Feminist Collective*, August 14, 2012. http://www.crunkfeministcollective.com/2012/08/14/ratchet-feminism.

95. Lewis Heidi, "Exhuming the Ratchet before its buried," *The Feminist Wire*, January 7, 2013. http://thefeministwire.com/2013/01/exhuming-the-ratchet-before-its-buried/.

96. Cooper, "Ratchet Feminism."

97. Ibid.

98. hooks, *Talking Back*, 9.

99. Morgan, *Home to Roost*, 62.

# TEN

# The "Down Ass Bitch" in the Reality Television Show *Love and Hip Hop*

*The Image of the Enduring Black Woman and Her Unwavering Support of the Black Man*

## Antwanisha Alameen-Shavers

Within Spoken Soul, better known as Ebonics, the term *down* can be used as an adjective to describe a person that willingly yields a tremendous amount of support to another person. The "Down Ass Bitch" (DAB) is a controlling image of the black woman that calls for her unwavering support of the black man, even when it is pernicious to her best interest. In fact, we can see this in the black community on many levels: (1) from black women faithfully waiting years for men to be released from prison; (2) hiding domestic abuse or rape at the hands of black men for the sake of protecting the race; or (3) sexually exploiting our bodies for the financial benefit of black men. However, what is most interesting about this particular stereotype of the black woman being "down" for her man is that this is not an expectation that is asked of the black man. It is this author's contention that the "Down Ass Bitch" is obsequious to the powers of black men—though she is portrayed as being strong, aggressive, and assertive. Essentially, the "Down Ass Bitch," a highly celebrated image in the black community, is the black version of the submissive white woman, the Eurocentric construction of the idealized womanhood. Various controlling images of black womanhood—such as the mammy, the jezebel, and the welfare queen—served as justifications for the oppression of black women and have been discussed significantly by scholars.[1]

However, what seems to be missing from the literature is an in-depth analysis of the DAB stereotype. This perception has become a dominant image of black women in several popular reality television shows, explicitly the VH1 series *Love and Hip Hop*—both the original show in New York in 2011, and the spin off in Atlanta in 2012. This chapter analyzes the DAB stereotype in several characters on the reality show, with the aim of interrogating the implicit and explicit messages sent to the larger public about black womanhood.

## WHITE PATRIARCHY AND WHITE WOMANHOOD

African American culture and identity has been shaped by many factors that affect how we organize our communities, interact with one another, and how we behave as individuals. Though a significant amount of our cultural mores, idioms, and aesthetics can be attributed to our African inheritance, many other aspects have been influenced by the Eurocentric worldview. It is reasonable that after being subjected to four hundred years of European oppression, a significant number of African Americans would internalize aspects of European thought and culture. Some individuals even embrace it as "'normal,' 'natural,' or even worse, 'ideal.'"[2] One aspect of European culture that has been heavily absorbed by the African American community is European patriarchy.

Within the European worldview, human difference is categorized as being opposed to and opposite of each other, such as man/woman, white/black, reason/emotion etc., with the latter of each pair being inferior.[3] Women are reduced to their bodies, seen as weak and emotional, while men are of the mind and are characterized as rational and logical.[4] As a result, the categorical concepts such as man and woman or black and white have Western understandings attached to each that function to limit, control, and oppress women and people of color. This type of thinking is the foundation of the United States of America and is implicit in every aspect of life. Mark Kann (1999) states that the "practice of male domination and female subordination was traditional. It was embedded in the English laws and customs that governed British Americans."[5] White patriarchy was the controlling system of America's governance from its inception. Racial and gender hierarchies were built on the purported ideology that white women, African people, and the Indigenous were biologically inferior to white men. For example, white men were given complete legal authority over their wives. As legal patriarchs, men had total "domination of women in family life, religion, culture, economics, society and politics."[6]

As a White patriarchal society, the United States was controlled by and centered on white men, which granted institutional privilege to white men of all classes.[7] Once a white woman married, her identity was replaced with her husband and she was expected to be loyal and dependent. Her intelligence was not considered and was often overlooked, even if she "managed a large family, ran a complex household, farm or business."[8] Under the control of the white patriarch, the white wife did not have her own thoughts, but it was presumed that her thoughts, desires, and ideas were the same as her husband, or that she simply lacked the ability to have independent thinking due to her biological weakness. White women that did not marry were criticized by the society for being lascivious, evil, or unfeminine. Despite the inequality that came with marriage, many white women married in order to escape public shaming, gain economic security, and to procreate.

White men were indoctrinated with ideas about manhood that made many have a strong distrust and hate of women. Most importantly, white men feared that they would behave like women or become subdued by a woman's sexuality. "Real" manhood could only be achieved through establishing independence, maintaining self-control, ridding one's self of purported feminine qualities—such as dependency—and lastly, ruling over wives and children.[9] Similarly, white women were also restrained by a set of requirements that allowed them to be respected and viewed as "real" women. White women were encouraged to be honest, caring, gentle, modest, and loyal[10] as well as adhere to other virtues such as "piety, purity, submissiveness, and domesticity."[11] White men believed that white women could not take care of their families, defend themselves or protect the country without their help. The supposed innate dependency exhibited by white women was used as justification for white men to rule over them and to dictate the direction of the country. It was also presumed that the fulfillment of white women was "based on their *cheerful willingness to render obedience* to loving men as well as on their maternal desire to bear men's children."[12] In consequence, white female embodiment was established on obsequiousness, loyalty and diffidence. White patriarchy was paramount to how white men accessed manhood, enacted white male supremacy, and controlled white women.

## EXPLOITIVE IDEALS AND IMAGES OF BLACK WOMANHOOD

White patriarchy or white male supremacy, as system of governance in politics and culture dictated the lives of white women, as well as the lives of black men and black women. Whereas white women were considered the legal dependents of their white husbands, black people, on the other hand, were enslaved; seen as legal property of white male enslavers and deemed as nonhuman. Black women were denied access to "real" womanhood status because they were reduced to animals, whose sole purpose was to produce labor for white enslavers. In comparison to the traditional roles of white women during the period of enslavement, black women were rendered genderless, because they were made to work just as hard as enslaved black men.[13] Patricia Hill Collins contends that black women's oppression is characterized through three interdependent dimensions: the exploitation of their labor, the denial of political rights routinely granted to white male citizens, and controlling images that have been "attached to black women . . . to justify [their] oppression."[14] Such images or characteristics associated with black women—as described in previous chapters—have served as rational for their unjust treatment in American society, but it has also been used to silence their voice. Black women have not been able to control their own image or create a functional womanhood for their own benefit, but rather black womanhood has been historically fabricated by the white dominant society—and in some cases even by black men. However, black women are not without fault, given that a significant number of them have internalized these exploitive ideals and have used various controlling images as the barometer of their personhood. Exploitative images of Black womanhood have been generated through popular media, such as music, film, television, and print news. Although most of the media outlets that disseminate exploitative images of black women have been controlled by the white dominant power structure, some ideals of black womanhood have been crystalized through the Hip-Hop culture—dominated by black men— namely the "Down Ass Bitch" and "Ride or Die Chick" image. In order to fully grasp the historical trajectory of the DAB exploitive ideal, a brief synopsis of past exploitive ideals and images of black women will be discussed.

## THE MAMMY

During enslavement, black women and black men were subjected to the worse conditions imaginable. Their humanity was not their own, but rather it was controlled by white enslavers for the economic, social, and political advancement of America. Enslaved Africans did not control their bodies physically or sexually. Black people were made to work from sun up to sun down until they were too old to produce labor for their enslavers,[15] and they were forced to breed children to add to their enslaver's labor force.[16] Black women were relentlessly raped by white male enslavers. This viscous and inhuman treatment of a group of people for more than 200 years caused a great dilemma for the dominant white society. How could a group of people subject another group of people to a system so devilish and barbaric? Instead of critically addressing this question, white America attempted to revise history, so that their image went untainted.[17] Consequentially, the image of the mammy was carefully constructed to eradicate any notions that the enslavement of African men and women was short of hell itself. The mammy was depicted as a jolly, faithful and obedient servant[18] who worked for a kind and warm white family. She was portrayed as big and overweight with a dark complexion so that she was not seen as physically more attractive than the white mistress of the home. She was asexual and lacked any feminine qualities that would suggest that she would be desirable by the white patriarch. The mammy possessed "no personal needs or desires" of her own but rather she was completely devoted to loving and caring for her white family.[19] In the movie *Imitation of Life*,[20] the mammy literally gives her life to serving her white female boss. She rubs her feet, listens to her ails, takes care of her white daughter and even when she becomes financially secure enough to leave, the mammy preferred to stay to spend her last days as a servant. Her devotion and love for the white family was so deep that she would not only sacrifice her own life to take care of them, but she also elevated them above her own black children and family.[21]

The mammy image eased the tensions or guilt felt by whites about enslavement. By showing a happy black woman that was eager to serve white families, the discussion of human exploitation was muted. The mammy image justified the oppression of black women by keeping a disproportionate amount of them in low paying jobs, which served as another way to abuse their labor and control their life chances. Collins (2000) argues that "White families in both the middle class and working class were able to maintain their class position because they used black women domestic workers as a source of cheap labor while black families were constricted to poverty."[22] White women were discouraged from working domestic jobs because they were associated with black servants. When a white family had to choose the race of their domestic workers, they would most likely choose a black woman because she so-called looked the part.[23] Thus, black womanhood became synonymous with submission and an unwavering commitment to loving others, even those that played an active role in their exploitation.

The mammy exploitive ideal was used by popular media to silence black women and their actual experience as slaves and as domestic workers. Melissa Harris-Perry (2011) succinctly expresses the reality of black women that were enslaved:

> Enslaved women working as domestic servants in Southern plantations were taken from their families and forced to nurse white babies while their own infants subsisted on sugar water. They were not voluntary members of the enslaver's family; they were women laboring under coercion and the constant threat of physical and sexual violence. They had no enforceable authority over their white charges and could not even resist the sale and exploitation of their own children. Domestic servants often were not grandmotherly types but teenagers or very young women. It was white supremacist imagination that remembered these powerless, coerced slave girls as soothing, comfortable, consenting women.[24]

The controlling image of the mammy was one of the earliest images that required black women to self-sacrifice and place the needs of others above their own. It was the first exploitive ideal that demanded black women's unwavering love, devotion, and support even though they received nothing in return from such arrangement. While the mammy image was used to hide the oppression of black women, other images such as the black matriarch, was created to blame black women for oppression inflicted upon them.

## THE BLACK MATRIARCH

During Lyndon B. Johnson's presidency, the War on Poverty was launched in order to address the high rate of Americans living in extreme poverty. Daniel Patrick Moynihan was hired to conduct a thorough investigation of the issues that caused poverty in the black community. Instead of pinpointing racism and discrimination as the culprits, Moynihan concluded that the main issue was the deterioration of the black family structure and the black community as a whole.[25] He argued that there were too many black men unemployed, which left a significant number of them unable to run their households. Instead, black women were the head of household—*clearly* a dysfunctional arrangement. He further contended that black men needed "to strut" so that they can feel valuable and important to the black family structure. Moynihan recommended that "the government should not rest until every able-bodied Negro man was working even if this meant that some women's jobs had to be redesigned to enable men to fulfill them."[26] Where is the logic in taking a job that pays little to nothing and giving it to another person just so that it looks as if he is contributing? Undoubtedly, Moynihan's report had many holes and left many questions unanswered. At the heart of his analysis was the idea that somehow black women were to blame for black poverty because they had all the jobs, which allowed them to rule over men and children. The fact that black women were being economically exploited, earned less than Black men and White women on average was overlooked.[27] Paula Gidding (1984) further argues that Moynihan's conclusion suggests, "The black family stability could be achieved only if black men could 'strut,' even, if need be, at the *expense of [black] women*."[28] Once again, black women and their struggles were pushed to the background and disregarded in order to address the needs of others. The image of the black matriarch removed responsibility from the government and redirected it towards black women that allegedly refused to allow black men to rule in their households. The black matriarch was therefore seen as a bad mother that failed to fulfill her womanly duties by staying home and taking care of children while her man worked outside the home. She essentially denied him access to "real" manhood by making him dependent on her as opposed to the reverse—*clearly* a breach to the *optimal* male-female arrangement. Patricia Hill Collins (2000) argues that "the image of the black matriarch serves as a powerful symbol for both black and white women of what can go wrong if white patriarchal power is challenged."[29] In this case, black women were isolated, demonized, and held liable for the demise of the black family and the black community; a tactic to keep them in line and to force them to adhere to the traditional patriarchal family structure. Although the black woman was labeled the "bad black mother" by the white dominant society through the black matriarch image, conversely she was placed on a pedestal in her community for being a Super Strong Black Mother, an insidious *honor* at best.

## THE SUPER STRONG BLACK MOTHER

The Super Strong Black Mother exploitive ideal, unlike the black matriarch image of black women, seemingly celebrates black women and their work as mothers, but does more damage than good. The Super Strong Black Mother is applauded for raising children alone, working several jobs, and coming home to tend to household chores. She is praised for her self-sacrifice and devotion to caring for and loving her family, especially in less than ideal situations such as poverty. The black woman is encouraged to be a strong black mother even at the expense of her own mental and physical health. Due to the normalcy of the Super Strong Black Mother in the black community,[30] black women that do not fit this ideal are often labeled bad mothers—even when their conduct is identical to men that are not deemed as bad fathers. Collins asserts that in order for black women to "remain on their pedestal" they "must continue to place their needs behind those of everyone else, especially their sons."[31] Tupac's classic rap song, "Dear Mama,"[32] epitomizes the love and respect of the Super Strong Black mother exploitive ideal, as the rapper reminisces about the late hours his mother worked, yet still made sure to make hot meals for her children. And he rapped about the many challenges of raising children as a single black mother.

Tupac expresses his appreciation for his mother and the sacrifices that she was forced to make alone, but he fails to acknowledge his mother's individual suffering. The Super Strong Mother exploitive ideal asks black women to put others before themselves without question. Their desires and needs are insignificant. If this is a healthy expectation, why is this ideal not placed on black men? Why is self-sacrificing for your children a norm that is limited to black women? In the context of white patriarchy and the controlling standards placed on white women, we can begin to see how the African American community has been greatly influenced by Eurocentric thinking. The celebration of the Super Strong Black Mother by black male rappers can be quite perplexing since simultaneously some of their songs reduce black women to lascivious, sexually wanton animals. Nevertheless, black women that acquiesce to the various demands of black male rappers are described as ideal and are highly sought after.

## THE "DOWN ASS BITCH"/THE RIDE OR DIE CHICK

The image of the enduring black woman and her unwavering support of the black man was clearly defined by two Hip Hop artists—The Lox and Ja Rule. The Hip Hop group, The Lox, released a song entitled "Ryde or Die Chick" that described the ideal woman they required.[33] She was to be sexually attractive with a fat ass, fashionably dressed, and willing to do whatever for her man. She needed to be willing to have sex with all of her man's friends if he requested, engage in illegal activities—such as swiping fake credit cards, smuggling drugs, and supplying him with weed. She also was to be loyal and committed to her man so much that she would kill for him. Jadakiss, a member of The Lox and the sole rapper on the song, rapped about his power over a woman, who he could force to do anything he instructed her to do. Furthermore, in the song, he reduced the woman to a whore[34] demonstrating that the Ride or Die Chick was appreciated, but not highly respected. The definition provided by the Urbandictionary.com states that the Ride or Die chick is, "a chick that ain't afraid to be *down* [Emphasis added] with her man; she'll do anything her man needs her to do."[35] The Down Ass Bitch exploitive ideal is synonymous with the "Ride or Die chick" image. Ja Rule articulates the characteristics of such a woman in his song entitled, "Down Ass Bitch" featuring Charli Baltimore, an African American female rapper. Ja Rule states that the Down Ass Bitch must kill for him, live for him, die for him, comfort him, love him, have his back, protect his name and shoot at the police if necessary.[36]

The DAB was also expected to take care of his kids, cook for him, serve jail time for him, and to lease her body sexually for his economic gain. According to the Urbandictionary.com, the Ride or Die/Down Ass Bitch exploitive ideal was a woman that did the following:

> A female that ain't 'fraid of going to jail for her man. . . . Never rats him out and takes it all for him. . . . Is down for anything will scrap for him no matter how big the mofo is. . . . Is ready to go to whaeva lengths she has to ta make sure food is on the table . . . strip, sell . . . [you] name it. . . . Cleanz and cooks for him and takes care of the fam and lets no one come between what they have she would even kill for him.[37]

The image of the DAB falls in line with other exploitive ideals of black womanhood, such as the Mammy and the Super Strong Black Mother, because it demands that the black woman place the needs of others before her own, even when such actions are inimical to her well-being. As the DAB, the black woman is expected to serve prison time for her partner's illegal exploits, remain in a monogamous relationship with her partner when he is imprisoned for a lengthy amount of time, and love him unconditionally despite whether his actions are egregious. Much like the attributes that enveloped white womanhood, the DAB's primary features were also founded on loyalty, submission and self-denial. Under societal constraints and requirements, the black woman is either catering to the needs of the white family, the black family, or in this case, the black man—but never her own. The black woman is treated as the "mule of the world" and she is only appreciated when she is laboring, giving to someone else, or being sexually controlled.[38] Similar to her enslaved ancestors, the black woman's body is a tool that serves to sexually, economically, and emotionally benefit the person she is "down" for. As Ja Rule iterates, the DAB must live for him and die for him. As the DAB, the black woman is a silent participant in the black male's patriarchal fantasy of what a "real" woman should be. If she is not *down* for her man, she is criticized for not being understanding and supportive of him. Similar to the black matriarch, the black woman that refuses to sacrifice and do whatever her man requires, is culpable for breaking up her family and denying her kids a father. Her unwillingness to sacrifice her personal needs is seen as irresponsible and irrational especially when she has children with him. Many black women find themselves subjected to the DAB exploitive ideal even when they should question its validity. The reality television show *Love and Hip Hop* has become a popular median by which the DAB image is disseminated and is central to the identity of several black female cast members.

## METHODOLOGY

An in-depth content analysis of seasons one through four of *Love and Hip Hop*—set in New York—was conducted to observe the ways in which the DAB image was displayed in various characters. Key aspects associated with the DAB exploitive ideal was used as the barometer to determine if the stereotype in question was being projected in a given character. Extensive data was gathered from each cast member that fit into the DAB model; and written into short comprehensive storylines that specifically illuminates incidents or situations aligned with the DAB exploitive ideal. A separate content analysis of seasons 1–2 of *Love and Hip Hop-Atlanta*, the spin-off of *Love and Hip Hop*, was conducted in order to access the significance of the stereotype in the subsequent show.

## AN ANALYSIS OF VH1'S SERIES *LOVE AND HIP HOP*

The reality television show *Love and Hip Hop* first premiered on VH1, March 6, 2011, and quickly became one of the networks highest rated shows. The reality show followed the lives of several women involved or affiliated with the Hip Hop industry. As the identity of the cast members were outlined in the first season, it was evident that most of the all-female cast was either an ex-girlfriend or a current girlfriend of a former-ly popular rapper. Only one female cast member was actually pursuing a career as a Hip-Hop artist, while the others seem to lack an individual identity outside of their former or current male partners.

Emily was part Puerto Rican and part Dominican. She was a clothing stylist most known for her relationship with black male hip-hop artist Fabulous. Emily had been in an eight year relationship with Fabulous, who often is quoted as saying he was "single as a dollar bill."[39] They shared one child and also lived together. She repeatedly expressed her discontent with how he treated their relationship, particularly in public. Fabulous avoided walking on the red carpet with his girlfriend, because he associated public events with his work and often did not mention that he was in a relationship. Fabulous kept his relationship hidden from the public eye and also attempted to keep Emily hidden as well. According to Emily, he did not want her to attend parties with professional football or basketball players, because he believed such actions to be unmotherly. Throughout the first season, Emily is continuously reminded by cast member Olivia that her baby's father never claims her and avoids show-ing her in public. The accusations are used as evidence of his lack of love for her; and they challenge the validity of their relationship. By season two, Emily moves out of their home to establish her own residence, in hopes to gain a new level of respect from her now ex-boyfriend Fabulous. However, Emily is jolted with new information from a fellow cast mem-ber that her former boyfriend had sex with her two years prior—the same time Emily was pregnant with his son. Fed up with his actions, Emily seemingly embraces her new life without Fabulous by throwing a "mov-ing on" party to celebrate singlehood. Soon, however, we learn that she is struggling with the reality of being without him and is contemplating reentering the relationship. Emily states, "I'm not going to run back to him, there has to be some big changes but I'm also not going to give up hope." She continues by stating, "I think the problem that I had in my relationship with him is that I was always trying to *be down*, like I'm always there for him."[40]

Since Emily started dating Fabulous when she was twenty-one years old, she attributed her actions to her youth. However, according to her, as a thirty-year-old woman, she demanded and expected more from her child's father. When Emily decided that she would no longer function as his paramour, she was met with much resistance from other women that encouraged her to remain as his DAB. She was advised by her female friend, Winter, to remain with Fabulous despite her issues with him. Winter claimed that Fabulous was "a good guy" who "had a great heart" but he did not want anyone to see that side of him. Winter also claimed he was "going to come around" but Emily needed to be patient. She continued by questioning why Emily would give up on him after nine years, and stated "You know who he is so you knew what you were getting yourself into, you put up with him for nine years so why give up now? . . . You going to have to deal with whatever comes with it, I say *ride it out*."[41] Emily was expected to stay loyal and committed to rapper Fabulous after he had cheated on her and refused to acknowledge their relationship in public. Though Emily was not getting her primary needs met in the relationship, she was strongly encouraged to stay *down*.

Chrissy, an African American female cast member, much like Emily, was involved in a six-year relationship with rapper Jim Jones. Their relationship also had its issues. Chrissy's main problem was that their relationship lacked growth. They were not approaching marriage, had no children and Jim Jones seemed to be content with it all. Eventually, Chrissy decided to propose to Jim to get the ball moving in their stagnant relationship. Chrissy's assertive, unorthodox approach to fixing her relationship did not win the approval of Jim Jones's mother, Mama Jones. A feud ensued between Chrissy and her man's mother that proved to be stressful for Jim Jones and taxing on the relationships held with both women. Mama Jones was displeased with not being informed that Chrissy planned to propose to her son. Mama Jones questioned Chrissy about what her son was getting from the engagement because Chrissy has yet to give him children. Mama Jones, framed as the Super Strong Black Mother, was defending her son's right to string Chrissy along in a six-year relationship without a real commitment by chastising her for demanding one. Mama Jones also demanded grandchildren from Chrissy even though her son, Jim Jones, had yet to seriously consider marriage. Chrissy's lack of children with Jim Jones resulted in her diminished position as his DAB from Mama Jones' perspective. The show illuminated what can occur when you cross a Super Strong Black Mother and a DAB; an intense battle to prove who can be the most "down." Chrissy had a clear understanding of what her position entailed as a DAB. She stated "if you sign up for certain things, certain things come with the territory . . . but respect is never something that's up for question."[42] By season two, Chrissy had truly proved herself as the DAB by fighting other cast members on her man's behalf and protecting his name when people attempted to defame it. Perhaps Chrissy's efforts to be the most "down" were successful since she eventually received the engagement proposal from Jim Jones she so desired.

Yandy, an African American female cast member found herself being framed as the DAB by season three of *Love and Hip Hop*. Yandy entered the cast during season two, as Jim Jones' manager. She was young, career oriented and focused. Unlike the other cast members, she actually was connected to the hip hop industry through her own endeavors, as opposed to through a third party. By season three, however, the main focus in Yandy's story line was her relationship with her man, Mendeecee, an African American male. By the start of season three, it's clear that Mendeecee is not without flaws and in some cases his actions even read as irresponsible. Nevertheless, Yandy's frustration with Mendeecee did not outweigh her devotion to him. After a six year on and off relationship, Mendeecee proposes to Yandy on the show, stating that he was ready to marry her after she had been by his side through all his mistakes and up and downs. However, this fairytale ending was quickly interrupted when he was forced to turn himself in to the FBI for charges—unbeknownst to the viewers. Mona Scott, the producer of the reality show, asked Yandy "Are you prepared to wait as long as it takes?" Yandy quickly replied without hesitation, "Absolutely!"[43] Mona Scott encouraged Yandy to put herself first in this less than ideal situation. Yandy decided to stay "down" for her man by not only raising their son alone, but also taking care of his son from a previous relationship part time. Yandy's loyalty to her man can be seen as admirable, but in the context of the exploitive ideals of black womanhood, it is often a requirement that many cannot escape.

Kimbella, part black and white, first entered the cast of *Love and Hip Hop* in season two. She, like other cast members, was involved in a relationship with a former popular rapper, Juelz Santana. Kimbella was also a model and the mother of two children by Santana. Her two year relationship with Santana was not without issue, but she was committed to making it work in order to keep her family together. During one episode, Kimbella was driven off the edge when a cast member alluded to Santana being involved with other women. Kimbella immediately exculpated Santana of any wrongdoing. She defended her man's name by physically attacking his accuser. She exclaimed, "Don't ever in your life talk about me and my man . . . you don't know nothing about us . . . or else you gonna get a piece of that Kimbella I always warn everybody about."[44] Kimbella realized that she was in fact suffering from deep rooted issues that stemmed from her relationship with her mother, a white woman that devoted her life to caring for her black man, Kimbella's father. According to Kimbella, her mother endured a lot from her father. He often cheated on her mother; lost his money in gambling exploits, leaving her mother to pay all the bills alone, which placed a significant amount of stress and anguish on Kimbella's mother. At one point, her mother even considered suicide. Kimbella stated "my mom just invested everything into her relationship with my dad than she had with raising her children."[45] She also claimed that her mother did not provide her with guidance or relationship advice which Kimbella accredits as the reason she herself entered into so many bad relationships with men.[46] In order to justify her behavior, Kimbella's mother explained, "If you love a man you go through a lot."[47] Kimbella's desire to stay in her relationship with her man, Santana, despite his behavior can be traced back to her mother who laid the groundwork for being the DAB at any cost.

Tahiry, an Afro-Dominican female cast member, model and former girlfriend of Joe Budden—a popular rapper from the early 2000s—claim to the show was being the retired DAB. The first episode of *Love and Hip Hop* season three, the audience is introduced to the scars still left from Tahiry's past relationship with Budden. Joe Budden attempts to persuade Tahiry to be his friend, even though he is in a relationship with another woman. Tahiry states that her "life no longer revolves around Joe" and he needed to rely on his current girlfriend to be there for him. Tahiry was sent into an emotional rage after Joe Budden insinuated that she was being selfish not to agree to his request: "I was your fucking backbone, I'm tired of being taken advantage of. . . . You don't even know what giving is mother fucka because I gave you everything I fucking had. . . . I was your fucking backbone, I held you fucking down, and you gonna tell me the I don't know how to give? I do. I gave it all and I gave you all!"[48] Tahiry had become the scorned DAB; while Joe Budden's much younger, 20-year-old girlfriend, Kaylin, was proving herself to be his new DAB. Kaylin told Tahiry during a verbal altercation, "I've been the one holding us *down*. I've been holding us *down* making sure we are good and that we are clean . . . you haven't been doing shit!"[49] Kaylin was referring to her efforts to help Joe Budden stay off drugs after his recent relapse. As the new DAB, Kaylen was unbothered that Joe wanted to remain friends with his pervious girlfriend of five years, but soon her "downness" was tested when he told her that he was going on a vacation with Tahiry to see if he still had feelings for her. Upon his return, he told Kaylin that he still was in love with Tahiry and no longer wanted to be in a relationship with her. Kaylin responded with, "I've been sticking by your side and it's basically like a slap in the face."[50] At the start of season four, Tahiry and Joe had attempted to take a second run at their relationship. Soon, their relationship ended after Tahiry found a strand of hair from another woman in their bed. Tahiry refused to ignore what she believed was infidelity. She told Joe Budden that after ten years of being in each other's lives, she had made him a priority when he had only made her an option. In efforts to get her back, Joe proposed to Tahiry later in the season, but she declined because she felt that he had not actually done any real work to change. On the reunion show, Yandy is shown clapping as they reviewed clips of Joe proposing to Tahiry. Obviously, the DAB dream is to become the wife of the man that she has devoted her life to. Tahiry's actions were quite curious to the average DAB. Joe claimed that Tahiry left him at "thick" and that she was a runner. From Joe's perspective, she had not been "down" enough. Tahiry had officially given up her reign as the DAB.

Tara, an African American female cast member, and Amina, an Afro German female cast member, found each other in a less than desirable triangle with Peter Gunz, a former African American male rapper. The audience is introduced to Tara as Peter Gunz girlfriend of thirteen years and the mother of his two children. The love between Tara and Peter seemed passionate and undeniable. Peter Gunz repeatedly declared his love for his family and even referred to Tara as his soul mate. However, twenty minutes into *Love and Hip Hop*—episode one of season four—the reality of their relationship is revealed. Peter Gunz is having an affair with his new artist of one year, Amina. As the season progresses, we learn that Amina is not actually the "side chick" or the mistress, but she is the official DAB. Believing that Peter Gunz is not in a relationship with Tara but is only living with her to be close to his children, Amina tolerates Gunz questionable behavior in order to maintain their marriage. Amina pleads with him to stay at her home for the evening, as opposed to going home to his children and their mother. Gunz obliges her, but as a consequence, fails to take his son to school the next morning or pick him up from school. Tara, his girlfriend, is rightfully upset and determined to get answers from her man about his whereabouts. Gunz is not ready to be honest and simply says he was working late with Amina. Tara is sent a picture of Amina and Peter from an acquaintance—that Amina posted on Instagram—with the caption "where I wanna be."[51] This string of events pushed Tara to believe that something was not quite right in her relationship with Gunz. Amina is questioned by Peter Gunz' close friend, Rich Dollars, about her mixing business with pleasure, especially when Gunz has a family. Feeling up against the wall, Amina swiftly tells Dollars that she is in fact Peter Gunz' wife, proving that her relationship with him is legit and substantial. Peter Gunz, is outraged by his wife's actions. He claimed that she "snitched" by sharing their matrimonial status. He said "If you want to be treated like my wife, you have to act like my wife" by keeping her mouth shut.[52] Amina broke the code as the DAB by refusing to keep their marriage a secret. Amina would soon break the code again by revealing their secret to Tara. Under much pressure from Amina, Gunz tells his girlfriend Tara that he "fucked up," implying that he had sex with Amina. Tara, in tears and anger, replied "I've given you the best thing a woman could ever give, thirteen years of *loyalty*."[53] As a result of Peter Gunz unwillingness to be completely honest, Amina decided to expose to Tara, during a hostile discussion, that she was in fact married to Gunz. Though this action was against Gunz' request, Amina's purported betrayal can also be read as a strategic step to become Gunz' only DAB. Tara, completely devastated and appalled that her devotion was not fruitful, states "I've been holding this man *down* for thirteen years," even after he had cheated five years prior.[54] Tara later stated that, "Any woman with children will go above and beyond to make her household work even if she has to *sacrifice* more." [55] Although Peter Gunz' marriage to Amina was finally exposed, it did little to change how he treated her. Peter Gunz' behavior was not expressive of someone in a marriage. He had sex with Tara, even after their separation, and he frequently did not come home to his wife Amina. On the reunion show, Amina stated, "I believed he would change for me," but she eventually realized that she was in the same position Tara once was, as the dissatisfied DAB. [56]

The DAB exploitive ideal proved to be successful for the original series *Love and Hip Hop* in New York; so much so that it was central to the spin off series, *Love and Hip Hop Atlanta*. The show, much like the original, followed a group of women that were connected to the music industry, either directly or indirectly. The most explosive and perhaps most sensational character was Joseline, an Afro-Puerto Rican female cast member, and former exotic dancer turned musician. However, her claim to the show was less about her musical talents and more about her relationship with Stevie J, an African American male song writer and record producer. Stevie J. attempted to hide his affair with Joseline from his on and off girlfriend of twelve years, and the mother of one of his children, Mimi— another African American female cast member, and business woman. In *Love and Hip Hop* style, the triangle was exposed immediately to the audience and the battle of the DABs began. Joseline declared her love for her man, Stevie J., of only four months and attempted to remain "down" by keeping their relationship a secret, until she became pregnant and no longer wanted to be the side chick. Joseline wanted to make Mimi aware of her current status, despite the fact that she planned to have an abortion. Mimi, coming to the defense of her man, accused Joseline of being a "side chick" whose primary goal was to milk Stevie J. for money. Mimi's DAB position was further uncovered during a conversation with her good friend Ariane. She questioned Mimi about her relationship with Stevie J: "You still accepting his behavior" with so many women? "He doesn't have a reason to fight for you because you have *given him everything*, and that's not fair." Mimi's response was simply, "I know." [57] Even after Mimi ended her relationship with him, she agreed to go to therapy with Stevie J. and Joseline. Stevie J. wore a t-shirt with bold print that stated "I am God" to one of the therapy sessions, which alluded to the control he had over both women. The season was compacted with drama from this triangle, which captivated millions of viewers on a weekly basis. By season two, Joseline had become his main DAB, but was starting to experience all of the woes that came with such a position. By season three, her "downness" had paid off and she was married to Stevie J. However, like Amina from the cast of *Love and Hip Hop* New York, Joseline was now the disgruntled DAB.

Though many of the examples discussed dealt with infidelity, it would be a mistake to confuse the DAB controlling image with the scorned angry woman type. Though the DAB finds herself angry, especially when her loyalty and self-sacrifice does not pay off, the difference is that when she is wronged it is seen as acceptable and normal. Her position as the DAB does not allow her to hurt or to complain, because it is expected that she will take any abhorrent treatment in stride for the sake of maintaining her relationship with her black man. However, what is most glaring is that there is no such exploitive ideal placed on the black man. The black man is not asked to give his all and sacrifice for a woman to no end or tolerate her questionable behavior in order to save his family or prove his devotion. Fortunately, black men have managed to escape *one* unhealthy image of their manhood; conversely, this cannot be said for black women.

The Politics of Staying Down and the implications of the Down Ass Bitch Exploitive Ideal

Media serves as a powerful tool to disseminate ideas and ideals. Marci Littlefield (2008) contends that the "media strategically remake our picture of reality by controlling the images and the information that we receive. This process of selective reporting affects the ability of the populace to make objective, informed decisions, because the information presented is biased and controlled."[58] The media has been used to dictate ideas about African Americans that, in turn, impact societal views of them and thus determines how they are treated. The media also helps to shape the identity of young viewers.[59] This can be extremely problematic for young African American women, if the majority of the images displayed of them are rooted in racism and sexism. The DAB exploitive ideal has become a dominant image in reality television, specifically in *Love and Hip Hop*, and it can have grave consequences for the identity of black women. The explicit messages being sent to black women is that regardless of your tough exterior, assertiveness, or independent status, you are to 'be *down*' for your man at any cost. You are to put the needs, desires, and requirements of his before your own, even when it is to your detriment. You are to remain in relationships in which you find yourself giving everything while he is giving very little, in hopes that eventually he will see how committed and loyal you have been and decide to follow Beyoncé's instructions in her 2008 hit song, "Single Ladies (Put a Ring on it)."

Implicitly, this teaches black women that their personhood is not valid unless it is connected to a man, and that they must do what is necessary to 'stay *down*' to retain a man. If they fail to do so, they are criticized for not adhering to the virtues of 'real' black womanhood. Staying *down* implies remaining below or being at the bottom. Such a position is an oppressed position that was designated to white women by white men in the name of white male domination, which granted white men access to 'real' manhood. The difference is that the white woman was asked to be docile, meek and gentle, while the black woman is allowed to be loud, aggressive and assertive, as long as she remains "down" for the black man. The result for both groups of women is submission to male control. Asking black women to stay *down* is essentially requesting that they place themselves in an oppressed position. It also indirectly suggests that black women's value rests in their ability to give to others, remain silent, and to sacrifice at her own expense. The cost of "staying down" or remaining oppressed can be high. The damage can range from emotional and mental distress to physical and sexual violence.

The DAB is supposed to protect her man and his name if it is being defamed. Some cast members of *Love and Hip Hop* entered into verbal and physical altercations in defense of their men. Protecting the black man and his image has become an overall concern for the black community. Black women have not wanted to contribute negatively to the image of the black man, especially when it concerned sexual abuse, because it could aid in the white male's agenda to label him a rapist.[60] The consequence of protecting the black male's image often results in black women being further victimized and oppressed. McGuffey (2010) conducted a study with black male and female victims of rape. One of his participants responded as follows, when asked if she believed the black community required her to remain silent about her rape because her rapists were five black men:

> What? Are you trying to be funny or are you just fuckin' stupid? You know exactly why we can't talk about this. It's because of yo' black ass that I gotta keep my mouth shut! Black people are so concerned about black males that we let y'all . . . shit on us and black women are just supposed to keep quiet in order to protect the black male from lookin' bad in white people's eyes . . . plus everybody thinks everything is a conspiracy against black men when it comes to sex and rape. Just take a look at how everyone acted about Desiree Washington/Mike Tyson rape case. That was all about protecting black men and, literally and figuratively, fucking black women over for the sake of black men and supposedly for the sake of all black people.[61]

Black female scholars have long discussed the politics of racial solidarity which had historically boiled down to black women "taking sides against the self."[62] Collins further explains such a predicament as follows:

> Taking sides against the self requires that certain elements of black women's sexuality can be examined, namely, those that do not challenge a race discourse that historically has privileged the experiences of African American men. The cost is that other elements remain off-limits. Rape, incest, misogyny in black cultural practices, and other painful topics that might implicate black men remain taboo.[63]

The cultural requirement to protect black men does not only impact black women, but also black girls. Black families are less likely to report incidents of rape and molestation if the perpetrator is a black male as opposed to another race, which researchers theorize is connected to them wanting to avoid being stigmatized as race traitors.[64] Perhaps it is time to question the rationality of protecting individuals that deserve no such protection. Since black woman are socialized to put their needs second, it effects how they deal with domestic violence. Research shows that black women endure "more episodes of violence before leaving their partners and were more likely to have been hospitalized as a result of the abuse" as compared to their white female counterparts.[65] Black women enduring more acts of domestic violence at the hands of their partners can be related to the exploitive ideal that requires them to be compliant in their oppression by remaining 'down' and loyal. Such an ideal is not rooted in African thought and practice and thus stifles the growth of black women and therefore the entire community.

## RELOCATING BLACK WOMANHOOD

The DAB exploitive ideal derived from Eurocentric thought and practice. The African American community must operate from a center that is rooted in their cultural perspective rather than those that have sought to oppress them. Molefi Kete Asante argues that people of African descent must have *agency*.[66] He states "an agent, in our terms, must mean a human being who is capable of acting independently in his or her own best interest."[67] The exploitive ideals that have been placed on black women have not allowed them to operate as agents; in fact, it has placed them in oppressed positions or been used as justification for their unjust treatment. Asante further argues that Africans who are operating from a Eurocentric perspective are *dislocated*. They are removed from their own cultural center, which has been replaced with a Eurocentric understanding of who they are in the world.[68] Some black women have internalized the down ass bitch exploitative ideal or the racial politics of 'staying down' as acceptable forms of womanhood. Asante states that a person's psychological location is determined by whether they are *dislocated* or *located*.[69] If a person is *dislocated* then they are operating from a marginal place or within the confinements that their oppressor has outlined. The black community has been influenced by aspects of white male patriarchy which has resulted in the sexist treatment of black women. Therefore, it becomes imperative to relocate black womanhood from a cultural perspective that promotes the agency of black women, with healthy thriving male-female relationships based on self-determination and mutual cooperation. Maulana Karenga (1993) further explains the steps that need to be taken to relocate black womanhood and thus male-female relationships:

> . . . it is important that women continue to define and fight for the freedom, equality and the kind of relationships they need and want that they reconstruct their supportive links with each other and speak their own African truth of what it means to be a woman-in-community. Likewise, men must stand upright, assume a moral posture on the personal and the political level and reconstruct themselves in relationship with and in consideration of women.[70]

The DAB exploitive ideal necessitates an extreme level of unwavering support from black women to be given to black men even when such support is harmful. So the question begs—can black women be "down" for black men in a healthy way? Is there a healthy level of support that can be given to black men? Simply put: Yes! Black women and black men are engaged in various types of relationships with one another—from familial, romantic to platonic. In any relationship that the black woman shares with the black man, especially romantic, a deeply profound respect for each other's personhood and well-being must exist. Black male-female relationships thus have to be centered on respect and a shared commitment that includes the best interest of both parties. The degree to which African Americans will reach success in culturally re-defining black womanhood and black relationships will depend on our ability to acknowledge that sexism has impacted our community—a reality that many choose to abrogate in the name of focusing primarily on race.

## CONCLUSION

The current norm that pushes the needs and concerns of more than half the black community (i.e. black women) to the background by reason of acquiescing to the other half of the community (i.e. black men) is one that is not rooted in African ideals and is counterproductive to black unity and progress. The DAB controlling image functions to maintain systems of domination that were created to keep power in the hands of white men and out of the hands of people of color and white women. Black women happen to fall into both categories so the reality is further exacerbated. Constructions of patriarchy, rooted in European thought, adapted and refashioned in the black community, will result in our lack of agency and highly dysfunctional male-female relationships based of false power and exploitation. Reality television shows such as *Love and Hip Hop* help to contribute to the long history of destructive exploitive images attached to black womanhood that reduce us to self-sacrificing, subservient, sexual objects. We must critique, challenge and work to change this current reality.

## NOTES

1. Patricia Hill Collins. *Black Feminist Thought Knowledge, Consciousness, and the Politics of Empowerment*. Rev. 10th Anniversary ed. (New York, NY: Routledge, 2000); Melissa V Harris-Perry. *Sister Citizen: Shame, Stereotypes, and Black Women in America* (New Haven, CT: Yale University Press, 2011); Deborah G White. *Ain't I a Woman?: Female Slaves in the Plantation South* (New York, NY: Norton, 1985).

2. Ama Mazama. *The Afrocentric Paradigm* (Trenton, NJ: Africa World Press, 2002), 4.

3. Oyèrónkẹ́ Oyěwùmí. *The Invention of Women: Making an African Sense of Western Gender Discourses* (Minneapolis, IN: University of Minnesota Press, 1997).

4. Oyěwùmí. *Invention of Women*, 4.

5. Mark E Kann. *The Gendering of American Politics: Founding Mothers, Founding Fathers, and Political Patriarchy* (Westport, CT: Praeger, 1999).

6. Kann, *Gendering of American Politics*, 4.

7. Judith M Bennett. *History Matters: Patriarchy and the Challenge of Feminism* (Philadelphia, PA: University of Pennsylvania Press, 2006).

8. Bennett, *History Matters*, 5.

9. Kann, *Gendering of American Politics* (1999).

10. Ibid.

11. Collins. *Black Feminist Thought*, 72.

12. Kann. *Gendering of American Politics*, 10.

13. Angela Y. Davis. *Women, Race & Class*. New York, NY: Vintage Books, 1989.

14. Collins. *Black Feminist Thought*, 5.

15. White. *Ain't I a Woman?* (1985).

16. Davis. *Women, Race & Class* (1983).

17. Collins. *Black Feminist Thought* (2000); Harris-Perry. *Sister Citizen* (2011); White. *Ain't I a Woman?* (1985).

18. Donald Bogle. Toms, Coons, Mulattoes, Mammies, and Bucks; an Interpretive History of Blacks in American Films (New York, NY: Viking Press, 1973).

19. Harris-Perry. *Sister Citizen*, 72.

20. *Imitation of Life*. USA: Universal Pictures, 1934. Film.

21. Collins. *Black Feminist Thought* (2000).

22. Collins. *Black Feminist Thought*, 74.

23. Davis. *Women, Race & Class* (1983).

24. Harris-Perry, *Sister Citizen*, 72.

25. Paula Giddings. *When and Where I Enter: The Impact of Black Women on Race and Sex in America*. New York, NY: W. Morrow, 1984.

26. Giddings. *When and Where I Enter*, 328.

27. Giddings. *When and Where I Enter* (1984).

28. Giddings. *When and Where I Enter*, 328.

29. Collins, *Black Feminist Thought*, 77.

30. Collins, *Black Feminist Thought* (2000).

31. Collins, *Black Feminist Thought*, 174.

32. Shakur, Tupac. *Me Against the World*. Tupac. Death Row Records/Interscope Records, 1998, CD.

33. The Lox. *Ryde or Die Chick*. Jadakiss, Sheek Louch, and Styles P. Ruff Ryders. 1999. LP.

34. Ibid.

35. "Ride or Die Chick." Urban Dictionary. April 4, 2005. Accessed August 5, 2014.

36. Baltimore, Charlie. *Down Ass Bitch*. Ja Rule. Recorded 2000. Irv Gotti, 2002, CD.

37. "Down Ass Bitch." Urban Dictionary. April 4, 2009. Accessed August 5, 2014.

38. Collins, *Black Feminist Thought* (2000).

39. *Love & Hip Hop: New York*, VH1, Season 1: episode 1, March 14, 2011, producer Moni-Scott Young.

40. *Love & Hip Hop: New York*, VH1, Season 2: episode 7, December 26, 2011, producer Moni-Scott Young.

41. *Love & Hip Hop: New York*, VH1, Season 2: episode 9, January 16, 2012, producer Moni-Scott Young.

42. *Love & Hip Hop: New York*, VH1, Season 2: episode 10, January 23, 2012, producer Moni-Scott Young.

43. *Love & Hip Hop: New York*, VH1, Season 3: episode 12, April 1 2013, producer Moni-Scott Young.

44. *Love & Hip Hop: New York*, VH1, Season 2: episode 7, January 2, 2012, producer Moni-Scott Young.

45. *Love & Hip Hop: New York*, VH1, Season 2: episode 8, January 9, 2012, producer Moni-Scott Young.

46. Ibid.

47. Ibid.

48. *Love & Hip Hop: New York*, VH1, Season 3: episode 1, January 7, 2013, producer Moni-Scott Young.

49. Ibid.

50. Ibid.

51. *Love & Hip Hop: New York*, VH1, Season 4: episode 1, October 28, 2013, producer Moni-Scott Young.

52. *Love & Hip Hop: New York*, VH1, Season 4: episode 2, November 4, 2013, producer Moni-Scott Young.

53. *Love & Hip Hop: New York*, VH1, Season 4: episode 3, November 11, 2013, producer Moni-Scott Young.

54. *Love & Hip Hop: New York*, VH1, Season 4: episode 4, November 18, 2013, producer Moni-Scott Young.

55. Ibid.

56. *Love & Hip Hop: New York*, VH1, Season 4: episode 14, February 10, 2014, producer Moni-Scott Young.

57. *Love & Hip Hop: Atlanta*, VH1, Season 1: episode 3, July 9, 2012, producer Moni-Scott Young.

58. Marci, Littlefield. "The Media as a System of Racialization: Exploring Images of African American Women and the New Racism." American Behavioral Scientist (2008), 677.

59. Littlefield, "The Media as a System of Racialization" (2008).

60. McGuffey, C. Shawn. "Blacks and racial appraisals: Gender, race, and interracial rape." In J. Battle & S.L Barnes (Eds), *Black Sexualities: Probing Powers, Passions, Practices, and Politics* (p. 273–298). New Brunswick: Rutgers University Press, (2010).

61. McGuffey, "Blacks and racial appraisals," 275.

62. Collins, *Black Feminist Thought*, 124.

63. Ibid.

64. McGuffey, "Blacks and Racial Appraisals" (2011).

65. Hill, Shirley A. Black Intimacies: A Gender Perspective on Families and Relationships (Walnut Creek, CA: AltaMira Press, 2005), 192.

66. Asante, Molefi Kete. *An Afrocentric Manifesto: Toward an African Renaissance.* Cambridge, CA: Polity, 2007.

67. Ibid.

68. Ibid.

69. Ibid.

70. Karenga, Maulana. *Introduction to Black Studies.* Los Angeles: University of Sankore Press, 1993.

# ELEVEN

## Real Housewives or Real Lies?

### *New Constructions of "Housewives" on* The Real Housewives of Atlanta

### Shavonne R. Shorter

An old adage prescribed that "art imitates life." If one believes this to be true, then it is plausible that entertainment is a source from which information about everyday life can be gleaned? Can U.S. television shows provide a looking glass into how Americans perform certain aspects of their lives? For a "real" look into how careers are performed, I have examined content from a reality television show which bears a title that implies something about the cast—the Bravo Network's *Real Housewives of Atlanta* series.

This show was chosen for two reasons. First, *The Real Housewives of Atlanta* is the most popular show among the "Housewives" franchise.[1] Thus with each airing of the show, those who watch have the opportunity to learn more about the career aspirations, roles, and behaviors, of the cast members. Second, this is the only show within *The Real Housewives* franchise that features a primarily black cast. As such, the question emerges—can this show provide insight into the way black women construct their career roles?

Another goal of this study is to determine how cast members construct notions of housewifery. Hence, throughout this chapter, readers will see that these women are not the typical "housewives," rather they have reinvented what it means to be a housewife in the modern age.

213

## A HISTORICAL OVERVIEW OF THE HOUSEWIFE

Housewifery is perhaps the oldest job for women—both around the world and within the United States.[2] Within a U.S. context, the history of this career has been intertwined with what some might argue are old fashioned beliefs about the role of women in society, stemming back to the 1900's.[3] Housewives were women who were married to male partners,[4] and the man in the relationship was the provider for the family.[5] The man would work outside of the home and he was paid a wage for his labor; and while the man's work responsibilities were outside of the home, it was the job of his wife to make sure that everything within the home was taken care of.[6]

### Duties of a Housewife

The most obvious duties of a housewife were ones that were directly related to the upkeep of the home. Responsibilities included keeping the home tidy by performing housework, such as washing dishes, sweeping floors, and other domestic tasks.[7] In addition to this, housewives were expected to take the lead role in caring for the family.

A housewife was expected to tend to the needs of both her spouse and their children. And she was responsible for her family's most basic need—nourishment. The housewife prepared meals for breakfast, lunch, and dinner—usually from scratch.[8] She was also the one who saw the children off to school or drove them there each day.[9] After caring for home and family, some housewives filled their days with volunteer work in the community.

Housewives were known for being very active within their neighborhoods. One of the places that they were most influential was in the schools that their children attended; often taking positions within Parent Teacher Associations (PTAs).[10] In addition to this, they also volunteered at local non-profit organizations, places of worship, or anywhere else that their help might have been needed.[11] Moreover, housewives handled all of these responsibilities while remaining pleasant, cheerful, and happy.[12] Hence, as previously noted, housewifery was seen as the primary career for women until the early 1900's, when women were encouraged to seek work outside of the home.[13]

### Decline of Housewifery as a Job

When the First World War began in 1914, men from the U.S. were called upon to leave their fulltime jobs and travel overseas to fight.[14] Thus, many U.S. women were called upon to work fulltime, labor intensive, jobs outside of the home—in order to keep the economy stable.[15] During the time of World War I, women made up 20.7 percent of the workforce.[16] After the war, the amount of women in the workforce continued to grow. During the 1950's, women made up about 32.7 percent of the workforce.[17] In the 1980's, women in the United States made up 44.2 percent of the workforce.[18] Today, women have become the gender majority within the workforce.[19]

As women entered the workforce in record numbers, opinions about housewifery as a job also changed. What was once viewed as one of the foremost careers for women, became one that was seen as being less than desirable. In fact, one study found that young girls had no aspirations to be housewives when they grew up. Instead they desired to be out in the workforce making money.[20] So why do modern girls who are just shy of womanhood feel this way about housewifery? The work of Clair (1996)[21] may be able to help explicate why this career path fell out of favor.

In her study, Clair (1996)[22] polled college-age students to get a sense of what they meant when they quipped that they desired to work a "real job." She found that a real job was constructed as work that is done outside of the home; and usually in a corporate setting. In short, "real" work is considered to be white collar, office-based work that is engaged in for at least forty hours a week—typically 9 am to 5 pm. According to this description, the work of a housewife is not what is desired by young women. Although the idea of being a housewife is somewhat passé in today's modern age, television programs that chronical the experiences of housewives have become quite popular within the media.

## THE RISE OF THE HOUSEWIFE IN POPULAR MEDIA

From 2006–2010, *Desperate Housewives* was the most watched comedy series across all television networks.[23] This show provided a fictional account of the lives of four housewives. The core themes of the show revolved around the women engaging in trysts with men who lived in their neighborhood; scenes in which the women gossiped about the lives of the other wives; and instances where the women plotted revenge on people who wronged them.[24] If art is supposed to imitate life, then this show was not exactly an accurate representation of what housewives do on a daily basis, according to the aforementioned literature. Unlike this fictional series, the Bravo Network created a series of shows premised upon the idea of showing the "true," lived experiences of housewives.

In 2005, the network began airing a television show titled, *The Real Housewives of Orange County*.[25] In this show, a camera crew followed around six "actual housewives" to see what they did in their daily lives. Bravo then went on to produce several spin-offs of the show.[26] *The Real Housewives of New York City, The Real Housewives of DC, The Real Housewives of New Jersey, The Real Housewives of Beverly Hills, The Real Housewives of Miami* and *The Real Housewives of Atlanta*.

*The Real Housewives of Atlanta* has become the most popular show in the franchise.[27] And this show is quite different from the others for one glaring reason; it is the only *Housewives* show that features a primarily black cast. As such this show affords the opportunity for viewers to learn more about how black women perform their duties as housewives. This chapter focuses on the women featured in the third season of *The Real Housewives of Atlanta*.

The cast of the third season was comprised of a motley crew of six very different women.[28] NeNe Leakes was one of three women in the third season who remained from the original cast of season one. She began the season married to Real Estate tycoon, Gregg Leakes; and the couple had two sons. Kim Zolciak was another member of the original cast; and she was the only Caucasian housewife on the show. Even still, Kim had much in common with the black housewives—such as an affinity for music, hair extensions and wigs, and gossip. Although not a member of the black community, during her time on the show her life was discussed in tandem with the other women's lives. It truly seemed as if she had been lumped into the category of a black housewife, just by virtue of her presence on the show. At the start of season three, she was divorced with two daughters. Sheree Whitfield was the last of the remaining members of the original cast. She was also divorced in season three; and she had three children—two daughters and one son. Kandi Burruss joined the show in season two. She was unmarried and had one daughter. Phaedra Parks joined the cast in season three; she was married with one son. Finally, the last housewife, and newcomer to season three, was Cynthia Bailey. Bailey began the season unmarried; and she had one daughter. Aside from understanding more about how black women perform housewifery, this show affords the opportunity for viewers to learn more about if and how these women identify with previously discussed conceptions about what housewives do on a daily basis.

## IDENTITY AND HOUSEWIVES

The concept of identification is premised upon the idea of connecting with another person or group of people through common shared experiences.[29] Language is the conduit through which the process of identification takes place.[30] Indeed Rhetorician Kenneth Burke argued that, "You persuade a man only insofar as you can talk his language by speech, gesture, tonality, order, image, attitude, idea, identifying your ways with his."[31] After watching a few episodes of the third season of *The Real Housewives of Atlanta*, I began to wonder what notions of housewifery these women were identifying with. Did their constructions of the career resonate more with the domestic, demure notions of housewifery from the early 1900's; or did they exemplify a new image of what it means to be a housewife, possibly as shown in *Desperate Housewives?*[32] While previous studies in communication have analyzed the perpetuation of minority stereotypes on housewife shows,[33] to date none have applied Burkean Identification Theory to the study of housewives. This chapter enters the conversation at this point, guided by the following research questions.

1. Research Question One: How are the cast of the third season of *The Real Housewives of Atlanta* constructing the aspirations, roles, and behaviors of a housewife?
2. Research Question Two: How realistic are the aspirations, roles, and behaviors of the cast of the third season of *The Real Housewives of Atlanta*?

## Method

I examined each episode from the third season of *The Real Housewives of Atlanta* prior to the halfway mark of the season[34] (9 episodes in total[35]). This season was selected for analysis because at the time this chapter was written, it was the most current season. Episodes were examined via live television and/or YouTube rebroadcast. I transcribed relevant data from each episode. These transcripts served as the text that was analyzed.

The data were analyzed via thematic analysis. A thematic analysis is the means through which recurring patterns (themes) are identified within a text.[36] In order to conduct a thorough textual analysis, the author must be familiar with the text. Since I transcribed the data, I was quite familiar with it. Even still, I re-read the text multiple times to ensure that I had a complete understanding of the text. The next stage is to engage in initial coding, or the finding of recurring keywords or interesting pieces of data.[37] This is the first step in the process of developing potential themes. Next themes were established guided by the work of Owen.[38]

According to Owen (1984),[39] a theme is present when it is repetitive — meaning that it shows up time and again within the data; forceful — meaning that it has an overwhelming presence within the data; and recurring — meaning that it appears frequently within the data. Lastly the themes were examined once more, given names, and matched to supporting quotes and/or descriptions from the text. Upon the completion of this process, I determined that the housewives in the show were portraying their role in four different ways.

## Findings

After viewing each episode of the third season of *The Real Housewives of Atlanta*, it was discovered that the housewives constructed their aspirations, roles, and behaviors in four ways, as: (a) a job that is available to women of differing marital statuses, (b) a job in which domestic work is rarely performed by housewives, (c) a job in which primary employment takes place outside of the home, and (d) a job in which loud, rude, and brash attitudes are commonplace.

## A JOB THAT IS AVAILABLE TO WOMEN OF DIFFERING MARITAL STATUSES

By the nature of the word, in order to be a housewife, it is assumed that a woman in this position is legally married. However, on the third season of *The Real Housewives of Atlanta*, the term housewife was used to represent married women, women who have never been married, and divorcees alike. In the third season there was only one woman who began and ended the season married—Phaedra Parks. There were also two women who had never been married, yet who had both been previously engaged—Kandi Burruss and Cynthia Bailey. Burruss became engaged to be married during the second season, but tragically, her fiancé was killed in a fight at the nightclub where he worked.[40] Like Burruss, Bailey had never been married, but had been engaged multiple times.

On the second episode of the season,[41] Bailey disclosed to fellow cast member, NeNe Leakes, that she had been engaged three times before. Leakes, who appeared utterly shocked, asked Bailey why she had never followed through on the engagements and married any of the men. Bailey quickly replied, "I just like the thought of men wanting to marry me."[42] Indeed Bailey stayed true to this quote over the course of the season, by becoming engaged for a fourth time.

On the *She Can Dance?*[43] episode, Bailey's then boyfriend—Peter—proposed to her on their three-year anniversary. As he was down on bended knee, Peter, who was very familiar with her non-marital history asked, "You're not going to back off, you're not going to run? You're going to marry me? You promise?" to which Bailey remarked "yes,"[44] And true to her word, in the last episode of the season, Bailey did marry Peter in an elaborate ceremony—joining Parks as a fellow married woman who could legally be considered as a true housewife. On the other hand, some of the cast members were divorcees.

Two women began the season divorced. One was Sheree Whitfield. Before the show began, Whitfield was married to former National Football League (NFL) player, Bob Whitfield.[45] During season three, Whitfield began to date again, striking up a relationship with Tiy-E Muhammad—a popular love psychologist and radio show host in Atlanta. Aside from Whitfield, Zolciak was also divorced. Prior to the show, Zolciak was previously married to Dan Toce.[46] Over the course of the season, Zolciak was involved in a lesbian relationship with a woman known as DJ Tracy

Young; yet, she ended the season dating Troy Biermann, an NFL player for the Atlanta Falcons.[47]

Lastly, there was the marital status of NeNe Leakes, who began the season happily married to her husband Gregg. However, as the season progressed, viewers quickly learned that there was trouble in paradise. For instance, in one episode, Leakes invited Bailey and her boyfriend to her home for a double date.[48] Throughout the date, Leakes was seen drinking copious amounts of alcohol; and by the end of the episode she disclosed to Bailey that she and Gregg were having marital problems. As they were just a few feet away from Gregg, Leakes turned to Bailey and said, "I'm going to divorce Greg." [49] Over the course of the season, Leakes did just that.

As the findings show, at given points within the season, only half of the cast members were in a position to be legally referred to as a "housewife." One wonders what this means about the term housewife. Can one be unmarried and still consider themselves as such? This will be discussed in the latter portion of this chapter. Aside from having varying martial statuses, these women were all adverse to the idea of engaging in domestic work.

## A JOB IN WHICH DOMESTIC WORK IS RARELY PERFORMED BY HOUSEWIVES

During the third season, the cast demonstrated their disdain for engaging in domestic tasks. They did not put their hands to work making meals or cleaning their houses, instead they employed an alternative; contracting someone else to do the tasks for them. An example, of this behavior was found in the first episode of the season. During this episode, Leakes invited Zolciak over to her home for a special luncheon, because the two had gotten into a big fight in the previous season. Leakes wanted to talk to Zolciak and resume their friendship. As Zolciak made her way into the house, Leakes informed her that she wanted the meeting to be perfect for them. Leakes exclaimed, "I even hired a Chef."[50] Leakes did not cook for this special occasion, as arguably many housewives would. Moreover it is essential to note that Leakes' idea of the perfect way to entertain company coincided with someone else doing the grunt work. This instance begged the question, are modern housewives now turning to trained professionals to complete their tasks? Also one wonders what the implications would be for a housewife who could not afford the services of a professional. Would her luncheon be less than perfect because she cooked everything herself? If so, one wonders what type of image this casts on housewifery as a job.

In another episode, Zolciak, like Leakes, showed that she too did not cook. On the *Contract Player*[51] episode, Zolciak decided that it was time for her to get back in good physical shape. However, instead of going to the gym, she decided to try out a new in-home laser weight loss treatment. She also invited the other housewives to come over and try it out with her; and as any good housewife knows—a decent social gathering requires food. Zolciak provided food by ordering Papa John's pizza, chicken tenders, and soda for her guests and her children to eat, while she had the procedure done.[52] These examples suggest that anytime there is a social gathering, the women prefer to have their events catered. One can only surmise why this could be. Do modern housewives not enjoy cooking? Do they just not have the time to cook? Whitfield provided insight into why the housewives may turn to professionals for their domestic needs in yet another episode.

On their second date, Tiy-E Muhammad invited Whitfield over to his home for dinner.[53] Once she arrived, he informed her that they would be making dinner together. She immediately scrunched up her nose and exclaimed to the camera, "Oh, this is not exactly what I had expected. I mean usually men are taking me out to fine dinners."[54] According to this statement, Whitfield believed that she was above engaging in the domestic task of cooking. She was not pleased that she was expected to do the work for herself, as she had become accustomed to others doing it for her. If a good date was equated with going out for a fine dinner, this date was certainly destined for disaster from the start. In addition to being generally unwilling to cook, the housewives were also not interested in cleaning.

In the *Model Behavior*[55] episode, Leakes chastised her twenty-three year old son Bryson for his irresponsible lifestyle. At the time, he was unemployed and spent his days hanging out around the neighborhood. As a result, Leakes was considering asking him to leave the household, because he was not contributing money, time, or labor. As she lectured him and shared her thoughts about his behaviors she said, "You don't pick up nothing around here, I pay the maid service."[56] In her speech she accused him of doing nothing to tidy the house, while at the same time voicing that she was not engaging in housework either. This was a not so subtle indication that the house cleaning was not done by her, but by outside persons. Leakes was exasperated with her son because of his lack of desire to engage in domestic work, yet she was unwilling to do this kind of work herself. Perhaps her son believed that he would not have to do domestic work because he did not see his mother—the housewife—doing any. Is it then fair for her to become upset with her son?

It appears as though the housewives have constructed themselves as women who do not cook or clean, but who utilize outside trained professionals to complete these tasks. One could argue that this is a very business savvy move, as it allows the housewives to focus on other tasks and interests. The women featured in season three would more than likely agree, as all of the women maintained additional jobs that were outside of the home.

## A JOB IN WHICH PRIMARY EMPLOYMENT
## TAKES PLACE OUTSIDE OF THE HOME

Previous literature noted that a housewife's work was mainly located inside of the home.[57] However, this was not the case for the housewives of season three. All of the housewives maintained lucrative primary employment that was outside of the home. For example, Parks was a defense attorney, who was known to work on the cases of celebrities in and around the Atlanta area.[58] Bailey had a successful career as an international supermodel, who received her start by appearing on the cover of the popular black women's magazine—*Essence*.[59] Burruss was a professional singer and Grammy award winning producer, who was best known for her role in an all-female singing group—XSCAPE—popular in the late 90's. Moreover, Burruss created her own music and produced musical tracks for up-and-coming artists, like her fellow housewife—Kim Zolciack. Inspired by Burruss' success as a singer, Kim Zolciak embarked upon her own solo singer career. At the conclusion of the season, she had recorded one hit song titled, *Tardy for the Party*.[60] This song became number one on the iTunes download list for many weeks.[61] In addition to this, Zolciak also launched her own line of wigs.[62]

Leakes also worked outside of the home. Throughout the course of the season, Leakes was in the process of pursuing two jobs. The first was that of an author—Leakes had recently wrote and published her first book titled, *Never Make the Same Mistake Twice: Lessons on Love and Life Learned the Hard Way*.[63] In addition to this, she also procured a job as an entertainment segment co-host at local Atlanta news station—*11 Alive*.[64] Finally, Sheree Whitfield divided her time working two jobs as well. Whitfield developed her own line of clothing called *She by Sheree*[65] She later decided to shift her focus away from fashion, and instead work towards becoming an actress. In season three, she began taking acting lessons and even had her first opportunity to portray a small role in a local play called, *The Child Support Man*.[66] One wonders why these housewives elected to primarily work outside of the home. It may indeed be less about these women pursuing their passions and more about them providing for their families.

Unlike traditional housewives, all of the women on the cast were the breadwinners in their households. Phaedra Parks was married to a man—Apollo Nida—who was an ex-convict, recently serving time in jail for auto title fraud.[67] He was not employed at all during the season. Leakes was married—and later divorced—to Gregg, who had recently run into financial troubles and needed to borrow thousands of dollars from a friend just to make ends meet.[68] Bailey's fiancé, Peter, was a struggling entrepreneur who had to close one restaurant that he opened—through a loan provided by Bailey.[69] Burruss, Whitfield, and Zolciak, on the other hand, were all single women who were the heads of their households. Additionally, all of these women were mothers who needed to provide income to care for their children. As seen in these examples, modern housewives are being constructed as self-sufficient and independent women, who do not need to depend on men to survive and thrive. Lastly, the women were also characterized as being loud, brash, and sometimes downright rude.

## A JOB IN WHICH LOUD, RUDE,
## AND BRASH ATTITUDES ARE COMMONPLACE

When one thinks of a housewife, one may conjure up images of a pleasant woman.[70] However, it was commonplace to see *The Real Housewives of Atlanta* from season three fighting, cursing, and acting out of control in public settings on the show. For example, there was an altercation that ensued between Leakes and a close friend. On the *New Attitude*[71] episode, Leakes and Zolciak were invited to the grand opening of a high fashion shoe store in downtown Atlanta. When they arrived at the store, they noticed that all the other housewives had been invited and brought guests as well. Parks' guest was Dwight Eubanks, a close friend of both her and Leakes. Earlier in the episode, it had been disclosed that Leakes heard that Eubanks was spreading rumors that she and her soon-to-be-ex-husband, were going broke; and the reason Eubanks cited for knowing about their financial woes was that Gregg asked to borrow $10,000 from him. These rumors made Leakes furious and she had no problem telling Eubanks exactly how she felt in front of everyone.

When Leakes saw Eubanks, she immediately marched over to him. Without hesitation, she proceeded to get in his face so close that his nose almost touched hers. She then yelled at him saying, "You really need to come correct honey and stop . . . trying to act fabulous when you know you're not! Gregg borrowed $10,000 from you? Let me know friend, let me know. Did Gregg borrow $10,000?"[72] She repeated the last sentence over and over again getting louder, until security finally escorted her off of the premises. This behavior was far from the docile, demure, image that is associated with that of a housewife in the past; but Leakes was not the only housewife who had a loud, brash, and rude attitude during the course of the show.

As mentioned earlier, Whitfield was dating a psychologist by the name of Tiy-E Muhammad. Over the course of the season, viewers learned that his academic credentials had been called into question. Leakes, who had formerly worked with him, informed Whitfield that Muhammad had received his degree from an online, unaccredited, institution. As a result, he was not actually a licensed psychologist, as he had also been proclaiming during the season. Because of this lie, he had been fired from the radio station where he was working as a disc jockey giving out love advice to callers.[73] Angered by this discovery, Whitfield—who thought that she was dating a well-paid, prestigious, man—made a final date with him to confront him about his fake title and to break off their relationship.

The pair went to have lunch at a busy restaurant. They chose to sit at an outside table. As they were dining, Whitfield questioned him on why he had not been honest about his credentials or lack thereof; yet he continually alleged that he was, in fact, a real doctor. At one point in the episode, Whitfield became so enraged with him that she yelled, "Show me the proof then! Show me your transcripts!"[74] As can be seen from the previous two incidents, these housewives have no problem acting out in public for the world to see. They are not embarrassed by their behaviors, rather they brandish them at any chance they get.

Zolciak also made some very rude comments during the course of the show. One of the focal points of the season was Parks' pregnancy. During the season, Parks made comments about her upcoming bundle of joy that left the women baffled. For instance, when asked by the other women when her baby was due, Parks remarked that she did not know.[75] At one point, she even told the women that her pregnancy was going to be induced at seven months.[76] It did not take long for the women to figure out that the details of her pregnancy were very complicated.

At a social event, Zolciak questioned Eubanks about the details of Parks' pregnancy, commenting, "She is going to have the baby at seven months? Is it an alien baby?"[77] Later on in the season, viewers discovered that Parks made these comments because her child was conceived before she got married. However, she did not want her mother—who was a pastor—to know.[78] This insensitive comment would not be expected from a housewife, let alone a fellow mother. Yet, as seen from the previous examples, modern housewives—such as those portrayed on this show—seem to have no problem sharing exactly what is on their minds. Some may argue that this was liberation from the false guise of happiness that old-school housewives ascribed to,[79] while others may argue that their behavior was out of line and unnecessary.

## DISCUSSION

At the beginning of this analysis, I sought to understand more about how the cast of *The Real Housewives of Atlanta* from season three were constructing the aspirations, roles, and behaviors of a housewife. In short, I discovered that these are not your typical housewives who identify with previous notions of housewifery. Rather in the spirit of *Desperate Housewives*, these women redefine what it means to do housewifery in the modern age.

Whereas in the literature Neuhaus (2011)[80] would prescribe that housewives should be married, these women have differing martial statuses. It is widely known that housewives complete the domestic tasks within their homes,[81] yet these women have no desire to lift a finger to engage in this type of work. A housewife's primary work was her domestic responsibilities,[82] however, all of these women maintain primary employment that is outside of the home. And lastly, scholars have argued that housewives are cheerful, happy, and pleasant in demeanor;[83],[84] but the women in this study have proven that they have no issues with becoming rude, loud, or brash. After analyzing the data, I speculated just how these women could fancy themselves to be housewives, when they displayed little to none of the traits that traditionally accompanied this job.

What notions of housewifery are these women identifying with? Seemingly none. They do not desire to mimic past housewives in the spirit of Burke, but instead—in the spirit of *Desperate Housewives*—they have created a new genre regarding how housewives act. They desire to eschew the idea of identification, as we know it to create their own category of housewifery to which others may look to as a new career paradigm. But where did this new concept of the modern housewife come from, if not from what is currently known about housewifery? I would argue that these new modern housewives have re-envisioned what this career looks like from the perspective of women who ascribe to the beliefs found in the discourse of women's empowerment within the media.

Perhaps the most prevalent way in which this rhetoric has been disseminated is through entertainment mediums, such as radio. One need look no further than to the lyrics of popular songs throughout recent years, to get a better understanding of how women come to view themselves and their place within society. In short the modern woman is independent, self-sufficient, and savvy.

In *Independent Women Part I*, Destiny's Child[85] sang about being women who can buy their own items, including homes, rings, and shoes, without the help of anyone else—namely men. Thus, it would be assumed that an "Independent Woman" was one who worked a "real job"[86] that paid her very well. This woman was not looking to depend on the income of a man, as she made her own income and spent it accordingly. An independent, well paid, woman also had professionals do domestic work for her.

For example, in her song *No Matter What They Say*, Lil' Kim rapped about being a woman who lived a leisurely life, got paid by others to have her photos taken, and have maid service.[87] According to this lyric, the modern woman is too busy making money to do her own domestic work. Instead she used her well-earned money to have other people do her domestic duties for her. Destiny's Child also provides insight into how the modern woman views relationships.

In *Independent Women Part I*, the group implied that their relationships with men were based upon casual flings and one-night stands.[88] Similarly, The Pussycat Dolls, in their song *I Don't Need A Man*, echoed these sentiments, saying directly that they didn't need men to make them happy or buy them rings.[89] According to these lyrics, the modern woman eschewed marriage as a mechanism to make insecure women feel better about themselves. The modern woman was confident enough to define relationships on her own terms. She does not need a man, but she can get one if she wants one. She is independent and free thinking enough on her own to make these decisions for herself. As such, today's modern woman is more liberal in how she conducts herself publically.

In lyrics from her song, *Smack You*, Kimberly Cole sings casually about how she would physically assault another woman by slapping her in the face.[90] This suggests that the modern woman is not afraid to show her anger and fight if need be. All of these attributes describe *The Real Housewives of Atlanta*. Their new brand of housewifery is bold, brazen, and completely different than old conceptions of what it means to be a housewife. It's new, it's different, and it is based on the experiences of today's modern woman. Thus it comes as little surprise that this show is so beloved by viewers.[91] This show is connecting with viewers through a message of modernity that they enjoy and can appreciate. Interestingly enough, since the creation of this show that has been so successful, other networks have created spinoff shows with similar plots and storylines about black "housewives" (i.e. *Basketball Wives, Football Wives, Love and Hip Hop*). *The Real Housewives of Atlanta* franchise has become a model that other networks look to when creating shows that black women can identify with and enjoy, even if it is not the most accurate representation of what people come to expect of women within this career. However, this leads to a larger overarching question, how realistic are the portrayals of housewifery by the cast? I would argue that it is questionable, at best, due to two key reasons.

The housewives, and all the aforementioned entertainers, have one unique trait in common, they are financially well off. Arguably it is very easy to live the life of an independent woman who can provide for herself in the absence of a man, when one has the consistent financial means to do so. Could money be the real reason why these housewives behave so differently from the literature? This argument is supported when one considers what some of the cast members were doing before they became stars of the show.

Before the show, only half of the housewives had careers that paid them enough to allow them to live the independent, luxurious, lives discussed in the aforementioned songs—Parks (high profile lawyer), Bailey (international supermodel), and Burruss (Grammy award winning singer/songwriter/producer). Prior to the show, however, Whitfield, Leakes, and Zolciak were all gainfully unemployed (Whitfield and Leakes were married to wealthy men); but upon being cast on the show (and being paid large sums of money to be filmed as found by Samantha Darcy[92]), these women magically morphed into the modern independent women from the songs—complete with their own business ventures, new marital statuses, and the ability to pay others to do work for them. While money is arguably a determining factor in the casts' portrayal of housewifery, the reality television format may also have influenced the portrayal.

Reality television has become a wide sweeping phenomenon in the United States since the early 1990's.[93] These shows claim to portray the true life experiences of the characters that star in them. However, previous research has shown that many of these shows are in fact not as real as they may claim. They maintain that they are unscripted, but they often provide flawed, inaccurate, accounts of reality—just like fictional shows.[94]

In her work, Signorielli (1991)[95] found that sitcoms tended to portray marriages as more stable and loving than they actually are in real life. Conversely, soap operas portray relationships as being more volatile and prone to divorce, adultery, and violence than they were in reality.[96] In addition to an inaccurate portrayal of relationships, research has found that careers are not always portrayed as accurately on television. For example, Waldeck, Pullins, & Houlette (2010)[97] found that the media portrayed sales jobs in a very negative fashion, which was influencing the opinions of high school students, who watched these shows and came to understand sales jobs in a negative way. These portrayals influenced students not to consider sales jobs in the future.

Additionally, show writers have an impact on a show's content. The storylines writers produce may be influenced by such factors as the need to achieve high ratings, and the need to provide material for an interesting show.[98] Previous research has shown that American television watchers are more entertained by sensational, fantasy style, storylines.[99] These plots are exciting, entertaining, and make every day lived experiences seem exceedingly bland. This provides more insight into why and/or how the cast members may be comfortable with portraying themselves as loud-mouthed, rude, volatile women who are unconventional housewives. In today's age, for some the idea of being a typical housewife is seen as being the antithesis of a career that young women desire.[100] Thus it makes sense that the women of *RHOA* have created their own, new, exciting genre of housewifery. They are being paid to entertain.[101] It may not be exactly who they truly are, but it may explain why so many people watch the show; and the more people watch the show, the longer Bravo will decide to air the show. The longer the show airs, the more money these women will receive. Thus, it is easy to see how this too feeds into the vicious cycle of materialism as the impetus behind how these "housewives" are portrayed.

As mentioned earlier, this show also provides commentary on what it means to be a modern black housewife. After perusing the themes and determining that materialism and the format of the show may have a major impact on how the women perform their "duties," one wonders if the cast realizes the implications of their behaviors on black women? At the end of the season, only one cast member was still married. Thus these women's marital statuses could be seen as contributing to the notion of the broken black family, which some point to as a reason for the various economic, social, and political ills that blacks face today. [102] Their desire to not engage in domestic work could be read, not as having the means to pay others to do work for them, but as laziness — a pejorative term that has been associated with blacks' work habits since the days of slavery; and one that still persist today. [103] Their new form of housewifery could be read as incompetence, yet another pejorative term that has been associated with blacks. [104] Can one truly be a housewife if they are unmarried or if they do not work inside the home? One could argue that this show has nothing to do with housewives at all and would best be recast as a show that chronicles the fictitious lives of modern day black women a la the show *Single Ladies*. Is the cast truly comfortable with the fact that they are being paid to be loud and rude, markers of what some would argue are unfeminine behaviors associated with the image of the black "bad" girl? [105] One wonders if they realize that they are just feeding into the aforementioned discourses surrounding the negative images of blacks historically and on television. Because this is the number one show of the franchise, these women have the power, opportunity, and platform to break the cycle of how black women are portrayed; yet they choose not to—likely because being too "normal" might cause a cast member's dismissal from the show and loss of subsequent income as it did in a past season. [106] It is also no wonder that due, in part to the themes that permeate the show, *The Real Housewives of Atlanta* is still airing and is currently in its seventh season.

## CONCLUSION

In sum, the authenticity of what it means to be a housewife in the modern age, as portrayed on *The Real Housewives of Atlanta*, should be interpreted with caution. The women of the cast are not identifying with the old notions of what it means to be a housewife—as found in the literature— and are perhaps redefining what it means to be a housewife who also happens to be black. [107] Based on the findings from this chapter, housewives do not necessarily have to be married to maintain this career; they are averse to domestic work; they are more known for the careers that they maintain outside of the home; and they are loud, rude, and disrespectful. Moreover the performances of the women on the show may serve to build upon the harmful images that the media broadcast of black women.

The majority of these housewives are black women who are portrayed as unmarried, single mothers, who spend most of their time socializing. They are categorized as women who would rather pay housekeepers than complete the domestic duties associated with being a housewife. And they are packaged as business minded women that still fall back on their ghetto girl, in your face, confrontational communication style when they need to "read" (confront) someone who has wronged them. The show effectively markets the women as having a variety of negative stereotypes associated with black women, which contrasts with the empowered woman image that they may be intending to send—as previously noted. Reality television is popular due to its dependence on exciting, dramatic storylines. Thus, one wonders if this show is so popular, in part, because of America's affinity toward negative images of black women? This is a problematic question, because it implies that viewers may internalize these images and believe them to be reflective of how all black housewives—and women—behave.

Furthermore, the women's new version of housewifery is inaccessible, at best, to most women who are actual housewives. This is because most do not have the financial resources that the cast depict, in order to live the lives that the cast members lead. And although some modern day wealthy or upper middle class housewives may be able to live like the cast—to some extent—what about middle class and lower class housewives, who do not have the financial means to live like these women do? As such, one wonders how non-televised housewives interpret the behaviors of the "Real Housewives."

Do non-televised housewives feel as though they are not a good representation of what it means to be a housewife—particularly black women who are housewives? Or, on the other hand, do non-televised housewives regard the women from this show as women to be false representations of the position? In a future study, I intend to speak with non-televised housewives of varying social and economic statuses in order to gauge their opinions on the show. Additionally, it will be interesting to ascertain what percentage of housewives are actually black women, given the continued financial disparities that exist between black and white households. And if that number is small, won't that call into question any level of reality represented on *RHOA*?

## NOTES

1. Rodney Ho, Bravo Renews "Real Housewives of Atlanta," Two Related Spinoffs. *AJC.com,* April 8, 2014, http://radiotvtalk.blog.ajc.com.

2. Center For Information on America, *Vital Issues, Volumes 9–14* (Washington, CT: Center For Information on America, 1959).

3. Kirstin Olsen, *Chronology of Women's History* (Westport: Greenwood Publishing, 1994), Google Books.

4. Jessamyn Neuhaus, *Housework and Housewives in American Advertising: Married to the Mop* (New York: Palgrave McMillian, 2011), Google Books.

5. Center For Information on America, *Vital Issues, Volumes 9–14* (Washington, CT: Center For Information on America, 1959).

6. Glenna Matthews, *Just a Housewife: The Rise and Fall of Domesticity in America* (New York: Oxford University Press, 1989), Google Books.

7. Ibid.

8. Kathleen Anne McHugh, *American Domesticity: From How-to Manual to Hollywood Melodrama* (New York: Oxford University Press, 1999), Google Books.

9. Sherri Caldwell and Vicki Todd, *The Rebel Housewife Rules: To Heck with Domestic Bliss* (Boston: Conari Press, 2004), Google Books.

10. Betty Friedan, *The Feminine Mystique* (50th Anniversary Edition) (New York: W.W. Norton Company, 2013), Google Books.

11. Ibid.

12. Sarah Ahmed, *The Promise of Happiness* (Durham: Duke University Press, 2010), Google Books; Kathleen Anne McHugh, *American Domesticity: From How-to Manual to Hollywood Melodrama* (New York: Oxford University Press, 1999), Google Books.

13. Kirstin Olsen, *Chronology of Women's History* (Westport: Greenwood Publishing, 1994), Google Books.

14. Ibid.

15. Ibid.

16. Ibid.

17. Ibid.

18. Ibid.

19. Hanna Rosin, "The End of Men," *Atlantic*, July/August 2010, http://www.theatlantic.com.

20. Andrew Helwig, "Occupational Aspirations of a Longitudinal Sample From Second to Sixth Grade," *Journal of Career Development* 24, no. 1 (1998): 247–265.

21. Robin Patric Clair, "The Political Nature of the Colloquialism, 'A Real Job': Implications for Organizational Socialization," *Communication Monographs* 63, no. 3 (1996): 249–267.

22. Ibid.

23. Nellie Andreeva and Nikki Finke, "Shocker: Desperate Housewives to End in May," *TV Line*. August 5, 2011, http://tvline.com.

24. Kristy Miller, Kevin Murtha and Sam Svedlund, Themes and Motifs, *The Scandalous Lives of Desperate Housewives*, accessed July 1, 2015, http://scandalousdh.blogspot.com.

25. John Kenneth Muir, *TV Year Volume 1: The Prime Time 2005–2006 Season* (New York: Applause Theater & Cinema Books, 2007), Google Books.

26. Dana Schuster, "How The 'Housewives' Franchise Spiraled into Dullsville," *New York Post* (New York, NY), July 28, 2014.

27. Rodney Ho, Bravo Renews "Real Housewives of Atlanta," Two Related Spinoffs. *AJC.com*, April 8, 2014, http://radiotvtalk.blog.ajc.com.

28. Diane Anderson-Minshall, "'The Real Housewives of Atlanta': Meet The RHOA Cast," *About Entertainment*, accessed June 24, 2015, http://realitytv.about.com.

29. Kenneth Burke, *A Rhetoric of Motives* (Berkeley: University of California Press, 1969), p. 55.

30. Ibid.; Gary C. Woodward, *The Idea of Identification* (Albany: State University of New York Press, 2003).

31. Kenneth Burke, *A Rhetoric of Motives* (Berkeley: University of California Press, 1969), p. 55.

32. Kirstin Olsen, *Chronology of Women's History* (Westport: Greenwood Publishing, 1994), Google Books.

33. Debra Merskin, "Three Faces of Eva: Perpetuation of the Hot-Latina Stereotype in Desperate Housewives," *Howard Journal of Communications* 18, no. 2 (2007): 133–151.

34. I became disgruntled because of the negative nature of the themes found in the show and decided to stop watching the show at this point.

35. Two episodes were discarded as they were not relevant.

36. Virginia Braun and Victoria Clarke, "Using Thematic Analysis in Psychology," *Qualitative Research in Psychology* 3, no. 2 (2006): 77–101.

37. Ibid.

38. W. F. Owen, "Thematic Metaphors in Relational Communication. A Conceptual Framework." *Western Journal of Communication 49*, no. Winter (1984): 1–13.

39. Ibid.

40. Chris Witherspoon, "Kandi Burress Opens up About Getting Married 5 Years After Death of Ex-Fiancé," *The Grio*, June 24, 2014, http://thegrio.com.

41. *The Real Housewives of Atlanta*, "Model Behavior," Bravo, October 11, 2010, written by Scott Dunlop.

42. Ibid.

43. *The Real Housewives of Atlanta*, "She Can Dance?," Bravo, November 14, 2010, written by Scott Dunlop.

44. Ibid.

45. "Sheree Whitfield's Ex-Husband Bob, on Divorce from the Atlanta 'Housewife': 'I Could Have Paid Her Child Support,'" *Huff Post OWN Video*, April 24, 2013, http://www.huffingtonpost.com.

46. Samantha Leffler, Who is Kim Zolciak's Ex-husband Daniel Dominic Toce?, *Wetpaint.com*, June 23, 2013, http://www.wetpaint.com.

47. Cristina Everett, "'Real Housewives' Star Kim Zolciak Calls Lesbian Fling With DJ Tracy Young a 'One-Time Deal,'" *NY Daily News* (New York, NY). March 31, 2010.

48. *The Real Housewives of Atlanta*, "Trashed Collection," Bravo, November 7, 2010, written by Scott Dunlop.

49. Ibid.

50. *The Real Housewives of Atlanta*, "Model Behavior," Bravo, October 11, 2010, written by Scott Dunlop.

51. *The Real Housewives of Atlanta*, "Contract Player," Bravo, December 12, 2010, written by Scott Dunlop.

52. Ibid.

53. *The Real Housewives of Atlanta*, "Hot Mama's Day," Bravo, November 1, 2010, written by Scott Dunlop.

54. Ibid.

55. *The Real Housewives of Atlanta*, "Model Behavior," Bravo, October 11, 2010, written by Scott Dunlop.

56. Ibid.

57. Glenna Matthews, *Just a Housewife: The Rise and Fall of Domesticity in America* (New York: Oxford University Press, 1989), Google Books.

58. *The Real Housewives of Atlanta*, "New Attitude," Bravo, October 4, 2010, written by Scott Dunlop.

59. *The Real Housewives of Atlanta*, "Model Behavior," Bravo, October 11, 2010, written by Scott Dunlop.

60. *The Real Housewives of Atlanta*, "New Attitude," Bravo, October 4, 2010, written by Scott Dunlop.

61. Ibid.

62. Ibid.

63. Nene Leakes and Denene Millner. *Never Make the Same Mistake Twice: Lessons on Love and Life Learned the Hard Way* (New York: Touchstone, 2009), Google Books.

64. *The Real Housewives of Atlanta*, "Nene Get Your Gun," Bravo, November 28, 2010, written by Scott Dunlop.

65. *The Real Housewives of Atlanta*, "New Attitude," Bravo, October 4, 2010, written by Scott Dunlop.

66. *The Real Housewives of Atlanta*, "Contract Player," Bravo, December 12, 2010, written by Scott Dunlop.

67. Natalie Abrams, "Real Housewives of Atlanta Apollo Nida Sentenced to Eight Years in Jail," *TV Guide*, July 8, 2014, http://www.tvguide.com.

68. *The Real Housewives of Atlanta*, "New Attitude," Bravo, October 4, 2010, written by Scott Dunlop.

69. Natasha, "RHOA" Stars Cynthia Bailey & Peter Thomas' Wedding Pic, Cynthia Talks Peter's Bad temper and Money Woes, *TheYBF.com*, January 24, 2011, http://theybf.com.

70. Barbara Bergmann, "The Economic Risks of Being a Housewife," *University of Minnesota Libraries*. May, 1981, http://blog.lib.umn.edu; Kathleen Anne McHugh, *American Domesticity: From How-to Manual to Hollywood Melodrama* (New York: Oxford University Press, 1999). Google Books.

71. *The Real Housewives of Atlanta*, "New Attitude," Bravo, October 4, 2010, written by Scott Dunlop.

72. Ibid.

73. *The Real Housewives of Atlanta*, "Is There a Doctor in the House?," Bravo, November 21, 2010, written by Scott Dunlop.

74. *The Real Housewives of Atlanta*, "Nene Get Your Gun," Bravo, November 28, 2010, written by Scott Dunlop.

75. "Phaedra Parks Expecting: 'Real Housewives of Atlanta' Star Pregnant with Baby No. 2." *HuffPost Celebrity*, December 31, 2012, http://www.huffingtonpost.com.

76. Nina Hammiel Turner, "RHOA: Phaedra Lies About Due Date; Gives Birth to a Baby Boy in May 2010," *Examiner.com*, November 7, 2010, http://www.examiner.com.

77. *The Real Housewives of Atlanta*, "Nene Get Your Gun," Bravo, November 28, 2010, written by Scott Dunlop.

78. "Phaedra Parks Expecting: 'Real Housewives of Atlanta' Star Pregnant with Baby No. 2." *HuffPost Celebrity, December* 31, 2012, http://www.huffingtonpost.com.

79. Betty Friedan, *The Feminine Mystique* (50th Anniversary Edition) (New York: W.W. Norton Company, 2013), Google Books.

80. Jessamyn Neuhaus, *Housework and Housewives in American Advertising: Married to the Mop* (New York: Palgrave McMillian, 2011), Google Books.

81. Glenna Matthews, *Just a Housewife: The Rise and Fall of Domesticity in America* (New York: Oxford University Press, 1989), Google Books.

82. Ibid.

83. Sarah Ahmed, *The Promise of Happiness* (Durham: Duke University Press, 2010), Google Books.

84. Kathleen Anne McHugh, *American Domesticity: From How-to Manual to Hollywood Melodrama* (New York: Oxford University Press, 1999). Google Books.

85. *Independent Women Part I*, Recorded by Destiny's Child, New York, NY: Columbia Records, 2001, CD.

86. Robin Patric Clair, "The Political Nature of the Colloquialism, 'A Real Job': Implications for Organizational Socialization," *Communication Monographs* 63, no. 3 (1996): 249–267.

87. *No Matter What They Say*, Recorded by Lil' Kim. New York, NY: Atlantic Records, 2000, CD.

88. *Independent Women Part I*, Recorded by Destiny's Child, New York, NY: Columbia Records, 2001, CD.

89. *I Don't Need a Man*, Recorded by Pussycat Dolls, Santa Monica, CA: A&M Records, 2001, CD.

90. *Smack You*, Recorded by Kimberly Cole, New York, NY: Atlantic Records, 2010, CD.

91. Rodney Ho, Bravo Renews "Real Housewives of Atlanta," Two Related Spin-offs. *AJC.com*, April 8, 2014, http://radiotvtalk.blog.ajc.com.

92. Samantha Darcy, "Reality Pays! You Won't Believe What Your Most Loved—And Hated—Housewives Earn," *OK!* May 2, 2013, http://okmagazine.com.

93. Annette Hill, *Reality TV: Audiences and Popular Factual Television* (New York: Routledge, 2005). Google Books.

94. Stephanie Cottrell Bryant, *Videoblogging for Dummies* (Hoboken: Wiley Publishing, 2006), Google Books.

95. Nancy Signorielli, "Adolescents and Ambivalence Toward Marriage: A Cultivation Analysis," *Youth and Society 23*, (1991): 121–149.

96. Ibid.

97. Nancy Waldeck, Ellen Bolman Pullins, and Melissa Houlette, "Media as Factor in Student Perceptions of Sales Jobs: A Framework for research," *Journal of Personal Selling and Sales Management* 30, no. 4 (2010): 343–354.

98. Horace Newcomb. *Encyclopedia of Television* (New York: Fitzroy Dearborn, 2004), Google Books.

99. Tom Engelhardt, "How Sensational News Stories Distract us from Real Crises," *Thenation.com*, April 3, 2014, http://www.thenation.com.

100. Robin Patric Clair, "The Political Nature of the Colloquialism, 'A Real Job': Implications for Organizational Socialization," *Communication Monographs* 63, no. 3 (1996): 249–267.

101. Jack Benza, So You Wannabe on Reality TV? (New York: Allworth Communication, 2005), Google Books.

102. Julia S. Jordan-Zachery, *Black Women, Cultural Images, and Social Policy* (New York: Routledge, 2009), Google Books.

103. Joe R. Feagin, *Racist America: Roots, Current Realities, and Future Reparations* (New York: Routledge, 2001), Google Books.

104. Ibid.

105. Nikki Jones, *Between Good and Ghetto: African American Girls and Inner City Violence* (Piscataway: Rutgers University Press, 2010), Google Books.

106. theJasminebrand, What Happened to Fired Atlanta Housewife DeShawn Snow? *TheJasminebrand.com*, April 3, 2014, http://thejasminebrand.com.

107. With the exception of Kim Zolciak who is white.

# Conclusion

## *Discussion and Implications*

## Donnetrice C. Allison

According to Nellie Andreeva, in her March 24, 2015 article, *Pilots 2015: The Year of Ethnic Castings—About Time or Too Much of Good Thing*, there has been a "noticeable shift toward minority castings . . . with more parts opening up to ethnic actors."[1] The author implies, however, that there may be a down side to this growing trend. She states:

> But, as is the case with any sea change, some suggest that the pendulum might have swung a bit too far in the opposite direction. Instead of opening the field for actors of any race to compete for any role in a color-blind manner, there has been a significant number of parts *designated* as ethnic this year, making them off-limits for Caucasian actors, some agents signal.[2]

Is she suggesting some sort of "reverse discrimination," as is often the presumption made when people of color "take opportunities away" from whites? Furthermore, assuming this upswing in "ethnic" roles is true, what types of roles are being secured—particularly for black women?

As noted in chapter one, Shonda Rhimes is responsible for a Thursday night line-up filled with black leading ladies—on *Grey's Anatomy*, *Scandal* and *How to Get Away with Murder*. Then Lee Daniels and Danny Strong made a splash on Wednesday nights with the runaway hit, *Empire*—a modern-day *Dynasty*, focused on a black family that made its fortune in hip hop. The show features all the essentials of a successful primetime soap opera—excess, materialism, sex, back-stabbing, murder and homophobia. *Empire* premiered January 7, 2015 in the same time slot—9 p.m.— as the hit sitcom *Black-ish*, starring Anthony Anderson and Tracee Ellis Ross.[3] *Being Mary Jane*, starring Gabrielle Union, premiered in September of 2013 with solid ratings and the show is currently in its third season.[4] Several additional shows are set to premiere in the fall of 2015, featuring black women—*Quantico* (featuring Aunjanue Ellis), *Minority Report* (featuring Meagan Good), *Blindspot* (featuring Marianne Jean-Baptiste), *CSI: New Orleans* (featuring CCH Pounder), *The Flash* (featuring Candice Patton), *Chicago Med* (featuring S. Epatha Merkerson) and *Rosewood* (featuring Lorraine Toussaint).[5] While all of these women are not lead charac-

233

ters in their respective shows, their roles range from doctors and nurses, to police officers and investigators. It is uncertain how long any of these shows will last and if they will garner the ratings success of a Shonda Rhimes production. Moreover, it is uncertain whether any of these shows will garner the ratings success and staying-power of the reality television shows covered in this book. Nonetheless, an important question to emerge from this examination of black women on television is the question of whether a series of "positive" new roles for black women on scripted television can undo the harm done by the stereotypical depictions of black women on reality television. The question also remains whether these new images are "positive" or just repackaged mammies, jezebels and sapphires?

In this book, we analyzed a number of reality television shows featuring black women: *Preachers of L.A., Mary Mary, Tiny and Toya, T.I. & Tiny: The Family Hustle, Welcome to Sweetie Pie's, Raising Whitley, Mom's Got Game, Dance Moms, Tia and Tamera, Run's House, Bad Girls Club, The Apprentice, America's Next Top Model, Love & Hip Hop, Love & Hip Hop: Atlanta,* and *The Real Housewives of Atlanta.* There are several additional shows that we did not discuss—*Basketball Wives, R&B Divas, Blood Sweat and Heels, Preachers of Detroit, Love and Hip Hop: Hollywood, Sisterhood of Hip Hop, Braxton Family Values, Tamar and Vince,* and *Frankie and Neffe.* All of the above demonstrate the wealth of reality programming featuring black women and all bring us back to the question: Too much of a good thing? Or maybe too much of a bad thing?

As noted in chapter one, Ruby Dee, narrator for the documentary, *Color Adjustment,* contended that during the Civil Rights Era there were two black Americas—one demonstrated the dynamism of activists fighting for change and the other demonstrated buffoonery in the 1950s and unrealistic harmony in the 1960s. Those representations existed alongside one another.[6] Similarly, today exists the "ratchetness"[7] of black women on reality television alongside the professionalism of some of the black women portrayed on primetime dramas. So which image is most potent and has the most impact on the viewing public?

While little research has been conducted on others' perceptions of black women and the potential connection between those perceptions and media stereotypes of black women, countless personal narratives exist to suggest there is indeed a connection. The most commonly cited study on the subject is that of Weitz and Gordon (1993), who examined white college students' perceptions of black women and found that students view black women as primarily "loud, aggressive, argumentative, stubborn, and bitchy."[8] Yet, it has been more than two decades since this study was conducted, and little progress has been made in terms of additional research. Of particular interest would be to ascertain the origins of such negative perceptions. The implication of this collection of essays is that these notions largely come from media.

The overall contention of this collection of essays is that black women in reality television are portrayed negatively; primarily associated with decades old stereotypes of black women as Mammies, Matriarchs, Aunt Jemimas, Jezebels, Sapphires, bitches, hoes, ABW (angry black women) and SWAs (sistahs with attitudes). And while the chapters in section one maintain that there are some portrayals of black women on reality television that suggest positive characteristics and redeeming qualities—spiritual women, good mothers, good friends, supportive wives, smart business women—the authors note that most still fall back on negative stereotypes. For instance, though Tina and Erica Campbell of *Mary Mary* are often depicted praying, loving on their children, singing the gospel and professing their faith, they are also shown in dramatic conflicts with one another and—most often—with their ex-manager, Mitch. Similarly, the wives on *Preachers of L.A.* are depicted as women of faith, but also as women who gossip, backstab and flaunt materialism. Tiny is a devoted wife, mother, and business woman on one hand; but an immature, airhead on the other. And all of the women described in section one, no matter the degrees held (e.g. Dr. Holly), financial success (e.g. Miss Robbie) or business savvy (e.g. Pamela McGee), are shown finger-snapping and neck-rolling at some point in their respective shows.

Sections two and three of this collection primarily focus on portrayals of ABW, SWAs, bitches and hoes of reality television. And while chapter seven attempts to explain the reasons behind some of the anger displayed by black women on *Bad Girls Club*, the sad reality is that few viewers will labor to do so. They will simply see what they perceive as "typical" behavior of black women, as evidenced by much of the social media commentary about these shows. The women discussed in sections two and three engage in loud, verbal altercations regularly; and they even engage in physical altercations from time to time. One famous such altercation took place during the season 6 reunion special of *Real Housewives of Atlanta*, and the comments that followed the YouTube clip ran the gamut of insults, from calling the women "black bitches" and "whores" to labeling them "jungle bunnies."[9] In short, the likely impression of black women behaving in this way is an enduringly unflattering one.

As noted in several previous chapters, black women face the combined stigma of racism and sexism, thus leaving them often at the bottom of the social hierarchy to face the harshest treatment and most negative forms of stereotyping. In 1981, bell hooks wrote, "when black people are talked about the focus tends to be on black men; and when women are talked about the focus tends to be on white women."[10] More than three decades later, the same holds true. As noted in chapter nine, the 2015 article dissects why black women are often deemed "invisible" in corporate America today.[11] Both bell hooks and Valerie Purdie-Vaughns speak to the potential "impact" of these continued negative images of black women. Weitz and Gordon (1993) also spoke to the issue twenty years ago and several recent narratives continue to speak to this issue. In other words, constant negative depictions of black women in popular media equals negative perceptions by others, which results in poor treatment in school, at work and at home.

In terms of the impact on school-age girls, a 2011 study—conducted by Blake, Butler, Lewis and Darensbourg of Texas A&M University—determined that black girls are "twice as likely to receive in-school and out-of-school suspensions than all female students," (compared to white and Latina girls) and black girls are far more likely than white girls to receive "discipline practices that remove them from the classroom."[12] The authors assert that: "Many of the behaviors that black girls were cited for seemed to defy traditional standards of femininity and closely paralleled the behaviors of stereotypical images of black women as hypersexualized, angry, and hostile."[13] Additionally, the researchers found that black girls' involvement with in-school discipline "closely mirrored that of their Black male counterparts."[14] This falls in line with continuing notions that black women and girls are more like black men and boys, and can therefore be handled and engaged in the same way that one might handle and engage a man. Recent news accounts speak to this issue as well. For instance, a 14-year-old bikini-clad black female was slammed to the ground by a white police officer in McKinney, Texas on June 5, 2015, after officers responded to a call about a fight at a pool party. Although witnesses say the fight was instigated by a white female, it was the black female who was held down on the ground by her neck.[15]

This manhandling of black women and girls is nothing new, but in recent years, with the advent of camera phones and dashboard cameras (i.e., dash-cams), many others have become privy to these incidences. In July of 2014, a 51-year-old homeless woman was repeatedly punched by a white California Highway Patrol officer, who had accused her of behaving erratically and walking along the yellow line on the freeway.[16] Additionally, a 19-year-old black female, who had crashed her car, was fatally shot after she came onto a white man's porch looking for help.[17] And most recently, the name Sandra Bland made national headlines, as she died under mysterious circumstances after her confrontation with Texas State Trooper Brian Encinia was caught on his dash-cam video.[18] Police reported that the 28-year-old black female hanged herself in her cell, but her family maintains that there is no way she would have ever committed suicide.[19] Countless other such incidents have occurred in recent years, far too many to name in this chapter; but this speaks to the continued devaluation of black women. And while no study exists that makes a definitive connection between brutality against black women and negative stereotypes of black women in media, it is this author's contention that the constancy and consistency of these negative portrayals of black women have indeed impacted the treatment of black women in our society. Jacklyn Huey and Michael J. Lynch might agree, given that in their article, *The Image of Black Women in Criminology: Historical Stereotypes as Theoretical Foundation*, they state:

> Theoretical distortions are not accidental, but are a function of and necessity of domination. We need to be cognizant of the fact that criminologists, like others, influenced by systems of domination, reproduce these relations and myths in theoretical explanations involving black female offenders and victims.[20]

Again, although this does not offer a definitive connection between brutality against black women and media stereotypes about them, the notion that black women are not as feminine as white women—and therefore do not deserve respect and/or chivalry—has been around for generations. And, according to bell hooks, (1981) this notion began as soon as black women were stolen from Africa and brought to America. Hooks (1981) writes, "black women were forced to assume a 'masculine' role . . . the black female was exploited as a laborer in the fields, a worker in the domestic household, a breeder, and as an object of white male sexual assault." This idea was passed down from generation to generation and now seems to appear prominently in the fight scenes manufactured on shows like *Bad Girls Club*, *Real Housewives of Atlanta*, and *Love and Hip Hop: Atlanta*; and appear in the consciousness of white officers who encounter black women.

Even tennis phenom, Serena Williams, must contend with this notion of black female masculinity on a daily basis. Claudia Rankine poignantly asks readers—in her August 25, 2015 article, "The Meaning of Serena Williams"—to imagine that given all the extraordinary successes one might have in tennis, including twenty-one Grand Slam titles, that one would still have to contend with relentless racism and sexism. She writes:

> Imagine that, despite all this, there were so many bad calls against you, you were given as one reason video replay needed to be used on the courts. Imagine that you have to contend with critiques of your body that perpetuate racist notions that black women are hypermasculine and unattractive. Imagine being asked to comment at a news conference before a tournament because the president of the Russian Tennis Federation . . . has described you and your sister as "brothers" who are "scary" to look at. Imagine.[21]

Moreover, Rankine (2015) also spoke about the limited number of endorsement deals Serena receives. Even though she is the best in her sport, she ranks well behind the blond-haired white female, Maria Sharapova, in marketability—as ranked by the London School of Marketing.[22] The authors notes:

> There is another, perhaps more important, discussion to be had about what it means to be chosen by global corporations. It has to do with who is worthy, who is desirable, who is associated with the good life. As long as the white imagination markets itself by equating whiteness

and blondness with aspirational living, stereotypes will remain fixed in place. Even though Serena is the best, even though she wins more Slams than anyone else, she is only superficially allowed to embody that in our culture, at least the marketable one.[23]

Regarding black women's experiences in the workplace, the same holds true. Black women must contend with numerous stereotypes held about them by others—employers, peers and subordinates—within the workplace. According to Allen (2000), a black woman entering a predominantly white organization must contend with several stereotypes, such as the twofer or the token—where it is believed that she was only hired to fill an affirmative action quota; the mammy—where she is viewed as a nurturer and caretaker to the problems of others; and the matriarch—where she is viewed as aggressive, overbearing, arrogant, controlling, self-centered, and "uppity" as a result of her success.[24] In the late 1990s, Irene Browne and Ivy Kennelly conducted research on stereotypes employers held about black women and found that:

> The black woman, according to the white Atlanta employers interviewed, was a single mother who was either reliable in a suspicious sort of way or the most likely person to be late, distracted, and absent because of her child-care concerns.

More recently, a 2015 report by the Center for Talent Innovation found that in terms of pursuing middle and upper management positions: (1) black women's contributions often go unrecognized; (2) black women lack sponsors, who can assist in them acquiring middle and upper management positions; and (3) black women are more likely to "put their heads down," "make no noise," and hope that "hard work alone will pay off."[25]

This chapter opened with two questions: (1) Can a series of "positive" new roles for black women on scripted television undo the harm done by the stereotypical depictions of black women on reality television?; and (2) Are these new images of black women on recent scripted programming "positive" or just repackaged mammies, jezebels and sapphires? The chapter also poses the question of whether the wealth of black women on television—in both scripted and unscripted programs (i.e., reality television)—is too much of a good thing or too much of a bad thing? Lastly, the question was raised: which image of black women on television is most potent and impactful on the viewing public—the ratchet or the professional?

In answer to the first question, it is unlikely that a series of "positive" new roles for black women on scripted television can undo the harm done by stereotypical depictions of black women on reality television. We have no sense of how long these new shows might last, on the one hand; and, on the other, it took generations of negative imagery to build these views of black women and it will likely take generations to diminish them. Additionally, it would take a sustained effort on the part of television producers and executives to offer positive images of black women; and that is not likely to happen unless the viewing public stops watching the negative depictions and ratings drop. That too, would take a concerted effort—on the part of viewers—to demonstrate that they prefer the positive images over the negative images.

The next question asks whether the images on these new programs are indeed "positive." *Empire* brought FOX its highest ratings in years, with its steadily growing audience each week and a season finale that brought in more than 20 million viewers;[26] and the star of *Empire* is undoubtedly the female lead—Taraji P. Henson as Cookie Lyon. Cookie wears outlandish outfits that scream for attention—from leopard to leather, shoes and hats to match; and she is continually finger-pointing, neck-rolling, and name-calling—particularly toward her nemesis, Anika, the love interest of her ex-husband, Lucious Lyon. In fact, the show hit ratings gold, when the two finally engaged in a much-anticipated girl fight. Cookie is every bit the Sapphire and Jezebel of old, sprinkled with the ABW discussed in chapters seven and eight and the "Down-Ass Bitch" discussed in chapter 11—given that her devotion to Lucious ran so deep that she took the rap for their crimes and spent seventeen years in prison rather than rat him out.

A character on yet another show—*Grey's Anatomy*'s Miranda Bailey— was once known as "The Nazi," because, even though she was short in stature, she was tall on attitude and brought fear to the hearts of all of her interns. Rhimes has since softened Miranda's character significantly, but whether the new black female characters on upcoming shows will fit the profile of the ABW or SWA—with the black woman's sassiness that viewers seem to love—remains to be seen.

So is this wave of black women on television too much of a good thing or too much of a bad thing? This, too, remains to be seen. The growing onslaught of reality-based programming featuring loud, angry black women is certainly not a good thing, but the degree of negative impact from these images can only be inferred absent substantial extensive research. This addresses the last question: Which image of black women on television is most potent and has the most impact on the viewing public? Again this author maintains that extensive supplemental research is needed—longitudinal research that tracks what viewers watch and how the images of black women that they see on television impacts their real-world interactions with black women encountered in their daily lives.

This is the primary recommendation of this book. There is a wealth of research on the negative stereotypes of black women in media—currently and historically; but there is a dearth of research on the impact of such images. The primary contention of this book is that negative portrayals of black women on reality television negatively impact audiences, and induce them to perceive all black women as aggressive, angry, bitchy, uncouth, and LOUD! We can only hope that change will soon come.

## NOTES

1. Nellie Andreeva, "Pilots 2015: The Year of Ethnic Castings—About Time or Too Much of Good Thing," *Deadline Hollywood* (March 24, 2015), accessed August 2015, http://deadline.com/.

2. Ibid.

3. *IMDB.com*, accessed August 2015, http://www.imdb.com.

4. Ibid.

5. TVguide.com, accessed August 2015, http://www.tvguide.com/special/fall-preview/schedule/.

6. Ruby Dee (narrator), "Two Black Americas: News and Prime Time," *Color Adjustment*, directed by Marlon T. Riggs (San Francisco, CA: California Newsreel, 1991). Videocassette (VHS).

7. According to the Urban Dictionary, http://www.urbandictionary.com, ratchet is a diva, mostly from urban cities and ghettos, that has reason to believe she is every man's eye candy; unfortunately she is wrong. Synonyms for ratchet include—ghetto, hoe, bitch, slut, whore and thot—all negative connotations associated with black women. According to Merriam Webster's dictionary, http://www.merriam-webster.com, ratchet is a device made up of a wheel or bar with many teeth along its edge in between which a piece fits so that the wheel or bar can move only in one direction. Unclear how this term became associate with black women.

8. Rose Weitz and Leonard Gordon, "Images of Black Women Among Anglo College Students," *Sex Roles* 28 (1993): 33.

9. *RHOA: Kenya Moore/Porsha Williams Reunion Fight Video*, YouTube video, .09, posted by Diary of a Hollywood Street King, April 21, 2014, https://www.youtube.com/watch?v=xmyTY5d_rLg.

10. bell hooks, *Ain't I a Woman: Black Women and Feminism* (Boston, MA: South End Press, 1981), 7.

11. Valerie Purdie-Vaughns, "Why so few black women are senior managers in 2015," *Fortune Magazine* online (April 22, 2015), accessed August 2015, http://fortune.com/2015/04/22/black-women-leadership-study/.

12. Jamilia J. Blake, Bettie Ray Butler, Chance W. Lewis & Alicia Darensbourg, "Unmasking the Inequitable Discipline Experiences of Urban Black Girls: Implications for Urban Educational Stakeholders," *The Urban Review* 43, no. 1 (2011): 100.

13. Ibid.

14. Ibid. 99.

15. Ashley Fantz, Holly Yan & Catherine E. Shoichet, "Texas pool party chaos: 'Out of control' police officer resigns," *CNN.com* (June 9, 2015), accessed August 2015, http://www.cnn.com.

16. Artemis Moshtaghian and Sara Sidner, "$1.5 million settlement for woman beaten by California patrol officer," *CNN.com* (September 25, 2014), accessed August 2015, http://www.cnn.com.

17. Josh Levs and Ralph Ellis, "Detroit woman shot after apparently approaching home for help," *CNN.com* (November 8, 2013), accessed August 2015, http://www.cnn.com.

18. Polly Mosendz, "Family of Sandra Bland Files Wrongful Death Lawsuit Against Texas Trooper, Jailers," *Newsweek* online (August 4, 2015), accessed August 2015, http://www.newsweek.com.

19. Ibid.

20. Jacklyn Huey & Michael J. Lynch, "The Image of Black Women in Criminology: Historical Stereotypes as Theoretical Foundation," in *Justice with Prejudice: Race and*

*Criminal Justice in America*, eds. Michael J. Lynch & E. Britt Paterson (Guilderland, NY: Harrow and Heston, 1996), 86.

21. Claudia Rankine, "The Meaning of Serena Williams," *The New York Times Magazine* online (August 25, 2015), accessed August 2015, http://mobile.nytimes.com.

22. Ibid.

23. Ibid.

24. Brenda J. Allen, "'Learning the Ropes:' A Black Feminist Standpoint Analysis," in *Communication From Feminist Perspectives*, ed. Patrice M. Buzzanell (Los Angeles, CA: Sage Publications, 2000), 178.

25. Valerie Purdie-Vaughns, "Why so few black women are senior managers in 2015."

26. Rick Kissell, "Weekly Ratings: Huge 'Empire' Finale Lifts Fox to Demo Victory," Variety.com (March 25, 2015), accessed August 2015, http://variety.com.

# About the Editor

**Donnetrice C. Allison**, PhD, currently serves as an associate professor of both Communication Studies and Africana Studies at Stockton University in Galloway, NJ. Dr. Allison teaches numerous Africana Studies courses, which include—Introduction to Africana Studies, African American Movies, Introduction to Hip Hop Culture, and a Seminar on Representations of Race in Media; she has also developed a learning abroad course on Senegal, West Africa—whereby she will travel there with a group of students at the culmination of the course. In addition to Africana Studies, Dr. Allison also teaches for the Communication Studies program. Those courses include: Film Theory and Criticism, Communication Research Methods, Senior Seminar in Communication Studies, Mass Communication Theories, Television and Popular Culture, and Women, Minorities and the Media. Dr. Allison has been a Communication Studies scholar for more than two decades. Dr. Allison has published articles on Black professors at predominantly white institutions (PWIs), hip hop culture, and media portrayals of crises. Dr. Allison has also offered numerous conference presentations on hip hop culture and media portrayals of African Americans at national and international conferences—including the National Communication Association Convention, the National Council for Black Studies Convention, Cheikh Anta Diop International Conference, Eastern Communication Association Convention, The New Jersey Communication Association, The International Conference on Diversity in Organizations, Communities and Nations, The Alternative Soul Arts and Music Festival, and the Hawaii International Conference on Arts and Humanities.

# About the Contributors

**Antwanisha Alameen-Shavers**, PhD is an Assistant Professor at San Diego State University. She recently received her PhD from Temple University and her Masters of Arts from The Ohio State University in the discipline of Black Studies. Her research interests include the role of African women in African civilizations, Black female embodiment and gender politics in the Black community. She has presented her research at several conferences such as the Cheikh Anta Diop Conference, National Conference for Black Studies and Africana Womanism Conference. Her recent publications deal with the role of women in traditional Igbo government.

**Allison M. Alford** is a Doctoral Student in Communication Studies at The University of Texas at Austin with a focus on Interpersonal Communication. Ms. Alford studies relationships and closeness between adult daughters and their mothers in a variety of contexts. Using in-depth qualitative methodology, Ms. Alford has recently conducted interviews regarding adult daughters' perceptions of change in their daughter/mother relationships after relational turning points. Presently, she is expanding her inquiries to include Hispanic and Black daughters' perspectives. She has coordinated the multi-disciplinary Conflict Conference and Summer Symposium for Peace and Conflict Resolution and continues to promote peace work and healthy relationships. She hopes to eventually write a book on best relationship practices.

**Patrick Bennett** is an adjunct communications professor at the University of South Carolina-Aiken, where he teaches public speaking, interpersonal communication, and media and culture. He has a B.S. (magna cum laude) from Georgia Southern University (2012) in communications studies and an M.A. from Southern Illinois University Carbondale (2014) in speech communication. His research interests include intercultural communication, critical and cultural studies, and hip hop studies. Patrick Bennett was the recipient of Communications Studies student of the year at Georgia Southern University in 2012 and was awarded the PROMT fellowship upon entering Southern Illinois University Carbondale. He also has presented at the Women, Gender, and Sexuality Studies conference at Southern Illinois University Carbondale.

**Mia E. Briceño**, PhD is an Assistant Professor of Rhetorical Studies in the department of Communication Studies at Wilkes University. Prior to arriving at Wilkes in the fall of 2013, Dr. Briceño completed her PhD in Communication Arts and Sciences at Penn State University in 2012, where she also completed a graduate minor in Women's Studies. She earned her M.A. in Communication Studies from California State University, Northridge in 2007 and received her B.A. in Rhetoric in Communication and a certificate in Latin American Studies from the University of Pittsburgh in 2004. Dr. Briceño's research interests and teaching expertise are in the areas of rhetorical theory and criticism, feminist theory, and gender studies. Her research focuses on gendered communication broadly and includes topics like the rhetoric of pageantry in the United States, official discourses of women's health and healthcare, and the radical speech of activist figures like Lucy Parsons.

**Chetachi A. Egwu**, PhD is a Nigerian American professor, writer/producer, filmmaker, dancer/choreographer, artist and actor. She earned a BA in Communication from the University of Buffalo in 1996, then moved on to Howard University in Washington, DC, where she completed a Masters and PhD in Mass Communication. Dr. Egwu has served as a faculty member in the communication departments at Morgan State University, George Washington University and Nova Southeastern University in Fort Lauderdale, FL. She is currently teaching for the University of Maryland–University College. Her work has been featured in academic journals, newspapers and online publications such as *The Grio* and *The Burton Wire*, but her creative nature reaches beyond writing. An avid filmmaker, Dr. Egwu is currently co-producer and co-director for the documentaries *Runway Afrique* and *No Justice, No Peas: Getting a Veggie in the Hood*, and co-producer, director and cinematographer for the documentary *Sunshine Chic*.

**Evene Estwick**, PhD is an Associate Professor in the Communication Studies Department at Wilkes University in Wilkes-Barre, PA. She joined the Wilkes faculty in 2005. Originally from Barbados, Dr. Estwick's teaching responsibilities include Mass Media Literacy, Arts of Film, Introduction to Telecommunications, Intercultural Communications and Public Speaking. Her research interests include international media, globalization and the media, Caribbean media and developmental and international communication. Dr. Estwick has presented research papers at some of the largest professional organizations in the field, including the National Communication Association, International Communication Association and the Association for Education in Journalism and Mass Communication conferences. Dr. Estwick received her B.A. and M.A. from Howard University and her PhD in Mass Media and Communication from Temple University.

**Adria Y. Goldman**, PhD is currently an Assistant Professor of Communication at Gordon State College in Barnesville, GA. Dr. Goldman's research examines media representations of Black womanhood as well as groups that are underrepresented in media. She examines the way in which such representations impact viewers' construction of reality. Dr. Goldman is co-editor of the recent book, *Black Women and Popular Culture: The Conversation Continues* (2014).

**Rachel Alicia Griffin**, PhD is an Associate Professor in the Department of Communication Studies at Southern Illinois University (SIU), cross-appointed in Africana Studies and Women, Gender, and Sexuality Studies. As a critical intercultural scholar, her research interests span Black feminist thought, critical race theory, popular culture, sport, education, and sexual violence. From 2012 to 2015 Dr. Griffin was awarded the Judge William Holmes Cook Professorship by the Office of the Associate Chancellor for Institutional Diversity at SIU and in 2013 she was awarded the College of Liberal Arts Early Career Faculty Excellence Award at SIU. Dr. Griffin has published in several journals, including *Women's Studies in Communication*, *Critical Studies in Media Communication*, the *International Journal of Qualitative Studies in Education*, *The Howard Journal of Communications*, and the *Journal of International and Intercultural Communication*.

**Johnny Jones**, M.F.A. is an assistant professor of Theatre Arts at the University of Louisville, where he teaches black performance and script analysis. His research focuses primarily on the performance of black masculinity and black male identity in early 21st-century America and extends into the various ways that black male performance affects other aspects of black life, such as black womanhood or childhood. With scholarly and creative work that breaks down and questions black male oppression and how it transforms into black men's subjection of others on micro and macro levels, Johnny seeks to facilitate a discussion that reimagines progressive black American masculinity.

**Ryessia D. Jones** is a third year doctoral student at The University of Texas at Austin in the Department of Communication Studies with a focus on Rhetorical and Language Studies. Her research interests include portrayals of African Americans in reality television, specifically in the areas of Black fatherhood, Black motherhood, and gender performance. Furthermore, she has taken an interest in examining media representations of police brutality victims, specifically Black males.

**Madeline M. Maxwell**, PhD is Professor of Communication Studies at the University of Texas at Austin. Her research has been published in U.S. and international journals and books, and she has edited four books and monographs, including *Constructing (In)Competence: Disabling Evaluations in Clinical and Social interaction*, and co-authored *Storied Conflict Talk: Narrative Construction in Mediation*. Sample article titles include: "Metaphors of Hostile Communication," "Values Conflict in a Diagnostic Team," "Conflict Talk in a Professional Meeting," and "Evaluation in Everyday Interaction." She is on the editorial boards of the *Journal of Intercultural Communication and Mediation Theory and Practice*. Additionally, Dr. Maxwell studies the discourse of mediation and other situations of difficult communication, and she established the University of Texas Project on Conflict Resolution to focus on the roles of two approaches to communication for dispute resolution.

**Angelica N. Morris** is a doctoral student in Advertising at the University of Texas at Austin. She received a B.A. in Public Relations from Florida State University in 2008, and an M.A. in Advertising from UT Austin in 2012. Her primary research interests include consumer behavior, media effects, and diversity and inclusion. More specifically, she explores how consumer racial and ethnic identities affect self-perceptions, perceptions of reality, and the perceptions of advertising and marketing messages; and analyzes how these perceptions affect consumer product and brand preferences.

**Donyale R. Griffin Padgett**, PhD currently serves as Associate Professor of Diversity, Culture, and Communication in the Department of Communication at Wayne State University in Detroit, Michigan. Dr. Padgett holds a doctorate degree from Howard University, in Washington, D.C., in rhetoric and intercultural communication. She also holds a master's degree in organizational communication/public relations and a bachelor's degree in journalism — both from Wayne State University. Her research examines how crises are negotiated between institutional leaders and other audiences, particularly around issues of race and culture. She is specifically interested in the public dialogue that stems from crises and how meaning is shaped in the aftermath of these events.

**Tracey Owens Patton**, PhD is Director of African American & Diaspora Studies as well as a Professor of Communication in the Department of Communication and Journalism at the University of Wyoming. She earned her PhD in Communication at the University of Utah. Her area of specialization is critical cultural communication, rhetorical studies, and transnational studies. Her work is strongly influenced by critical theory, cultural studies, womanist theory, and rhetorical theory. She has authored a number of academic articles on topics involving the interdependence between race, gender, and power and how these issues interrelate culturally and rhetorically in education, media, policy, and speeches. Dr. Patton presents her research at numerous academic conferences and she recently published a co-authored book titled, *Gender, Whiteness, and Power in Rodeo: Breaking Away from the Ties of Sexism and Racism* (2012). Her academic articles include publications in top African American, Communication, Visual, and Women Studies journals, as well as in chapters in the following books: *The Handbook of Global Radio* (2012), *The Body Reader: Essential Social and Cultural Readings* (2010), *Fight the Power! The Spike Lee Reader* (2008), and *Emerging Issues in Contemporary Journalism: Infotainment, Internet, Libel, Censorship, Et Cetera* (2006).

**Shavonne R. Shorter**, PhD is an Assistant Professor in the Department of Communication Studies at Bloomsburg University. Shorter specializes in Organizational Communication. Her research focuses on the innately political nature of organizing. Shorter investigates the organizing processes in contexts such as education, politics, and within the media. Her scholarship has been published in Health Communication and presented at conferences sponsored by the International Communication Association, National Communication Association (Top Paper Recipient), Eastern Communication Association, and Maryland Communication Association. In her spare time she is committed to helping students take the steps to achieve their dreams.

**Siobhan E. Smith**, PhD is an Assistant Professor in the Department of Communication at the University of Louisville since August 2010. She teaches courses in mass media, race, and culture. Her general research interests include issues concerning people of color and how the media impact perceptions of people of color. She has produced critical analyses of race and gender portrayals in television texts such as *I Love New York*, *College Hill*, and *T.I. and Tiny: The Family Hustle*. She is also part of a team of interdisciplinary scholars who explored (sources of) food knowledge and access to healthy foods in Louisville and Hopkinsville, Kentucky. Smith is a proud graduate of Xavier University of Louisiana, Louisiana State University, and the University of Missouri.

**Elizabeth Whittington Cooper**, PhD is a graduate of Howard University. She is currently a Visiting Assistant Professor at Xavier University in New Orleans, Louisiana. Currently, she teaches public speaking with an emphasis on social justice issues, Introduction to Communication Studies, Intercultural Communication, and other classes dealing with race and gender within human communication. Her areas of research include race and gender dynamics in the perceptions of negotiations of sexual consent. She is currently examining how Black students at a Historically Black University (HBCU) negotiate sexual consent in casual sex relationships and the influence of parent and peer messages about sex. Her secondary research focuses on a critical, cultural examination of gender and sexual identities in the media portrayals. She has spent the last 10 years teaching undergraduate and graduate students. Currently, Elizabeth lives in between Atlanta and New Orleans with her wife and their new baby. Dr. Whittington Cooper is originally from a small suburb outside of Houston called Sugar Land, Texas.

**Julie Snyder-Yuly** holds a B.S. in psychology from the University of Iowa and an M.S. in Interdisciplinary Graduate Studies (communication, sociology, and industrial education) from Iowa State University. She is a third year doctoral student in the Communication Department at the University of Utah. Employing critical cultural and critical race theories, her academic work engages qualitative and rhetorical methods to examine textual and visual racial microaggressions in traditional and new media. Snyder-Yuly received an Iowa State University Research Excellence Award for her thesis "Harassment prevention training in higher education: Educating or silencing?" Additionally, she received the Iowa Task Force on Young Women's "Courageous Advocacy Award" and the Margaret Sloss Women's Center's "Margaret Sloss Gender Equity Award."